REFERENCE

SOURCES

IN HISTORY

SECOND EDITION

REFERENCE SOURCES IN HISTORY

AN INTRODUCTORY GUIDE

Ronald H. Fritze

Brian E. Coutts

Louis A. Vyhnanek

with the assistance of

Walter Bell and Jimmy Bryant

A B C · C L I O

Santa Barbara, California   Denver, Colorado   Oxford, England

Library of Congress Cataloging-in-Publication Data
Fritze, Ronald H., 1951–
Reference sources in history : an introductory guide / Ronald H.
Fritze, Brian E. Coutts, Louis A. Vyhnanek with contributions by Walter
Bell and Jimmy Bryant.—2nd ed.
p.   cm.
ISBN 0-87436-883-9 (hardcover : alk. paper) — ISBN 1-85109-522-5 (e-book)
1. History—Bibliography.   I. Coutts, Brian E.   II. Vyhnanek, Louis
Andrew.   III. Title.
Z6201.F72   2004
[D20]
016.909—dc22
2003025558

07   06   05   04   10 9 8 7 6 5 4 3 2 1

This book is also available on the World Wide Web as an eBook.
Visit abc-clio.com for details.

ABC-CLIO, Inc.
130 Cremona Drive, P.O. Box 1911
Santa Barbara, California 93116-1911

This book is printed on acid-free paper.
Manufactured in the United States of America

With Love to Our Parents

Harold[†] and Eleanor Fritze

George and Verna[†] Coutts

Louis[†] and Margaret[†] Vyhnanek

Nisi fuissetis, nihil esset★

★Unless you had been, there would be nothing.

CONTENTS

CHAPTER THREE
Book Review Indexes, 55

CHAPTER FOUR
Periodical Guides and Core Journals, 63

CHAPTER FIVE
Periodical Indexes, Abstracts, and Guides, 81

CHAPTER SIX
Guides to Newspapers, Newspaper Collections,
and Newspaper Indexes, 93

CHAPTER SEVEN
Dissertations and Theses, 113

CHAPTER EIGHT
Government Publications and Legal Sources, 123

CHAPTER NINE
Dictionaries and Encyclopedias, 151

CHAPTER TEN
Biographical Sources, 189

CHAPTER ELEVEN
Geographical Sources and Atlases, 219

CHAPTER TWELVE
Historical Statistical Sources, 243

PREFACE TO THE SECOND EDITION

Since *Reference Sources in History* was first published in 1990, much has changed in the world of historical reference materials. In spite of all the changes, however, the basic needs of researchers and students have remained fairly constant. The framing quotes from Lord Chesterfield and Ecclesiastes used in the preface to the first edition of this book continue to be just as valid as ever. Reference works give their users a foundation from which to start their research whether that foundation is bibliographical, biographical, geographical, chronological, archival, or whatever that case may be. Once the process of research is begun, they continue to guide historians and aspiring historians in their task of bringing some order to what Lord Chesterfield rightly described as a "confused heap of facts." Postmodernist colleagues will object to the term "facts" since they deny that such things exist. In contrast, unrepentant empiricists and undeconstructed positivists will continue to agree heartily with Lord Chesterfield. The Preacher's observation in Ecclesiastes 12:12 that, "Of making many books there is no end" is, if anything, more true than ever. The only qualification is that the many books are increasingly joined by CD-ROMS, microforms, Web sites, listservs, and other forms of new technology. Since 1990 many new reference sources have been published, some of which are destined to become classics. The massive *American National Biography* has superseded the old standard *Dictionary of American Biography* while the *Oxford Encyclopedia of the Reformation* and Scribner's *Encyclopedia of the Renaissance* have joined the great *Dictionary of the Middle Ages*. Other venerable reference works have been thoroughly updated in new editions—the *AHA Guide to Historical Literature*, the *Oxford Dictionary of the Christian Church*, and the *Oxford Classical Dictionary*. Even the grandsire of all multivolume biographical reference works, the century-old *Dictionary of National Biography,* is on the verge of publication in a completely revised, much improved, and expanded second edition. Furthermore, both *American National Biography* and the *New Dictionary of National Biography*, like many new works of reference, will be available in electronic formats that will also allow for continuous updating of content. Other exciting new forms of reference materials include the electronic *Centennia Dynamic Historical Atlas,* which depicts political and military expansion through boundary changes over time. These are just a sampling of the new reference works that have been created to make the task of historical research better and easier.

All of this means that the original *Reference Sources in History* also needed to be updated if it is to retain its usefulness. That is the purpose of this second edition. Like its predecessor, the second edition intends to provide an introduction to major historical reference works for all time periods of history and for all geographical areas, with a primary focus on English-language sources. The authors have again endeavored to include all of the most important and generally useful reference sources. In preparing this second edition many decisions needed to be made about what to add, what to exclude, what to keep, and what to drop. Such decisions were all the more difficult and imperative because we wanted to avoid having the second edition balloon into a far larger book than the first edition. *Reference Sources in History* is a one-volume guide or handbook. That means it should remain handy and portable and not evolve into a piece of equipment that belongs in the weight room of a gym.

The second edition of *Reference Sources in History* consists of 930 reference works listed in numbered bibliographic entries with annotations. Many new entries have been added. Some entries from the first edition have been dropped completely, others have been merged or shortened, and others have been reduced to a listing within a new entry. The first edition's organization into fourteen chapters on the basis of types of publications (e.g., bibliographies, atlases, microforms, journals) has been retained.

Works relating to various topics within the discipline of history (e.g., economic history, British history, psychohistory) can be found by using the index, which also lists all authors, editors, and titles mentioned throughout the text. Individual entries are numbered and are followed by complete bibliographic information and annotations that describe the contents of the works and provide some evaluation of their usefulness for the study of history. Whenever an annotation for one work mentions the title of another work with an entry in the guide, a bracketed see-reference including the item number of that work has been provided. Frequently annotations will also mention other similar or related titles that have not been given separate entries in the guide. Whenever this occurs, the authors have supplied the author's or editor's name, the title, place of publication, publisher, and date of publication. In this way the reference guide is able to list more titles by way of comparison than could have feasibly been listed separately.

As in the first edition, no arbitrary cutoff date for new publications has been used. The authors have continued to search for new, useful works of historical reference up to the submission of the manuscript in mid-2003. In some cases they were able to obtain advance information about important forthcoming reference sources such as the *Encyclopedia of Chicago History* and the *New Dictionary of National Biography*. Reference publishing appears to be accelerating rather than slowing down, so there will be many other new works of historical reference in the future. This situation is quite positive, reflecting the continuing vitality of the world of historical scholarship.

PREFACE TO THE FIRST EDITION

Never read History without having maps, and a chronological book,
or tables lying by you, and constantly recurred to; without which,
history is only a confused heap of facts.

That is what Philip Dormer Stanhope, the earl of Chesterfield, advised his son on 5 February 1750. It is a piece of advice that still retains its relevance in spite of the passage of time. The historian's job is to make sense of that "confused heap of facts," to recover and preserve knowledge of the past known as history, to organize it in an intelligible manner, and to explain or interpret it so that society can understand it. In the performance of that task the historian and the student of history are assisted by many different types of reference works: bibliographies, dictionaries, indexes, guides, and so on. There are so many of these works, in fact, that it might almost be said that for every question there is a reference book to answer it. Under these circumstances, it is impossible for practicing historians and librarians to maintain a working knowledge of the existing general reference literature for history in their heads. For the beginning student of history at the undergraduate or graduate level, the situation is even more bewildering. Hence the need for a reference guide that organizes, describes, and evaluates the basic reference works of interest to historians.

For many years the task of introducing the major reference works for history has been performed by Helen J. Poulton's excellent *The Historian's Handbook: A Descriptive Guide to Reference Works*. It was first published in 1972 and has gone through six printings. Since 1972, however, the enterprise of creating and publishing reference works has gone through several significant changes. The volume of excellent new reference titles appearing, particularly specialized historical dictionaries and encyclopedias, has increased and shows no signs of diminishing. New types of printed reference materials, particularly indexes, have appeared, such as *Biography and Genealogy Master Index* and *Arts and Humanities Citation Index*. Even more revolutionary has been the vast increase in the number of microform titles available to researchers. This change has been accompanied by vastly improved photographic reproduction. Still, the greatest changes have taken place in the field of electronic publishing. Most indexes are now available in computerized databases that can be searched by means of a telephone connection (i.e., online) from libraries throughout the country. Some of these online indexes are also available in the CD-ROM format (compact disc-read only memory), which is even more convenient for researchers. All of this means that the time has arrived for a new reference guide for history.

The present volume is designed to provide an introduction to the major reference works for all periods of history and for all geographical areas. At the same time, since the intended audience for this book is primarily English speaking, reference materials published in the English language have been emphasized. Publications in languages other than English have been limited to works in European languages that use the Roman alphabet and are outstanding or unique in their utility for historical research. Because the intended audience of this volume will largely be Anglo-American, the geographical coverage emphasizes British, Canadian, European, and U.S. history. Major works for African, Asian, Latin American, and Middle Eastern history, however, have been included.

The authors of this volume have attempted to include all of the most important and generally useful reference works for historians. They have also included various specialized publications that are particularly outstanding in their quality. In fact, the great majority of the items listed in this guide are publications of the highest distinction. The only time an unsatisfactory reference work appears in this guide is when it is the only work available on an important topic. All of the criteria used for the selection of the

works listed in this reference guide are somewhat subjective. The authors have no doubts that many readers of this book will find that find one or more of their favorite and most trusted reference works have been left out. For that omission, the authors apologize. Practical considerations of size and cost for this book caused the authors to forego listing many worthy reference works both old and new.

685 reference works and related titles have been listed and annotated in this reference guide. The entries have been organized into fourteen chapters on the basis of types of publications (e.g., bibliographies, atlases, microforms, journals). Works relating to various topics within the discipline of history (e.g., economic history, British history, psychohistory) can be found by using the index, which also lists all authors, editors, and titles mentioned throughout the text. Individual entries are numbered and followed by complete bibliographic information and annotations that describe the contents of the works and provide some evaluation of their usefulness for the study of history. Whenever an annotation for one work mentions the title of another work with an entry in the guide, a bracketed see-reference including the item number of that work has been provided. Frequently annotations will also mention similar or related titles that have not been given separate entries in the guide. Whenever this occurs, the authors have supplied the author's or editor's name, the title, place of publication, publisher, and date of publication. In this way the reference guide is able to list more titles than could have possibly been listed separately.

Regarding the continuing appearance of new books, the authors established no arbitrary cutoff date for the inclusion of recent publications. Instead, they continued to sift through catalogs, reviews, book exhibits, publishers' advertisements, and new acquisitions well into early 1990. Thanks to the wonders of word processing, the chosen fruits of this labor could be added to the guide with minimal trouble. And without a doubt, something will have been overlooked anyway. The Preacher spoke most truly in Ecclesiastes 12:12 when he said, "Of making many books there is no end."

ACKNOWLEDGMENTS FOR THE SECOND EDITION

As was the case with the first edition of this book, many people have helped us with the completion of this new edition of *Reference Sources in History*. We would like to thank them along with the people we thanked in the first edition. Once again we are grateful to ABC-CLIO for agreeing to publish a second edition and for patience in waiting for the manuscript. The people who work at ABC-CLIO are always a joy to work with. Alicia Merritt has been a wonderful acquisitions editor who gently prodded us to stay on the straight and narrow path to completion. Kay Mariea, the project editor, and Chrisona Schmidt, the copy editor, did a wonderful job of preparing the manuscript for publication. The libraries and their staff of Lamar University, the University of Central Arkansas, Western Kentucky University, and Washington State University all provided access to the resources that helped make this book possible. Ron was assisted in his work on the book by the award of a development leave from the faculty senate of Lamar University and several summers teaching at his alma mater, Concordia University in River Forest, Illinois, which gave him access to the libraries of Chicago, particularly the great Newberry Library. Brian's editorship of the "Best References Sources of the Year" featured in *Library Journal* for the past 15 years afforded him the luxury of seeing virtually all of the new reference works in history and auxiliary sciences. Lou was assisted by receiving a brief grant of leave to work on the book from the Washington State University Libraries.

ACKNOWLEDGMENTS FOR THE FIRST EDITION

Many people have helped us in the writing of this book. First, we would like to thank Heather Cameron of ABC-CLIO. No one could ask for a better person to help develop a project. She is patient, attentive, and full of sound advice and suggestions. John Grenville, professor of history at the University of Birmingham, read and evaluated our original proposal. He stayed on to provide advice and consultation. His suggestions were always sensible and his criticisms were invariably polite and constructive. Donald Davis of the Graduate School of Library and Information Science at the University of Texas steered us to Heather at a crucial moment. Charles Patterson and Lee Shiflett of the Graduate School of Library and Information Science at Louisiana State University introduced all of us to the librarian's point of view on reference materials. John Loos of the Department of History at Louisiana State University introduced us to reference and research materials from the historian's side. He was aided in this task by Paul Hoffman, Burl Noggle, and Fred Youngs, all of the Department of History at Louisiana State University. Dr. Rudolph Heinze and Professor Sir Geoffrey Elton also contributed significantly indispensably to Ron's education as a historian. Various colleagues from the libraries of Lamar University, Washington State University, and Western Kentucky University assisted with the location and acquisition of needed materials, in particular Mary Frances White. Many thanks to Lisa Andreason of Kelly High School, Beaumont, Texas, for providing the Latin epigram on the dedication page and saving an always poor and now quite rusty Latinist from embarrassment. Brian's wife, Karen D. Greene, was a constant source of support. Lou would like to thank his wife, Kay, and his daughter, Rachel, who always gave him the motivation and support to complete this project.

1

GUIDES, HANDBOOKS, AND MANUALS FOR HISTORY

This chapter brings together some basic reference books concerned with different aspects of the study of history that are important to anyone beginning research. A selection has been made of basic guides, handbooks, dictionaries, encyclopedias, and bibliographies that are likely to prove most useful. English-language texts have been preferred if available.

HISTORIOGRAPHY

Historiography is a term that can be used in several different ways. Here it is used to mean the study of the development of historical scholarship or the critical analysis of conflicting interpretations of a given period or problem in history. Historical scholarship has changed in both its methods and its concerns over the years and continues to change. For a full understanding of the study of history, it is important to know how it has developed and what are the different current trends.

001. *Historiography: An Annotated Bibliography of Journal Articles, Books, and Dissertations.* **Edited by Susan K. Kinnell.**

Santa Barbara, CA: ABC-CLIO, 1987. 2 vols. 458pp. ISBN 0-87436-168-0. Containing some 8,500 entries, this work is drawn from the databases for *America: History and Life* and *Historical Abstracts.* The first volume deals with individual historians, schools of history, and the various types of history: economic, social, political, etc. The second volume covers the geographical and national divisions of history (e.g., France, Soviet Union, and the United States). Within the broad divisions listed above, the individual entries are listed alphabetically by author and are numbered. A complete citation to the written work is provided. Most entries are annotated and signed by the abstracter. The many foreign-language entries are given with the original title followed by an English translation. This is an excellent source for beginning historiographical research but it does not include the older literature.

002. *Historiography: A Bibliography.* **Edited by Lester D. Stephens. Metuchen, NJ: Scarecrow, 1975. 271pp. Index. ISBN 0-8108-0856-0**
The purpose of this bibliography is to provide a comprehensive, although not complete, reference source for the beginning

student of historiography. It contains almost 2,300 entries books and journals, some of which are lightly annotated. These are divided into four sections: theories of history, historiography, historical methods, and reference works. Stephens's work has a strong emphasis on American history. A similar and more recent bibliography with a British emphasis is R. C. Richardson, *The Study of History: A Bibliographical Guide* (Manchester: Manchester University Press, 1988). Also see Attila Pok, *A Select Bibliography of Modern Historiography* (Westport, CT: Greenwood Press, 1992). These volumes are a good complement to *Historiography: An Annotated Bibliography* [see 001].

003. *Dictionary of Concepts in History.* By Harry Ritter. Westport, CT: Greenwood, 1986. 490pp. Index. ISBN 0-313-2270-4.

004. *The Routledge Companion to Historical Studies.* By Alan Munslow. London: Routledge, 2000. 271pp. Index. ISBN 0-415-18494-0.
These two works consist of alphabetized, encyclopedic entries that are really historiographical, critical essays dealing with various ideas and words commonly used by historians (e.g., frontier, modernization, and revolution). Each entry consists of a definition or definitions of the term followed by a critical essay with a list of references; entries end with suggestions for further reading. Munslow's book also includes some biographical entries for influential historians and philosophers and reflects the latest thinking of postmodernism. Both books will stimulate thinking about the meaning and implications of words commonly used among historians.

005. *A Global Encyclopedia of Historical Writing.* Edited by D. R. Woolf. New York: Garland, 1998. 2 vols. Index. ISBN 0-8153-1514-7.
For an up-to-date, comprehensive, highly scholarly, and easy-to-use reference work on the history of historical writing, students should consult this two-volume set first. The geographical scope of the *Global Encyclopedia* is the entire world, while its chronological scope is all eras where historical writing occurred. The 1,262 entries, which include suggestions for further reading, are signed by the expert who wrote them and are almost uniformly well written. 1,008 of the entries are biographical, while 167 are topical (e.g., "Annales School" to "Whig Interpretation") and 87 deal with national and regional historiographies. The historiographical articles range from something as familiar as "American Historiography" to the much more obscure "Sinhalese Historiography." While topical and historiographical entries only number 20 percent of the total, they comprise almost 50 percent of the total pages of the encyclopedia. A detailed index for persons and subjects completes this work.

006. *Historiography: Ancient, Medieval, and Modern.* By Ernst Breisach. 2d ed. Chicago: University of Chicago Press, 1995. 482pp. Index. ISBN 0-226-07278-9.
As a pioneering work, this narrative work provides in one volume a survey of the development of Western historical scholarship from the ancient Greeks to the 1970s. The author sees the writing of history as an activity that is a fundamental part of western culture; history helps to provide a balance between continuity and change in human society. The detailed index allows

specific topics and historians to be located easily, while the endnotes and the selective bibliography provide guidance for further reading. An older, two volume work that traces in great detail the development of both Western and non-Western historical scholarship from ancient times to 1900 is James Westfall Thompson, *A History of Historical Writing* (New York: Macmillan, 1942), while a short, up-to-date work is Mark T. Gilderhus's *History and Historians: A Historiographical Introduction*, 4th ed. (Englewood Cliffs, NJ: Prentice Hall, 1999). Many periods and historical topics have their own specialized histories of historical writing.

METHODOLOGY

007. *Church History: An Introduction to Research, Reference Works, and Methods.* By James Bradley and Richard A. Muller. Grand Rapids, MI: Eerdmans, 1995. xvi+236pp. ISBN 0-8028-0826-3.
Although this methodological guide was written to guide Ph.D. and Th.D. candidates in their graduate studies, it contains much that is of interest to undergraduate researchers and practicing historians, even those not engaged in the study of church history. Consisting of six chapters, the book covers the history of church history, the general philosophy of history, the use of basic bibliographic and research tools, the nature and use of primary sources, techniques of scholarly writing, and advice for the beginning professor. Particularly useful is the book's discussion of online catalogs, electronic bibliographic resources, and computerized primary collections like *Thesaurus Linguae Graecae* and the *Eighteenth*

Century Short Title Catalog. Hopefully this useful volume will be regularly updated.

008. *The Craft of Research.* By Wayne C. Booth, Gregory G. Colomb, and Joseph M. Williams. 2d ed. Chicago: University of Chicago Press, 2003. xii+294pp. ISBN 0-226-06567-7.
While the three authors of this excellent guide to research and the writing of research are all literary scholars, their book is still of great interest and relevance to people engaged in historical research. Fifteen chapters take the reader through the various stages of the creation of a research paper: formulating the topic, researching, organizing the results, writing the first draft, and revising. Examples dealing with historical topics are commonly employed. An appendix lists important reference works for various disciplines.

009. *The Modern Researcher.* By Jacques Barzun and Henry F. Graff. 6th ed. Belmont, CA: Wadsworth/Thomson, 2004. 322pp. Index. ISBN 0-15-505529-1.
The classic manual for research and writing for almost fifty years, *The Modern Researcher* has been regularly updated in every edition and so remains fresh and relevant. Written by two historians, the book's scope is wide; it provides a useful guide for all researchers and writers in the humanities and the social sciences. The reader is shown the way to develop a research topic, to use the library, to take notes, to organize research materials, and to write up the findings. Barzun and Graff write with style and much thought, making this work the best available. The length of the sixth edition has been considerably shortened by the elimination of three chapters dealing with the

philosophy of history and historiography. New material has been added on using the internet, electronic databases, and the computer.

010. *The Historian's Toolbox: A Student's Guide to the Theory and Craft of History.* By Robert C. Williams. Armonk, N.Y.: M. E. Sharpe, 2003. 170pp. ISBN 0-7656-1093-0.

011. *A Short Guide to Writing About History.* By Richard Marius and Melvin E. Page. 4th ed. New York: Longman, 2001. 240pp. ISBN 0-321-09300-3.

012. *Writing History: A Guide for Students.* By William Kelleher Storey. New York: Oxford University Press, 1999. 118pp. ISBN 0-19-512220-8.

These three brief guides do specifically for history what *The Craft of Research* [see 008] does for the humanities and social sciences in general. They discuss the types of historical writing, thinking and analyzing historically, types of historical evidence, techniques and pitfalls of writing, and the mechanics of the research paper. The *Short Guide* even includes a sample research paper while *The Historian's Toolbox* includes a brief history of historical writing.

013. *The History Handbook.* By Carol Berkin and Betty S. Anderson. Boston, MA: Houghton Mifflin, 2003. 144pp. ISBN 0-618-12285-0.

014. *A Student's Guide to History.* 8th ed. By Jules R. Benjamin. New York: St. Martin's, 2000. 233pp. ISBN 0-312-24765-6.

All undergraduate history students, whether majors, minors, or nonmajors, would do well to read either or both of these valuable

textbooks on how to study history and to learn its lessons. Those lessons are applicable to more than just history courses. Both books show their readers how to do reading assignments for class, to take notes in class, to study for an exam, to write a book review, and to write a research paper. Guidance on using computers, the Internet, and online research make this new edition particularly useful. Benjamin's work includes a helpful classified bibliography of reference books found in most college libraries.

CHRONOLOGIES, CALENDARS, AND LISTS OF RULERS

015. *Calendrical Calculations: The Millennium Editions.* By Nachum Dershowitz and Edward M. Reingold. Cambridge: Cambridge University Press, 2001. 456pp. ISBN 0-521-77167-6.

In *Calendrical Calculations* the authors first describe the world's calendars, both current and historical, and then present simple algorithms for calendrical calculations, supplemented with code to implement many of the algorithms. In *Calendrical Tabulations* the authors achieve what some had thought virtually impossible, the simultaneous display of a date on thirteen different calendars over a 300-year period. Represented are the Gregorian, ISO, Hebrew, Chinese, Coptic, Ethiopic, Persian, Hindu Lunar, Hindu Solar, and Islamic calendars. The author's precise computer calculations make this work more accurate than previous sources.

016. *Cronologia, Cronografia, e Calendrio Perpetuo Dal Principio Dell'Era Cristiana ai*

Nostri Giorni: Tavole Cronologico-Sincrone e Quadri Sinottici per Verificare le Date Storiche. By A. Cappelli. 3d ed., expanded and amplified. Milan: Ulrico Hoepli, 1969. 602pp. Index.

Although written in Italian, much of the information found in this guide is still accessible to English-speaking readers. Basically, it is a handbook which gathers together information that is useful for dating documents. The perpetual calendar for both the Julian and Gregorian systems supplies the date, day of the week, and religious holidays as they occurred in individual years. Further lists of saints' days and religious feasts are also supplied. Other tables allow conversions from the Islamic calendar based on Hegira and the French Revolutionary calendar. Another large section of the book provides chronological lists of various European dynasties, including quite minor states as well as the major dynasties of Egypt, China, Islam, and Japan. Most of this information can be found in various English-language publications, particularly the *Handbook of Dates for Students* [see 024], but Cappelli brings it all together in one convenient place. An English translation of this work would be useful.

017. *Chronologies in Old World Archaeology.* Edited by Robert W. Ehrich. 3rd ed. Chicago: University of Chicago Press, 1992. 2 vols. ISBN 0-226-19447-7.

018. *Chronology of the Ancient World.* By E. J. Bickerman. 2nd ed. Ithaca, NY: Cornell University Press, 1980. 223pp. Index. ISBN 0-80-141282-X.

019. *Handbook of Biblical Chronology: Principles of Time Reckoning in the Ancient World and Problems of Chronology in the Bible.* By Jack Finegan. Princeton, NJ: Princeton University Press, 1964. 338pp. Index.

Ehrich's chronology is a guide to the dating of prehistory and the most ancient historical developments among the Old World civilizations. It combines both breadth and depth of coverage. Focusing more on later ancient history, Bickerman's *Chronology* is a much revised English translation of his original German work. Its historical focus is the classical Greek and Roman era from about 800 BC to AD 476. Three chapters discuss the various ancient calendars, chronography (i.e., the techniques used to determine the amount of time between an ancient event and the present) and applied chronology (i.e., the supplying of a modern date, BC or AD, to some ancient event). These chapters are followed by various tables that can be used for converting ancient dates to modern equivalents (e.g., astronomical new moons from 605 BC to AD 308); a synchronistic listing of Olympic years; years from the founding of Rome; Egyptian mobile years with the BC or AD equivalent; and lists of various rulers, Athenian archons, and Roman consuls. Finegan is not as detailed as Bickerman for Greek and Roman systems of dating. But as the title indicates, this work spends more time on biblically related topics such as ancient Egyptian, Mesopotamian, and Hebrew chronology and datings used by the early Christians. It includes many tables and, unlike Bickerman, supplies a useful bibliography. *A Companion to Greek Studies,* edited by Leonard Whibley, 4th ed. (1931; New York: Hafner, 1963) and *A Companion to Latin Studies,* edited by Sir John Edwin Sandys, 3rd ed. (1935; New York: Hafner,

1963) also contain useful sections on dating and chronology along with much other information.

020. *Chronology of World History.* **Edited by H. E. L. Mellersh and Neville Williams. Santa Barbara, CA: ABC-CLIO Press, 1999. 4 vols. ISBN 1-57607-155-3.**
Named a *Choice* outstanding academic title and a *Library Journal* Best Reference Source in 1999. This four-volume set, which includes 70,000 events compiled by 27 contributing editors, is the best and most current chronology of world history. Volume 1 covers *The Ancient and Medieval World* (Prehistory to AD 1491), volume 2 is *The Expanding World* (1492–1775), volume 3 is *The Changing World* (1776–1900), and volume 4 is *The Modern World* (1901–1998). Entries range from Art to Technology and cover both major and minor events throughout world history. See also *Timelines on File*, rev. ed. (New York: Facts on File, 2000). This very popular and widely available source has been thoroughly revised and updated with 500 new plates. Volume 1 covers ancient and medieval history, volume 2 describes the history of the expanding world, volume 3 examines the 20th century, and volume 4 presents a brief history of each U.N. member.

021. *Handbook of British Chronology.* **Edited by E. B. Fryde, D. E. Greenway, S. Porter, and I. Roy. 3rd ed. London: Royal Historical Society, 1996. 6,645pp. ISBN 0-521-56350-X.**
Serious students of British history will want to have their own personal copy of this book. It is a series of lists of the major office holders for the British Isles from about AD 400 to the present. The work begins with the monarchs and rulers for England, Scotland, Wales, and the Isle of Man but not the complicated subject of Irish kings. Next comes lists of the major officers of state for England, Ireland, and Scotland. The largest section of this work lists the archbishops and bishops for England, Wales, Scotland, and Ireland. The various dukes, marquesses, and earls for England, Scotland, and Ireland are listed. Finally, there are lists of the meetings of Parliament and the provincial and national councils of the English church before 1536. This work is an excellent aid for assigning approximate dates from internal evidence to undated documents.

022. *Handbook of Oriental History.* **Edited by C. H. Philips. London: Royal Historical Society, 1963. 265pp. Index.**
Most Western students are unfamiliar with much of the basic historical terminology and the cultural practices of the Near East, Middle East, and Far East. This volume seeks to alleviate that problem for the entire Orient excluding the pre-Islamic Near and Middle East. It is divided into five geographical sections, each written by an expert on the region: Near and Middle East, India and Pakistan, Southeast Asia and the Archipelago, China, and Japan. Each section supplies useful information on the romanization of that area's words, local naming practices and titles, a glossary of frequently used terms, systems of dating and calendars (e.g., the Islamic calendar dating from Hegira [AD 622]), and lists of dynasties and rulers. This clear and handy guide is a must for any student of Oriental history.

023. *Monarchs, Rulers, Dynasties, and Kingdoms of the World.* **Compiled by R. F.**

Tapsell. New York: Facts on File, 1983. 511pp. ISBN 0-87196-121-0.
Who ruled when and where are the questions answered by this fascinating book. Its scope is international and includes all periods of history back to the beginning of written records. U.S. presidents are the one group of nonmonarchial rulers included in this work. Popes are also listed but not Orthodox patriarchs. The volume is divided into two sections. Section 1, an "Alphabetical Guide to Dynasties and States," consists of some 1,200 dictionary-length entries with some genealogical charts. About 1,000 dynastic lists make up section 2. The lists are arranged in geographical and chronological order and provide the name, dates for the reign, and brief family information for approximately 13,000 rulers. This book's great utility is that it provides easy access to information on many minor European rulers and major and minor non-European states. A similar title is John E. Morby, *Dynasties of the World: A Chronological and Genealogical Handbook* (Oxford: Oxford University Press, 1990), which became available in a paperback edition in 2002.

024. *Handbook of Dates for Students of English History.* Edited by C. R. Cheney and revised by Michael Jones. New ed. Cambridge: Cambridge University Press, 2000. 246pp. Index. ISBN 0-521-77095-5.
Originally published in 1945 and regularly updated, this revised edition thoroughly updates, revises, corrects, and expands the previous editions. This handy little book functions for students of English history as Adriano Cappelli's *Cronologia* . . . [see 016] does for general European history. It explains the Julian (Old Style) and the Gregorian (New Style) calendars along with

the concept of the year of grace for beginning a new year. There are lists of English rulers along with tables of regnal years beginning with Henry II in 1154 and lists of popes. Various saint's days and Christian festivals are also listed. The dating and chronology used in the English legal system is explained, as is the Roman calendar, and has been greatly expanded. A series of tables provides all possible dates for Easter in both Old and New Style from AD 400 to 2100. Finally, there is a chronological listing of Easter dates from AD 400 to 2100. New tables list the dates of adoption of the Gregorian calendar by the various European countries and provide detailed information about the French Revolutionary calendar. For a similar electronic source, there is Ian's English Calendar at www.albion.edu/english/Calendar. It provides calculations for (1) Easter dates, (2) Old and New Style dating conversions, (3) the day of the week for any date Old or New Style, and (4) conversions of regnal years of English monarchs into AD dates. This electronic source is fine for those who do not own a copy of Cheney, although it is much less detailed.

HISTORICAL METROLOGY: WEIGHTS, MEASURES, AND EXCHANGE RATES FOR MONEY

025. *British Weights and Measures: A History from Antiquity to the Seventeenth Century.* By Ronald Edward Zupko. Madison, WI: University of Wisconsin Press, 1977. 248pp. Index. ISBN 0-299-07340-8.
In addition to the three chapters providing a narrative history of the evolution of stan-

dardized weights and measures in England from Roman times to 1603, the remaining half of the volume consists of four valuable appendixes for students of European economic history. Appendix A lists alphabetically goods imported and exported by the English from 1150 to 1800 and how they were bulk-rated (i.e., measured in groups). British preimperial units are given in tabular form in Appendix B and include all units set up by statute in England, Scotland, and Ireland prior to the Imperial Weights and Measures Act of 1824. Appendix C provides tables for the units established in the British Isles by the Imperial Weights and Measures Act of 1824. Finally, Appendix D, "Pre-Metric Weights and Measures in Western and Eastern Europe," alphabetically lists the unit and supplies where it was used and what its English and metric equivalents were. The classified and occasionally annotated bibliography updates the one found in Zupko's *Dictionary of English Weights and Measures* [see 027] and includes a large number of relevant dictionaries and glossaries. Also worth consulting is Zupko, *A Dictionary of Weights and Meaures for the British Isles: The Middle Ages to the Twentieth Century* (Philadelphia: American Philosophical Society, 1985).

026. *Diccionario Universalde Monedas.* By Jose Manuel Coelho de Paula. Vigo: J. M. Coelho, 1997. 458pp. *Diccionario Universal de Monedas: Especializado.* By Jose Manuel Coelho de Paula. Vigo: J. M. Coelho, 2000. 1 vol. Various paging.
The author has spent almost two decades examining 6,000 "monedas" worldwide from all periods of time and of all types. Beautifully bound and illustrated. See also Alan K. Craig, *Spanish Colonial Silver Coins*

in the Florida Collection (Gainsville: University Press of Florida, 2000) for an intriguing discussion of the minting and transportation of these unique handmade coins.

027. *A Dictionary of English Weights and Measures: From Anglo-Saxon Times to the Nineteenth Century.* By Ronald Edward Zupko. Madison, WI: University of Wisconsin Press, 1968. 224pp. LC 68-14038.
The purpose of this very helpful book is to clear up ambiguities and confusions concerning the English weights and measures used in the past. Each main entry consists of the name of the unit of measure, alternative spellings with the approximate century they were in use, an etymology of the word, and a general definition and history of the unit, including its metric equivalent whenever it can be determined. There are also numerous see-references from alternative spellings to the main entry. The information in each entry is documented by references to items in the extensive and sometimes annotated bibliography.

028. *A Dictionary of Weights, Measures, and Units.* By Donald Fenna. Oxford Paperback Reference. Oxford: Oxford University Press, 2002. 342pp. ISBN 0-19-860522-6.
This comprehensive dictionary provides definitions of units, prefixes, and styles of weights and measures within the Systeme International (SI), as well as traditional and industry specific and traditional terms currently in usage. It describes the evolution of the basic metric system into the SI and parallel developments with other units of measure.

029. *French Weights and Measures before the Revolution: A Dictionary of Provincial and Local Units.* By Ronald Edward Zupko. Bloomington, IN: Indiana University Press, 1978. 208pp. ISBN 0-253-32480-7.

If historical English weights and measures are confusing, the French situation is even more complex, as France is a larger country with even more regional variations. Individual entries are listed alphabetically by name of the unit. Alternative spellings are cross-referenced to the main entry. The body of the entry supplies the century in which the unit was first used, variants in later centuries, an etymology of the word, and the definition of the unit with its dimensions, along with citations to the appropriate sources listed in the partially annotated bibliography.

030. *Glossary of Medieval Terms of Business: Italian Series, 1200–1600.* By Florence Edler. Cambridge, MA: Mediaeval Academy of America, 1934. 430pp. Index.

Italians dominated much of the international trade of the Middle Ages and early modern era. Therefore, an understanding of their business terminology and methods is essential for students of the economy and society in those time periods. The extensive glossary provides both definitions and citations to primary sources. Nineteen classified lists of terms for money, various measures, types of tolls, and other related subjects supplement the glossary. A further nine appendixes provide information on business and industrial terms and practices. This book provides clear guidance through a highly complex subject. Also see Ronald Edward Zupko, *Italian Weights and Measures from the Middle Ages to the Nineteenth Cen-*

tury (Philadelphia: American Philosophical Society, 1981).

031. *Handbook of Medieval Exchange.* By Peter Spufford. London: Royal Historical Society, 1986. 468pp.

Determining the relative value of money throughout history is often an impossible task. After years of research in both archives and printed documents, Peter Spufford has managed to produce a volume that provides European exchange rates for the period 1250–1500. Since the Florentine florin was the medieval equivalent of the U.S. dollar, its exchange rates form the basis for most of the tables in this book. Individual chapters are organized on a geographical basis. Commercially advanced Italy, not surprisingly, is covered in three chapters, while far more primitive Muscovy has no listings. Besides the rest of Europe, Byzantium, Levant, and the Barbary States are given detailed listings. As a tool for comparing the financial situation of the many kingdoms, regions, and cities of medieval Europe, this volume is a unique and superb work of reference. A companion volume of exchange rates for post-1500 Europe is under preparation by Professor F. C. Spooner.

032. *Historical Metrology: A New Analysis of the Archaeological and Historical Evidence Relating to Weights and Measures.* By A. E. Berriman. London: J. M. Dent, 1953. 224pp. Index.

As an introduction to the study of weights and measures throughout history, this encyclopedic survey is excellent. Each chapter gives a history of various historical weights and measures and explains how they convert into modern English units. Besides the expected chapters on Classical and western European nations, there are discussions of Russian, Chinese, and Indian systems of weights and measures. Particularly useful are the chapters on ancient Egyptian and Babylonian measuring systems, which are often neglected in other works on historical metrology.

033. *Scales and Weights: A Historical Outline.* By Bruno Kisch. New Haven, CT: Yale University Press, 1965. 297pp. Index. LC 65-12545.
While this work is not strictly a reference work, it provides an encyclopedic survey of its subject. Clearly delineated chapters and subsections supply readily comprehensible explanations and histories of the metric system, various types of scales, and specialized systems of weights (e.g., carat, pharmaceutical, and Byzantine). Particularly useful are the three appendixes: "Ancient Weight Units," "Weight Standards of the World before the Metric-Decimal System," and "Weight Standards of the World with Gram or Kilogram Equivalents." These appendixes are worldwide in their scope. The bibliography is superseded by those found in Zupko's works [see 025, 027, and 029].

034. *The Weights and Measures of England.* By R. D. Connor. London: Her Majesty's Stationery Office, 1987. 422pp. Index.
This encyclopedic survey of English weights and measures covers from earliest times to the present metric system. Its detailed subject index and numerous subheadings within chapters make it easy to locate information on specific topics. Besides discussions of the history of the mile, the foot, the acre, the gallon, and many other weights and measures, the British system of coinage is also described. Various appendixes detail how weights and measures were regulated, tell the history of the metric system, and provide a table of premetric British measures. A useful glossary of unit terms follows along with a helpful bibliography.

035. *Weights, Measures, and Money of All Nations.* Compiled by F. W. Clarke. New York: Appleton, 1894. 117pp.
The purpose of this work is to supply the metric equivalent for measures of length, liquid measures, dry measures, weights, and the gold or U.S. dollar equivalent for coinages of various nations around the world. The first part of this work is arranged alphabetically by country. In the second part, tables are provided for measures of length, road, square measures, dry measures, weights, and money. These are arranged alphabetically by the name of the measure followed by its locality and its English, U.S., and metric equivalent. Although it is dated, this work can still supply difficult-to-find information for the historian. For a recent study of early medieval Russian weights and money, see *The Origins of the Old Rus' Weights and Monetary Systems,* by Omeljan Pritsak (Cambridge, MA: Harvard University Press, 1998).

AUXILIARY SCIENCES OF HISTORY

Archaeology

036. *Archaeology. A Bibliographical Guide to the Basic Literature.* By Robert F. Heizer, Thomas R. Hester, and Carol Graves.

New York: Garland, 1980. 434pp. Index.
ISBN 0-8240-9826-9.
Although this guide has a definite bias
toward New World archaeology, it is still a
very useful resource for beginning research
in the general subject of archaeology. Listing
4,818 books, articles, and other materials, it
is divided into five broad sections: the nature
and purpose of archaeology, its history,
methods and subfields of archaeology, the
teaching and profession of archaeology, and
reference materials. Entries are listed alphabetically by author within the many subsections. There are no annotations and there is
an author index but no subject index.

037. *The Cambridge Encyclopedia of
Archaeology.* **Edited by Andrew Sherratt.
New York: Crown/Cambridge University
Press, 1980. 495pp. Index.
ISBN 0-517-53497-5.**
Written for an educated nonspecialist and
attractively illustrated, this work provides an
authoritative introduction to the many
aspects of the discipline of archaeology. It
has since been joined by a number of more
specialized and scholarly reference works.
For a more detailed multivolume work, see
the *Encyclopedia of Archaeology: The Great
Archaeologists,* edited by Tim Murray (Santa
Barbara, CA: ABC-CLIO, 2000), which
consists of two volumes containing 58
biographical essays, and the *Encyclopedia of
Archaeology: History and Discoveries,* edited by
Tim Murray (Santa Barbara, CA: ABC-
CLIO, 2001) in three volumes covering
such topics as discoveries, concepts, museums, geographical regions, and cultures. Of
particular interest to both archaeology and
classical studies is the two-volume *An Encyclopedia of the History of Classical Archaeology,*
edited by Nancy Thomson de Grummond

(Westport, CT: Greenwood, 1996). There
are also the two multivolume sets: *The New
Encyclopedia of Archaeological Excavations in
the Holy Land,* 4 vols. (New York: Simon &
Schuster, 1993) and *The Oxford Encyclopedia
of Archaeology in the Near East,* edited by
Eric M. Meyers, 5 vols. (New York: Oxford
University Press, 1997). Maurice Robbin,
The Amateur Archaeologist's Handbook, 3rd ed.
(New York: Harper & Row, 1981) is a prac-
tical introduction to the field and research
techniques used by archaeologists.

038. *The Oxford Companion to Archaeology.*
**Edited by Brian M. Fagan et al. New York:
Oxford University Press, 1996. 844pp.
Index. ISBN 0-19-507618-4.**
This handy, comprehensive dictionary of
archaeology—its history, concepts, and
practitioners—is a good place to begin
research or simply to answer a question. Its
scope is global with hundreds of entries
written by specialists, although there is a
discernible British bias. The index and
cross-references help readers locate topics
not covered in separate entries. Similar in
scope but not quite as recent is the *Collins
Dictionary of Archaeology,* edited by Paul
Bahn (Santa Barbara, CA: ABC-CLIO,
1993). Also see Molly Raymond Mignon,
Dictionary of Concepts in Archaeology (Westport, CT: Greenwood, 1993).

Genealogy

Printed Sources

039. *Genealogical Research and Resources:
A Guide for Library Use.* **By Lois C. Gilmer.
Chicago: American Library Association,
1988. 70pp. Index. ISBN 0-8389-0482-3.**

040. *The Genealogist's Handbook: Modern Methods for Researching Family History.* By Raymond S. Wright III. Chicago: American Library Association, 1995. 190pp. Index. ISBN 0-8389-0625-7.

Guides on how to do genealogical research compose one of the minor growth industries of book publishing. Many are available and many are good. Lois C. Gilmer's guide, published as an inexpensive paperback by the American Library Association, has the virtues of being recent, sensible, concise, and intended for the beginning genealogist. It is also designed to help librarians faced with frequent genealogical questions. Techniques of genealogical research are outlined. Next comes discussions of the primary and secondary sources used by genealogists. An appendix supplies the names and addresses of various archives, societies, libraries, and publishers of interest to genealogists. There is a brief subject index. Wright's volume is a concise but comprehensive introduction for the beginner. Its eight chapters describe getting started in genealogical studies, organizing research, using the computer, and the nature of the various sources used by genealogists. Also helpful is *Handy Book for Genealogists*, 9th ed. (Logan, UT: Everton, 1999). Focusing on the resources of one great research library, but with much material applicable to research in general, is James C. Neagle, *The Library of Congress: A Guide to Genealogical and Historical Research* (Salt Lake City, UT: Ancestry, 1990).

041. *American and British Genealogy and Heraldry: A Selected List of Books.* Compiled by P. William Filby. 3rd ed. Boston: New England Historic Genealogical Society, 1983. 736pp. Index. ISBN 0-88082-004-7.

Although there are many genealogical bibliographies, this one is an excellent place to start research. Almost 10,000 titles concerning genealogy, heraldry, and local history are listed in this fine bibliography. While the emphasis is American and British genealogy, this latest edition has begun listing works in English on other countries. The cutoff date for inclusion of a book is the fall of 1981. Individual entries are arranged into geographical sections: United States, the individual states, Latin America, Canada, England, Ireland, Scotland, Wales, other former British territories, and the world. There are also sections for heraldry and chivalry. The detailed index lists authors, titles, and subjects.

042. *Compendium of Historical Sources: The How and Where of American Genealogy.* By Ronald A. Bremer. Rev. ed. Bountiful, UT: AGLL, 1997. 914pp. Index. ISBN 1-877677-15-9.

This massive work is an excellent detailed starting point for genealogical research or historical research using family and local history types of materials. It provides detailed how-to information on locating and obtaining information, taking notes, and using interlibrary loan. Various sources of records are discussed in individual chapters. While the focus is American genealogy, Canadian and overseas sources are also discussed . There is also a glossary of useful terms.

043. *The Dictionary of Genealogy.* By Terrick V. H. FitzHugh and Susan Lumas. 5th ed. London: A. C. Black, 1998. 320pp. ISBN 0713648597.

The focus of the over 1,000 terms listed in this dictionary is British genealogy. All sorts of technical terms like gavelkind and virgate that a person might come across in the course of genealogical research are lucidly defined. Furthermore, sources of potential information like patent rolls and useful repositories of genealogical materials such as Dr. Williams's Library in London are described. This is a useful dictionary for students of genealogy and history. A much shorter and less detailed dictionary that is intended for an American audience and lists only terms commonly found in the historical documents used by genealogists is Frances Dunfee Larson, *The Genealogists's Dictionary* (Bellevue, WA: By the author, 1986, 1987). More recent is Paul Drake's excellent *What Did They Mean by That? A Dictionary of Historical Terms for Genealogists* (Bowie, MD: Heritage Books, 1994). Of interest for research relating to the British Isles is *The Oxford Companion to Local and Family History*, edited by David Hey (New York: Oxford University Press, 1996).

044. *Printed Sources: A Guide to Published Genealogical Records.* Edited by Kory Meyerink. Orem, UT: Ancestry, 1998. 840pp. Index. ISBN 0-916489-70-1.

045. *The Source: A Guidebook of American Genealogy.* Edited by Loretto Dennis Szucs and Sandra Hargreaves Luebking. Rev. ed. Salt Lake City, Utah: Ancestry, 1997. 834pp. Index. ISBN 0-916489-67-1.
These two related titles are premier resources for the serious genealogist and as such they also provide excellent introductions to both printed and archival sources of interest to historians. Both works consist of chapters describing the various materials of interest to historians and genealogists, ranging from church records to military

records and from bibliographies to biographies to journals. *Printed Sources* is particularly helpful and many historians teaching historical research might want to get their own copy.

Web Sites Frequently Searched by Historians

046. *Cyndi's List of Genealogical Sites on the Internet.* http://www. Cyndislist.com
What began as a hobby seven years ago has grown to be one of the largest genealogical sites on the Web. Maintained by Cyndi Howells, it lists 185,450 links arranged in 150 categories. Indexes include main, topical, alphabetical, "no frills," and text-only index. More than 34 million people have visited this site since its launch in March 1996. This is the best place to begin any genealogical search. *Cyndi's List* (the book) second edition was published in two volumes in 2001 by the Genealogical Publishing Company.

047. *CWGC: Commonwealth War Graves Commission.* http://www.cwgc.org
1.7 million men and women of the British Commonwealth forces died in the two world wars. Of these approximately 1 million were found. A headstone marks their graves. Others are commemorated in memorials. There are graves in 150 different countries. A commission established in 1917 endeavors to maintain graves and records.

048. *Ellis Island On-Line.* http://www. ellisisland.org
Between 1892 and 1924 more than 22 million immigrants, passengers, and crew members came through Ellis Island and the Port of New York. You can search by name,

view the original ship manifest, and even see a picture of the ship the immigrants arrived on.

049. *Family Search.* http://www. familysearch.org

This massive search engine maintained by the LDS Church searches for records in ancestral, census, and other vital records sources, including U.S. Social Security Death Index, Vital Records Index, 1880 U.S. Census, 1881 Census of the British Isles, and the 1881 Canadian Census. Click on "Search for Ancestors" to begin your search.

050. *The Ships List.* http://theshipslist. com/index.html

A vast collection of links to ships and shipping companies. The list was established to assist those seeking information on the vessels that brought settlers to Canada, the United States, Australia, and other parts of the world. Provides ships, passenger lists, fleet lists, ship decrypting schedules, wreck data, voyage accounts, and other related information.

051. *The USGenWeb Project.* http://www. Usgenweb.com

This noncommercial site was founded in 1996 and is maintained entirely by volunteers. It endeavors to provide Web sites for genealogical research in every county and every state of the United States. This is a great jumping-off spot for searching state archives.

052. *1901 Census (United Kingdom) Web Site.* http://www.census.pro.gov.uk/welcome. html

This census was taken on March 31, 1901,

and provides a comprehensive name index to 32 million individuals. While the basic search is free, there are fees for the actual documents. You can even search by place such as a barracks or school. There is a minimum fee of £5 for prints. See also Census of Canada, 1901, http://www.archives.ca/ 02/02020205_e.html. More cumbersome to search than the British census, the census of Canada was undertaken on March 31, 1900, and consisted of 11 questionnaires and 561 questions. These were published between 1902 and 1906. The census of population declared the population of Canada to be 5,371,051. The originals were destroyed in 1955. This digitized version provides access to the microfilmed version.

Heraldry

053. *Bibliotheca Heraldica Magnae Britanniae: An Analytical Catalogue of Books on Genealogy, Heraldry, Nobility, Knighthood, and Ceremonies with a list of Provincial Visitations, Pedigrees, Collections of Arms, and Other Manuscripts; and a Supplement, concerning the principal Foreign Genealogical Works.* By Thomas Moule. 1822. Reprint, London: Heraldry Today, 1966. 668pp. Index.

Originally published in 1822, this bibliography has remained a standard for students of heraldry. It includes 810 annotated entries that are arranged in chronological order by date of publication and describe books on English heraldry. Another 221 entries merely list various books on Continental heraldry. The index is a simple subject one and does not list titles, although it does list authors. This work should be used in conjunction with the bibliographies found in modern books on heraldry. A plan to extend this bibliography past 1822 up to the present has not yet been realized.

054. *A Dictionary of Heraldry.* Edited by Stephen Friar. New York: Crown, 1987. 320pp. ISBN 0-517-56665-6.
Intended to satisfy the needs of beginning and advanced students of heraldry, this attractive volume is an important basic resource for its subject. Its entries deal with the subject of heraldry in general and also with the subject of armory, which is the system of symbolism and presentation used in heraldry. While English topics dominate the entries, Continental heraldry is also discussed. Since heraldry was an important part of the feudal system that formed the basis for the European social structure in the Middle Ages and early modern period, this dictionary contains much to interest historians.

055. *The Oxford Guide to Heraldry.* By Thomas Woodcock and John Martin Robinson. Oxford: Oxford University Press, 1988. 288pp. ISBN 0-19-211658-4.
Everyone knows of heraldry because coats of arms and other heraldic paraphernalia are frequently used in trademarks and decorations. Few people, however, realize the actual complexity and diversity of true heraldry. Furthermore, the English practice of heraldry was considerably different from that of Continental Europe. Fortunately, beginning researchers can now turn to *The Oxford Guide to Heraldry* for the answers to most of their basic questions. Besides providing a clear and readable overview of the subject enhanced by many attractive illustrations, this book also supplies a useful glossary of terms and a brief introductory bibliography of modern books that can be

used to supplement *Bibliotheca Heraldica* [see 053].

Numismatics

056. *Numismatics.* By Philip Grierson. Oxford: Oxford University Press, 1975. 211pp. Index. ISBN 0-19-888098-7.
Coins and medals are an important form of historical evidence, especially for the ancient and medieval periods. Numismatics is the study of coins and medals, and Grierson's book is an excellent introduction and overview of the subject. It discusses both western and eastern systems of coinage, the making of coins, numismatic methodology, and the importance of numismatics to the historian. There is a short glossary of numismatic terms and a brief bibliography to guide further reading. This work is available in paperback.

057. *The Macmillan Encyclopedic Dictionary of Numismatics.* By Richard G. Doty. New York: Macmillan, 1982. 355pp. ISBN 0-02-532270-2.
Numismatics is a vast and complicated subject with a specialized vocabulary and much obscure lore. The scope of this work is the terminology of coinage from ancient times to the present, including tokens, medals, and paper money along with various technical subjects regarding the making of coins. There are some 500 entries with ample cross-referencing, which tend to be about 200–1,000 words in length. There is a brief bibliography for the volume. Any student of history seeking a more detailed knowledge of numismatics will want to consult this book. Complementing and supplementing this volume is the more

recent *International Encyclopedic Dictionary of Numismatics,* by R. Scott Carlton (Iola, WI: Krause, 1996).

058. *Numismatic Bibliography.* By E. E. Clain-Stefanelli. Munich: Battenberg, 1985. 1,848pp. Indexes. ISBN 3598075073. Numismatics is a busy field in which new writings are appearing all the time. As a result, the publication of an exhaustive general bibliography is impossible. Instead, the present work with its over 18,000 entries is designed to be an introduction for both historians and coin collectors. Although its scope is worldwide and all eras of history, the emphasis is on Europe and the United States. The entries are arranged quite logically beginning with general reference works and broad monetary topics, followed by three large sections on the ancient, medieval, and modern periods, which are arranged geographically. These are followed by specialized chapters on tokens, medals, decorations, the production of coins, important numismatic collections, the history of numismatics, and numismatic methodology. Six detailed indexes to authors, collectors, personal names, geographical terms, numismatic terms, and public collections greatly assist users of this bibliography. It updates and replaces Philip Grierson's *Select Numismatic Bibliography* (Washington, DC, 1965). A less expensive and more accessible bibliography containing some 1,100 numismatic items, which, however, is more oriented toward coin collecting, is Richard H. Rosichan, *Stamps and Coins* (Littleton, CO: Libraries Unlimited, 1974). The most recent writings on the subject can be found through the twice yearly *Numismatic Literature* (1947–), a current index and bibliography.

Paleography, Diplomatics, Epigraphy, and Sigillography

The topics composing this section are concerned with the written word and its authentication. Paleography is the study of the handwritings of former eras. Before the advent of typewriters, handwriting was a more precise and regulated skill. It also evolved over time, so there is a need to learn how to read the scripts of the medieval and early modern eras even when they are written in English. Diplomatics is the study of the form of standardized official documents. Many government documents of the past concerning frequently occurring situations were stereotyped in their form and phrasing. A knowledge of those forms and phrases will allow the historian to read and to understand many such documents better. Epigraphy is the study of engraved inscriptions. Sigillography is the study of the seals used to authenticate documents in the past.

059. *Bibliografia Paleografica.* By Josefina Mateu Ibars and Dolores Mateu Ibars. Barcelona: University of Barcelona, 1974. 932pp. Index. ISBN 84-600-1760-5. This massive work contains some 10,000 entries and is the most complete bibliography available. Although it is in Spanish, with patience and a Spanish-English dictionary, the non-Spanish speaker can still find it quite useful. There are entries from all the major European languages. While its scope is all of Europe, western Europe, particularly the Iberian Peninsula, dominates. Furthermore, this bibliography goes beyond works simply on the study of paleography and includes guides to various manuscript collections for various nations and subjects.

There are indexes for authors, repositories, places, and journals.

060. *English Court Hand A.D. 1066 to 1500: Illustrated Chiefly from the Public Records, Part I: Text* and *Part II: Plates*. **By Charles Johnson and Hilary Jenkinson. Oxford: Clarendon, 1915.**

061. *The Later Court Hands in England: From the Fifteenth to the Seventeenth Century*. **By Hilary Jenkinson. Cambridge: Cambridge University Press, 1927. Reprint 1962. 200pp. + plates.**
Beginning researchers will want to examine these two works on the paleography of English historical documents from the Norman Conquest through the early modern era. Their coverage is detailed, particularly in the earlier Johnson and Jenkinson volume. Introductory texts explain the history and methods of historical English handwritings. This material is followed by a large number of facsimiles of documents along with annotated transcriptions. A very detailed Italian textbook on paleography and diplomatics is Jole Mazzoleni, *Paleografia e Diplomatica e Scienze Ausiliare* (Naples: Libreria Scientifica, 1970). L. C. Hector, *The Handwriting of English Documents* (London: Edward Arnold, 1966), is a smaller but still useful and more affordable version of Johnson and Jenkinson, as is C. E. Wright, *English Vernacular Hands from the Twelfth to the Fifteenth Centuries* (Oxford: Oxford Paleographical Handbooks, 1959).

062. *Ductus: An Online Course in Paleography*. **http://www.medieval.unimelb.edu.au/ links.html**
"Ductus," from the Latin *ducere,* "to lead," is a Web-based, interactive multimedia pro-gram designed to facilitate the teaching of paleography, in particular the history of western European handwriting. The course won the Australian 2000 Award for Excellence in Tertiary Educational Publishing. Individuals can purchase a CD-ROM version, which includes 60 sample scripts. The URL above provides their free list of links on paleography, codicology, and early printed book sites.

063. *A Formula Book of English Official Historical Documents, Part I: Diplomatic Documents*, and *Part II: Ministerial and Judicial Records*. **Edited by Hubert Hall. 1908–1909. Reprint, New York: Burt Franklin, 1969. 170pp. and 229pp.**
This two-volume work is a collection of examples of the format and phraseologies used in the major official English historical documents. Actual primary documents have been transcribed along with introductions and notations. Chronologically the documents range from Anglo-Saxon times to the 19th century, although medieval documents predominate. While only English documents, of which most are written in Latin, appear in this collection, it is still an excellent place for any beginning student of the Middle Ages to start learning about the structure and format of official documents. Many similar works exist for other countries. The first volume consists of "diplomatic documents" such as royal charters, warrants, writs, confirmations, letters, and proclamations by which the government communicated its orders and policies. In the second volume, the documents transcribed are the various ministerial and judicial inquisitions by which the government gathered fiscal, military, and legal information and resources. There is a very informa-

tive essay on the study of diplomatics (i.e., the formulaic structure or organization of official documents) in Hubert Hall, *Studies in English Official Historical Documents* (1908; New York: Burt Franklin, 1969).

064. *Guide to Seals in the Public Record Office.* **London: Her Majesty's Stationery Office, 1954. 67pp.**

Sigillography, the study of the seals used to authenticate official documents, is a highly technical subject within medieval studies on which little has been written in English. This short study is an admirable and lucid introduction for beginners. It focuses on the types of seals found in the Public Record Office of Great Britain while including some discussion of foreign seals and private seals. While this study does not have a bibliography, references to further reading can be culled from its footnotes.

065. *Handbook of Greek and Latin Paleography.* **By Edward Maunde Thompson. London: Kegan, Paul, Trench, Trubner, 1906. 361pp. Index.**

Most students of history will never need to read handwritten manuscripts from the Classical period of Greek and Roman history. But for those who do need to decipher the mysteries of ancient scripts, this older work is a useful introduction. Its scope is actually both ancient and medieval Greek and Latin hands. Many similar works, however, exist for the medieval and early modern periods. The techniques and implements of writing are first described and then various chapters discuss the different forms of Greek and Latin writing. A helpful, but very dated, bibliography identifies collections of facsimiles of documents.

066. *Heraldry, Flags, and Seals: A Select Bibliography, with Annotations, Covering the Period 1920 to 1945.* **By S. Trehearne Cope. London: Association of Special Libraries and Information Bureaux, 1948. 146pp. Index.**

Although dated, the 445 annotated entries for books and articles in this bibliography are a useful introduction for students. The listings for seals are particularly helpful, since sigillography is little written about in the English language. A detailed subject index allows the user to find easily all materials of potential interest.

067. *Illustrated Introduction to Latin Epigraphy.* **By Arthur E. Gordon. Berkeley: University of California Press, 1983. 264pp. Index. ISBN 0-520-03898-3.**

Monumental inscriptions are an incredibly important source of historical information for Greco-Roman Classical civilization, which declined in significance, however, by the early medieval period. This volume consists of a short introduction which describes the nature of these inscriptions, their subject matter, their format, and supplies a bibliographic essay on the literature of epigraphy. A selection of 100 Latin inscriptions dating from the sixth century BC to AD 525 makes up the remainder of the book. E. G. Turner's *Greek Manuscripts of the Ancient World* (Oxford: Oxford University Press; Princeton, NJ: Princeton University Press, 1971) performs a similar function for Greek sources. While *Illustrated Introduction to Latin Epigraphy* is an excellent starting place for the beginning student, still useful and more detailed is John Edwin Sandys, *Latin Epigraphy: An Introduction to the Study of Latin Inscriptions*, 2nd ed. (Cambridge: Cambridge University Press, 1927; reprint, 1969).

068. *The Record Interpreter: A Collection of Abbreviations, Latin Works, and Names Used in English Historical Manuscripts and Records.* **Compiled by Charles Trice Martin. 2nd ed. 1910. Reprint, Dorking, U.K.: Kohler & Coombes, 1976. 464pp.**

Old documents from the Middle Ages and the early modern periods are usually written in a Latin that is idiosyncratic and frequently abbreviated. Martin's book is a guide to deciphering and understanding these peculiarities. It contains a series of alphabetical lists: abbreviations of Latin words, abbreviations of French words, a glossary of medieval Latin, and the Latin forms of various place-names, bishoprics, surnames, and Christian names used in England. A more detailed Italian work is *Lexicon Abbreviaturarum: Dizionario di Abbreviature Latin et Italiane* by Adriano Capelli, 5th ed. (Milan: Hoepli, 1954). It is easily accessible to students with an elementary knowledge of Latin. Its entries include a facsimile of a handwritten abbreviation as well as printed versions of the abbreviations and their extended forms. There is an English translation of the introduction of Cappelli's book: *The Elements of Abbreviation in Medieval Latin Paleography* (Lawrence, KS: University Press of Kansas, 1982).

069. *Two Select Bibliographies of Medieval Historical Study: I. A Classified List of Works Relating to the Study of English Paleography and Diplomatic. II. A Classified List of Works Relating to English Manorial and Agrarian History from the Earliest Times to the Year 1660.* **Edited by Margaret F. Moore. London, 1912. Reprint, New York: Burt Franklin, 1967. 185pp. Index.**

The 428 items listed in the paleography and diplomatic section are what continues to make this older volume valuable to students of medieval history. Although it was originally published in 1912, this bibliography remains helpful because the study of paleography and diplomatic have not changed dramatically since the beginning of the 20th century. While the focus of this book is the British Isles, the paleography sections also deal with other western European nations. There is an accompanying index for titles, authors, and subjects.

2

BIBLIOGRAPHIES

Once a subject has been selected, the next logical step is to compile a bibliography of books, articles, Web sites, and any other sources relevant to the topic. Where older generations of students mined the bibliographies and footnotes of other books, articles, or theses on the same topic, today's student can search a vast array of electronic databases, online catalogs, and specialized Web sites.

This chapter looks at bibliographies and bibliographic guides of value and interest for historical research. A bibliography is an organized list of books, articles, or other materials that focus on some topic, sometimes a fairly general one, such as Latin American history, or a specific one, like Brazil in the 19th century. The individual entries may also provide further brief information in the form of annotations. Bibliographic guides tend to be more heavily annotated and contain additional introductory and explanatory information to guide the researcher's choice. Another type of bibliographical listing is the periodical index, but that will be discussed in a separate chapter.

The variety and number of bibliographies and bibliographic guides that are available are very large, with more being added every day. The introduction of World Wide Web access to the Internet in 1993 and easy-to-use browsers such as Netscape and Microsoft Explorer has added a whole new dimension to bibliographic research in some areas.

This chapter begins with a description of bibliographic guides to reference works. It then describes bibliographic utilities such as OCLC and RLIN, which now dwarf all national bibliographies. These are followed by a section that looks at national bibliographies, with an emphasis on books published in the United States and Britain. National libraries in Europe and North America are discussed, followed by library Web catalogs of major research collections. The sixth section deals with general historical bibliography. This is followed by sections dealing with regional bibliographies, some of the more significant bibliographies for chronological periods, and finally a selection of bibliographies on important subfields of history.

BIBLIOGRAPHIES OF REFERENCE WORKS

070. *American Reference Books Annual*. Westport, CT: Libraries Unlimited (an

imprint of Greenwood Publishing Group), 1970–. ISSN 0065-9959. Annual.

072. *ARBAonline.* Westport, CT: Greenwood, 2002–.

For more than three decades ARBA has been one of the principal reviewing sources of new reference books. Under the capable editorship of Bohdan S. Wynar ARBA has provided descriptive and evaluative reviews for nearly 1,800 reference sources from 400 reviewers. Reviews written by librarians, scholars, and subject specialists average 250 words in length, are signed, and include references to reviews of the same work in other publications. These are arranged by subject from general reference to science and technology. Many sources of interest to historians appear in sections other than history. Each volume includes an author/subject/title index. Cumulative indexes have been published every five years. In August 2001, Libraries Unlimited was acquired by the Greenwood Publishing Group.

ARBAonline premiered at the ALA Annual Conference in Atlanta in June, 2002. Accessible via subscription at www.arbaonline.com, it includes more than 9,000 reviews of reference works published since 1997. In February 2003 all of the reviews featured in the print version of ARBA 2003 were added to the database. In 2002 Dr. Martin Dillon, former executive director of the OCLC Institute, became editor in chief of ARBA and ARBAonline.

072. *Bibliographic Index: A Cumulative Bibliography of Bibliographies.* New York: H. W. Wilson, Vol. 1–. 1937–. ISSN 0006-1255. Also on Wilson Web, 2003–.

Published in April and August, with a bound cumulation each December. New bibliographies appear constantly. The purpose of this publication is to provide a current listing of them. Originally *Bibliographic Index* appeared every three years, but in 1969 it started to appear annually. It is organized by detailed subject categories. The types of items listed include not only separately published bibliographies, but also bibliographies that appear as parts of books, pamphlets, and journals. A recent annual examined 2,800 periodicals for bibliographic material. A bibliography has to contain 50 or more entries for inclusion. The listing focuses on works published in English, German, Dutch, Swedish, Danish, Norwegian, French, Italian, Spanish, Portuguese, Russian, Polish, Czech, and other languages in the Roman alphabet. *Bibliographic Index on Wilson Web* offers faster digital searching with retrospective coverage back to 1984. Libraries can also provide links to their OPAC. Weekly updates are planned.

073. *Bulletin of Bibliography.* Westport, CT: Greenwood, 1897–. Vol. 1–. Quarterly. ISSN 0190-745X.

This is the oldest quarterly devoted solely to bibliography. The current editor is Bernard F. McTigue at D. H. Hill Library, North Carolina State University. The *Bulletin* publishes bibliographies on a wide range of topics in the humanities, social sciences, and the fine arts. A recent issue featured bibliographies on Adrienne Kennedy, Taylor Caldwell, T. H. White, and Josephine Baker. Some issues contain book reviews. An author-article index to the preceding volume appears in the first issue of the succeeding volume.

074. *Canadian Reference Sources: An Annotated Bibliography: General Reference*

Works, History, Humanities. Compiled and edited by Mary E. Bond with Martine M. Caron. Vancouver: UBC Press, 1996. 1,076pp. Index. ISBN 0-7748-0565-X.
This impressive work is much more than an update of Dorothy Ryder's *Canadian Reference Sources* (1981). It is an entirely new work. With 4,194 entries rendered in both English and French, this bibliography includes reference sources of all types, in all formats, about Canada. Reference sources of a general nature as well as works in history and the humanities are included. Annotations are descriptive rather than critical. There are four indexes: names, titles, and English and French subjects. Entries in the subject headings follow Canadian subject headings. Mary E. Bond and Martine M. Caron are both of the National Library's Reference and Information Division. This is a major advance in Canadian bibliography. Future editions are promised.

075. *Essay and General Literature Index.* New York: H. W. Wilson, 1900–. Published twice yearly; the second part is an annual cumulation that later is incorporated into a five-year cumulation. ISSN 0014-083X. Also available with quarterly updates on WisonWeb and WilsonDisc.
Unlike most other Wilson indexes, this subscription service is not concerned with periodicals. Instead, it indexes collections of articles appearing in books on subjects in the humanities and social sciences. Such collective books include Festschriften, for example, collections of essays published in honor of a famous scholar. More than 300 volumes are indexed annually. Additionally, more than 20 annuals or serial publications are indexed. The *Essay and General Literature Index* provides full bibliographic informa-

tion on collective titles indexed. The Web version provides access to 64,843 essays from 5,317 collections published in the United States, Canada, and Great Britain back to 1985.

076. *Guide to Reference Books.* Edited by Robert Balay. 11th ed. Chicago: American Library Association, 1996. 2,020pp. Index. ISBN 0-8389-0669-9.
This is the best general bibliography for locating reference works on all subjects. It used to be known as "Winchell," after an earlier editor and then "Sheehy," after a subsequent editor. Five broad sections divide the volume: general reference works, humanities, social sciences, history and area studies, and pure and applied sciences. These sections are further divided by subject, disciplines, or geographical areas such as newspapers, philosophy, law, the Americas, and chemistry. Within these divisions, more specialized categories, appropriate to that context, are used. Individual entries are given an alphanumeric designation, followed by the bibliographic citation and a descriptive and evaluative annotation. The 15,875 titles were selected by 50 general reference and subject specialist librarians from major universities across the United States. The index, almost one-quarter of the total volume, is vastly improved over prior editions. All students of history will find this work helpful.

077. *Reference Books Bulletin* (Annual Cumulations). Chicago: American Library Association, 1967–. ISSN 8755-0962.
Reference Books Bulletin, currently edited by Mary Ellen Quinn, is one of the premier sources of reference reviews in the United States and appears bimonthly in *Booklist.*

The 34th annual cumulation for 2001-2002 was published in 2002. The unsigned reviews are a collective effort of the editorial board and contributing reviewers that originally appeared in the journal *Booklist*. The most recent edition includes a special section "Reference on the Web," an "Encyclopedia Update," "Core collections," "Another Look At," and other *RBB* features. There are separate subject and title indexes.

078. *Walford's Guide to Reference Materials.* Vol. 1, *Science and Technology;* Vol. 2, *Social and Historical Sciences, Philosophy, and Religion;* and Vol. 3, *Generalia, Language and Literature, the Arts.* 8th ed. London: Library Association, 1999–. ISBN 1-85604-341-X. Originally edited by A. J. Walford, a British language and linguistics librarian, each volume now has separate editors. An edition cycle runs 3–4 years. Vols. 2–3 in the seventh edition were published in January 1998 and October 1998. Volume 1 in the eighth edition was published in October 1999. Archaeology, area studies, geography, and history are treated in volume 2. *Walford* follows a subject arrangement based on the Universal Decimal Classification with history falling in the 900s. Numerous CD-ROMs and databases are listed. All entries are annotated, albeit some very briefly. Michael Walsh and the library staff at Heythrop College, University of London, edited the nonhistory sections while Alan Day edited the 900s. There are separate author/title and subject indexes in each volume, as well as an online and database services index. An essential reference source.

079. *A World Bibliography of Bibliographies and of Bibliographic Catalogues, Calendars,* *Abstracts, Digests, Indexes, and the Like.* By Theodore Besterman. 4th ed. Lausanne, Switzerland: Societas Bibliographica, 1965–1966. 5 vols. Index.

080. *A World Bibliography of Bibliographies, 1964–1974; A List of Works Represented by Library of Congress Print Catalog Cards.* A Decennial Supplement to Theodore Besterman, *A World Bibliography of Bibliographies.* By Alice F. Toomey. Totowa, NJ: Rowman & Littlefield, 1977. 2 vols. ISBN 0-87471-999-2. Together these massive works list 117,000 and 18,000 separately published bibliographies and lists of manuscripts and patents published through 1974. They represent one of the last great efforts in the precomputer era to describe world bibliography.

BIBLIOGRAPHIC UTILITIES

081. *OCLC Online Union Catalog.* http://www.oclc.org/home
This is the largest bibliographic utility in the world. As of January 2003 it had 49,130,208 unique records. From 2001 to 2002 the OCLC WorldCat grew by 2.7 million records, and was used to arrange 8.9 million interlibrary loans. Staff and users conducted 35.6 million searches of WorldCat via FirstSearch for research and reference. WorldCat is most frequently searched through FirstSearch, a proprietary gateway offering a common search front for 72 databases in 14 topic areas. The WorldCat database includes books, journals, musical scores, datafiles, magazines, newspapers, manuscripts, sound recordings, films and slides, maps and videotapes. You can search

by subject, author, title, publication place, publisher, ISBN or ISSN, or subject heading. Most searches for monographs should begin here.

082. *RLG Union Catalog.* http://www. rlg.org

This union catalog lists 42 million titles in comprehensive research libraries and special libraries in the Research Library Group (RLG) member institutions plus over 100 additional law, technical, and corporate libraries. It includes records cataloged by the Library of Congress, the National Library of Medicine, the U.S. Government Printing Office, CONSER (Conversion of Serials Project), the British Library, the British National Bibliography, the National Union Catalog of Manuscript Collections, and RLG members and users. Coverage is comprehensive for books published since 1968. The RLG catalog is searchable via Eureka, RLIN, and Zephyr. A Web version of Eureka has been available since January 1997. There were 23 RLG files in 2003, including the Online Avery Index to Architectural Periodicals, the English Short Title Catalog, and the National Library of Australia Catalog.

NATIONAL BIBLIOGRAPHIES AND NATIONAL LIBRARIES

In 1977, under the auspices of IFLA (International Federation of Library Associations and Institutions) and UNESCO, the heads of national bibliographic services met in Paris to formulate recommendations for defining the basis of adequate bibliographic control for each country. Their aim was the eventual creation of the Universal Bibliographic Control (UBC). Principles agreed on included the desirability of legal deposit legislation, a national bibliography, and the bibliographic agency or national library. There are few countries that do not have at least one of these components.

United States

083. *American Bibliography: A Chronological Dictionary of All Books, Pamphlets and Periodical Publications Printed in the United States of America from the Genesis of Printing in 1639 down to the Year 1800; with Bibliographical and Biographical Notes.* By Charles Evans. Chicago: By the author; Worcester, MA: American Antiquarian Society, 1903–1959. Reprint 1941–1967. 14 vols. Index. ISBN 0-8446-1175-1.

084. *Supplement to Charles Evans' American Bibliography.* By Roger Pattrell Bristol. Charlottesville, VA: University Press of Virginia, 1970. 636pp. ISBN 0-8139-02878-8.

085. *National Index of American Imprints Through 1800: The Short-Title Evans.* By Clifford Kenyon Shipton and James E. Mooney. Worcester, MA: American Antiquarian Society, 1969. 2 vols. Charles Evans is one of the giants of historical bibliography in the United States. His bibliography provides a chronological listing of almost 36,000 books from the beginning of North American printing in 1639 through 1800. Besides being available at those libraries that own original copies of these books, they are also on the microcard and microfiche collection *Early American*

Imprints 1639–1800 [see 917, 918]. Originally Evans planned to go to 1820, but he had completed only about half of the year 1800 at the time of his death. The works of Bristol and Shipton and Mooney supplement and amplify that of Evans. Of related interest is J. Sabin's *Bibliotheca Americana* and its associated titles [see 088].

086. *American Bibliography: A Preliminary Checklist for 1801–1819.* By Ralph Robert Shaw and Richard H. Shoemaker. New York: Scarecrow, 1958–1966. 22 vols. ISBN 0-8108-1607-5.

087. *A Checklist of American Imprints for 1820–1886.* By Richard H. Shoemaker, Gayle Cooper, Scott Bruntjen, and Carol Rinderknecht. Metuchen, N.J.: Scarecrow, 1964–. Author and Title Indexes for 1820–1829 by M. Frances Cooper, 1972–1973. Author and Title Indexes for 1830–1839 by Carol Rinderknecht, 1989.

088. *Bibliotheca Americana: A Catalogue of American Publications Including Reprints and Original Works, from 1821 to 1861.* By Orville Augustus Roorbach. New York: Roorbach, 1852–1861. Reprint 1939. 4 vols.

089. *The American Catalogue of Books (Original and Reprints), Published in the United States from Jan. 1861 to Jan. 1871, with Date of Publication, Size, Price, and Publisher's Name.* By James Kelly. New York: Wiley, 1866–1871. Reprint 1938. 2 vols.

090. *American Catalogue Founded by F. Leypoldt, 1876–1919.* New York: Publishers Weekly, 1880–1911. Reprint 1941. 8 vols. in 13 parts. Title varies.
The modern work of historical bibliography for the United States begun by Evans

has been continued by that of Shaw, Shoemaker, and others. Books are listed chronologically by year of publication. Much of the 19th century remains to be completed. Until that time Roorbach, Kelly, and Leypoldt will continue to be useful.

091. *Bibliotheca Americana: A Dictionary of Books Relating to America.* By Wilberforce Eames and R. W. Vail. New York: Joseph Sabin, 1868–1892. Reprint, New York: Bibliographical Society of America, 1928–1936. 28 vols.
This classic bibliography, often known simply as "Sabin," contains 106,413 numbered items as well as mentioning many others in its notes. Its purpose is to list by author all books concerned with America, including in some cases the libraries where they can be found. The books were not necessarily published in the United States. An aid for using Sabin is provided by J. E. Molnar, *Author-Title Index to Joseph Sabin's 'Dictionary of Books Relating to America,'* 3 vols. (New York: Scarecrow, 1975); L. S. Thompson, *The New Sabin: Books Described by Joseph Sabin and His Successors, Newly Described Again on the Basis of Examination of the Originals, and Fully Indexed by Title, Subject, Joint Authors, and Institutions and Agencies,* 10 vols. (Troy, NY: Whitson, 1974–1986) is merely a set of lists and indexes to large-scale microform collections. *European Americana: A Chronological Guide to Works Printed in Europe Relating to the Americas 1493–1776,* edited by J. Alden and D. C. Landis (New York: Readex, 1980–), is a chronological guide to works printed in Europe related to the Americas.

092. *European Americana: A Chronological Guide to Works Printed in Europe Relating to the Americas, 1493–1750.* Edited by John

Alden and Dennis C. Landis. Readex/ Newsbank, 1979–1997. 6 vols.

With the completion of volumes 3 and 4 covering the period 1651–1700 this set, begun almost 20 years ago, was finally finished. It largely supersedes Joseph Sabin's *Bibliotheca Americana* and can be considered the most comprehensive bibliographical guide to the entire printed record of European awareness of the Americas from Columbus to the mid-18th century. With more than 30,000 entries, it includes three to four times the number of entries in Sabin. Extensive subject indexes provide access by topic to this vast literature. It represents several decades of effort by the John Carter Brown Library in Providence, RI.

093. *Books in Print.* **New York: R. R. Bowker, 1948–. 9 vols. ISSN 0068-0214.**

R. R. Bowker was founded in New York City in 1872. In 1872 it introduced *Publishers Weekly* and in 1876 *Library Journal,* still two of the leading magazines about books for libraries. In 1873 it published the first national guide to available books, the *Publishers Trade List Annual*, which later evolved into *Books in Print* in 1948. In 1968 Bowker became an official ISBN agency. A CD-ROM version, *Books in Print Plus,* premiered in 1986 and an online version, *books inprint.com,* became available recently. In August, 2001 the R. R. Bowker publishing operations were acquired by the Cambridge Information Group from Reed Elsevier. The print version of BIP, long a mainstay of libraries and bookstores, is published annually in September. Its nine-volume set of approximately 28,000 pages includes entries for 1.9 million citations to adult, juvenile, popular, scholarly, and reprint titles with 180,000 new titles added annually. It provides basic information for every title from

pages, price, and publisher to edition, binding, and ISBN. Each new addition includes some 1 million price and entry revisions. A stand-alone publisher index lists 70,000 firms. A supplement is issued in March, and *Forthcoming Books* anticipates thousands of forthcoming titles in bimonthly issues from February to December. A *Subject Guide to Books in Print* in 6 volumes indexes the more than 1.8 million nonfiction titles in BIP under more then 83,000 Library of Congress subject headings, 1,500 of which are new in the latest edition.

094. *booksinprint.com*

With over 43 million records this subscription-based Internet source provides bibliographic information on 3.7 million books, 320,000 videos, and 130,000 audio cassettes plus 628,000 full-text reviews from 14 sources. You can use the "Quick Search" to locate items by key word, author, title, ISBN or you can browse by general subject, index, check publisher's home pages, or even look for new books from previous award winners. The "Advanced Search" function provides more targeted searching and allows you to limit results by type of book (hardcover, softcover, e-book), by fiction/nonfiction, or even by audience. You can even limit to items discussed on television programs like *Good Morning America* or reviewed in magazines like the *New Yorker*. Smaller libraries may subscribe to *Books in Print* on *DISC,* which is issued monthly.

R. R. Bowker also publishes or distributes:

095. *Whitaker's Books in Print*

This is the definitive source of bibliographic reference for English-language titles published in the United Kingdom, Ireland,

and Europe. The most recent annual edition in five volumes includes 978,000 titles from 41,273 publishers by author and title.

096. *Australian Books in Print (Thorpe's)*
A comprehensive reference source published annually in April and organized by title and author for more than 110,000 in-print books and series published under Australian imprints or written by Australian authors.

097. *New Zealand Books in Print (Thorpe's)*
Contains updated bibliographic information on all in-print books from New Zealand and many South Pacific island states. Published annually in February, the most recent edition includes 14,000 book entries listed by author and title from more than 900 New Zealand and Oceanian publishers.

098. *globalbooksinprint.com*
This massive international bibliographic database includes information from Bowker's *Books in Print* database of U.S. and Canadian titles, *Australian Books in Print,* and a leading U.K. database. It provides online subscription access to 6.8 million editions from the United States, United Kingdom, Canada, and Australia. New Zealand titles are being added in 2003. Like booksinprint.com, on which it is modeled, it provides "Quick" and "Advanced" searches. Added features include 650,000 reviews, 40,000 review citations, 200,000 cover images, and 60,000 tables of content.

Other listings of books in print include *African Books in Print* (Bowker-Saur), *French Books in Print* (Cercle dela librarie), *German Books in Print* (K. G. Saur), *Italian Books in Print* (Editrice Bibliographica), and *International Books in Print.*

099. *Canadian Books in Print.* **Toronto: University of Toronto Press, 1967–. ISSN 0068-8398; 0315-8398.**
Originally published with the parallel title *Catalogue des livres canadiens en librairie* from 1967–1972 in two volumes. Volume 1 included an author and publisher index. Volume 2 was the title index. After 1973 the French version was dropped. Since 1980 it has appeared in an annual author and title index published in March plus quarterly updates on microfiche. The most recent edition has 48,000 titles indexed under 800 different subject categories from 4,800 publishers.

100. *AcqWeb's Verification Tools: In Print and Price Listing Resources.* **http://acqweb. library.vanderbilt.edu/acqweb/verif_ip.htm**
For books and other materials published in countries not listed above, be sure to check out this valuable online resource that groups bookstores and vendors in categories from "Arabic" to "Venezuela."

101. *Library of Congress Online Catalog.* http://catalog.loc.gov
Launched in late 1999, the new Library of Congress Online Catalog is a database of approximately 12 million records representing books, serials, computer files, manuscripts, cartographic materials, music, sound recordings, and visual materials. The Library of Congress mainframe-based online catalog LOCIS was closed on August 12, 1999. The new online catalog can be browsed by subject, name, or call number, and searched by title or serial title. Guided key word (using words or phrases) and command key word (using Boolean operators) searching is available. Searches can be limited by language, date, type of material, or place of

publication. This is a terrific place to begin any bibliographic search. It is available 24 hours a day, 7 days a week, and it is free.

Other LC online catalogs include:

102. *Prints and Photographs (P&P) Online Catalog.* http://www.loc.gov/rr/print/catalogabt.html

The Prints and Photographs Online Catalog (PPOC) contains catalog records and digital images of a cross-section of still pictures held by the Prints and Photographs Division and other units of the Library. The catalog provides access through group or item records to about 50 percent of the Division's holdings. About 90 percent of the records are accompanied by one or more digital images. Copies of most images can be ordered from the Library of Congress Photo duplication service.

103. *SONIC: Sound Online Inventory and Catalog.* http://www.loc.rr/record/soniccont.html

Among the collections in the Recorded Sound section's SONIC database include: 78s, 45s, copyright cassettes, and recordable compact discs as well as many broadcast and archival recordings, including 68,000 records from the NBC Radio Collection dating back to the early 1930s.

104. *National Union Catalog, pre-1956 Imprints. A Cumulative Author List Representing Library of Congress Printed Cards and Titles Reported by Other American Libraries.* [London] Mansell, 1968–1980. 685 vols. and supplement. [London]: Mansell, 1980–1981. Vols. 686–754.

Referred to as Mansell, the NUC, or simply the "Pre-56," this magnum opus lists 13 million books, pamphlets, maps, atlases, and music held by the Library of Congress and other research libraries in the United States. Individual items are listed alphabetically by personal or corporate author. Large as this bibliography is, it has been surpassed by the Library of Congress's own online catalogs and by Union catalogs like OCLC's WorldCat and RLG's RLIN. *The National Union Catalog: A Cumulative Author List* continued coverage of the pre-1956 imprints volumes until 1983 with various cumulations when it was succeeded by *NUC: Books.* Published in five parts: register, monthly; name index, title index, series index, subject index, quarterly with annual and larger cumulations. *NUC: US Books* extracts records for books published in the United States. The NUC was last published in 1994. Access from 1995 on is available only through OCLC WorldCat.

United Kingdom

105. *The British Library General Catalogue of Printed Books to 1975.* London: Bingley; London: K. G. Saur, 1980–1987. 260 vols. ISBN 0-86291-006-4.

This set is the British version of the *National Union Catalog, pre-1956 Imprints,* and it cumulates and supersedes the previous *British Museum, Department of Printed Books, General Catalogue of Printed Books, Photolithographic Editions to 1955* and its various supplements. The set has been supplemented for acquisitions through 1985. Books are basically listed under personal or corporate author, although there are some subject entries. In some ways, like its American counterpart, this large print collection has been surpassed by the British Library's online catalogs [see 106, 107].

106. *BLPC: The British Library Public Catalogue.* http://blpc.bl.uk
This is the catalog of the library's major collections held at its main sites in both London and Boston Spa containing records for over 10 million items dating back to the 15th century.

107. *British Library Catalogues on the Web.* http://www.britishlibrary.net/webcats.html
In addition to the BLPC the British Library offers free access to a number of other diverse catalogs:

> Current Serials Received—records for over 60,000 journals currently received by the Document Supply Centre at Boston Spa and the Science, Technology and Business Service in London
> Manuscripts Catalogue—a catalog of the Department of Manuscripts collection of manuscripts, private papers, and archives acquired since 1753
> Microform Research Collections
> National Sound Archives
> Newspaper Library Catalogue—a catalog of over 50,000 newspapers dating back to the 17th century

Nineteenth Century

108. *Short Title Catalogue of Books Printed and of English Books Printed Abroad, 1475–1640.* Compiled by Alfred W. Pollard and G. R. Redgrave. Revised and enlarged by W. A. Jackson, F. S. Ferguson, and Katherine F. Pantzer. 2d ed. Oxford:

Oxford University Press, 1976–1986. 2 vols. ISBN 0-19-721789-3; 0-19-721790-7.

109. *Short-Title Catalogue of Books Printed in England, Scotland, Ireland, Wales and British America, and of English Books Printed in Other Countries, 1641–1700.* 2d. ed., rev. and enl. Compiled by D. G. Wing and T. J. Crist. New York: Modern Language Association, 1972–1998. 4 vols. Also available on CD-ROM (Chadwyck-Healey).
Early English Books: Series I, 1475–1640 ("Pollard and Redgrave," or STC I), which includes over 30,000 titles in microfilm, is now complete. Early English Books: Series II, 1641–1700 ("Wing" or STC II) is still in progress. When completed it will include 50,000 titles. These short-title catalogs are guides to books published in England or in English from the beginning of printing until 1700. Individual works are listed by author and provide a bibliographic citation, besides giving the locations of various British and American libraries that own copies. Early English Books Online is placing English books published between 1485 and 1700 into a database of images. Selected titles are being produced in a searchable format.

110. *English Short-Title Catalogue* (ESTC); formerly the *Eighteenth Century Short Title Catalogue.* London: British Library; Riverside: University of California. In progress. http://cbsr26.ucr.edu//estcabot.html
The ESTC is a product of the joint efforts of the British Library, the Center for Bibliographical Studies and Research, and the University of California at Riverside, with the cooperation of the American Antiquar-

ian Society and over 1,600 libraries around the world. It is mounted on the Research Libraries Information Network (RLIN) and on the British Library's Automated Information Service (BLAISE). There are also CD-ROM and microfiche editions. When complete it will contain bibliographic records for virtually every item printed in England or one of her dependencies, 1473–1800. It currently contains 400,000 records; appended to each record is a list of libraries holding the title.

111. *Nineteenth Century Short Title Catalogue (NSTC)*. Newcastle-upon-Tyne: Avero, 1984–.
Series I, Phase I, 1801–1815. 6 vols.
   1984–1986 (also on CD-ROM)
Series II, Phase I, 1816–1870. 56 vols.
   1986–1995 (also on CD-ROM)
Series III, 1871–1919. 1997. (CD-ROM only)
This massive project attempts to record all books printed between 1801 and 1919 in Great Britain, her colonies, the United States, and in English from the rest of the world, and in translation from English. Chadwyck-Healey, now part of ProQuest Information, is publishing selected items in the microfiche series "Nineteenth Century."

Canada

112. *Library and Archives of Canada.* http://www.nlc-bnc.ca
In October 2002 the minister of Canadian heritage, Sheila Copps, announced the creation of the Library and Archives of Canada. This new agency will see the convergence of the collections of the National Library of Canada and the National

Archives of Canada. Click on "National Library of Canada" to get to AMICUS Services. From the AMICUS Web you can search over 25 million records from 1,300 Canadian Libraries and access the entire database, including National Library records. You can browse the title, name, or subject or search by key word, ISBN, or ISSN. This is the best place to begin any search for items about Canada.

France

113. *Bibliothèque Nationale de France (BNF).* http://www.bnf.fr
The collections of the BNF have been redistributed in the two main library buildings. The new François Mitterrand Library houses the collection of printed books, periodicals, audiovisuals, and computer materials. Manuscripts, engravings, photographic materials, maps and plans, coins, medals, and performing arts and music collections are housed in the Richelieu Library. An online catalog was launched in 1999. Click on "Catalogues et resources electroniques" to access BN-OPALE Plus which since March 2002 provides access to the entire book and serials collections; or BN-OPALINE to access the special collections in the Richelieu Library.

Spain

114. *Biblioteca Nacional.* http://www.bne.es
The catalogs of Spain's National Library are publicly accessible through a Web interface, ARIADNA. Eleven different files can be searched: modern books published after 1931 (1.9 million), books published up to

1831 (31,029), maps and plans (32,046), etc. Searching can be done by name, title, collection, subject, place of publication, and ISBN. Searches can be limited by date or range of years. There are browsable author and subject files. They have recently added an English-language interface. You can also search the Spanish collective catalog of periodical publications or serials owned by 1,100 Spanish libraries.

Other European

115. *Gabriel: Gateway to Europe's National Libraries.* http://portico.bl.uk/gabriel/en/opacs.html
Online public access can be gained to the following European National Libraries: Austria, Belgium, Croatia, Czech Republic, Denmark, Finland, France, Germany, Hungary, Iceland, Italy, Lithuania, Republic of Macedonia, The Netherlands, Norway, Portugal, Russia, Slovak Republic, Slovenia, Spain, Sweden, Switzerland, Turkey, United Kingdom, and Vatican City.

LIBRARY SERVERS VIA WWW

116. *Libweb-Library WWW Servers.* http://sunsite.berkeley.edu/Libweb
The Berkeley Digital Library SunSITE currently lists over 6,500 pages from libraries in over 115 countries. Their files are updated daily at midnight Pacific time. A key word search can be made for location, library type, name, or other information. For the United States the following groups can be searched: Academic Libraries, Public

Libraries, National Libraries, State Libraries, Regional Consortia, and Special and School Libraries.

LIB-WEB-CATS

117. *lib-web-cats: A directory of libraries throughout the world.* http://www.librarytechnology.org/libwebcats
Marshal Breeding, library technology officer for the Jean and Alexander Heard Library at Vanderbilt University, maintains this very helpful directory of more than 4,000 libraries world wide. Each listing includes links to the library's Web site and online catalog. Other information available includes the location, address, library type, current and previous library automation systems used, and the size of the library's collection.

GENERAL HISTORICAL BIBLIOGRAPHIES

Bibliographies of Bibliographies

118. *Bibliographies in History.* Vol. 1, *An Index to Bibliographies in History Journals and Dissertations Covering the U.S. and Canada;* vol. 2, *An Index to Bibliographies in History Journals and Dissertations Covering All Countries of the World Except the U.S. and Canada.* Santa Barbara, CA: ABC-CLIO, 1988. 459pp. ISBN 0-87436-521-X.
This two-volume set contains 5,000 entries. Volume 1 describes 1,461 items on subjects about the U.S. and Canada, Volume 2 consists of 3,437 entries about the rest of

the world. Individual entries are numbered and supply complete bibliographic information. Since the entries for these volumes are drawn from ABC-CLIO online databases—*America: History and Life* [see 219] and *Historical Abstracts* [see 220]—they can be updated by searching the same databases.

Current Bibliographies

119. *Annual Bulletin of Historical Literature.* London: Historical Association. Vol. 1–. 1911–.
Intended for teachers and students in both secondary and higher education, librarians, and the general reader, this publication consists of bibliographic essays surveying the significant publications (books and articles) of the previous year. Each essay is authored by one or more experts in the field. After an essay on general works, most of the remaining chapters cover chronological periods in European history. There are also regional chapters for other continents. Individual chapters are further subdivided into sections on regions, nations, or topics. There is a name index for authors. An American counterpart, *Recently Published Articles,* published since 1976 by the American Historical Association, ceased in 1990. A related publication is the annual *International Bibliography of Historical Sciences* (New York: K.G. Saur), which runs several years behind and is difficult to use.

Guides

120. *The American Historical Association's Guide to Historical Literature.* Edited by Mary Beth Norton and Pamela Gerardi. 3rd ed. New York: Oxford University Press, 1995. 2 vols. 0-19-505727-9.
Designed to be an inventory of the best historical literature extant at the time of compilation, this work serves as an introductory bibliography to guide further study in all fields of history. It contains 26,926 bibliographic citations and is divided into 48 sections. Each section includes an introductory essay, a guide to contents, and an annotated bibliography. Each citation includes appropriate bibliographic information and a brief annotation. Following the bibliographies in volume 2 is a list of journals that publish articles in history, an author index, and a subject index. To quote *Booklist/RBB*, "the new edition remains a splendid achievement and is sure to be heavily consulted for years to come."

121. *WWW-VL History: Central Catalogue.* http://www.ukans.edu/history/VL
The World Wide Web Virtual Library's History Index began operations in March 1993. In September of that year it became the first of WWW's Virtual Library index sites. The central catalog is located at the University of Kansas. Links are arranged first for methods and materials (bibliographies, guides, indexes, etc.), then by eras and epochs and by historical topics, and finally by countries and regions. The VL is the oldest catalog of the Web, started by Tim Berners-Lee, the creator of html and the Web itself. VL Pages are recognized as being among the highest-quality guides to particular sections of the Web.

122. *History: The Web Site of the Institute of Historical Research.* http://ihr.sas.ac.uk
Since the summer of 1993, the IHR

History Web site has served as a comprehensive Web site for history in the United
Kingdom and beyond. You can search over
30,000 records and find information on
books in print, journal articles, theses completed in the United Kingdom, and semi-
nars and conference papers presented annually at the Institute. In 2003 the IHR and
Blackwell Publishing plan to create History
Compass, a subscription-based online service designed to keep readers abreast of the
latest research.

123. *History Guide.* http://www.
HistoryGuide.de/hist_main.html
The History Guide is an Internet-based
subject gateway to the scholarly literature of
history with a focus on Anglo-American
history and the history of Central and
Western Europe. It is maintained in cooperation between Göttingen State and
University Library and the Bavarian State
Library. You can search for sources by
region, time period, and subject. The catalog provides links to and descriptions of
158 electronic journals, 440 source materials and collections, and 36 general
bibliographies.

124. *Best of History Web Sites.* http://www.
besthistorysites.net
Best of History Web Sites is a portal created
for students, teachers, and enthusiasts. It
identifies sites and rates them for usefulness
and accuracy. There are currently links to
800 history-related Web sites arranged by
period and area. It also recommends sites
for lesson plans, multimedia, and research
and is the winner of numerous Web awards
itself.

SPECIALIZED HISTORICAL BIBLIOGRAPHIES: REGIONS AND COUNTRIES

United States

General

125. *Reader's Guide to American History.* By
Peter J. Parish. London: Fitzroy Dearborn,
1997. 880pp. ISBN 1-884964-22-2.
The aim of this guide, claims the editor, is
to offer some help to those who wish to
explore the riches of American historical
writing. The guide, through a series of
essays, describes the secondary literature
(books) on some 600 different topics.
Entries review events, individuals, and
themes and issues. The essays are well constructed and provide useful, balanced suggestions for further reading on most of the
key topics in American history. Parish is
the Mellon Fellow in American History
at Cambridge.

126. *Handbook for Research in American
History: A Guide to Bibliographies and Other
Reference Works.* Revised by Francis Paul
Prucha. 2nd ed. Lincoln: University of
Nebraska Press, 1994. 214pp.
ISBN 0-8032-3701-4.
Prucha's *Handbook* is an excellent resource
for all students of American history, and it is
available in an inexpensive paperback edition. Its 1,000 items are discussed in 20 different chapters, beginning with chapter 1,
"A Revolution in Access" and ending with
chapter 20, "Picture Sources." Each chapter
is a combination of a bibliographic essay
and bibliographic listing. Individual items

are assigned a reference number. Part 2, "Bibliographies of Bibliographies," in the first edition is omitted in this addition. While mentioning the Internet as a source, this guide was written prior to its development as a significant research tool. Prucha is a distinguished professor of American History at Marquette University.

127. *United States History: A Multicultural, Interdisciplinary Guide to Information Sources.* By Ron Blazek and Anna H. Perrault. 2nd ed. Westport, CT: Libraries Unlimited, 2003. 688pp. ISBN 1-56308-874-6. Blazek, a professor of library science at Florida State, and Perrault, of the University of South Florida, have combined their talents to produce this helpful guide to U.S. history.

This edition has been revised and expanded with the addition of online databases, Web sites, and CD-ROM titles. It identifies and describes hundreds of reference books useful to the student of American history. After an opening chapter on general sources the authors discuss sources for politics and government, diplomatic history, foreign affairs, military history, social, cultural, and intellectual history, regional history, and economic history.

Specialized by Regions or Chronological Period

Bibliographies of the States of the United States. Westport, CT.: Greenwood, 1992–.

128. *Kansas History: An Annotated Bibliography.* Compiled by Homer E. Socolofsky and Virgil W. Dean. 1992. 616pp. ISBN 0-313-28238-2.

129. *South Dakota History: An Annotated Bibliography.* Compiled by Herbert T. Hoover and Karen P. Zimmerman. 1993. 552pp. ISBN 0-313-28263-3.

130. *North Carolina History: An Annotated Bibliography.* Compiled by H. G. Jones. 1995. 824pp. ISBN 0-313-28255-2.

131. *Illinois History: An Annotated Bibliography.* Compiled by Ellen M. Whitney, Janice A. Petterchak, and Sandra M. Stark. 1995. 640pp. ISBN 0-313-28235-8.

132. *Arkansas History: An Annotated Bibliography.* Compiled by Michael B. Dougan, Tom W. Dillard and Timothy G. Nutt. 1995. 392pp. ISBN 0-313-28226-9.

133. *Nebraska History: An Annotated Bibliography.* Compiled by Michael L. Tate. 1995. 576pp. ISBN 0-313-28249-8.

134. *Alabama History: An Annotated Bibliography.* Compiled by Lynda W. Brown, Donald B. Dodd, Lloyd H. Cornett Jr. and Alma D. Steading. 1998. 462pp. ISBN 0-313-28223-4.

135. *Wisconsin History: An Annotated Bibliography.* Compiled by Barbara Dotts Paul and Justus F. Paul. 1999. 448pp. ISBN 0-313-28271-4.

136. *Kentucky History: An Annotated Bibliography.* Compiled by Ron D. Bryant. 2000. 592pp. ISBN 0-313-28239-0.

137. *Louisiana History: An Annotated Bibliography.* Compiled by Florence M.

Jumonville. 2002. 810pp.
ISBN 0-313-28240-4.
This series has drawn widespread praise
from reviewers. Writing about the North
Carolina volume, the reviewer for *Choice*
called it "the most comprehensive and user-
friendly bibliography of North Carolina
History to date." Commenting on the
Alabama volume, a reviewer wrote, this is
"the first comprehensive scholarly bibliography of Alabama . . . since 1898." About
the Louisiana volume a reviewer in *Choice*
noted "this is destined to be the standard
bibliography for many years." Volumes in
the series generally cite journal articles,
theses, dissertations, books, and compilations. The volume on North Carolina has
11,399 entries; Louisiana 6,800; Illinois
has 4,620 and Alabama more than 3,000.
For additions to this series, see the
Greenwood Press Web site at http://
www.greenwood.com.

138. *Bibliography of American County
Histories.* **Compiled by P. William Filby.
Baltimore: Genealogical Publishing, 1985.
449pp. ISBN 0-8063-1126-6.**
This remains the most current guide to
county histories. It includes 5,000 entries
for all states except Alaska and Hawaii
published prior to 1985. Works dealing
with more than one county are listed in a
"regional" section. Arrangement is alphabetical by state and within each state
alphabetical by county. Filby is more current but less comprehensive than Marion J.
Kaminhow's classic *United States Local
Histories in the Library of Congress: A Bibliography,* 5 vols. (Baltimore: Magna Carta,
1975).

139. *Bibliographies of New England History.*
**Prepared by the Committee for a New
England Bibliography. Hanover: University
Press of New England, 1976–.**
The *Bibliographies of New England History*
began publishing volumes on individual
states with Massachusetts in 1976. Con-
necticut, published in 1986, was the last of
the state volumes. Volume 7 lists materials
dealing with the region as a whole. Volume
8 updates the individually published state
volumes. Both were published in 1989.
Volume 9 contains 4,231 citations to
books, dissertations, pamphlets, and magazine and journal articles published between
1989 and 1994. Volume 10, part 1, provides
updates to 1997. The 10 volumes published
to date provide 67,650 citations on the history of New England or its component
states, counties, and towns.

140. *The New Netherlands Project—
Bibliography.* **http://www.nnp.org/project/
bibliography.html**
This project of the New York State Library
is to create an exhaustive online bibliography of primary sources, secondary sources,
articles, and dissertations that relate to the
Dutch settlements in North America.

141. *WestWeb.* **http://www.library.csi.cuny.
edu/westweb**
WestWeb is a topically organized Web site
about the study of the American West created and maintained by Catherine Laven-
der, a history professor at the College of
Staten Island, City University of New York.
From her "Hand-Picked Sites" to the "Irri-
gated Garden: Water in the West," this is a
wonderful guide to sources on the West.

United Kingdom and Ireland

142. *Royal Historical Society Annual Bibliography of British and Irish History.* Oxford: Oxford University Press, 1975–. ISSN 0308-4558. http://www.rhs.ac.uk/bibwel.html

Starting its coverage with 1974, this bibliography was first published in 1975 under the editorship of Sir Geoffrey Elton, and is now edited by Austin Gee. It provides, in annual volumes, a comprehensive and authoritative survey of books on historical topics published in a single calendar year. Coverage spans the history of England, Ireland, Scotland, and Wales through the Classical period, Middle Ages, Renaissance, and modern times. The main headings are Auxiliary; General; Roman Britain; England 450–1066; England 1066–1500; England and Wales 1500–1714; Britain 1714–1815; Britain 1815–1914; Britain since 1914; Medieval Wales; Scotland before the Union; Ireland to c.1640; Ireland since c. 1640; and Empire and Commonwealth post-1783. Subheadings within chapters include General, Politics, Constitution, Administration and Law, External Affairs, Religion, Economic Affairs, Social Structure and Population, Naval and Military, Intellectual and Culture, and Science and Technology. Earlier volumes were published by Harvester Press in the United Kingdom and St. Martin's in the United States. There are author, place, personal name, and subject indexes. A CD-ROM version, *Royal Historical Society Bibliography*, provides comprehensive coverage of references from 1901 to 1992. Its core sources are *Writings on British History* (1901–1974) and the *Annual Bibliography* (1975–1992). A new online edition of the database was published in July 2002. This now contains 330,000 titles and incorporates the annual bibliographies for 1993–2001. In January 2003 records from *London's Past* online were incorporated.

143. *A Bibliography of British History, 1914–1989.* Compiled and edited by Keith Robbins. Oxford: Clarendon, 1996. 918pp. ISBN 0-19-822496-6.

This latest retrospective cumulation of the Royal Historical Society provides scholars with a comprehensive survey of British history in the 20th century. Its 27,000 entries describe all aspects of British life and culture from constitutional and political history to foreign policy, economics, and religion. The lack of a subject index forces reliance on the extensive table of contents. Bibliographic citations sometimes lack series information and physical descriptions. Still, this is an important tool for any student of 20th-century British history. Also helpful is Peter Canterall, *British History, 1945–1987: An Annotated Bibliography* (Oxford: Blackwell, 1991.) Because of delays in the above volume, Catterall produced his guide to post–World War II Britain. His bibliography includes 8,644 entries. Other volumes in this series include:

144. *A Bibliography of English History to 1485.* Compiled by E. B. Graves. Oxford: Clarendon, 1975.

145. *Bibliography of British History: Tudor Period, 1485–1603.* Compiled by Conyers Read. 2nd ed. Oxford: Clarendon, 1959.

146. *Bibliography of British History: Stuart History, 1603–1714.* Compiled by G. D. Davies and M. F. Keeler. 2nd ed. Oxford: Clarendon, 1976.

147. *Bibliography of British History: The Eighteenth Century, 1714–1789.* Compiled by S. Pargellis and D. J. Medley. Oxford: Clarendon, 1951.

148. *Bibliography of British History, 1789–1851.* Compiled by L. M. Brown and I. R. Christie. Oxford: Clarendon, 1977.

149. *Bibliography of British History, 1851–1914.* Compiled by H. J. Hanham. Oxford: Clarendon, 1976.

Canada

150. *Bibliography of Canadian Bibliographies.* By Ernie Ingles. 3rd ed. Toronto: University of Toronto Press, 1994. 1,178pp. ISBN 0-8020-2837-3.
This outstanding compilation lists 7,375 Canadian bibliographies (in French and English), more than three times as many as the second edition. Entries are arranged by subject class, year of publication, and author. The combined English and French indexes provide 50,000 additional access points. Coverage is from 1789 to mid-1993. Ingles is associate vice president, learning systems, and chief librarian at the University of Alberta.

151. *Introducing Canada: An Annotated Bibliography of Canadian History in English.* By Brian Gobbett and Robert Irwin. Metuchen, N.J.: Scarecrow, 1998. 392pp. ISBN 0-8108-3383-2.

Gobbett, a doctoral candidate in history at the University of Alberta, and Irwin, a Ph.D. graduate of the same school, have combined their talents to produce a detailed look at works on Canadian history since 1970. It is organized alphabetically by author and focuses on scholarly works. In addition to brief descriptions of 1,000 historical monographs, the authors explore recent historiographic debates. There are author-subject indexes. Still useful is *Canada: A Reader's Guide: Introduction Bibliographique,* by J. A. Senecal, prepared for the International Council for Canadian Studies (1991).

152. *Canadian Library Web Sites and Catalogues.* http://www.nlc-bnc.ca/canlib/eindex.htm
The Interlibrary Loan Division of the National Library of Canada maintains this exhaustive list of Canadian libraries and library catalogs. Sites are organized both by region (from Alberta to Yukon) and also by library type: academic, government, public, and special.

153. *Canadian Studies: A Guide to the Sources.* By John Blackwell and Laurie C. Stanley-Blackwell. This bibliographic essay originally appeared as "Canadian Studies: A Core Collection," *CHOICE: Current Reviews for Academic Libraries,* September 1997, 71–84. It was revised in June 1999 for the International Council for Canadian Studies World Wide Web Service, http://www.iccs-ciec.ca/blackwell.html.
Written with a flair, this 37-page bibliographic essay describes the emergence of Canadian studies as a subject of study in the United States and Europe and then reviews

important sources for history, literature, government, politics, etc. With chapters like "Due North," "Culture High and Low," and "The True North Strong and Free," the authors Blackwell give you the "best of recent Canadiana" with lots of hot links to send you on your quest. Frequently updated by John D. Blackwell, who is director of the Research Grants Office, and Laurie Stanley-Blackwell, a historian, both at St. Francis Xavier University in Antigonish, Nova Scotia.

By Continent

Africa

154. *Africa Bibliography*. Manchester: Manchester University Press, 1985–. ISSN 0266-6731.
Published in association with the International African Institute, this annual lists scholarly works written about the continent, arranged by geographical area and country. This is a good place to begin any search for recent printed works.

155. *Reference Guide to Africa: A Bibliography of Sources*. By Alfred Kagan and Yvette Scheven. Lanham, MD: Scarecrow, 1999. 262pp. ISBN 0-8108-3585-1.
Designed for humanities and social science researchers interested in African studies, this guide provides more than 900 annotated bibliographic citations for publications related to continental Africa. An introductory section covers indexes, bibliographies, handbooks, guides, and directories, as well as electronic resources and Web sites. Continuing chapters discuss statistics, current events, biography, primary sources, and gov-

ernment publications. The main body of the guide is an annotated overview of sources for 17 disciplines in the humanities and social sciences plus agriculture and ecology. Typical chapters include overview information, annotated entries with full bibliographic citations and selected LC Subject Headings. Kagan is the African studies bibliographer at the University of Illinois-Champaign, a position held by Scheven from 1969 to 1992.

156. *Africa: A Guide to Reference Material*. By John McIlwaine. London: Hans Zell, 1993. 507pp. ISBN 0-905450-43-4.
This is the first in a series of volumes planned by Hans Zell that will provide detailed annotated guides to reference works that exist for particular regions of the world. Exclusive of bibliographies, the compiler's intent is to provide a guide to the major reference sources which relate to Africa south of the Sahara. The author first describes sources related to Africa in general: handbooks, yearbooks, statistics, directories, biographical sources, and atlases and gazetteers. Similar sources are examined for each country, arranged first by region: northeast, east, central, west, and southern Africa. The 1,766 unannotated sources reflect the rich reference literature of the region. McIlwaine teaches at the School of Library, Archive and Information Studies, University of London.

157. *Bibliography for African Studies, 1970–1986*. By Yvette Scheven. London: Hans Zell, 1988. 615pp. ISBN 0-905450-33-7.
This is a bibliography of 3,277 annotated bibliographies, published separately, relating to sub-Saharan Africa in the social sciences

and humanities. It cumulates earlier volumes from the same author. Scheven says her purpose in writing the guide was to simplify and shorten literature searches by eliminating the multistep process usually necessary. Bibliographies are arranged by subject (from agriculture to women) and geographically, by region and by country. Entries include both books and articles. The chapter on ethnic groups includes sources on groups from Akan to Zulu. Scheven was African studies bibliographer at the University of Illinois. This book won the African Studies Association Conover-Porter Award for the "most outstanding achievement in Africana reference works."

158. *Bibliographies for African Studies, 1987–1993.* Compiled by Phyllis Bischof et al. Edited by Yvette Scheven. London: Hans Zell, 1994.

Updates the latter's bibliography of bibliographies with 834 additional sources for the past eight years.

159. *Central and Equatorial Africa Area Bibliography.* By Gordon Harris. Lanham, MD: Scarecrow, 1999. 256pp.
ISBN 0-8108-3606-8.

Harris, director of the Orchard Learning Resources Centre of Selly Oak Colleges in Birmingham and editor of the quarterly *International African Bibliography,* here presents information about texts relating to eleven states in the heart of Africa: Chad, Central African Republic, Sao Tome and Principe, Equatorial Guinea, Gabon, People's Republic of the Congo (formerly Congo-Brazzaville), Democratic Republic of the Congo (formerly Congo-Kinshasa and Zaire), Rwanda, Burundi, Zambia, and

Malawi. References are organized first by general subject heading and then by more specific headings or the states themselves. An excellent place to begin for a novice researcher. Hector Blackhurst uses a similar approach in his *East and Northeast Africa Bibliography* (Lanham, MD: Scarecrow, 1996), to describe 3,838 sources for East and Northeast Africa, which includes Djibouti, Eritrea, Ethiopia, Kenya, Somalia, Sudan, Tanzania, and Uganda. Reuben Musiker and Naomi Musiker list significant books on Angola, Botswana, Lesotho, Malawi, Namibia, Mozambique, South Africa, Swaziland, Zambia, and Zimbabwe published since 1945 in their *Southern African Bibliography* (Lanham, MD: Scarecrow, 1996).

160. *Africabib.org.* http://www.africabib.org
Africabib is the cumulation of 25 years of Africana research by David Bullwinkle, director of the Institute for Economic Advancement Research Library at the University of Arkansas–Little Rock. In 1989 Greenwood Press published his three-volume *Bibliography on Women in Africa.* The site consists of two bibliographic databases covering Africana periodical literature and African women's literature as well as a comprehensive bibliography on women travelers and explorers to Africa. The periodical database indexes 40,000 items from 325 periodical titles.

Asia

161. *Asian Studies WWW Virtual Library.* http://coombs.anu.edu.au/wwwVL-AsianStudies.html
A massive collection of Asian-Pacific global resources, this Web site was launched March

24, 1994, and is edited by Dr. T. Matthew Ciolek and a team of 44 coeditors. The WWW server is provided by the Research Schools of Social Sciences and Pacific and Asian Studies at the Australian National University. Regional files for the Middle East, Caucasus, South Asia, Southeast Asia, South China Sea, East Asia, Pacific Ocean, and the Asian continent are maintained on files at other institutions. Of particular note are the Middle East Studies Internet Resources, http://www.columbia.edu/cu/web/indiv/mideast/cuvlm, and SARAI: South Asia Resources Access on the Internet, http://www.columbia.edu/cu/lweb/indiv/southasis/cuvl, both at Columbia University. Each features an ongoing compilation of electronic bibliographic resources and research materials. The main Asian studies site at ANU provides coverage of resources on individual countries from Afghanistan to United Arab Emirates.

162. *Bibliography of Asian Studies.* http://www.aasianst.org/bassub.htm
The online version of the *Bibliography of Asian Studies* (BAS), a subscription service, contains more than 450,000 records on all subjects pertaining to East, Southeast, and South Asia. It includes full data from print editions issued through 1997 (for 1991), as well as thousands of entries compiled since. Since 1992 no individual monographs are being added to the database. Instead, staff have identified the 100 or so key periodicals in Asian studies and have made indexing of them a high priority. In addition to the "Search" function, users can also browse by country/region, by subject, or by journal title. This is the premier database for Asian studies produced by the Association for

Asian studies. The online version promises to end the considerable delays in indexing.

163. *Bibliography of South Asia.* **By David N. Nelson. Lanham, MD: Scarecrow, 1994. 484pp. ISBN 0-8108-2854-5.**
A useful compilation that describes recently published materials on South Asia, Afghanistan, Bangladesh, Bhutan, India, Maldives, Nepal, Pakistan, and Sri Lanka.

164. *Middle East Bibliography.* **By Sanford R. Silverburg. Metuchen, N.J.: Scarecrow, 1992. 564pp. ISBN 0-8108-2469-8.**
This is the first volume in a new series of area bibliographies. Silverburg is a political science professor specializing in Middle Eastern politics. He lists major bibliographies and sources for research in an opening essay. This is followed by 4,435 entries covering the literature from 1980 to 1991. These are arranged by author in subject categories. There is no table of contents and no running heads, which makes browsing more difficult. Coverage is limited to books.

165. *Online Bibliographies for Chinese Studies.* **http://sun.sino.uni-heidelberg.de/igcs/igbiblio.htm#history**
Part of the Internet Guide for China Studies at the University of Heidelberg, this collection designed by Fabrizio Pregadio, and maintained since 1998 by Hanno Lecher, contains 93 entries for bibliographies (scanned) in 15 categories, including reference works, history, geography, and 13 others. For each entry there is a brief description and comments about language and encoding. Sources are ranked essential or assigned stars. A very valuable site.

Australia and Oceania

166. *Australasia and South Pacific Islands Bibliography*. By John Thawley. Lanham, MD: Scarecrow, 1997. ISBN 0-8108-3240-2. This title in Scarecrow's Area Bibliographies series includes almost 6,000 unannotated sources in the sciences, social sciences, and humanities on Australia, Melanesia, Micronesia, and Polynesia. All references are to books published since World War II, mostly in English. Arrangement is first by region, country, or island group, and then by subject. There is an author index but no subject index.

Europe

167. *The American Bibliography of Slavic and East European Studies*. Urbana-Champaign, IL: American Association for the Advancement of Slavic Studies, 1956–. Annual. ISSN 0094-3770. http://gateway. library.uiuc.edu/absees
The American Bibliography of Slavic and East European Studies (ABSEES) has been published since 1957. Through 1966 it was published with the support of the Russian and East European Institute at Indiana University. Since 1968 it has been sponsored by the American Association for the Advancement of Slavic Studies (AAASS), first at the Library of Congress (1973–1989) and more recently at the University of Illinois. The bibliography comprehensively covers materials in the humanities, social sciences, and sciences relating to East Central Europe and the former Soviet Union. It contains citations for books, articles, government publications, conference proceedings, dissertations, and book reviews published in the United States or Canada. Chapter 8, "History," in the 1994 print volume (published in 1999) includes entries on historiography, Byzantine Empire, Ottoman Empire, the Holocaust, Russia/USSR, Territories and Adjacent States, and then East Central Europe from Bulgaria to Yugoslavia. *ABSEES Online* has been available over the Internet on a subscription basis since 1992. Coverage begins in 1990 with monthly updates. Approximately 53,000 records were searchable by key word, author, title, publisher, date of publication, and subject heading in early 2003. A demo file is at http:// carousel.lis.uiuc.edu/~absees/absees_online. html. For European publications, consult *The European Bibliography of Slavic and East European Studies (EBSEES)*. EBSEES, http://www1.msh-paris.fr/betuee/BD_ Bibl_Est_Presentation_angl.htm, was originally a tool for research on the Soviet Union and the Communist countries of Eastern Europe. It now includes information on 27 independent countries. The database lists books, journal articles, reviews, and theses on Eastern Europe published in eight western European Countries.

168. *Bibliographie annuelle de l'histoire de France du cinquieme siecle à 1958*. Paris: Centre National de la Recherche Scientifique, 1955–. Annual. ISSN 0067-7043.
Aiming to provide a comprehensive listing of new research in French history, this bibliography is reasonably current. Coverage begins in the fifth century AD to 1958. Items listed include books, journal articles, essays in collective works, and conference proceedings. Although written in French, non-French publications are also listed.

Items are organized under broad sections like general, political, institutional, economic and social, religious, imperial, cultural, and local history. Within sections there are chronological and topical subdivisions. Entries are numbered and there are separate subject and author indexes.

169. *Bibliographie internationale de l'humanisme, et de la Renaissance.* **Federation Internationale des societes et instituts pour l'etude de la Renaissance. Geneva: Librairie Droz, 1965–.**
An annual publication, which runs three to four years behind (the 1997 annual covered literature published in 1993), focuses on the literature of the 15th and 16th centuries. A list of journals precedes the bibliography, arranged by country. The bibliography itself is arranged in two parts: a bibliography of persons and anonymous works on Humanism and the Renaissance arranged alphabetically, followed by a bibliography of subjects arranged by systematic classes. DROZ issued a CD-ROM covering the years 1969–1998 in 1999 to commemorate the 30th anniversary of the index. It includes 20,000 pages and 200,000 notes.

170. *Jahresberichte für deutsche Geschichte.* **Leipzig: K. F. Koehler, 1927–. Issued in Pt. 1, Bibliographie, and Pt. 2, Forschungsberichte. Annual. ISSN 0075-286X.**
Part 1 covers all periods of German history in German. Individual entries are numbered and are organized under detailed chronological, geographical, and topical categories, which make for easy browsing. Part 2 lists works in progress, in-press, or recently published materials, including dissertations. An online version of this guide is available in some German libraries. See, for example, http://bibliothek.bbaw.de/my_html/header_jdg.htm. A CD-ROM version covering the period 1991–1995 is available in some North American libraries. It contains approximately 50,000 references.

171. *European History.* http://www.library. yale.edu/rsc/history/european/home.html
While there are many fine research guides and bibliographies of European history on the Internet, those done by Susanne Roberts, librarian for European History, Research Services, and Collections, Sterling Memorial Library at Yale, are among the best. She currently maintains bibliographies for British, French, German, Portuguese, and Spanish history. For each there is a table of contents and then detailed coverage by type of materials. The recently updated "A Select Bibliography for the Study of French History 1500–Present" is 49 pages long.

172. *West European Studies Section: WESSWEB.*
The Western European Studies Section of the Association of College and Research Libraries maintains a helpful list of WESSLinks for European Studies.

173. *Bibliography of the Soviet Union, Its Predecessors and Successors.* **By Bradley L. Schaffner. Lanham, MD: Scarecrow, 1995. ISBN 0-8108-2860-X.**

174. *Reinterpreting Russia: An Annotated Bibliography of Books on Russia, the Soviet Union, and the Russian Federation, 1991– 1996.* **By Steve D. Boilard. Lanham, MD: Scarecrow, 1997. ISBN 0-8108-3298-4.**

Schaffner's work provides subject access to recent titles on the region's social, political, and cultural development. It is especially valuable for research during the transition period from Gorbachev's Soviet Union to Yeltsin's Russia. Boilard lists, categorizes, and describes 600 recent books concerning Russia, the Soviet Union, and the post-Soviet Russian Federation.

Latin America

175. *A Bibliography of Latin American and Caribbean Bibliographies, 1985–1989,* Supplement to No. 5: Social Sciences and Humanities. Edited by Lionel V. Lorona. Metuchen, NJ: Scarecrow, 1993. 330pp. ISBN 0-8108-2702-6.
This fifth supplement to Arthur E. Gropp, *A Bibliography of Latin American Bibliographies* (1968), covering bibliographies published 1985–1989 and those published earlier but not noted in previous supplements, includes 1,867 unannotated citations.

176. *A Bibliography of the Caribbean.* By Marian Goslinga. Lanham, MD: Scarecrow, 1996. 368pp. ISBN 0-8108-3097-3.
This helpful bibliography, the first comprehensive bibliography of the Caribbean since the 1970s, includes all the islands from Bermuda to Trinidad, as well as mainland countries identified with the Caribbean such as Belize, Guyana, Suriname, and French Guiana. Goslinga, a librarian at Florida International University, arranges 3,600 entries (books) by region, and within regions by historical materials (pre–20th century), reference materials, and contemporary works. There are separate geographical, title, and author indexes. Although useful for broad regional studies, for country studies researchers should turn to CLIO

Press's *World Bibliographical Series* [see 180] or Scarecrow's *Latin American Historical Dictionaries Series* [see 616].

177. *Handbook of Latin American Studies Online (HLAS Online).* Washington, DC: Library of Congress. http://memory.loc.gov/hlas. Handbook of Latin American Studies. Austin, TX: University of Texas Press, 1935–. Annual. ISSN 0072-9833.
With the advent of HLAS Online in 1999, the handbook is available in three formats: the original print volumes, published by the University of Texas Press; a CD-ROM produced and updated by the Fundación Histórica TAVERA (Madrid, Spain); and the Internet version. The Handbook is a bibliography on Latin America consisting of works selected and annotated by scholars. The Handbook alternates annually between the social sciences and humanities. Each year some 130 academics select 5,000 new works for inclusion. The advantages of the online version should be obvious; it provides rapid, comprehensive access to future, current, and retrospective volumes of the Handbook. Recent enhancements are links to full-text databases like JSTOR and Project Muse.

178. *Latin America and the Caribbean: A Critical Guide to Research Sources.* Edited by Paula H. Covington. New York: Greenwood, 1992. 924pp. ISBN 0-313-26403-1.
Conceived at a meeting of the Committee on Bibliography of the Seminar on the Acquisition of Latin America Library Materials (SALALM) in 1984, this collaborative project was designed to provide an introduction to the nature of research and recent research trends in each discipline, followed by a guide to the principal sources for research and, selectively, description of spe-

cialized resources held in various libraries. The book is divided into 15 chapters, beginning with a chapter on interdisciplinary resources and ending with women's studies. History in chapter 8 begins with a general bibliography, followed by colonial history, history 1750–1850, history since 1950, and history of Brazil. Each opens with a lengthy historical review of the literature and is followed by a bibliography. Contributors include a "Who's Who of Latin American bibliographers in the United States," as well as practicing historians and other academics. This is the best place to begin researching a topic in Latin American history.

World

179. *World Bibliographies on CD-ROM.* http://www.saur.de/cdbibwo.htm
In collaboration with the Research Library Group (RLG), K. G. Saur, now a Thomson-Gale Company, has created a set of bibliographies recording titles published since the 15th century in the major languages of the world. The following were available in early 2003:

Italian Bibliography, 15th Century–1999, 2nd ed.

French Bibliography, 15th Century–2000, 2nd ed.

English Bibliography, 1901–1945

English Bibliography, 15th Century–1901

International Bibliography of Maps & Atlases, 2nd ed.

Spanish Bibliography, 15th Century–2002, 4th ed.

Portuguese Bibliography, 15th Century–1999

Latin Bibliography, 15th Century–2001, 2nd ed.

Russian Bibliography, 16th Century–1999

The number of records contained in each bibliography ranges from 250,000 to 2.5 million. Five user languages are included: English, German, French, Spanish, and Italian. User menus are identical for the whole series, and for bibliographic searches the same search criteria are available. Future updates are planned.

180. *World Bibliographical Series.* **Robert Neville, executive editor. Oxford: CLIO.** http://www.abc-clio.com
The number of titles in this series exceeds 200. While it originally focused on countries, it was later expanded to include the world's principal regions, islands, and cities. Each volume focuses on a single country/region/ocean/city and introduces its culture, history, place in the world, and unique qualities. There is an introductory essay and a map. Most volumes contain 500–1,000 entries. The last volume for Rome was published in October 2000. No new volumes are planned. E-versions are available from netLibrary, a division of OCLC.

SPECIALIZED HISTORICAL BIBLIOGRAPHIES: CHRONOLOGICAL PERIODS

181. *Ancient Greece and Rome: Bibliographical Guide.* **Compiled by Keith Hopwood. Manchester: Manchester University Press, 1995. 450pp. ISBN 0-7190-2401-3.**
This is the first book-length bibliography on classical history in 25 years. *Ancient*

Greece and Rome is intended for both academic and general audiences. It includes
8,000 citations to English-language books,
chapters, proceedings, and journal articles
written in the past 200 years. Entries are
arranged first in chronological sections covering the period 950 BC to AD 565 and
then in topical sections. Entries for recent
monographs cite book reviews. A final section lists 199 Festschriften, conference proceedings, and collective works. There is an
author index but no subject index. Also
helpful is *Classical Studies: A Guide to the Reference Literature*, by Fred W. Jenkins (Littleton, CO: Libraries Unlimited, 1996), which
includes 700 annotated entries and a special
chapter (now dated) on electronic sources.

182. *Exploring Ancient World Cultures.*
http://eawc.evansville.edu
Designed as an introduction to ancient
world cultures on the World Wide Web, this
source features its own essays and primary
texts. The eight "cultures" represented are
Near East, India, Egypt, China, Greece,
Rome, Early Islam, and Medieval Europe.
Chapters are planned for Rome and
Greece. EAWC also includes a substantial
index of Internet sites divided into five
subindexes: a chronology, an essay index, an
image index, an Internet site index, and an
electronic test index.

Other useful guides to Internet resources
include ABZU: Guide to Resources for the
Study of the Ancient Near East, available on
the Web at http://www.etana.org/abzu and
maintained by the Research Archives of the
Oriental Institute of Chicago, and the
Ancient World Web, http://www.julen.net/
aw, a personal page developed by Julia Hay-
den that indexes 1,223 sites.

183. *International Medieval Bibliography.*
Leeds, U.K.: University of Leeds, 1967–.
Published twice yearly. Index.
ISSN 0020-7950. Also on CD-ROM.
Appearing in January and July, this excellent serial bibliography lists articles, notes,
and essays, but not books, on medieval topics. Focus is on the European Middle Ages
(c. 1450–1500). About 1,000 journals and
some 100 Festschriften and collections of
essays are surveyed for relevant materials.
The organization is topical with geographical subdivisions. There are separate author
and general indexes. The CD-ROM database comprises over 220,000 articles from
around 4,000 journals and 5,000 miscellaneous conference proceedings, essay collections, and Festschriften.

An online version, IMB-Online from
Brepolis Publishers, premiered in 2001 with
quarterly updates.

184. *Iter: Gateway to the Middle Ages and
Renaissance.* http://www.intergateway.org
Iter, meaning a journey or a path in Latin,
is a nonprofit research project with partners
in Toronto, New York, and Tempe, AZ.
Its goal is to increase access to all published
materials pertaining to the Middle Ages
and Renaissance (400–1700) through the
creation of online bibliographic databases.
The journal database is available on a subscription service while the books database
is under construction. Future enhancements promise coverage of conference proceedings, dissertations, Festschriften, collections of essays, and digitized music and
artwork. Also in the planning stages is a
directory of Renaissance scholars, their
research projects, and their organizations/
institutions.

185. *The Labyrinth: Resources for Medieval Studies.* http://www.labyrinth.georgetown.edu

Sponsored by Georgetown University, the Labyrinth provides free, organized access to electronic resources in medieval Studies through a WWW server. The project not only provides an organizational structure for electronic resources in medieval studies but also serves as a model for other fields of study. You can search by category from archaeology to women, or by category and type of material.

186. *The Eighteenth Century: A Current Bibliography.* New York: AMS Press, 1978–. New Series. Vol. 1–. Annual. Index. ISSN 0161-0996.

This excellent interdisciplinary publication's coverage of scholarly literature begins with the year 1975. It has been plagued by long delays in publication. Books, journal articles, and essays in collective works are listed. All aspects of the 18th century—literary, artistic, historical, and intellectual—are covered. Geographic scope is international, with Western European and American topics predominating. Most items listed are in English, although materials in other languages are included. Many of the books are reviewed, while others and some of the articles are briefly annotated. There is a personal name index of authors and editors. This bibliography is the successor to the listing in "English Literature 1660–1800," which appeared in the *Philological Quarterly* from 1926 to 1970. From 1970 to 1974 the listing was expanded and made interdisciplinary, although it was still published as part of the *Philological Quarterly*.

187. *Eighteenth-Century Resources.* http://newark.rutgers.edu/~jlynch/18th

This extensive list of Internet resources developed by Jack Lynch, assistant professor of English at Rutgers University (Newark), is divided into the following categories: Art, Architecture, Landscape Gardening, etc.; History, Literature; Music; Philosophy; Religion and Theology; Science and Mathematics; Other Fields; Professional Resources and Journals; and Home Pages (of people working on the 18th century). The history section is subdivided into general resources, British history, American history, Canadian history, European history, and Other history. Lynch focuses on reliable, noncommercial sites. This is a good place to begin any 18th-century search.

SPECIALIZED HISTORICAL BIBLIOGRAPHIES: SUBJECTS

188. *The American Civil War: A Handbook of Literature and Research.* Edited by Steven E. Woodworth. Westport, CT: Greenwood, 1996. 751pp. ISBN 0-313-29019-9.

The American Civil War is one of the most written about periods in American history. One reviewer estimates that more than 70,000 books have been written about the conflict, about one a day since the war ended. This wonderful guide is designed to help both the novice student and experienced Civil War scholar wend their way through the vast literature on the conflict, its causes, and its aftermath. It includes 47 bibliographic essays from noted scholars, divided into 11 subject areas: general secondary sources, general primary sources, illustrative materials, causation, international relations, leaders, strategy and tactics, conduct of the war, the home front, reconstruction and beyond, and popular media. The essays average 15 pages in length and include a bibliography. The essays cite 3,960 books, articles, dissertations, and media. An appendix lists 516 publishers. There are author, title, and subject indexes. Also excellent is *The Civil War in Books: An Analytical Bibliography*, by David Eicher (Urbana: University of Illinois Press, 1997). Eicher, the managing editor of *Astronomy* magazine and an avid Civil War student, describes 1,100 books in lengthy annotations under the following subjects: Battles and Campaigns, Confederate Biographies, Union Biographies, General Works, and Unit Histories. To keep current on Civil War history, check out two excellent Web sites: American Civil War home page at http://sunsite.utk.edu/ civil-war began as a class project at the University of Tennessee School of Information Sciences. Today maintained by George H. Hoemann and Mary Myers, its stated purpose is to gather together hypertext links to the most useful identified electronic files about the Civil War. Resources are arranged in 10 categories from general to state/local studies. The United States Civil War Center at Louisiana State University, Baton Rouge, http://www.cwc.lsu.edu, identifies its mission as "to locate, index and make available all appropriate private and public data on the Internet regarding the Civil War." It had 7,000 links in early 2003.

189. *American Indian Studies: A Bibliographic Guide.* **By Phillip M. White. Englewood, CO: Libraries Unlimited, 1995. 163pp. ISBN 1-56308-243-8.**

This short but succinctly organized guide from Phillip White, bibliographer for American Indian studies at San Diego State University, is designed to guide college students and other researchers in utilizing library resources on American Indians/Native Americans. The primary focus is Indians of North America. It is organized by type of publication: books, guides, encyclopedias, bibliographies, periodicals indexes, newspaper indexes, American Indian periodicals/newspapers/newsletters, biographical, dissertations/theses, government publications, and microform collections. White describes 400 works published between 1970 and 1993. The longest chapter, "Bibliographies," is arranged alphabetically by topic or tribe.

190. *American Military History: A Guide to Reference and Information Sources.* **By Daniel K. Blewett. Englewood, CO: Libraries Unlimited, 1995. 295pp. ISBN 1-56308-035-4.**

The literature on the American military is voluminous. Blewett, bibliographer for history and political science at Loyola University, Chicago, has designed this selective guide as a first reference to that vast literature. The guide covers all branches of the services from the colonial period to the Persian Gulf War. The 1,284 entries (books) are arranged in 23 chapters. Within each section chapters are arranged chronologically by war or period. In the post–world War II period Blewett discusses resources for arms control, terrorism, intelligence, and espionage, as well as electronic information sources. For additional research, he recommends Robin Higham, *A Guide to the Sources of United States History* (Hamden, CT: Shoe String, 1975) and supplements with Donald J. Mrozek in 1981, 1986, and 1993; Susan K. Kinnell, *Military History of the United States: An Annotated Bibliography* (Santa Barbara, CA: ABC-CLIO Press, 1986); and Jack Lane, *America's Military Past: A Guide to Information Sources* (Detroit: Gale, 1980). On a narrower topic the Naval Historical Center has published *United States Naval History: A Bibliography*, revised by Barbara A. Lynch and John E. Vajda, 7th ed. (1993) at their Web site: http://www.history.navy.mil/biblio/biblio1/biblio1.htm. It includes more than 450 titles chosen from the literature since the bibliography's sixth edition in 1972.

191. *Arctic Studies Center.* http://www.mnh.si.edu/arctic

Since 1988 Congress has provided funding for the Arctic Studies Center, as a permanent program for northern research and education within the National Museum of Natural History of the Smithsonian Institution. The center is dedicated to the study of northern peoples, their history, and environment. The center works closely with native communities and scientists from Russia, Japan, Canada, and Europe to facilitate research and international communication. Click "Resources" and then "Web Links" for an extensive bibliography of Arctic resources in the following categories: Archeology/Anthropology/Sciences; Education; General Resources; Museums, Exhibits, and Collections; and Native Sites and Native Resources. This is a very attractive and colorful site!

192. *Asian American Studies: An Annotated Bibliography and Research Guide.* **By Hyung-Chan Kim. Westport, CT: Greenwood, 1989. 504pp. ISBN 0-313-26026-5.**

Asian American studies did not really emerge as a field of study in the United States until the 1970s, in part fueled by vast new waves of Asian immigrants. This is the most comprehensive bibliography of Asian American studies ever published. Kim, a professor of education and Asian American studies at Western Washington University, includes 3,334 annotated entries drawn from a variety of sources (books, articles, dissertations). The work is organized in 27 chapters under two broad sections: Historical Perspectives and Contemporary Perspectives, with entries in each section organized by topic. The 1960s serve as the transition point; subject and author indexes provide additional access points.

193. *International Bibliography of Business History.* **Edited by Francis Goodall, Terry Gourvish, and Steven Tolliday. London: Routledge, 1997. 668pp. ISBN 0-415-08641-8.**

The aim of this bibliography is to assemble an authoritative international bibliography containing much of the best work in business history, written mainly in book form. The overall arrangement of the bibliography is based on broad chapters: primary and extractive industries (e.g., oil, agriculture); traditional and heavy industries (e.g., iron and steel); light manufacturing industries (e.g., electrical and computers); trade and distribution (e.g., department stores); banking and finance; utilities, transport, and other services; strategy and structure (e.g., approaches to business history); and entrepreneurship and management. All entries are annotated and there are numerous cross-references in addition to indexes of authors and firms. More comprehensive than previous bibliographies, this is an excellent place to begin any research in international business history.

194. *International Institute of Social History (IISH).* http://www.iisg.nl/instuk.html The IISH was founded in 1935 and today is one of the world's largest research institutions in the field of social history in general and the history of the labor movement in particular. The IISH holds almost 2,000 archival collections, 1 million printed volumes, and an equal number of audiovisual items. The collections are accessible through an online catalog and an online index of archives and inventories. The *International Review of Social History* is published for the Institute by Cambridge University Press. An attractive bibliographic feature of the IISH Web site is a collective listing of the tables of contents of 54 journals from 1997 forward. The IISH also maintains the award-winning Labour History section of the WWW Virtual Library at http://www. iisg.nl/~w3vl, with more than 1,500 links to organizations, institutions, resources, journals, exhibitions, conferences, profiles, and reference sources. Recently the Economic and Business Section of the Virtual Library was separated and is now maintained in Amsterdam by the Netherlands Economic History Archive. There is also an alphabetical list of sites. On a smaller scale, Michael Lonardo, Social Sciences librarian at Memorial University of Newfoundland, maintains the Canadian Labour History Bibliography at http://www.mun.ca/ geii/labour/index.php. He lists books, pamphlets, articles, and theses.

195. *ISIS Current Bibliography of the History of Science and Its Cultural Influences.* Edited by John Neu. Chicago: University of Chicago Press, Journals Division, 1913–. ISSN 0021-1753.
The *Current Bibliography* appears as a fifth issue of *ISIS,* the oldest and largest circulating journal of the history of science. The most recent annual bibliography provides a guide to 4,100 publications relevant to the history of science and related fields culled from 600 journals in all languages. It also lists recently published books and book reviews. The *ISIS Cumulative Bibliography, 1986–1995,* edited by John Neu, was published in 1997 in 4 volumes. This is the third supplement to the *ISIS Cumulative Bibliography, 1913–1965,* edited by Magda Withrow. The *ISIS Current Bibliography from 1975* to the present is now available online at RLIN. The bibliography joins the *Current Bibliography in the History of Technology,* published annually in *Technology and Culture* and the *Bibliografia Italiana di Storia della Scienza,* published by the Institute e Museo di Storia della Scienza in Florence, as a single file (HST) in RLIN's CitaDel database (available as an institutional subscription). History of Science Society members can access the HST file for free. The *Current Bibliography in the History of Technology,* mentioned above, is published as a supplement to *Technology and Culture* (John Hopkins University Press). The most recent issue for 1996–1997, published in 1999, is the largest ever with 3,300 entries organized first in five chronological divisions and then in one of 17 classifications. The history of medicine is covered in HISTLINE (History of Medicine Online), a National Library of Medicine (NLM) online bibliographical database. Updated weekly, it has some 190,000 citations. Also valuable is *Current Work in the History of Medicine,* a quarterly international bibliography of articles on the

history of medicine published since 1954 by the Wellcome Institute for the History of Medicine. Each issue contains approximately 1,500 recent articles arranged by broad subject area. Since 1991 *Current Work* has been produced electronically. It can be browsed on WILDCat (Wellcome Institute Library Database and Catalogue) at http://wihm.ucl.ac.uk.

In January 2000 the Research Libraries Group's History of Science and Technology database was expanded to include medicine.

196. *The Kaiser Index to Black Resources, 1948–1986.* Brooklyn: Carlson, 1992. 5 vols. ISBN 0-926019-60-0.
The Schomburg Center for Research in Black Culture, a research unit of the New York Public Library, has long been in the forefront of institutions dedicated to the preservation of the black past. In the absence of adequate reference sources about Afro-Americans or blacks, Schomburg Library Staff developed an in-house reference file of 3x5 slips, handwritten citations to books, articles, newspapers, etc. describing the black experience. By 1986 this file had grown to 174,000 items and was referred to as the Kaiser Index after Ernest Kaiser, longtime contributor to the file. Remembering that this is an idiosyncratic index with incomplete bibliographic citations, it is nonetheless a rich resource about black Americans. The index is arranged alphabetically by subject based on Library of Congress headings. It complements the *Dictionary Catalog of the Schomburg Collection* published in 1962 with supplements published in 1967 and 1972. From Cameroon—History to Roy Campanella, this is an incredibly rich bibliographic

resource on the black experience, not only in the United States but worldwide.

197. *African American Studies Reference Sources.* http://www.library.cornell.edu/africana/Library/AA_Studies.html
This is a selective list of available resources on African American studies in the John Henrik Clarke Africana Library at Cornell University. It can be used as a guide to find more extensive materials in this and other libraries.

198. *Oral History: A Reference Guide and Annotated Bibliography.* By Patricia Pate Havlice. Jefferson, NC: McFarland, 1985. 140pp. Index. ISBN 0-89950-138-9.
Oral history is a relatively new (post–World War II) methodology used by historians. This bibliography lists 773 books, dissertations, and articles that have appeared on the topic from the 1950s to 1983. It should be supplemented by more recent Web links. Oral History Links on the Web, http://bancroft.berkeley.edu/ROHO/ohlinks.html, a site maintained by the UC-Berkeley Library, includes a very complete list of U.S. and international sites. See also the "Selected Oral History Bibliography" at http://www.indiana.edu/~ohrc/bibliogr.htm.

199. *The Psychohistorian's Handbook.* By Henry Lawton. New York: Psychohistory, 1988. 241pp. ISBN 0-914434-27-6.
Psychohistory is one of the more controversial subfields of history. This book, consisting of 11 chapters, covers key topics such as psychoanalytic theory, psychohistorical methodology, psychobiography, and teaching psychohistory. Each chapter includes a narrative essay interspersed with sections of

annotated bibliography. The author is a
practitioner and defender of the scholarly
validity of psychohistory. The Institute for
Psychohistory is a New York–based research
and publication institute. Its Web site at
http://www.psychohistory.com contains
extensive material reproduced from the
Journal of Psychohistory and from books
published by Psychohistory Press. It also
includes the *25-Year Index to the Journal of
Psychohistory* by Lloyd deMause, published
as issue 4 of the journal, spring 1998.
A major Web Directory of Psychohistory
Links is at http://www.geocities.com/
RainForest/vines/6074/psyhohis.htm.

200. *Reader's Guide to Women's Studies.*
**Edited by Eleanor B. Amico. Chicago:
Fitzroy Dearborn, 1998. 732pp.
ISBN 188496477X.**
Women's history and women's studies have
exploded since the late 1960s. Women's
studies research has taken place in virtually
every field of academic endeavor. Like the
earlier *Reader's Guide to American History*, this
book is designed to provide the reader with
brief discussions of important books on over
500 topics and individuals. Only books
available in English are listed. Entries are
listed in alphabetical order. In addition, there
is a thematic list, a Booklist index, a general
index, and numerous cross-references.
Regrettably, many prominent women who
have not been the subject of monographs,
but only of articles, are excluded. For each
person/subject a list of books with complete bibliographic citations is included, followed by a comparative analysis of each by a
women's studies scholar. More limited in
scope but more comprehensive in coverage
is *The Women's Movement: References and
Resources,* by Barbara Ryan (New York: G.

K. Hall, 1996). This comprehensive annotated bibliography of critical resources
includes 1,301 entries arranged in six sections: First Wave Feminism, Second Wave
Feminism, Women Activists, Feminist Dis-
course, Issues, and Guide to Sources. There
are subject, author, and title indexes. Ryan
is an associate professor of sociology and
coordinator of women's studies at Widener
University. Also valuable is *CHOICE
Reviews in Women's Studies, 1990–1996*
(Chicago: ACRL, 1997), which includes
reviews of more than 2,000 recent women's
studies titles. These are arranged alphabetically by subject matter.

201. *Term Paper Resources Guide to
Twentieth-Century United States History.* **By
Robert Muccigrosso, Ron Blazek, and Teri
Maggio. Westport, CT: Greenwood, 1999.
310pp. ISBN 0-313-30096-8.**
A librarian, historian, and library science
professor have combined their talents to
produce this handy guide to sources on 100
important events in 20th-century U.S. history. They begin with the Spanish American War (1898) and end with the North
American Free Trade Agreement (NAFTA)
in 1993. Each of the 100 entries includes
15–35 items under seven categories: general
sources, specialized sources, biographical
sources, periodical articles, audiovisual
sources, and World Wide Web. There is also
a brief summary of the event suggestions
for term paper topics. This source has been
designed to meet the needs of high school
and undergraduate students. It certainly
leaves nothing to chance.

202. *The United States and Latin America:
A Select Bibliography.* **By John A. Britton.
Pasadena, CA: Scarecrow; Englewood**

Cliffs, NJ: Salem, 1997. 277pp.
ISBN 0-8108-3248-8.

This book is part of the Magill Bibliographies Series. Britton, a professor of History at Francis Marion University in South Carolina, intended this volume to be a convenient description of the content of books and articles in U.S.-Latin American relations. After contrasting diplomatic history with international history he arranges sources under the following headings: general studies, the 19th-century, the 20th century, and nations and diplomacy. The annotations are lengthy and evaluative, although limited largely to books. There is a very short section on video documentation and author and subject indexes.

203. *The History Highway 3.0: A Guide to Internet Resources.* By Dennis A. Trinkle and Scott A. Merriman. Armonk, NY: M. E. Sharpe, 2002. 702pp. ISBN 0-765609-04-5. Also on CD-ROM.

Now revised, expanded, and updated, this third edition describes more than 3,000 Web sites useful to historians with a brief description of the contents. It includes a CD-ROM with links to the sites. A very helpful resource.

3

BOOK REVIEW INDEXES

Since the historical literature on many topics is vast, making qualitative decisions regarding the best books to read on a particular topic is often predicated on how well those books were received by the critics. Prior to 1970, locating reviews of historical monographs was a difficult task largely confined to searching book review sections of major historical journals. That task has been rendered a good deal easier in recent decades with the development of new historical indexes like *America: History and Life*, expanded coverage of historical journals in Wilson indexes like *Humanities Index*, the publication of several retrospective indexes to book reviews in scholarly journals, and the appearance of a number of electronic products. Standard book review indexes like *Book Review Digest* and *Book Review Index* have increased their coverage of historical reviews, and sophisticated online and compact disc versions of many periodical and newspaper indexes have made it easy to locate reviews of current books.

GENERAL

204. *Book Review Digest*. New York: H. W. Wilson, 1905–. Monthly except for

February and July with annual cumulations. ISSN 0006-7326.
This title, commonly abbreviated as *BRD*, is the oldest and best known of the general reviewing indexes. It provides excerpts of and citations to reviews of current fiction and nonfiction. Reviews are selected from more than 109 periodicals in the humanities, social sciences, and general sciences from titles published in the United States, Canada, and the United Kingdom. Most major historical journals are included and coverage was expanded in 1989. To qualify for inclusion, a book must be published or distributed in the United States or Canada. A work of fiction must have received reviews in at least three periodicals while a work of nonfiction must have been reviewed at least twice. All of the reviews must have appeared within eighteen months after publication. Reviews are listed alphabetically under the author's last name. There is also a subject and title index. The cumulative *Author/Title Index 1905–1974* was published in 1976.

205. *Book Review Digest Plus*. New York: H. W. Wilson, 2002–. Online database.
On November 21, 2002, H. W. Wilson launched its newest book review index. Far more than an online version of the print

digest, it draws thousands of reviews from other Wilson e-products such as Readers' Guide Full Text, Wilson Business Full Text, Humanities Full Text, Education Full Text, Art Full Text, General Science Full Text, Library Literature and Information Science Full Text, Applied Science and Technology Full Text, Biological and Agricultural Index Full Text, Index to Legal Periodicals Full Text, and Social Sciences Full Text. Plans call for daily updates with retrospective coverage back to 1983. It uses the new Wilson Web interface, which permits natural language searching, full-text searching, and relevancy-ranked results. They anticipate publishing review excerpts and book summaries for more than 8,000 English-language titles a year.

206. *Book Review Index.* **Detroit: Gale Research, 1965–. Three paper issues with annual bound cumulations. ISSN 0524-0581.**

Often referred to as *BRI,* this index provides broad access to book reviews in the social sciences, humanities, and sciences. Begun as a monthly in 1965, publication was briefly suspended from 1969 to 1972. A retrospective index for these years was published in 1975. *BRI* includes citations to reviews of any type of book that has been or is about to be published that is at least 50 pages long. All reviews in 500 indexed journals are cited, including contents notes and collection recommendations. Entries are arranged alphabetically by the name of the author of the book. The information included in an individual entry includes author, title, source, date, and page on which the review appears. There is a title index. Unlike *BRD* [see 204], there is no subject indexing. A recent cumulation of

BRI listed 133,000 reviews of 77,700 titles. *Master Cumulation, 1965–1984* was published in 1985 providing title access to 1.6 million citations. Cumulations for 1985–1992 and 1993–1997 have also been published. Online access has been available through Dialog File 137 since 1969 with the file being updated three times yearly.

207. *booksinprint.com.* **New York: Bowker, 2000–. Online database.**

This is a greatly improved version of the former *Books in Print with Book Reviews Plus.* In addition to providing bibliographic information for more than 4 million in print items and 1.4 million out of print items, it includes 628,000 full-text reviews from 25 sources, including *Booklist, Choice, Kirkus, Library Journal, Publishers Weekly, Quill & Quire, School Library Journal, Sci-Tech Book News,* and *Voya,* as well as newspapers ranging from the *Boston Globe* to the *Wall Street Journal.*

208. *Canadian Book Review Annual.* **Toronto: CBRA, 1975–. Annual. ISSN 0383-770X.**

This is an evaluative guide to Canadian-authored, Canadian-published English-language books. A recent annual includes 1,700 reviews arranged in six categories from reference to children's literature. All reviews are signed. The French Canadian equivalent, *Livres et Auteurs Quebecois,* has ceased publication.

209. *Academic Search Premier.* **EBSCOhost. Ipswich, MA: EBSCO Publishing, 1990–. Online database.**

Designed specifically for academic institutions, this multidisciplinary database contains full text for nearly 3,600 scholarly publications and indexing and abstracting for all 4,500 journals in the collection. While most major history journals are included, not all are available full text. Available in many academic libraries, this is a rich source of book reviews.

210. *Infotrac: Expanded Academic ASAP.* Detroit: Thomson/Gale, 1996–.
This is Gale's premier database for research in academic disciplines. It provides broad coverage of social science journals, humanities journals, sci-tech journals, national news periodicals, general interest magazines, and indexing for the *New York Times.* Currently it includes indexing to 3,000+ titles with full-text coverage of 1,900 of those. Coverage begins with 1980 for some titles.

211. *National Library Service Cumulative Book Reviews Index, 1905–1974.* Princeton, NJ: NLS, 1975. 6 vols.
This publication supplies a cumulative index to the book reviews appearing in *Book Review Digest* (1905–1974), *Library Journal* (1907–74), *Saturday Review* (1924–1974), and *Choice* (1964–74). The titles listed for the *Book Review Digest* refer to its digests and not the complete review. Over 1 million reviews are given author and title access in this index.

212. *Periodical Abstracts Research II.* Ann Arbor, MI: ProQuest Information and Learning, n.d.
This general reference database provides abstracts and indexing for articles in 2,190 periodicals as well as current coverage of articles in the *New York Times* and *Wall Street Journal.* Journals included are drawn from *Magazines for Libraries* and are also designed

to correspond to the most popular college majors. In addition to full-text coverage of many titles, for each article cited in the database an abstract of up to 75 words is provided.

HUMANITIES

213. *Arts and Humanities Citation Index.* Philadelphia, PA: ISI/Thomson Scientific, 1976–. Internet via the ISI Web of Science updated weekly; CD-ROM updated triannually; Arts and Humanities Search via DIALOG and OCLC.
This once difficult to search source with its multivolumes of small print is a breeze to search online. Multidisciplinary, it provides access to current and retrospective bibliographic information and cited references found in nearly 1,130 arts and humanities journals including 193 history journals. Book reviews can be located quickly in the general or advanced search modes by limiting your search to "Book Reviews." Searchable abstracts were added after January 2000. The Internet version provides back files to 1975, the CD-ROM version to 1990; DIALOG or OCLC files date from 1980.

214. *Combined Retrospective Index to Book Reviews in Humanities Journals, 1802–1974.* Edited by Evan I. Farber. Woodbridge, CT: Research Publications, 1983–1984. 10 vols. ISBN 0-89235-061-X.
This helpful compilation provides one of the best sources for retrospective book reviews. Reviews are drawn from 150 humanities journals including some that were founded before 1850, such as the

American Oriental Society Journal, Dublin Review, Edinburgh Review, North American Review, Punch, and *Spectator*. The first nine volumes provide access to more than 500,000 reviews arranged in alphabetical order by the name of the author of the book. When known, the names of the authors of the reviews have been included. The final volume is an alphabetical list of books reviewed by title and provides cross references to the author entries.

215. *Humanities Index/Humanities Full Text.* New York: H. W. Wilson, 1974–. Quarterly with annual cumulations. ISSN 0095-5981. Online access via Wilson Web.
This easy-to-use, readily available publication indexes book reviews from 502 periodicals including about 80 major historical periodicals published in the United States, Great Britain, and Canada. These book review citations follow the main body of the index in a separate alphabetical listing. Reviews of less than one page in length or for books more than five years old are excluded. Originally this index formed part of the *Social Sciences and Humanities Index* (1965–1974) which had formerly been titled the *International Index* (1907–1965). Neither of these indexes included book reviews. Humanities Full Text provides full text coverage of 182 titles back to 1995.

216. *An Index to Book Reviews in the Humanities.* Williamston, MI: Philip Thomson, 1960–1990. Annual. ISSN 0073-5892.
Initially this publication was a selective index of book reviews in the humanities. With volume 12 (1974), however, it began to index all the reviews published in the journals it covered. Limited to books in

English, it includes about 400 reviews arranged alphabetically by author. Reviewer's names are listed when known and periodical titles are coded to a master list. Coverage of history is spotty. More attention is given to interdisciplinary period journals like *Victorian Studies* and *Eighteenth-Century Studies*. The index ceased in 1990.

SOCIAL SCIENCES

217. *Combined Retrospective Index to Book Reviews in Scholarly Journals, 1886–1974.* Edited by Evan I. Farber. Arlington, VA: Carrollton, 1979–1982. 15 vols. ISBN 0-8408-0157-2.
A spin-off from earlier CRIS indexes to the journal literature of history, sociology, and political science, this cumulation provides access to more than 1 million reviews in 458 scholarly journals in the fields of history, sociology, and political science. The first 12 volumes provide author access while the last three provide title access. Citations include an abbreviated journal title, volume number, year, issue number, and page. Unlike the *CRIS Index to Book Reviews in Humanities Journals* [see 214], no reviewers' names are listed in this index. It is, however, a very useful guide to reviews published in national, regional, and state historical journals.

218. *Social Sciences Citation Index.* Philadelphia, PA: ISI/Thomson Scientific, 1969–. Internet via the ISI Web of Science updated weekly; CD-ROM updated monthly; Social SciSearch via DIALOG updated weekly.
Organized exactly like its sister index, the

Arts and Humanities Citation Index [see 213], this publication's historical coverage includes approximately 15 history titles plus others on the history and philosophy of science and the history of social sciences. It provides access to current and retrospective bibliographic information, author abstracts, and cited references found in over 1,700 scholarly social science journals. Book reviews can be located much quicker online by limiting your search to "book reviews." Coverage varies by format. The CD-ROM version has back files to 1981. Print volumes date to 1969.

HISTORY

219. *America: History and Life.* Santa Barbara, CA: ABC-CLIO, 1964–. Semiannual. ISSN 0097-6172. Print. CD-ROM. Online.

Provides comprehensive coverage of U.S. and Canadian history from prehistory to the present. Most commonly searched online, it covers 2,000 journals published worldwide. In addition to the articles, the database adds 6,000 citations of book and media reviews from a selection of 100 key journals. To locate reviews use the "Advanced Search" mode and combine "Document Type=Book Review" with your search. In early 2003 the database contained 138,858 book review citations.

220. *Historical Abstracts.* Santa Barbara, CA: ABC-CLIO, 1954–. ISSN 0363-2725. Print. CD-ROM. Online.

Provides comprehensive coverage of world history (exclusive of Canada and the United States) since 1450. Most commonly

searched online, it covers 2,000 journals published worldwide in a multitude of languages. In addition to articles, each year approximately 3,000 citations to book reviews are added to the database. To locate these reviews use the "Advanced Search" mode and combine Document Type=Book Review with your search. In early 2003 the database contained 60,776 book review citations.

NEWSPAPERS

221. *InfoTrac Custom Newspapers.* Detroit: Thomson/Gale. Online.

The earliest version of this database dates to 1979, was on microfilm, and covered five national U.S. dailies. Today you can select from more than 100 different papers. Thus access varies by library. Retrospective coverage, particularly for the early 1990s, was negatively impacted by the Tasini decision, especially where papers had not acquired electronic distribution rights from authors.

222. *LexisNexis Academic Universe.* Bethesda, MD: LexisNexis Academic and Library Solutions.

LexisNexis, an expensive online subscription database, is available in most research libraries. It provides access to articles from hundreds of newspapers, most of which are full text. To locate book reviews, select the "News" category from the main screen. Then select "Arts & Sports." Be sure that "Book, Movie, Music, and Play Reviews" is highlighted in the source category.

223. *New York Times Index.* New York: NYT Co., 1913–. Semimonthly with

quarterly and annual cumulations. ISSN 0147-538X.

Book reviews have always formed an important part of this index since its creation. Retrospective volumes produced for the period 1851–1912 include book reviews written after 1862 under the heading "book reviews and books" or simply "reviews." Currently they are listed alphabetically by title under the subject heading "book reviews." Authors appear in the main A–Z sequence of the index with cross references to the book review section. The volume of titles reviewed has remained consistent over the years. The 1913 index listed 2,045 reviews while the 1998 index lists 2,319 reviews. A five-volume cumulation, the *New York Times Book Review Index, 1896–1970,* was published by Arno Press in 1973. It provides author, title, and subject access to more than 100,000 reviews. Available on CD-ROM since 1992.

224. *New York Times: Books.*

Like many newspapers that are available on the Web, the *NYT* makes its Sunday book review available. The major difference is that the *New York Times* reviews more books than any other paper. Archiving is limited.

225. *ProQuest Newspaper Abstracts.* Ann Arbor, MI: ProQuest Information and Learning, 1987–. Online. CD-ROM.

An early form of this database appeared on CD-ROM in 1987 and covered eight major U.S. dailies. Today ProQuest provides coverage of 27 national and international papers. Three versions of the database are currently available:

Newspaper Abstracts Complete (all 27 primary and secondary papers)

Newspaper Abstracts National (nine major U.S. papers)
Newspaper Abstracts Major Papers (five top U.S. dailies)

Updated daily, archival coverage dates to 1989. Back files are available from 1985 to 1988.

226. *ProQuest Historical Newspapers.*

This ongoing project provides full-text and full-image articles for newspapers dating back to the 19th century, including the *New York Times 1851–1999; Wall Street Journal 1889–1985;* and *Washington Post 1877–1987.* These provide access to thousands of book reviews.

227. *The Times Index.* Reading, U.K.: Research Publications, 1973–. Monthly with annual cumulations. ISSN 0260-0668.

This publication provides access to book reviews in *The Times, Sunday Times, Times Literary Supplement, Times Educational Supplement, Times Education Supplement: Scotland,* and the *Times Higher Education Supplement.* Earlier versions of this index, the *Annual Index* (1906–1913), the *Official Index* (1914–1957), and the *Index to the Times* (1957–1972) did not cover the various auxiliary publications of *The Times.* Coverage of book reviews in a special section "Book Reviewed and Noticed" appeared for the first time in the 1955 edition. In recent editions reviews appear under the heading "Books (Titles and Reviews)" in alphabetical order by title. Author entries with citations also appear in the main alphabetical index. More than 4,126 reviews were listed in the 1998 annual cumulation. See The Times Digital Archive, 1785–1985.

BOOK TRADE AND LIBRARY ASSOCIATION PUBLICATIONS

While virtually every country has special-ized book trade or library association publi-cations featuring advance reviews or notes of new books, the following selections are the most helpful sources for reviews of new history books.

228. *Booklist.* **Chicago: American Library Association, 1905–. Bimonthly except July and August, which are monthly. ISSN 0006-7385.**
One of the major U.S. reviewing sources, *Booklist,* which includes *Reference Books Bulletin,* is widely used as a selection tool in many libraries. Approximately 400 reviews of history titles written by staff reviewers appear each year in the adult non-fiction section. History reference sources are reviewed by the Editorial Board of *Reference Books Bulletin.* Semiannual combined author-title indexes appear in the February 15 and August issues.

229. *Choice.* **Middletown, CT: Association of College and Research Libraries, 1964–. 11 times a year. ISSN 0009-4978.**
This ACRL publication is the most impor-tant source of reviews for academic libraries in the United States. Each year *Choice* pub-lishes more than 7,000 reviews by subject experts of the reviews published. In 2000, 816 covered history titles. Each monthly print issue includes approximately 600 reviews of recent books and electronic resources, a bibliographic essay, and a special feature. Choice Reviews Online was launched in 1999 and now provides online

subscription access to 80,000 reviews dating back to 1988. You can search by title, by author, or by a word in the review. The development of this online resource marked a major step in expanding access to reviews of history books and electronic resources.

230. *Library Journal.* **New York: Reed Business Information, 1876–. 20 times a year.**
This is the oldest and most important library trade journal in its field. It combines the news typical of *American Libraries* and reviews of all formats common to *Booklist. LJ* publishes approximately 200 reviews of history titles each year in its social sciences section and reviews others under biography. History reference sources are reviewed sep-arately. Reviewers include librarians and other academics. All reviews are signed. Canadian publications performing a similar function are *Books in Canada* (Toronto: Canadian Review of Books, 1971; nine times a year) and *Quill & Quire* (1935–; 12 times a year). The British counterpart, *British Book News,* ceased in 1993. French books are reviewed in the *Bulletin Critique du Livre Français* (Paris: Association pour la Diffusion de la Pensee Francaise, 1945–; 11 times a year). The English-language edi-tion has ceased.

INTERNET REVIEWS

231. H-Net Reviews
H-Net Reviews in the humanities and social sciences is an online scholarly review resource. Reviews have been posted since 1993. Reviews are often posted at one of the many discussion group sites such as

H-South or H-Texas (there is one for virtually every region of the world and for many U.S. states) before being archived at H-Net. Discussion of books and the reviews is encouraged. To quote the publisher, "H-Net Reviews brings a new dimension to the world of academic publishing."

4

PERIODICAL GUIDES AND CORE JOURNALS

The scholarly historical journal appeared in the 19th century and quickly became a significant part of historical literature. Most journals publish articles, which generally are specialized studies about the length of a chapter in a book, and book reviews. During the 20th century the number of journals grew, along with a narrowing of their specialization. Now there are thousands of journals published throughout the world. Furthermore, advances in electronic technology have made possible electronic publishing of journals. This publishing phenomenon is making a big impact on the publishing of scientific journals and currently is affecting humanities and historical journals to a lesser degree. Historical journals continue to be published in the traditional print format, but back issues of journals are being offered electronically through JSTOR and Project Muse. This chapter begins by listing important sources for finding out about historical journals. Next, it lists and describes a selection of journals commonly found in college and university libraries. This list is intended to be representative rather than comprehensive.

PERIODICAL GUIDES

232. *Historical Journals: A Handbook for Writers and Reviewers.* **By Dale R. Steiner and Casey R. Phillips. 2nd ed. Jefferson, NC: McFarland, 1993. 274pp. ISBN 0-89950-801-4.**

Historical Journals is basically a writer's and a book reviewer's guide to journals of interest to historians. The second edition lists 700 journals compared to the first edition's mere 350 listings, and includes British journals as well as American and Canadian. While Steiner's volume lists about the same number of journals as Fyfe [see. 234], the two guides do not always list the same titles. Furthermore, since Steiner is specifically oriented toward writers and reviewers, its entries provide more specific publication information: type of manuscript style required by each journal, preferred length of manuscripts, length of time needed to consider a manuscript, and proportion of manuscripts accepted for publication. Two chapters at the beginning of the book provide guidelines and advice on preparing an article for submission and the writing of book reviews. These have been updated to take into consideration the impact of personal computers and other new electronic technology. Another more comprehensive publication that provides almost identical information for humanities journals in general is the *MLA Directory of Periodicals: A Guide to Journals and Series in Languages and Literatures*, 9th ed. (New York: Modern Language Association of America, 1999). An abridged paperbound version of the *MLA Directory* is available but only lists journals published in the Americas. Steiner's volume has the virtues of being specifically historical in its focus and readily affordable for a personal library in a paperback edition.

233. *Historical Periodicals Directory.* **Edited by Eric H. Boehm, Barbara H. Pope, and Marie S. Ensign. Santa Barbara, CA: ABC-CLIO, 1981–1986. 5 vols. ISBN 0-87436-022-6.**
Volume 1: *USA and Canada.*
Volume 2: *Europe: West, North, Central, and South.*
Volume 3: *Europe: East and Southeast.*
Volume 4: *Latin America and West Indies.*
Volume 5: *Australia and New Zealand and Cumulative*
Subject and Geographical Index to Vols. 1–5.
International in its coverage, this directory lists well over 6,000 periodicals dealing with history from all over the world. The publications included may be published at regular or irregular intervals but they must have at least 30 percent of their contents devoted to history. Many local genealogical publications are included. Volumes are organized geographically and within each volume entries are listed alphabetically by title under the country where they are published. Each entry is numbered and gives the title, publisher, address, in-house indexing, language(s) of the publication, past

titles, coverage in indexing and abstracting services, and ISSN number. The final volume includes a geographical and subject index to the whole set. It supersedes Eric Boehm and Lalit Adolphus's *Historical Periodicals: An Annotated World List of Historical and Related Serial Publications* (1961).

234. *History Journals and Serials: An Analytical Guide.* **By Janet Fyfe. Westport, CT: Greenwood, 1986. LC 86-9986.**
This volume is an annotated listing of almost 700 English-language journals specializing in history from all over the world. Its purposes are basically to help librarians select journals for their collections and to aid historians in deciding which journals they might be interested in submitting manuscripts to or reading. Virtually all important historical periodicals are listed. Each entry supplies information about location, indexing, scope, and format for each title. The journals are arranged under broad subject or geographical headings. Indexes for geographical location, title, publisher, and subject greatly assist the reader.

235. *The History Journals Guide.* **By Stefan Blaschke. http://www.history-journals.de**
This online directory of historical journals had its start as a student project at the University of Cologne in Germany during 1997. Stefan Blaschke maintains the Web site, which switched from German to English in 1998 and became part of the WWW-Virtual Library in 1999. Visitors to the home page of the *History Journals Guide* will see that it consists of five sections: the *History Journals News*, the periodicals directory, the discussion lists directory, the online articles directory, and the online reviews directory. *History Journals News* is a biweekly

newsletter concerning historical journals. The four directories are all indexed to be searched in a number of different ways such as topical, chronological, geographical, alphabetical, and other appropriate search fields. The most useful section is the periodicals directory, which lists some 4,000 periodicals from around the world. Contact and subscription information are listed, and links to home pages of the periodicals are provided when available. Frequently the home page will provide tables of contents for current and back issues. The discussion list directory does the same thing but in spite of Blaschke's continual efforts to keep his Web site up-to-date, users will find many dead links. That is the fleeting nature of many discussion groups. The online articles index and the online reviews index both provide access to articles, reviews, conferences, exhibits, and collections on the Internet. *The History Journals Guide* is a wonderful example of how an electronic publication format through the Internet can provide very valuable information.

CORE JOURNALS

236. *Agricultural History.* 1927–. Quarterly. Berkeley: University of California Press. ISSN 0002-1482.
Sponsored by the Agricultural History Society, this journal encompasses all periods and geographical areas. At the same time, the majority of articles published in it deal with American history. Special topics issues appear frequently. A normal issue contains four to seven articles while a special topic issue can have over 20 articles. About 25 books are reviewed in an average issue. The first issue of each volume includes a feature

"Significant Books on Agricultural History," discussing the previous year's publications. A table of contents for the entire volume is supplied in the fourth issue, along with an index of authors, titles, and subjects and a list of books reviewed. The British equivalent of this journal is called the *Agricultural History Review* and is published twice yearly.

237. *American Historical Review.* 1895–. 5 issues/year. Washington, DC: American Historical Association. ISSN 0002-8762.
All periods and all geographical areas fall within the scope of this journal as befits the diverse interests of the members of its parent organization, the American Historical Association. It has the widest circulation of any academic historical journal in North America. Each issue contains four to five articles, notes and comments, and review articles along with about 200 signed book reviews arranged into broad categories of time period and area. Authors of books under review are allowed to respond to their critics. The scholarly standards of this publication are of the highest order. A detailed author, title, and subject index is printed in the fifth issue of each volume. Every nation that is historically conscious to even a moderate degree will have a general historical journal similar to the *American Historical Review*. The *English Historical Review* [see 251] performs that role for the United Kingdom, while France has its *Revue Historique* and Germany produces *Historia Zeitschrift*.

238. *American Journal of Legal History.* 1957–. Quarterly. Philadelphia, PA: Temple University. ISSN 0002-9319.
The focus of this journal is the history of American and English law. There are usually

three to five articles in an individual issue, along with occasional short notes. Between eight and fifteen signed book reviews are normally published in each issue. There is a simple index of authors and titles in the fourth issue of each volume. The equivalent British publication is called the *Journal of Legal History*. In 1983 an excellent new American journal, *Law and History Review*, began to appear twice yearly.

239. *American Quarterly.* **1949–. Quarterly. Philadelphia, PA: Johns Hopkins University Press for the American Studies Association. ISSN 0003-0678.**
Although this is an interdisciplinary journal devoted to American studies, it has a strong emphasis on the historical approach to social and cultural topics. Furthermore, the articles published tend to be interesting and provocative as well as being soundly researched, clear, and entertaining. Each issue has four to eight articles, with occasional theme issues. There are six to eight long signed book reviews in most issues.

240. *The Americas: A Quarterly Review of Inter-American Cultural History.* **1944–. Quarterly. Washington, DC: Catholic University of America Press/Academy of American Franciscan History. ISSN 0003-1615.**
Ranking just behind the *Hispanic American Historical Review* [see 255] in importance among Latin American history journals, this journal has for many years been edited by Antonine S. Tibesar, OFM, who died in 1992. The current editor is Judith Ewell of the College of William and Mary. Four to five articles and 25 book reviews are published in each issue. High-quality articles, timely reviews, and an excellent section

called Inter-American Notes characterize this veteran journal.

241. *Bulletin of the Institute of Historical Research.* **See** *Historical Research.*

242. *Business History Review.* **1926–. Quarterly. Cambridge, MA: Harvard Business School. ISSN 0007-6805.**
Called the *Bulletin of the Business History Society* from 1926 until 1953, this publication is the foremost journal specializing in business history in the English language. Its scope is international with the modern period in the United States and Europe tending to predominate. Each issue contains three or four articles and one archival essay that discusses the resources for business history in a selected repository. Several review articles are published every year and every issue contains about 30 signed book reviews. The fourth issue contains a simple index for the whole volume. *Business History* is the British journal that corresponds to *Business History Review* and it naturally has a strong British focus.

243. *Canadian Historical Review.* **1920–. Quarterly. Toronto: University of Toronto Press. ISSN 0008-3755.**
The focus of this journal is Canadian history with no restrictions as to era, subject, or region. As such, it is the Canadian equivalent of the *Journal of American History*. An issue usually contains three or four articles and 20 reviews of new books. A special section, "Recent Publications Relating to Canada," provides a current bibliography of newly available material useful in the study of any aspect of Canadian history. The fourth issue of a volume includes a simple index. It should not be confused with the

Canadian Journal of History, which publishes articles on all aspects of history. Other journals that focus on Canadian studies include *The International Journal of Canadian Studies* and the *Journal of Canadian Studies.*

244. *Church History.* 1935–. Quarterly. Red Bank, NJ: American Society of Church History. ISSN 0009-6407.
The entire range of the history of Christianity in all times and places forms the scope of this journal. It is the premier religious history periodical in North America. There are usually five articles in each issue with occasional review articles. From 30 to 60 books are given substantial signed reviews in each issue, and another 10 books are mentioned in shorter book notes. The simple index appearing in issue four lists articles and book reviews alphabetically by author. *Journal of Ecclesiastical History* is the well-edited English periodical concerned with general church history. In addition, it is important to remember that most major, and even many minor, church denominations publish their own historical journals and that these are generally very scholarly and objective publications.

245. *Civil War History: A Journal of the Middle Period.* 1955–. Quarterly. Kent, OH: Kent State University Press. ISSN 0009-8078.
This journal has a considerably broader scope than its title might suggest. It not only deals with the Civil War years; it also has an interest in topics ranging from the events of the 1840s through the 1870s and in all aspects of history, not just military. Each issue contains four to five articles. The number of signed book reviews varies from as few as four to as many as fifteen. There is

a detailed author, title, and subject index in the fourth issue of every volume.

246. *CLAHR: Colonial Latin American Historical Review.* 1992–. Quarterly. Albuquerque, N.M.: Spanish Colonial Research Center, NPS. ISSN 1063-5769.
In recent decades the study of colonial Latin American history has taken on renewed importance in the United States. To recognize the Spanish colonial past in the area of the present-day United States and in commemoration of the Columbus Quincentennial in 1992, the National Park Service established the Spanish Colonial Research Center in 1986 and launched CLAHR in 1992. Articles describe the history of Luso-Hispano America in the colonial era, 1492–1821, as well as the Caribbean and the Philippines through 1898. Each issue features three to four articles, approximately five book reviews, a section of shorter book notes, and news notes. Also focusing on the study of the colonial period in Latin America is the *Colonial Latin American Review,* an interdisciplinary journal founded in 1992.

247. *The Classical Journal.* 1905–. Quarterly. Ashland, VA: Classical Association of the Middle West and South. ISSN 0009-8353.
Classical studies is a field blessed with many distinguished journals, of which *Classical Journal* is the best known in the United States. Since the focus of this journal is the classics, its contents are multidisciplinary, although history figures prominently. Each issue contains four to nine articles. There is a special section called "Forum," which consists of about four short articles dealing with the teaching of the classics at the high school and college level. The book review

section is comparatively skimpy with only one to six signed reviews being standard. A simple index is compiled for every two volumes. The Classical Association in Great Britain publishes a similar, although more sophisticated journal called *Classical Quarterly,* which is published twice a year and only contains articles. *Classical Review,* a companion publication, supplies the other two parts of the quarterly and also publishes over 50 signed reviews plus another 50 short notices in each issue. Also useful is the semiannual *Greece and Rome.*

248. *Current History.* 1914–. 9 issues/year. Philadelphia, PA: Current History. ISSN 0011-3530.

The purpose of this long-running periodical is to provide assessments from experts concerning the current political, economic, and military situations in various foreign countries. Individual issues are arranged around a geographical or national theme and contain seven to eight articles. The books reviewed in each issue also relate to its subject theme. There is no index.

249. *Diplomatic History: The Journal of the Society for Historians of American Foreign Relations.* 1977–. Quarterly. Malden, MA: Blackwell. ISSN 0145-2096.

American foreign relations in all of its aspects—diplomatic, cultural, and intellectual—forms the special interest of this periodical. Each issue includes four or five articles with occasional review essays. The second, or Spring, issue of each volume includes a section called "Doctoral Dissertations in U.S. Foreign Affairs," which is a classified listing of recent dissertations relevant to the readership of *Diplomatic History.* It does not publish book reviews and there is no index.

250. *Eighteenth-Century Studies.* 1967–. Quarterly. Baltimore, MD: Johns Hopkins University Press for the American Society for Eighteenth-Century Studies. ISSN 0013-2586.

Like most journals dealing with the 18th century, this one is interdisciplinary although the basic orientation is historical. Generally an issue will contain four articles and 15 to 20 signed book reviews. It is not indexed by its editors. There is a British counterpart titled the *British Journal for Eighteenth Century Studies.*

251. *English Historical Review.* 1886–. Quarterly. Oxford: Oxford University Press. ISSN 0013-8266.

The oldest English-language periodical devoted solely to history, the *English Historical Review* has maintained the highest standards of scholarship throughout its over 100 years of publication. Its historical interests are the medieval and modern periods for all geographical areas and subjects. British and European topics are preponderant. Each issue contains three to four articles and one to three shorter "Notes and Documents." There are 15 to 20 longer signed book reviews and over 100 signed short book notices. The July issue includes the valuable "Notices of Periodical and Occasional Publications," which lists, with brief summaries and occasional evaluative comments, historical articles from some 80 periodicals published during the previous year. The notices are arranged geographically. There is a simple annual index at the end of each volume. A general and more detailed index for the years 1956–1985 was published in 1986. Similar journals for the rest of the British Isles are *Irish Historical Studies* (2 issues/year), *Scottish Historical Review* (2 issues/year), and *Welsh Historical Review* (2 issues/year).

252. *Ethnohistory.* 1954–. Quarterly. Durham, NC: Duke University Press. ISSN 0014-1801.
This unique journal is sponsored by the American Society for Ethnohistory. Basically it is an interdisciplinary publication that integrates the disciplines of history and anthropology. There is a strong emphasis on subjects dealing with contacts between European and non-European cultures and most articles concern themselves with non-Western cultures, particularly the Indians of North and South America. Each issue contains five to seven articles and 15 to 25 signed book reviews. There is no in-house index. This journal has had a difficult time maintaining its production schedule, especially during the early 1980s, but now seems to have stabilized.

253. *French Historical Studies.* 1958–. 2 issues/year. Durham, NC: Duke University Press for the Society for French Historical Studies. ISSN 0016-1071.
All periods and aspects of French history fall within the scope of this scholarly journal. There are four to five articles in most issues with occasional short notes, but no book reviews. Instead, each issue has a section, "Recent Books on French History," which is a classified bibliography. News items of interest to French historians are also listed, and it is not indexed by the editors. *French History,* which just began publishing in the 1980s, is the British equivalent.

254. *German Studies Review.* 1978–. 3 issues/year. Tempe, AZ: German Studies Association. ISSN 0149-7952.
German and Austrian history, political science, and literature form the focus of this journal. Individual issues contain approximately five articles and 50 to 60 book reviews. The English equivalent is titled *German History* (3 issues/year) and began publishing in 1982.

255. *Hispanic American Historical Review.* 1918–. Quarterly. Durham, NC: Duke University Press. ISSN 0018-2168.
The grandfather of all journals on Latin American history, *HAHR* continues to publish lengthy scholarly articles on all periods and aspects of Latin American history. The editorial office rotates among leading Latin American Studies centers in the United States. Each issue contains three or four articles and about 50 signed book reviews along with occasional interviews with noted scholars. The fourth issue of each volume includes an index of articles, authors, books reviewed, and reviewers. Covering the same region from a Spanish perspective is the *Annuario de Estudios Americanos,* a biannual publication of Seville's Escuela de Estudios Hispano-Americanos.

256. *The Historian: A Journal of History.* 1938–. Quarterly. East Lansing, MI: Michigan State University Press/Phi Alpha Theta. ISSN 0018-2370.
As the official journal of Phi Alpha Theta, the academic honor society for history, the *Historian* naturally makes the history of all areas, all periods, and all subjects its province. However, subjects dealing with American history appear more frequently than any other area. Each issue has five to six articles with an occasional review article. There is an extensive section of 50 to 60 book reviews in each issue. News items of interest to members of Phi Alpha Theta are also published. There is no index for individual volumes, although simple five-year cumulative indexes are regularly compiled.

257. *Historical Journal*. 1928–. Quarterly. Cambridge: Cambridge University Press. ISSN 0018-246x.

This journal covers all areas of historical study from the 15th century to the present, although its contents are largely concerned with British and European topics. It was originally entitled *The Cambridge Historical Journal* from 1923 to 1958. This well-edited and highly scholarly journal typically contains seven to eight long articles, two to four communications (shorter articles), one to three review articles or historiographical reviews, and several signed book reviews. The fourth part of each volume includes a simple index.

258. *Historical Research*. 1923–. 3 issues/year. Oxford: Basil Blackwell. ISSN 0020-2894.

The year 1987 marked a change for the venerable journal *Bulletin of the Institute of Historical Research*. It became simply *Historical Research* and started publishing three issues a year instead of two. Apart from a change in the cover design, little else is different other than that selected papers from the Anglo-American Conference of Historians will be published in the June issue. The scope will remain British and European history from the Middle Ages to the present. Typically an issue consists of four to six articles and a "Notes and Documents" section, which publishes short contributions on methodology and archives or significant documents with scholarly notes and commentary. There are no book reviews and the journal has no in-house index.

259. *History and Theory: Studies in the Philosophy of History*. 1960–. Quarterly. Oxford: Blackwell. ISSN 0018-2656.

The purpose of *History and Theory* is to pro-vide a forum for debate, discussion, and research into "what is history?" Historiography, methodology, and philosophy of history are some of the broad subjects appearing in this periodical. There are no restrictions on time periods or geographical areas. Each issue consists of three or four articles and four to six review articles, which usually focus on only one book. There is also a section called "Books in Summary," in which eight to ten books are briefly noted. The third issue of each volume contains the index for the first three issues of the year. The fourth number of each volume is called a *Beiheft* and consists of either a monographic or bibliographic study of some topic falling within the interests of *History and Theory*.

260. *History of Education Quarterly*. 1961–. Quarterly. Slippery Rock, PA: History of Education Society. ISSN US-0018-2680.

All aspects of education at all levels in all countries and all periods fall within the scope of this impressive journal. There are more contributions dealing with American history than anything else. Separate issues contain articles, review essays, and book reviews, although the proportions can vary greatly. In the past, review essays appear to have been favored but the new editors are using more single book reviews of 600–1,000 words. Occasionally issues include "forums," which are debates among scholars, and "retrospectives," which are historiographical overviews. There is no in-house indexing.

261. *History: The Journal of the Historical Association*. 1912–. 3 issues/year. Oxford: Blackwell/Historical Association. ISSN 0018-2648.

The Historical Association is an English

organization consisting primarily of history teachers in secondary and higher education, but also including anyone with a strong interest in history. Therefore, the scope of its journal takes in all periods, all areas, and all subjects with the exception of classical antiquity. British and European topics predominate, reflecting the interests of contributors and readers. Because of its broad-based readership, there is a strong emphasis on well-written articles of wide interest. Each issue contains three articles and one or two review articles. There is also an "Editorial Notes" section containing news items and announcements of publications. The large number of book reviews and short notices (150–200 per issue) are particularly useful. There is no annual index. Other journals published by the Historical Association are the *Historian,* which is a sort of newsletter and popular magazine, and *Teaching History,* which is the British equivalent version of the *History Teacher* [see 262].

262. History Teacher. 1967–. Quarterly. Long Beach, CA: Society for History Education. ISSN 0018-2745.

This interesting and useful journal is unique in that its concern is with good teaching and that it is not run by education specialists. As a result, the prose is readable and the ideas presented are realistic and intellectually sound. Each issue contains about five to seven articles. They are divided into three categories. The first is the "Craft of Teaching," which consists of methods or how-to articles. Articles in the section "State of the Profession" are concerned with the role of teachers or the role of history in education. "Historiography" contains articles that discuss ideas and interpretations in various historical writings.

Basically, most issues of concern to history teachers from the upper elementary grades through college level form the focus of this journal. Its "Reviews" section is divided into "Media," commenting on movies and audiovisuals, "Textbooks and Readers," which provides useful evaluations of current materials, and "Books," which reviews historical monographs. There are about 20 to 30 reviews in each issue. An index at the end of the volume supplies the locations for authors, titles, reviewers, and a few broad subjects.

263. Isis: An International Review Devoted to the History of Science and Its Cultural Influences. 1912–. 5 issues/year. Chicago, IL: University of Chicago Press/History of Science Society. ISSN 0021-1753.

All fields and periods in the history of science are covered by *Isis.* It is also the oldest and most widely read of the journals specializing in this subject. The contents of this journal are evenly balanced in terms of the subjects of the articles published. Each issue contains two to four articles and one or two review essays. Other occasional features include "Critiques and Contentions," "Documents," and "Notes and Correspondence." Professional news items are also printed, and each issue contains approximately 50 signed book reviews. The fourth issue of the year has an index, while the fifth issue in each volume is an annual critical bibliography for the history of science, a feature that makes this journal particularly valuable to researchers. *Annals of Science* is a bimonthly journal from Great Britain that is most similar to *Isis* in its scope.

264. Journal of African American History. 1916–. Quarterly. Silver Springs, MD: Association for the Study of African

American Life and History.
ISSN 0022-2992.
Formerly titled the *Journal of Negro History*, this periodical takes black history for all periods and places as its scope, although it primarily publishes articles dealing with the United States. Each issue contains four to six articles. Documents are also published two or three times in each volume. The number of signed book reviews ranges from 10 to 25 per issue. A section called "Notes and Announcements" prints news items of interest to black history specialists. Until 1970 there was a detailed index published at the end of each volume, but that practice has been abandoned.

265. *Journal of African History.* 1960–.
3 issues/year. Cambridge: Cambridge University Press. ISSN 0021-8537.
This journal attempts to cover all parts of Africa and all periods of its history, although it publishes a disproportionate number of articles on the colonial period or on economic topics. Occasionally it publishes special issues focusing on a particular theme. Each issue includes approximately seven articles, with review articles appearing several times each year. There are roughly 20 signed and titled book reviews in each issue as well as some signed book notes. The end of each volume has a "Contents List and Index." In volume 27 (1986) the journal switched from a quarterly to a thrice yearly publication schedule due to a decline in the number of submissions.

266. *Journal of American History.* 1914–.
Quarterly. Bloomington, IN: Organization of American Historians. ISSN 0021-8723.
Formerly known as the *Mississippi Valley Historical Review* (1914–1964), the *Journal of*

American History is the largest scholarly periodical to take general American history as its focus. Three to four articles appear in each issue and usually one historiographical piece called a "Perspective." There are occasional review essays and research notes and comments. Other useful features are classified listings of recent articles and dissertations. The fourth (March) issue of each volume includes an excellent detailed index to authors, titles, and subjects.

267. *Journal of Asian Studies.* 1941–.
Quarterly. Ann Arbor, MI: Association for Asian Studies. ISSN 0021-9118.
Originally titled *Far Eastern Quarterly*, this journal is the leading academic periodical specializing in Asian studies. Its scope is all of Asian history and culture in all periods. Three to four articles and a review article are standard for most issues. Abstracts of the articles appear at the front of the issue. There are about 50 signed book reviews in every issue and news items are printed in the section called "Editor's Note." A simple index is provided in the fourth issue of each volume.

268. *Journal of Black Studies.* 1970–.
Quarterly. Beverly Hills, CA: Sage. ISSN 0192-513X.
Although this is an interdisciplinary journal, articles on historical topics or using a historical approach predominate. All geographical areas and all periods of time fall within the scope of this journal. Each issue contains five to seven articles with an occasional review article appearing. Signed book reviews sometimes appear, although they are not a regular feature of the journal. A simple author-title index is provided in the fourth issue of each volume.

269. *Journal of British Studies.* 1961–.
Quarterly. Chicago: University of Chicago
Press. ISSN 0021-9371.

With the appearance of volume 24 (1985),
the *Journal of British Studies* shifted from a
twice yearly to a quarterly publication
schedule. It is sponsored by the North
American Conference on British Studies,
along with another quarterly journal,
Albion. Both journals take British history
dealing with all subjects and in all periods
as their focus. Neither is a truly interdisciplinary "studies" periodical. Each issue
of the *Journal of British Studies* publishes
three or four articles and two to four
review articles. These review articles are
another new feature that was added in 1985.
Previously the journal did not contain
book reviews. There is usually at least one
theme issue published each year. The fourth
issue includes an alphabetical listing of articles, review articles, and books reviewed by
author.

270. *Journal of Contemporary History.* 1966–.
Quarterly. London: Sage.
ISSN 0022-0094.

Contemporary history is defined by this
journal as the 20th century, with occasional
forays into the 19th. Although there is a
heavy concentration on British and European topics, articles on other parts of the
world often appear. Special theme issues are
frequently published. Typically, an issue
consists of approximately eight articles.
They are well researched and usually well
written. There are no book reviews
although a list of books received is published. An annual index appears in issue
four of each volume, and volume 21, no. 4
(1986) contained a cumulative author-
subject index for volumes 1–21.

271. *Journal of Economic History.* 1941–.
Quarterly. Cambridge: Cambridge
University Press for the Economic History
Association. ISSN 0022-0507.

Although this journal is international in
scope, inevitably it publishes a larger portion of articles dealing with U.S. history
than any other region or country. Individual issues contain seven to twelve articles.
Shorter "Notes and Discussion" pieces and
review articles appear frequently. The second issue of the year (June) publishes papers
from the annual meeting of the Economic
History Association. It also provides summaries of recent dissertations on economic
history. There are approximately 50 signed
book reviews in each issue. The fourth issue
of the year includes a simple index. A
British journal called *Economic History
Review* has the same international scope,
although it publishes more articles on
United Kingdom topics. It does contain,
however, two unique features of particular
interest to researchers. The first issue of
each volume has a "Review of Periodical
Literature," which gives an evaluative discussion of selected periodical literature
from two years earlier. In the fourth issue, a
"List of Publications on the Economic and
Social History of Great Britain and Ireland"
appears, which is a classified list of books
and articles from the previous year.

272. *Journal of Interdisciplinary History.*
1970–. Quarterly. Cambridge, MA: MIT
Press. ISSN 0022-1953.

The purpose of this innovative journal is to
link the findings and methods of other disciplines to the advancement of historical
knowledge. All geographical areas and historical periods fall within its scope. Special
theme issues are common. Normally, an

individual issue of the journal will contain four long articles, a research note, a review article, and about 30 signed book reviews. However, if it is a theme issue, it could have about 10 articles. The fourth issue of each volume contains a complete table of contents, but there is no index.

273. *Journal of Latin American Studies.* 1969–. 2 issues/year. Cambridge: Cambridge University Press. ISSN 0022-216X.
Published under the sponsorship of the various institutes and centers of Latin American studies in Great Britain, the principal focus of this journal is the study of Latin American social sciences (including history). A typical issue includes seven or eight articles, a review article, and approximately 40 signed book reviews. Currently edited at the Institute of Latin American Studies, University of London, articles on history and political science predominate. A cumulative index for volumes 1–15 (1969–1983) was published in 1986.

274. *Journal of Library History.* See *Libraries & Culture.*

275. *Journal of Modern History.* 1929–. Quarterly. Chicago: University of Chicago Press. ISSN 0022-2801.
The focus of this excellent journal is European history from the Renaissance to the present. It maintains a good balance in the topics that it publishes. There are occasional theme issues. A typical issue includes two or three articles and two or three review articles. In addition, there are 30 to 40 signed book reviews appearing in each issue. The fourth issue has an index to articles, books reviewed, and authors for the entire volume.

276. *Journal of Near Eastern Studies.* 1884–. Quarterly. Chicago: University of Chicago Press. ISSN 0022-2968.
The history of the ancient and medieval Near East is well served by this impressive but somewhat technical journal. Subjects dealing with archeology and ancient languages appear frequently. Each issue contains four or five articles and about ten signed book reviews. It will also publish contributions in German and French as well as English.

277. *Journal of Negro History.* See *Journal of African American History.*

278. *Journal of Psychohistory: A Quarterly Journal of Childhood and Psychohistory.* 1973–. Quarterly. New York: Institute for Psychohistory. ISSN 0145-3378.
Formerly entitled *History of Childhood Quarterly* (1973–1976), this journal has broadened its scope to include the application of psychoanalytical methods to any appropriate historical setting, not just childhood. An average issue will have four to seven articles, one or two review articles, and three to ten signed book reviews. There is a simple index for the volume in the fourth issue, which lists articles and books reviewed.

279. *Journal of Social History.* 1967–. Quarterly. Fairfax, VA: George Mason University Press. ISSN 0022-4529.
As the most prestigious journal specializing in this type of history in the United States, its scope is necessarily broad and unrestricted by time period or geographical area. Contributions focusing on the United States predominate. Each issue contains five to seven articles, one or two review essays,

and 25 to 30 signed book reviews. Issue 4 (summer) of each volume contains a simple author-title index for the articles and review essays but not the book reviews. There is a similar British journal called *Social History* (3 issues/year) that has a much stronger British and European focus. Two other relatively new journals in the field of social history are *Continuity and Change* (3 issues/year) and the *Journal of Historical Sociology* (quarterly).

280. *Journal of Southern History.* 1935–. Quarterly. Athens, GA: Southern Historical Association. ISSN 0022-4642.
One of the oldest and best of the regional historical journals in the United States, it specializes in all periods and aspects of southern history. An individual issue will contain three or four articles, with review articles occasionally appearing. There is an extensive book review section of about fifty reviews per issue along with some shorter book notes. News items and notices of interest to members of the Southern Historical Association are also printed. The fourth issue of the year includes a detailed index of authors, titles, and subjects. Finally, the second issue of each year contains a useful classified survey of recent periodical literature on southern history.

281. *Journal of Sport History.* 1974–. 3 issues/year. Columbus, OH: North American Society for Sport History. ISSN 0094-1700.
The history of sport in all countries and all time periods forms the focus of this well-produced journal. Coverage of subjects from within the traditional area of Western Civilization is quite balanced, although there is a definite but understandable lack

of articles dealing with traditional Asia and Africa. A normal issue will consist of three or four articles, with an occasional review article. Seven to twelve signed book reviews are published in each issue. A useful section called "Recent Dissertations" is published in the second (summer) issue of the journal and lists relevant new dissertations. Each issue contains another valuable feature—the "Journals Survey," which lists articles on sports history appearing in other journals. There is no in-house index.

282. *Journal of the History of Ideas: An International Quarterly Devoted to Intellectual History.* 1940–. Quarterly. Baltimore, MD: Johns Hopkins University Press. ISSN 0022-5037.
As the leading English-language journal for intellectual history, the *Journal of the History of Ideas* maintains the expected standards of rigorous and sometimes rarefied scholarship. Each issue publishes six to eight articles and one to three shorter notes. Several review articles are published in each volume, although there are no book reviews. There is a list of books received. A simple index of authors and broad subjects appears in the last issue of each volume.

283. *Journal of Urban History.* 1974–. Quarterly. Thousand Oaks, CA: Sage. ISSN 0096-1442.
All periods and all geographical areas fall within the scope of this periodical devoted to the history of cities and urban studies. The bulk of the contributions deal with American history. Each issue normally contains three articles, one interview, and about three signed book reviews. The growing interest in urban history is further reflected by the existence of the British *Urban His-*

tory Yearbook and the Canadian *Urban History Review* (3 issues/year).

284. *Journal of World History.* 1990–.
2 issues/year. Honolulu: University of
Hawai'i Press for the World History
Association. ISSN 1045-6007.
The World History Association originated
for the purpose of encouraging historical
research and interpretation that takes a
global perspective. Its journal publishes articles that do just that. Each issue contains
four to five articles, which can vary greatly
in length. The table of contents conveniently includes a brief abstract of each article. There are seven to ten book reviews per
issue and the individual reviews frequently
review more than one book. Review articles also are occasionally published. The
second issue of each volume includes an
index of authors and titles of articles and
books reviewed for the entire volume.

285. *Labor History.* 1960–. Quarterly.
New York: Tamiment Institute.
ISSN 0023-656X.
The focus of this journal is the history of
labor, both organized and unorganized,
during all periods of American history. It
also publishes comparative studies when
appropriate. Each issue has four or five articles. Notes and documents are frequently
published, while review essays appear on
occasion. The fourth (fall) issue of each volume contains the useful features "Annual
Bibliography of American Labor History,"
a classified listing of new publications, and
"Recent Dissertations in American and
European Labor History," which lists new
dissertations along with an author-pro-
duced abstract of 175–200 words. There are
between 15 and 30 signed book reviews in

each issue. The fourth issue also includes a
simple index for the volume, which separately lists articles, books reviewed, contributors, and book reviewers.

286. *LARR: Latin American Research Review.*
1965–. 3 issues/year. Austin, TX: University
of Texas. ISSN 0023-8791.
LARR is the official journal of the Latin
American Studies Association. Its primary
goal is to publish top-flight research on
Latin America from a multi- and/or interdisciplinary perspective. After two decades
at the University of New Mexico, in 2003
LARR returned to the University of Texas
at Austin where it began in 1964. Each
issue includes five articles, several research
reports, and a series of review essays in
which five to seven books are discussed.
The new editors hope to expand the number of articles by publishing shorter manuscripts. *The Journal of Latin American Studies*
published quarterly by Cambridge University Press is the most important U.K. Latin
American studies journal. With a heavy
emphasis on history, it publishes the best
British scholarship on Latin America. See
also *Bulletin of Latin America Research,* published by Blackwell for the Society of Latin
American Studies in the United Kingdom,
and the *Canadian Journal of Latin American
and Caribbean Studies. Mesoamerica* is a multidisciplinary journal in Spanish covering the
region from Mexico to Panama.

287. *Libraries & Culture.* 1966–. Quarterly.
Austin, TX: University of Texas Press.
ISSN 0894-8631.
Originally titled *The Journal of Library His-
tory: Philosophy & Comparative Librarianship*
(ISSN 0275-3650), in 1987 this journal
assumed its present title. Its interdisciplinary

and international focus is the interaction of books, libraries, culture, and society throughout history. Special issues focusing on a theme or publishing the proceedings of conferences appear frequently. Normally an individual issue contains three to six articles and one to three shorter notes. Regular issues will have 15 to 20 signed reviews. The fourth (fall) issue of each volume contains a detailed author, title, and subject index. *Library History* is a similar British journal.

288. *Oral History Review.* 1966–. Annual. Berkeley, CA: University of California Press for the Oral History Association. ISSN 0094-0798.

As the oldest and largest circulation journal devoted to oral history, this journal takes all aspects, geographical areas, and time periods as its scope. At the same time, topics dealing with American history appear most frequently. A normal issue publishes four articles, two to three review articles, and another 20 signed book reviews. Notices and news items of interest to specialists in oral history are also printed. The British equivalent is a twice yearly publication called *Oral History.*

289. *Pacific Historical Review.* 1932–. Quarterly. Berkeley, CA: Pacific Coast Branch, American Historical Association. ISSN 0030-8684.

Articles on the West, the Pacific Coast region, and U.S. foreign policy and expansionism predominate in the contents of this journal. But it is more than a regional journal since it also publishes articles on historiography and methodology and because its area of specialization is so broad as to be of general interest to other American histori-

ans. Three or four articles appear in each issue. One or two items normally appear in the "Notes and Documents" section. Occasional review essays and historiographical essays are published. About 30 signed book reviews appear in each issue. The fourth (November) issue of each year contains a detailed author, title, and subject index.

290. *Past & Present: A Journal of Historical Studies.* 1952–. Quarterly. Oxford: Oxford University Press for the Past and Present Society. ISSN 0031-2746.

As one of the most stimulating and readable of all historical journals, *Past & Present* tries hard to make all historical periods and geographical areas part of its focus. Articles on British and European topics still dominate its pages, as might be expected from a periodical based in England. Six to nine articles tends to be the range of material contained in each issue. Furthermore, this journal has a policy of publishing articles that are often considerably longer than normal. Frequently, debates concerning controversial articles will develop and produce lively exchanges. There are no regular book reviews, although sometimes review articles are published. A classified list of the contents of issue numbers 1–100 is available (each issue is numbered separately) and an alphabetical listing by author of the contents of each year's issues is sent out with the fourth (November) issue.

291. *Renaissance Quarterly.* 1947–. Quarterly. New York: Renaissance Society of America. ISSN 0034-4338.

Devoted to the study of the European Renaissance between the years 1399 and 1660, this highly respected journal has a broader chronological range than *Sixteenth*

Century Journal [see 294], while the range of subjects covered is narrower since intellectual, cultural, and literary studies are preponderant. Three articles are usually published in each issue, along with about forty signed book reviews. It also contains a useful section of news items and announcements. There is no index. A similar British publication is the quarterly *Renaissance Studies*.

292. *Reviews in American History.* 1973–. Quarterly. Baltimore, MD: Johns Hopkins University Press. ISSN 0048-7511.
Instead of publishing articles, the purpose of this unique journal is the publication of review articles. These lengthy reviews can discuss a single book or a group of related books. Several retrospective bibliographic surveys also appear in each issue. There are normally 25 to 30 essays in an issue. A *Reviews in European History* began at the same time as this journal but, due to lack of interest, failed to sustain itself.

293. *Signs: Journal of Women in Culture and Society.* 1975–. Quarterly. Chicago: University of Chicago Press. ISSN 0097-9740.
This scholarly journal is devoted to the interdisciplinary study of women. Although it contains articles dealing with nonhistorical topics, historical articles and book reviews are quite common. Each volume has a simple contents index. *Feminist Studies* is quite similar in its approach and scope.

294. *The Sixteenth Century Journal: A Journal for Renaissance and Reformation Students and Scholars.* 1972–. Quarterly. Kirksville, MO: Sixteenth Century Journal Publishers. ISSN 0361-0160.
All aspects of the 16th century fall within

the scope of this interesting journal, although the approach is always historical, even when a literary or theological topic is being discussed. The coverage of subjects is well balanced. Each issue has five to seven long articles and 25 to 45 signed book reviews. A detailed author, title, and subject index is printed in the fourth issue of each volume. Very similar in scope is the highly regarded international annual *Archive for Reformation History / Archiv für Reformationsgeschichte,* publishing English and German articles under the sponsorship of the American Society for Reformation Research, and the quarterly *Journal of Early Modern History.*

295. *Slavic Review: American Quarterly of Soviet and East European Studies.* 1941–. Quarterly. Cambridge, MA: American Association for the Advancement of Slavic Studies. ISSN 0037-6779.
From 1941 to 1961 this journal was known as the *American Slavic and East European Review.* There are three or four articles in each issue. In addition, this journal publishes short items called "Discussions," which function as notes or comments. Review articles appear occasionally. The book review section is large, with about 75 signed reviews per issue. There is a simple volume index divided into lists of contributors (authors of articles and reviews) and books reviewed (listed by author). *Slavic Review* is the foremost American academic journal dealing with Eastern European and Russian topics. The British counterpart is the older *Slavonic and East European Review,* which is also a quarterly.

296. *Speculum: A Journal of Medieval Studies.* 1926–. Quarterly. Cambridge, MA:

Medieval Academy of America.
ISSN 0038-7134.
This highly academic journal is the oldest and most widely read periodical specializing in medieval history in the English language. The number of articles in a single issue ranges from four to six, with review articles appearing on occasion. Shorter "Notes and Documents" items also appear frequently. There is a large book review section containing about 60 signed reviews and from 20 to 60 shorter notices. A simple annual volume index lists articles by their authors, and then book reviews.

297. *Western Historical Quarterly.* 1970–. Quarterly. Logan, UT: Western Historical Association. ISSN 0043-3810.
This is the foremost academic journal focusing on the regional history of the American West. A normal issue contains three articles and about 30 signed book reviews. The third (July) issue publishes a classified list of recent dissertations. Other regular features appearing in each issue are lists of new books, recent articles, and news items of interest to historians of the West. Each volume includes a simple list of authors, reviewers, articles, books reviewed, and broad subjects.

298. *William and Mary Quarterly: A Magazine of Early American History and Culture.* 1892–. Quarterly. Williamsburg, VA: Omohundro Institute of Early American History and Culture. ISSN 0043-5597.
This well-edited, readable journal specializes in American history from its colonial beginnings through the early republic. It was originally titled the *William and Mary College Quarterly Historical Magazine* until 1944. An individual issue will contain three to five articles and one to three shorter notes or documents. There are 15 to 20 signed book reviews in each issue. The fourth issue (October) includes an extensive index of authors, titles, and subjects for the volume.

5

PERIODICAL INDEXES, ABSTRACTS, AND GUIDES

During the first half of the past century, the indexing of historical periodical literature was extremely limited. Historians were largely confined to using the bibliographies at the backs of monographs or published separately. The appearance of the first genuine historical periodical indexes, i.e., *America: History and Life* and *Historical Abstracts*, in the 1960s, along with expanded coverage by the Wilson indexes, ushered in a revolution in historical bibliography. By the 1970s sophisticated citation indexes like the *Social Sciences Citation Index*, along with their online versions, allowed for the first computerized searching of historical databases. Database accessibility expanded during the 1980s with the emergence of search services such as Dialog and Bibliographic Retrieval Services (BRS), along with the development of compact disc versions of the index providing rapid searching at no cost. The development of the Internet and the World Wide Web in the 1990s has meant that electronic databases formerly available only through CD-ROM or fee-based search services are now more accessible and less expensive through online Web-based products. Many of the publishers mentioned below continue to produce

print versions but are increasingly developing and marketing Web-based services that may eventually supplant their printed sources. An important development in this first decade of the 21st century has been the emergence of digitized journal collections and retrospective indexes.

GUIDES

Guides to scholarly periodicals, popular magazines, and other serials are numerous. Some print sources, such as *Ulrich's Periodicals Directory* and *Magazines for Libraries* are still publishing. Increasingly, however, general guides, such as *Ulrich's* and *The Serials Directory* have become available through Web-based products.

299. *Gale Directory of Databases.* Vol. 1, *Online Databases.* Vol. 2, *CD-ROM, Diskette, Magnetic Tape, Handheld, and Batch Access Database Products.* Detroit: Thompson/Gale, 1993. ISSN 1066-8934. Print and online versions.
The *Gale Directory of Databases* was formed in 1993 by the merger of three database

directories acquired by Gale Research: *Computer-Readable Databases,* the *Directory of Online Databases,* and the *Directory of Portable Databases.* The three directories were merged into the new *Gale Directory of Data-bases,* which is published twice a year in two volumes. The 2003 edition published in 2002 contains contact and description information for more than 15,600 databases and database products of all types in all subject areas produced worldwide in English and other languages by more than 4,000 database producers. These databases are offered by some 3,100 online services and database vendors and distributors. An online version is available from GaleNet or as File 230 on Thomson/Dialog.

300. *The Serials Directory (via EBSCOHost).* Online.
Provides up-to-date bibliographic information as well as current pricing for popular serials. It contains over 182,500 U.S. and international titles, including newspapers, historical data for an additional 20,000 titles, data from 85,000 publishers world-wide including e-mail and Internet addresses, and Library of Congress and Dewey Decimal Classifications for every entry. A title search for *Louisiana History* reveals the journal began publishing in 1960, has the abbreviation La. hist, ISSN 0024-6816, and is a U.S. periodical published four times a year in Lafayette, Louisiana. It's indexed in *America: History and Life* and several other indexes, includes book reviews, and can be found at F366 .L6238. An index is issued in the fourth issue.

301. *Ulrich's Periodicals Directory.* New Providence, NJ: R. R. Bowker, 1932–. Annual. ISSN 0000-2100.

One of the premier serials reference sources in the world, the 41st edition for 2003 contains information on over 172,000 serials published worldwide classified and cross-referenced under 896 subject headings. Each entry is assigned a Dewey Decimal Classification number. It lists serials that are currently available, issued more frequently than once a year and usually published at regular intervals, as well as publications issued annually or less frequently than once a year, or irregularly. Some 55,000 titles are indexed by at least one of 550 abstracting and indexing services. Over 86,000 e-mail addresses and 78,000 URLs (uniform resource locators on the World Wide Web) are also included. Volumes 1–3 include the classified list of serials. Volumes 4–5 contain the indexes. Since 1999 an online version has been available at www.ulrichsweb.com with a variety of search modes. The online version allows you to sort results, create lists, download, and send e-mail. In 2003 Bowker launched the *Ulrich's Serials Analysis System,* which allows you to compare your library's serials against industry benchmarks.

302. *Magazines for Libraries.* Edited by Cheryl LaGuardla. New Providence, NJ: R. R. Bowker, 1969–. ISSN 0000-0914.
Created by Bill Katz in 1969, the first 10 editions were coedited with Berry Richards (1st–3rd) and Linda Katz (4th–10th). Cheryl LaGuardla, head of instructional services at Harvard College Library, assumed editorship with the 11th edition (2002). *Magazines for Libraries (MFL)* is a selected annotated list arranged by subject of more than 6,950 journals selected by subject specialists. Eighty-five print history journals are reviewed, from *Alaska History* to *Wisconsin Magazine of History.* Three

electronic journals are listed. For each, complete bibliographical information is included, along with indexing information and the intended audience. This is a very helpful guide frequently used by libraries to select new serials.

GENERAL

303. *Academic Search Premier.* Ipswich, MA: EBSCOHost Research Databases. Online. Billing itself as the world's largest academic multidisciplinary database, Academic Search Premier provides full text for more than 3,900 scholarly publications, including full text for nearly 3,050 peer-reviewed journals. Two search modes are available: basic and advanced. The latter allows you to use Boolean operators; limit your search to articles available in full text, in a particular journal or only in peer-reviewed journals; or even limit to articles with graphics. Coverage of journals varies considerably. The *American Historical Review* dates back to 1975 and includes 230 articles. The *Canadian Historical Review* is covered back to 1989 in 20 articles; 252 articles from *Past & Present* are indexed dating to 1993 but none are available full text.

304. *Canadian Business and Current Affairs: Reference.* Micromedia ProQuest. Online database. Micromedia is Canada's largest developer, publisher, and distributor of reference information. Founded in 1972, it joined with *ProQuest Company's Information and Learning Unit* in January 31, 2002. While they market a number of databases, the CBCA Reference is the most comprehensive. It provides

indexing to 650 periodicals covering current events, business, science, the arts, and academic information. Thirty-six new titles were added in 2003. Approximately one-third are available full text. The *Canadian Historical Review* is indexed from 1993 but no full text is available. Repere is a companion database that indexes 561 periodicals in the French language, including *L'Histoire* and *Histoire Sociale.*

305. *Canadian Periodical Index.* CPI.Q. Toronto: Gale Group/Thomson Learning. Online database. Updated weekly. Since 1921 this has been the principal index to Canadian periodicals. CPI.Q on InfoTrac Web provides indexing of more than 400 Canadian periodicals (English and French) with full text available for 165 of these. Using the familiar InfoTrac interface searches can be done in basic or advanced modes. In the advanced mode you can search by subject or key word and use the Boolean operators "and," "or," and "not." Older print collections published by a variety of publishers are available in many libraries.

306. *Expanded Academic ASAP.* Detroit: Gale Group/Thomson. Online database. 1996–. This is Gale's premier database for research in academic disciplines. It provides broad coverage from every academic discipline. It currently indexes 3,000 journals, of which more than 1,650 are refereed. Full-text coverage is available for 1,900 of these in the social sciences, humanities, science and technology, news, and general interest magazines. A 20-year back file is available with your subscription. Other databases marketed by Gale include Academic ASAP,

General Reference Center Gold, General Reference Center and InfoTrac OneFile. InfoTrac OneFile includes more than 3,700 full-text titles, five newspaper indexes, and coverage of 7,200 periodicals, newspapers, and news wires.

307. *OCLC Article First.* **Dublin, OH: OCLC Online Computer Library Center. Online database. Updated daily.**
This general interest database indexes periodicals in business, humanities, medicine, popular culture, science, social science, and technology. Covering more than 12,000 sources it currently provides access to 12.7 million records from 1990 to the present. Access is available on subscription through OCLC FirstSearch interface. Basic and advanced search modes are available. From the advanced mode you can search by author, first page, issue, publisher, source, standard number, title, and volume. You can also rank by relevance of date.

308. *Periodicals Abstracts Research II.* **Ann Arbor, MI: ProQuest Information and Learning, 1988–.**
Similar in coverage to Academic Search Premier [see 303] and Expanded Academic ASAP [see 305], this is a general interest database marketed to academic libraries. It is currently abstracting and indexing articles in 2,190 periodicals as well as recent articles from the *New York Times* and *Wall Street Journal*. Many are available full text. Journals selected for inclusion are drawn from *Magazines for Libraries* [see 302] and correspond to the most popular college majors. For most titles coverage dates from 1990. For some, back files are available to 1971. Smaller versions of the database are available as *Periodicals Abstracts Research I* and *Periodicals Abstracts Library.*

309. *Periodicals Contents Index.* **Ann Arbor, MI: ProQuest Information and Learning.**
Developed by Chadwyck-Healey, now part of the ProQuest family, PCI is an electronic index to millions of articles published in over 4,079 periodicals in the humanities and social sciences. PCI combines broad subject coverage of 37 key areas with deep chronological coverage going back over 200 years. It currently indexes 13 million articles dating from the 18th century to 1995. Coverage includes publication in 40 languages and dialects. Each year index records for 300 to 500 journals are added providing access to more than 1 million articles. You can search by key word, article title key word, author, language, journal title, and journal subject. Participants in JSTOR's Arts and Science I–II collections can link directly from the relevant index records in PCI to articles in the JSTOR archive. Links to 130 journals are currently available. *PCI Full Text* is making a growing number of the back files of periodicals available electronically. Already 234 titles with access to 3.9 million article pages are available.

310. *Reader's Guide to Periodical Literature.* **New York: H. W. Wilson, 1900–. Semimonthly in September, October, December, March, and April and monthly in January, February, May, June, July, August, and November, with a bound annual cumulation. ISSN 0034-0464.**
Three years after the founding of the H. W. Wilson Company in Minneapolis, Halsey Wilson issued the first *Reader's Guide (RG)* in 1901, initially as a supplement to the *Cumulative Book Index.* The infant publication indexed just seven periodicals. When the first five-year cumulation was issued in 1905 it was organized in a dictionary

arrangement with uniform subject headings. Since that time, the *RG* has remained the standard guide to general English language periodicals published in the United States and is most often found in school, public, and undergraduate college libraries. Now indexing 306 titles, *RG* provides a cumulative author subject index to mainstream general interest periodicals. The entries are arranged alphabetically with citations to book reviews following the main body of the index. Like all Wilson indexes, *RG* uses its own subject authority file. Numerous "see" and "see also" references guide the reader to appropriate or additional subject entries. The titles indexed are frequently revised on the basis of recommendations from the Committee on Wilson Indexes of the Reference and Adult Services Division of the American Library Association and the polling of subscribers. Online access (from January 1983–) is now available through WilsonWeb, including access to more than 160 publications in full text, and a CD-ROM version is available through Wilsondisc. The Reader's Guide Retrospective: 1890–1982 database was completed in the fall of 2002. It indexes 526 magazines, some as far back as 1890, and provides citations to more than 3 million articles. It's the equivalent of searching 44 printed Reader's Guide Cumulations.

HUMANITIES

311. *Arts and Humanities Citation Index.* Philadelphia, PA: Thomson/ISI, 1976–. Via Internet weekly; includes author abstracts from 1999 forward; back files to 1975. CD-ROM updated triannually; subscription includes annual cumulation on one disc; back files to 1990. Arts and humanities Search via DIALOG, DataStar, and OCLC updated weekly; back files to 1980.

In 1958 Eugene Garfield started the Institute for Scientific Information (ISI) by borrowing $500 from Household Finance to launch *Current Contents of Chemical, Pharmaco-Medical, and Life Sciences.* It covered 200 journals in about 32 pages per issue. Forty years later in 1998 ISI employed 800 people in seven countries and indexed 8,000 titles in 35 languages. ISI was acquired by Thomson Business Information in 1992. The *A&HCI* was the third major index to be launched by ISI when it premiered in 1978 following the *Science Citation Index* in 1961 and *Social Sciences Citation Index* in 1972. It provides access to current and retrospective bibliographic information and cited references found in nearly 1,130 arts and humanities journals. Relevant items are also added from another 7,000 science and social science journals. The unique feature of this database is its cited reference searching which enables users to track the literature forward, backward, and through disciplinary and geographic boundaries. Searching the printed version of this index requires patience and a magnifying glass. Searching the online version is a breeze. Use the "form search" to locate articles by topic (article title, key words, or abstract), authors, source title (journal), or address (author's affiliation). Use the "concept search" to search by word, phrase, or sentence. Once an article is located you can click on "cited references" to see an author's references or footnotes, or click on "find related records" to display a list of articles whose cited reference list includes at least one of the sources cited in the original article. The *A&HCI* currently indexes 193 journals in history and an additional 32 under history and philosophy of science.

312. *BHI: British Humanities Index*. London: Library Association Publishing, 1962–. Quarterly with bound annual cumulations. ISSN 0007-0815. Online version from the Cambridge Scientific Abstracts (CSA) Internet Database Service.

This is an alphabetically arranged subject index to primarily British journals in the fields of politics, archeology, architecture, language, history, music, economics, philosophy, art, folklore, and books and publishing. Its predecessors, the Athenaeum Subject Index (1915–1918) and the Subject Index to Periodicals (1919–1961), indexed as many as 500 British and American periodicals. When the Subject Index ceased publication in 1961, it was succeeded by the *British Humanities Index* [BHI] and the *British Technology Index*. Unlike the Humanities Index [see 314], authors and subjects are not integrated in the main index although there is a special author index in the annual cumulation. *BHI* currently indexes over 320 titles, including daily newspapers, weekly magazines, and academic journals of international standing. These are mostly British but include occasional titles from Australia and New Zealand. *BHI* also indexes articles from *The Times* (London) and the *Times Literary Supplement*.

On August 21, 2001, the Cambridge Information Group acquired the R. R. Bowker publishing operations from Reed Elsevier. Bowker had formerly published the print version of *BHI* for the Library Association. Soon after, they launched an online version through Cambridge Scientific Abstracts (CSA) Internet Database Service. The online version covers the period from 1985 to the present—over 180,000 articles from humanities journals and weekly magazines published in the United Kingdom and other English-speaking countries as well as newspapers published in the United Kingdom. Updated monthly.

313. *Hispanic American Periodicals Index (HAPI)*. Los Angeles, CA: UCLA Latin American Center Publications, 1974–. Annual. ISSN 0270-8558. HAPI Online and CD-ROM.

This is a general index to the humanities and social sciences literature of Latin America. Currently indexing more than 400 periodicals, with its primary focus on titles published in Hispanic America, it has broadened its scope in recent years to include coverage of Hispanic groups in the United States. There are separate author and subject indexes. The latter uses a controlled vocabulary that was issued in the form of a thesaurus in 1983. Articles indexed are written in English, Spanish, Portuguese, and other Western European languages. The use of volunteer indexers has resulted in considerable delays in publication. The Seminar on the Acquisition of Latin American Library Materials (SALALM) serves as an adviser. A retrospective volume covering the years 1970–1974 was published in three volumes in 1984. Earlier coverage is available in the *Index to Latin American Periodical Literature, 1929–1960* and supplements for 1961–1965 and 1966–1970, all published by G. K. Hall. HAPI Online combines current information about Latin America with in-depth coverage spanning more than 25 years. Now containing 210,000 citations, it's growing at the rate of 8,000 records a year.

HAPI on CD-ROM is available from the National Information Services Corporation (NISC).

314. *Humanities Index.* **New York: H. W. Wilson, 1974–. Quarterly with bound annual cumulations. ISSN 0095-5981.** This publication is an alphabetically arranged integrated author and subject index to 503 periodicals in the humanities including over 100 history titles. The focus of the index, which was originally published as a supplement to the *Reader's Guide* [see 310] in 1907, is on English language periodicals. After a gentlemen's agreement between H. W. Wilson and R. R. Bowker, Bowker agreed to get out of the index business if Wilson would get out of the directory business. When Bowker's *Annual Library Index* ceased publication in 1910, the *International Index* was established by Wilson. It indexed 19 titles from *Reader's Guide* along with an additional 55 social sciences and humanities titles. Books were also indexed until 1914. The name was changed in 1965 to the *Social Sciences and Humanities Index*, and in 1974 the two broad subjects were separated into two different indexes. Since that time the coverage of the humanities has more than doubled. As with other Wilson indexes, the editors of *Humanities Index* receive suggestions from the American Library Association Committee on Wilson indexes. In recent years many new history journals have been added, including *Journal of Ecclesiastical History, Journal of Family History, Journal of Urban History,* and *Reviews in American History.* In 1988 coverage was extended to state historical journals like the *Southwestern Historical Quarterly* and the *Virginia Magazine of History and Biography.* Electronic versions of this index have been available in a variety of formats since 1984. Presently they include Humanities Full Text, which provides abstracting and indexing of 500+ titles back to 1984 and the full text of 160 publications back to 1995. Also available are *Humanities Abstracts,* which adds abstracts after 1994, and *Humanities Index,* which mirrors the print edition. Monthly updates are available on WilsonWeb and WilsonDisc. *Humanities and Social Sciences Index Retrospective: 1907–1984* will be available in late 2003, indexing more than 600 periodicals back to 1907 with citations to more than 1 million articles, including book reviews.

SOCIAL SCIENCES

315. *OCLC Public Affairs Information Service (PAIS).* **New York: OCLC PAIS, 1915–.** PAIS was established in 1914 for the purpose of chronicling the world's public affairs, public and social policies, international relations, and world politics. A year later the first *PAIS Bulletin* was issued. *PAIS Bulletin* and *PAIS Foreign Language Index* (1972–1990) were combined to form *PAIS International in Print* in 1991. In 2000 PAIS became OCLC PAIS. The PAIS International database contains references to more than 479,000 journal articles, books, government documents, statistical directories, gray literature, research reports, conference reports, publications of international agencies, microfiche, Internet material, and more. Newspapers and newsletters are excluded. Publications are drawn from 120 countries and include works in French, German, Italian, Portuguese, and Spanish, in addition to English. OCLC PAIS indexes more than 5,600 books, hearings, reports, and pamphlets, 900+ journals, and 900+ Internet documents annually. *PAIS International in Print* continues to be published. Since 2001, nearly 4,000 carefully evaluated public policy Web sites have been added to PAIS International. PAIS Archive, a retrospective database to contain the full content of *PAIS Bulletin,* 1915–1976, will be available in spring 2004.

316. Social Sciences Citation Index (SSCI). Philadelphia, PA: Thomson/ISI, 1972–.

Internet via the ISI Web of Science: updated weekly; back files to 1956. CD-ROM— with author abstracts: updated monthly, includes annual cumulations on one disc; available to 1992. Without author abstracts: updated quarterly, includes annual cumulation on one disc; available to 1981. Online via Social SciSearch: updated weekly; back files to 1972. SciSearch on DIALOG to 1972 and on STN back to 1973.

The older sister database to the *A&HCI* [see 311], the SSCI was launched in 1972 as a print index. It provides access to current and retrospective bibliographic information, author abstracts, and cited references found in over 1,700 scholarly social science journals covering 50 disciplines. Relevant items are also selected from an additional 3,300 of the world's leading science and technology journals. Search techniques mirror the *A&HCI.* Coverage of history is limited to 15 journals with a further 27 covering the history and philosophy of science and 18 more covering the history of social sciences.

317. *Social Sciences Index.* New York: H. W. Wilson, 1974–. Quarterly with bound annual cumulations. ISSN 0094-4920.

This is a general social sciences index providing broad indexing coverage of anthropology, economics, geography, international relations, law and criminology, political science, psychiatry, psychology, social work, and sociology. Coverage now includes 460 English language periodicals based on recommendations from the American Library Association committee on Wilson indexes. It was preceded by the *International Index,* 1910–1964 and the *Social Sciences and Humanities Index,* 1965–1974. Like other Wilson indexes, it is an alphabetically arranged integrated author and subject index using Wilson's own subject headings. While less useful to historians than the *Humanities Index* [see 314], it does provide indexing for such titles as *Economic History Review, Ethnohistory, Explorations in Economic History, Journal of Economic History, Journal of Latin American Studies, Journal of Social History,* the *Latin American Research Review,* and *Social History* among others. Coverage is particularly strong in the fields of area studies, ethnic studies, feminist studies, and urban studies.

Online access dates to 1983. *Social Sciences Full Text* adds abstracts from 1994 and the full-text coverage of 163 journals back to 1995. *Social Sciences Abstracts* and *Social Sciences Index* are also available on WilsonWeb: updates four times a week, and WilsonDisc: updated monthly. A British social sciences index, *ASSIA: Applied Social Sciences Index and Abstracts,* was launched in 1987 and published until recently by Bowker for the Library Association. Like the *BHI* [see 312] it was acquired by the Cambridge Information Group in late 2001. The Web version from Cambridge Scientific Abstracts (CSA) contains 312,000 records from 650 journals published in 16 countries covering health, social sciences, psychology, sociology, economics, politics, race relations, and education. It's updated monthly.

HISTORY

318. *America: History and Life.* Santa Barbara, CA: ABC-CLIO, 1964–. Online database.

Published since 1964, this is the index of first choice for the history of the United States and Canada. It is rather confusing to use in its original print format, but the online version is a dream. You can search by keyword, subject, author, and title and limit your search by language, document type, journal name, publication date, or time period. Annually the editors review more than 1,700 journals and add 16,000 new entries to the database. 75- to 120-word abstracts are contributed by historians. Citations to book/media reviews and dissertations are available. Recent enhancements include CLIO Notes—concise overviews of historical periods with detailed chronologies and topic suggestions for papers and class discussions—and CLIO Links—over 80,000 full-text links to JSTOR's Arts and Science I and II collections [see 322], full-text links to the journals of the History Cooperative [see 321], and full-text links to 60 journals from Project MUSE [see 323].

319. *C.R.I.S. The Combined Retrospective Index to Journals in History, 1838–1974.* Washington, DC: Carrollton, 1977–1978. 11 vols. ISBN 0-8480-0175-0.

Called the "great leap backward in retrospective indexing of social sciences litera-ture," this historical set was one of three sets to provide subject and author access to 400,000 articles in 530 journals in history, political science, and sociology. Historical coverage to 1974 is drawn from 243 English-language periodicals covering all periods and areas of history. The first nine volumes are arranged by subject and key word while the last two are organized alphabetically by author. The appearance of this set has greatly expanded retrospective searching of historical periodicals.

320. *Historical Abstracts.* Santa Barbara, CA: ABC-CLIO, 1955–. Online database.

Established by Eric and Inge Boehm in Vienna in 1955, the index moved first to Munich and finally to California in 1960. It is now the leading historical database for the history of the world from 1450 to the present (excluding Canada and the United States). Special emphasis is placed on English-language journal and book titles published worldwide. Every year 20,000 new entries are selected from over 1,700 journals published worldwide. Historians contribute 75- to 120-word abstracts for journal articles. Citations to books and dissertations are included. The database includes more than 600,000 entries. Since the print index covered only the period 1775–1945 until 1973 and did not include citations to books prior to 1980, these limitations are also reflected in the database. All the enhancements—CLIO Notes and CLIO Links available in *America: History and Life*—are also available in *Historical Abstracts.* They have also added a simple search screen to make searching easier. *World History Full Text* combines indexing and abstracts from *America: History and Life* and *Historical Abstracts* with the full text of

180 journals published since 1990. It's accessible through EBSCOHost.

DIGITAL COLLECTIONS

321. *History Cooperative.* http://www.historycooperative.org
On March 30, 2000, the American Historical Association, the Organization of American Historians, the University of Illinois Press, and the National Academy Press announced the launch of the History Cooperative. For the first time it made available electronically the full text of current issues of the *American Historical Review* (1999–) and the *Journal of American History* (1999–) to members of the *AHA* and *OAH* and to institutions that subscribe to print versions of the journals. The cooperative has now expanded to include: *Law and History Review* (1999–) (University of Illinois Press for the American Society for Legal History); *The William and Mary Quarterly* (2001–); *The History Teacher* (2000–); *Western Historical Quarterly* (2001–); *Common-Place* (2000–) (sponsored by the American Antiquarian Society and the Gilder Lehrman Institute of American History); *Labour-Le Travail* (2001–) (published by the Canadian Committee on Labour History); and *Labour History* (2002–) (published by the Australian Society for the Study of Labour History). If your institution's library participates in JSTOR [see 322] you can search in full-text for all issues of *JAH, AHR,* and the *William and Mary Quarterly* beginning with volume 1 of each up to 1997. By 2004 it is anticipated that all issues of these journals will be available in searchable electronic form. The Cooperative hopes to add five to

seven new journals per year, including both U.S. and international history journals. You can search an individual journal or all journals and limit your search by document type.

322. *JSTOR.* http://www.jstor.org
This subscription service was originally conceived by William G. Bowen, president of the Andrew W. Mellon Foundation. It began as an effort to ease the increasing problems faced by libraries seeking to provide adequate stack space for the long runs of back files of scholarly journals. The basic idea was to convert the back issues of paper journals in electronic formats that would allow savings in space while improving access to the journal content. Following a successful pilot project, JSTOR was established as an independent nonprofit organization in August 1995. Currently six complete collections are available: Arts and Science I–II, Business, Ecology and Botany, General Science, and Language and Literature. Several other collections are in the planning stages. The Arts & Science I collection includes 15 titles in history, including *American Historical Review* vols. 1–104, 1895–1999; *Journal of American History* and its predecessor, the *Mississippi Valley Historical Review,* vols. 1–85, 1914–1999; *Journal of Economic History* vols. 1–57, 1914–1997; *Journal of Modern History* vols. 1–71, 1929–1999; and *The William and Mary Quarterly* 1892–2000. The Arts and Science II collection adds 21 titles in history and nine titles in the history of science. Notable titles include the *English Historical Review* vols. 1–112, 1886–1997; *Hispanic American Historical Review* vols. 1–79, 1918–1999; *Past & Present* vols. 1–157, 1952–1997; and *Isis* vols. 1–92, 1913–2001. Searches can be conducted in

basic or advanced modes and must be limited to one or more disciplines. You can refine your search by limiting to type of document or publication date. A search for George Rogers Clark locates 143 items in A&S I, with the oldest an article by Frederick Jackson Turner from volume 1, no. 1 of the *American Historical Review*. In a very short time this has become an indispensable tool for the modern historical researcher.

323. *Project MUSE.* http://muse.jhu.edu
Project MUSE was launched in 1995 by Johns Hopkins University Press in collaboration with the Milton S. Eisenhower Library to offer the full text of JHU scholarly journals via the World Wide Web. In 1999 MUSE expanded to become a unique partnership of nonprofit publishers. It presently offers some 200 journal titles from 30 scholarly publishers, including the Brookings Institution, Duke University Press, University of Hawaii Press, Indiana University Press, University of Nebraska Press, University of North Carolina Press, Pennsylvania State University Press, and the University of Texas Press. Forty titles in history are covered. New titles added in 2003 include *French Colonial History, Holocaust and Genocide Studies, Journal of Military History,* and *Latin American Research Review.* Similar to JSTOR, basic and advanced searches can be conducted limited by type of document, date, or a particular journal title. In 2003 Project MUSE activated links from 14 of its journals to earlier issues of those titles available through JSTOR. The following MUSE history journals now include links to JSTOR: *Eighteenth-Century Studies, Hispanic American Historical Review, Journal of the History of Ideas,* and *Reviews in American History.* A nice complement to JSTOR.

6

GUIDES TO NEWSPAPERS, NEWSPAPER COLLECTIONS, AND NEWSPAPER INDEXES

Earlier generations of history students spent endless hours toiling over microfilm reels of 19th- and 20th-century newspapers. This task was rendered more laborious by the lack of many newspaper indexes. Researchers were often forced to travel long distances to major newspaper collections.

The development of the World Wide Web and Internet browsers such as Netscape and Explorer has made it possible for even the smallest newspaper to mount a home page and provide varying levels of full-text coverage. The *New York Times*, from its Web site, http://www.nytimes.com, after a free registration, allows you to search its index back to 1996 but provides access to full-text articles only for the past ten days. The others are available for a fee ranging from $1.05 to $2.95. Many other papers have similar arrangements.

Other major accomplishments over the past decade include the development of databases offering full-text and full-image articles for newspapers dating back to the 18th century. Primary Source, now a division of Thomson/Gale, hopes to complete the Times Digital Archive, 1785–1985, this year. UMI ProQuest has already completed work on the *New York Times*, 1851–1999; the *Wall Street Journal*, 1889–1985; the *Washington Post,* 1877–1987; and the *Christian Science Monitor,* 1908–1990. It is also digitizing the *Chicago Tribune* and the *Los Angeles Times.* Cold North Wind, a private company in Ottawa, Canada, is digitizing papers worldwide and providing access through its Paper of Record Web site at http://www.paperofrecord.com. Their collection is particularly strong for Canada, especially Ontario, and for late 19th- and early 20th-century Mexico.

The emergence of mega news gathering networks has made it possible to track recent historical events as described by the world press at the touch of a mouse. The LexisNexis Academic Universe will search your topic in 3,011 newspapers, while Dialog's NewsRoom, part of the Thomson empire, claims to have one of the world's largest single collections of news media with over 7,500 sources. If only one had time to read them all!

GUIDES TO NEWSPAPERS: GENERAL

324. *Journalism: A Guide to the Reference Literature.* By Jo A. Cates. 2nd ed. Englewood, CO: Libraries Unlimited, 1997. 317pp. Index. ISBN 1-56308-374-4.
The author is library director for Chicago's Columbia College Library. She was formerly director of the library at the Poynter Institute for Media Studies. She arranges her 800 sources in 14 chapters ranging from bibliographies and bibliographic guides to selected research centers, archives, and media institutes. For the history student seeking information about newspapers, chapter 6: "Biographical Sources"; chapter 10: "Catalogs"; and chapter 11: "Miscellaneous Sources," are the most helpful. See also Richard Schwarzlose, *Newspapers: A Reference Guide* (Greenwood, 1987). Chapter 1 on the histories of newspapers and chapters 2–4 on newspaper personalities are still helpful. A second edition is long overdue.

325. *The Newspaper Press in Britain: An Annotated Bibliography.* Edited by David Linton and Ray Boston. London: Mansell, 1987. 361pp. Index. ISBN 0-7201-1792-5.
Listing more than 2,900 books, articles, and theses about the British press, this bibliography is the most comprehensive guide available to British newspaper research. Entries are critically annotated and often provide biographical information on journalists and brief histories of newspapers. Appendix 1 gives a helpful chronology of British newspaper history.

DIRECTORIES

326. *Gale Database of Publications and Broadcast Media.* Detroit: Gale Research, 1869–. Online database.
For more than 130 years, the *Gale Directory of Publications and Broadcast Media* and its predecessors, *Ayer Directory of Publications* and *IMS Directory of Publications,* provided coverage of advertising rates, circulation statistics, local programming, personnel, and other key information about newspapers, periodicals, radio stations, television stations, and cable TV companies. Gale has combined this directory with its *Directories in Print* and *Newsletters in Print* in a new Web-based resource that provides access to information on more than 51,000 publications, including 24,000 general and special interest periodicals and newspapers of all types published in the United States and Canada. Also very helpful is *Burrelle's Media Directory,* which is available online or in print (Burrelle's Information Services). Burrelle's covers daily newspapers, nondaily newspapers, magazines and newsletters, television and cable, and radio in six volumes. It also publishes regional and state directories.

327. *Willings Press Guide.* East Grinstead, U.K. 1874–. Annual. ISSN 0000-0213.
This British equivalent to the Gale database is now published in three volumes. Volume 1 lists 18,000 entries for the United Kingdom, including national daily and Sunday newspapers, broadcast media, magazines and other periodicals, and special interest titles, journals, and directories. It even identifies e-zines and relevant Web sites hosted in the United Kingdom. Volume 2 covers the rest

of Europe in 26,000 entries. Volume 3, which includes an index to national and regional newspapers circulated in 150 countries, describes the rest of the world in 21,000 entries. Willings on the Web, a subscription service, provides access to 60,000 media outlets, publications, and organizations.

328. *Working Press of the Nation.* 3 vols. New York: Bowker, 1945–. Annual. Index. ISSN 0084-1323.
This three-volume annual publication, recently acquired by Bowker, provides U.S. coverage of 32 media centers organized in 40 easy-to-use sections. Volume 1 is the *Newspaper Directory.* Arranged alphabetically by state and city, it provides information similar to the *Editor and Publisher International Yearbook* [see 329] but uniquely adds an index of editorial personnel by subject and an index of papers by metro areas. There are also special sections for religious, black, and foreign-language newspapers published in the United States. The 2003 edition lists 8,000 daily, weekly, trade, and specialized newspapers, along with 130 news services and feature syndicates. Other volumes cover magazines, newsletters, TV and radio stations, networks, and local TV programs nationwide.

329. *Editor and Publisher International Yearbook.* New York: Editor and Publisher, 1921–. Annual. ISSN 0424-4923.
First published in 1921, this annual bills itself as the encyclopedia of the industry with comprehensive coverage of all U.S. and Canadian papers and additional coverage of others worldwide. Part 1 gives in-depth list-

ings for U.S., Canadian, and foreign daily newspapers. Part 2 covers the nondaily newspaper industry while part 3, "Who's Where," is a directory of professionals in the newspaper industry with phone numbers, titles, and newspaper and company names. E&P has recently launched its online edition with four different search engines that allow you to search by type of newspaper, frequency, market population, city, state, and many other categories. The database contains information on 1,600+ daily newspapers; 7,000+ weekly newspapers; 1,400+ shopper/TMC newspapers; and 1,300+ specialty newspapers.

NATIONAL UNION LISTS OF NEWSPAPERS

United States

330. *American Newspapers, 1821–1936: A Union List of Files Available in the United States and Canada.* Edited by Winifred Gregory. New York: Bibliographical Society of America, 1937. 791pp.
A monumental achievement for its time, this was the most complete list of American and Canadian newspapers for the 19th and early 20th centuries. Since microfilming was uncommon at that time, the list largely represents bound files of newspapers. Its arrangement is alphabetical by state and then by city with individual states. Canadian newspapers are listed in a similar fashion following the U.S. section. Information provided includes: titles, frequencies, dates, and libraries holding copies, which is

indicated by National Union Catalog symbols. Major holders of foreign newspapers are briefly noted in a concluding chapter.

331. *History and Bibliography of American Newspapers, 1690–1820.* **By Clarence S. Brigham. Worcester, MA: American Antiquarian Society, 1947. Reprint, Westport, CT: Greenwood, 1976. 2 vols. ISBN 0-8371-86773.**

Brigham began compiling data for these volumes in 1913 and published his findings in various installments of the *Proceedings of the American Antiquarian Society* with the last appearing in 1927. The present set is a revision of these installments with corrections and additions. It identifies 2,120 different newspapers published during the period of 1690–1820, with New York having the most (138), followed by Philadelphia (107) and Boston (73). Major collections of these early newspapers are described: the American Antiquarian Society (1,496 titles), the Library of Congress (936), and Harvard University (736). Unlike the brief entries in *American Newspapers, 1821–1936* [see 330], this work provides lengthy descriptions of each newspaper and notes early publishers and editors. Institutions holding runs of these papers are noted by brief title rather than symbols. Private collections are also listed. The complete file of titles listed by Brigham was microfilmed by Readex.

332. *United States Newspaper Program.* **http://www.neh.gov/projects/usnp.html**

Since the early 1980s, the Library of Congress and the National Endowment for the Humanities have collaborated in a partnership to fund and manage the United States Newspaper Program. The program is designed to locate, catalog, and preserve newspapers published throughout the United States. Projects have been established and funded in each state and territory. In addition to the state projects, NEH has funded the cataloging of newspapers at eight national repositories, each of which has extensive newspaper holdings. Cataloged records are being entered into a national database maintained by OCLC.

333. *United States Newspaper Program National Union List.* **5th ed. Dublin, OH: OCL, 1999. Microfiche.**

The most recent cumulative installment of microfiche provides: bibliographic information (135,000 records ranging from Public Occurrences 1690 to *USA Today*); volume-specific holdings information (410,000 listings) from USNP participants, arranged alphabetically by title; cross references from variant to actual titles; and four indexes—place of publication, publication date, subject topical, and subject geographic.

Canada

334. *Canadian Newspapers on Microform Held by the National Library of Canada.* **http://www.nlc-bnc.ca/8/18/index-e.html**

The National Library of Canada receives, through legal deposit, all newspapers filmed after January 1, 1988, for which more than three copies are produced. The National Library also participates in the Decentralized Program for Canadian Newspapers by acquiring and listing all newspapers filmed by the provincial/territorial institutions responsible for filming them. They are also attempting to acquire newspapers filmed commercially before 1988. The above list is organized by province/territory and city and

contains over 2,300 Canadian titles including ethnic, native, and student newspapers.

335. *Union List of Canadian Newspapers.*
Ottawa: National Library of Canada, 1993.
Microfiche. ISSN 0840-5832.
This microfiche collection issued by the
National Library of Canada provides the
most complete listing to date of Canadian
newspapers. The goals of this publication
are to serve as the definitive tool for locating Canadian newspapers, to provide sufficient publication information for reference
purposes, and to aid the interlibrary lending
of newspaper resources. The union list consists of a sequentially numbered register and
two indexes: a name-title index and a geographical index that lists the entries alphabetically by province and by city within the
province. Newspaper holdings for more
than 700 Canadian libraries are included.

Great Britain

336. *Bibliography of British Newspapers.*
London: British Library, 1975–. Vol. 1,
Wiltshire, edited by R. K. Bluhm, 1975;
vol. 2, *Kent,* edited by Winifred Bergess,
Barbara Riddell, and John Whyman, 1982;
vol. 3, *Durham and Northumberland,* edited
by F. W. D. Manders, 1982; vol. 4,
Nottinghamshire, edited by Michael Brook,
1987; vol. 5, *Derbyshire,* edited by Anne
Mellors and Jean Radford, 1987; vol. 6,
Cornwall and Devon, edited by Jean Rowles
and Ian Maxted, 1991.
These are the first volumes of an ongoing
project to provide a comprehensive listing
of British newspapers, national and local. It
includes those no longer published, along
with details of the location of files in Great

Britain and elsewhere. Published histories
of newspapers or bibliographic descriptions
are also noted. Initiated by the Library
Association, the project has now been taken
over by the British Library. The bibliography is being published in parts covering
each county. Although it was planned to be
completed in 20 years, it may take longer.

337. *The Waterloo Directory of Irish
Newspapers and Periodicals, 1800–1980.*
Edited by John S. North. North Waterloo
Academic Press. 1994. 840pp.
ISBN 0-921075-00-6.
This volume describes 3,900 newspapers
and periodicals in all fields: art, literature,
theater, science, music, agriculture, labor,
politics, trade, home, and church. Its indexes
list all periodicals published in each Irish
city and town and give locations for most
titles as well as a description of the political
and religious orientation of the title.

338. *The Waterloo Directory of Scottish
Newspapers and Periodicals, 1800–1900.*
Edited by John S. North. North Waterloo:
Academic Press. 1989. 2,200pp.
ISBN 0-921075-05-7.
Describes in detail over 7,300 Scottish Vic-
torian newspapers and periodicals with up
to 25 descriptors assigned to each title and
2,500 telefacsimile pages. The resources of
80 Scottish libraries were searched to pro-
vide locations. Every imaginable field of
Scottish history and culture is covered.
A monumental work.

Australia

339. *Newspapers in Australian Libraries:
A Union List.* 4th ed. Canberra: National

Library of Australia, 1985. 2 vols.
ISBN 0642993009.
This is the fourth edition of a union list
that was originally published in 1959.
It is divided into two sections. Section 1
describes overseas newspapers held by Australian libraries, while section 2 describes
Australian newspapers and their Australian
holders. The arrangement is alphabetical,
first by country and then by city or town.

- 19th–20th Century U.S. Newspapers
- 19th–20th Century Foreign
  Newspapers
- 18th Century American Newspapers
- 17th–18th Century Foreign
  Newspapers
- A variety of bibliographies and guides
  are available online, including "The
  Black Press Held by the Library of
  Congress"

GUIDES TO MAJOR NEWSPAPER COLLECTIONS (ARRANGED IN ORDER OF SIGNIFICANCE)

United States

340. *Newspaper and Current Periodical
Reading Room, Serial and Government
Publications Division, Library of Congress,
Madison Bldg., Independence and First St. SE.*
Washington, DC 20540-4760. http://www.
loc.gov/rr/news
The Library of Congress maintains one of
the most extensive newspaper collections in
the world. It is exceptionally strong in U.S.
newspapers, with 9,000 titles covering over
300 years. With 25,000 non-U.S. titles, it is
the largest collection of overseas newspapers in the world. Many lists formerly in
print are searchable online. Among the
most important:

- Current U.S. Newspapers
- Foreign Newspapers
- Historical Collections, microfilm
- Chronological lists 1940–1989
- Chronological lists 1801–1939 (under
  construction)
- Historical Collections, bound volumes

341. *State Historical Society of Wisconsin
Library.* Newspaper and Periodicals
Section, 816 State St., Madison, WI 53706.
http://www.wisconsinhistory.org/library/
collections/news.html
The State Historical Society of Wisconsin
owns the second largest collection of general newspapers in the United States. The
society library owns 11,740 bound volumes, 100,000 reels of microfilm, and
17,000 sheets of microprint spanning three
centuries of American newspaper history.
Particular strengths include Wisconsin
newspapers, colonial and early American
newspapers west of the Appalachians, and
the largest collection of labor and trade
union papers in the nation. Their holdings
of 1960s underground or alternative newspapers are also extensive. Most newspapers
and periodicals held by the society library
are available for Interlibrary Loan, photocopying, and general circulation. The society library has published periodical guides
to its collections; the most recent is:

342. *African-American Newspapers and
Periodicals: A National Bibliography.* Edited
by James P. Danky. Cambridge, MA:
Harvard University Press, 1999. 816pp.
ISBN 0-674-00788-3.
Danky is the longtime newspapers and

periodicals librarian for the society. This is the first comprehensive guide to all known newspapers and magazines by and about African Americans. Dating back to 1827, the bibliography lists some 6,500 titles in the United States, Canada, and the Caribbean. For each description the book identifies locations where the publication can be found. Danky has also coedited two earlier bibliographies: *Native American Periodicals and Newspapers, 1828–1982,* edited by James P. Danky and compiled by Maureen E. Hady (Greenwood, 1984); and *Women's Periodicals and Newspapers from the 18th Century to 1981,* edited by James P. Danky et al. (G. K. Hall, 1982).

343. *Center for Research Libraries.* 6050 South Kenwood Ave., Chicago, IL 60637-2804. http://www.crl.edu
From its founding in 1949 as the Midwest Inter-Library Center, the CRL has grown to include more than 130 participating libraries and research institutes in North America. CRL operates a global cooperative collection development program that assists academic and research libraries in making important research materials available to scholars and researchers. CRL's program is supported by a large centralized collection consisting of five major components: global newspapers, scholarly journals, area studies, international doctoral dissertations, and subject collections. CRL collects newspapers from each state in the United States, each country of the world, and specialized papers such as U.S. ethnic press titles. Major collections include black newspapers, including a core of 20 titles collected since 1965; ethnic newspapers—800 titles published in the United States from the 19th century to the present; foreign newspapers—6,100 titles in original format and microform; U.S. general

circulation newspapers, including at least one paper from each state plus newspapers from major metropolitan centers. For access, check the CRL catalog online at http://catalog.crl.edu. While all current titles are included, some retrospective newspaper files have not been cataloged yet.

Canada

344. *National Library of Canada, Reference and Information Services Division.* 395 Wellington St., Ottawa, Ontario, Canada K1A 0N4. http://www.nlc-bnc.ca
The National Library of Canada was created in 1953 to relieve the Library of Parliament of the responsibility of serving as Canada's National Library. Since that time, the National Library has grown to be the largest library in Canada. In 2003 a bill was introduced in the House of Commons to combine the National Library and the National Archives.

The National Library collects in hard copy a select number of Canadian current dailies, all Canadian ethnic papers, all Canadian native papers, and student newspapers. They have over 200,000 reels of Canadian newspapers on microfilm. Among the many online lists they maintain are Canadian ethnic newspapers currently received, Canadian newspapers currently received, Canadian newspapers online, Canadian newspapers on microform, Native newspapers currently received, non-Canadian newspapers currently received, and student newspapers currently received. The National Library of Canada (NLC) has developed and maintains AMICUS, an online database of over 25 million bibliographic records with 43 million holdings from over 1,300 Canadian libraries. For access in English, see http://

www.nlc-bnc.ca/amicus/index-e.html.
For access in French, see http://www.
nlc-bnc.ca/amicus/index-f.html.

Great Britain

345. *British Library, Humanities and Social Sciences Division.* Great Russell St., London WC1B, United Kingdom.
The British Library was founded in 1973 under the British Library Act. It combines the former library departments of the British Museum, the National Central Library, the British National Bibliography, and the National Lending Library for Science and Technology. The Public Services Division of the Humanities and Social Sciences Section administers the British Library Newspaper Library. The British Museum began collecting newspapers in the 1820s. By the end of the 19th century, out of space, a new site was purchased at Colindale in north London and a newspaper repository was constructed, opening in 1905. The repository building was destroyed by bombing in 1940. A new building was not completed until 1957. In 1996 the new reading room opened, which includes networked access to newspapers on CD-ROM. The newspaper library has some 600,000 bound volumes of newspapers, occupying 18 linear miles of shelving, plus 300,000 reels of positive microfilm. In all there are more than 37,000 separate titles. About 75 percent of the titles are British and Irish. The newspaper library acquires 3,100 titles a year, 350 from outside the British Isles. Additional titles are held in the British Library's Oriental and India Collections. In 1995 the newspaper library Web site was established on the British Library's online information server, and in 2000 the newspaper library catalog of over 52,000 newspaper and periodical titles was launched on the Web at http://progigi.bl.uk/nlcat. Each entry contains details of the title, place of publication, and dates held. For further information, contact The British Library Newspaper Library, Colindale Ave., London, NW95HE, United Kingdom or e-mail: newspaper@bl.uk

Australia

346. *National Library of Australia.* Canberra, ACT 2600, Australia, ABN: 28 346 858. http://www.nla.gov.au
The newspaper collection of the National Library of Australia consists of 8,000 titles (many no longer published). There are more than 700 current Australian titles, including all capital city dailies, major country newspapers, and newspapers published by ethnic groups. The National Library also collects foreign titles and has published *South Asian Newspapers in Australian Libraries: A Holdings List* based on a 1994 survey of academic libraries at http://www.nla.gov.au/asian/gen/saintro.html.

Others

347. *Subject Collections: A Guide to Special Book Collections and Subject Emphases as Reported by University, College, Public, and Special Libraries and Museums in the United States and Canada.* Compiled by Lee Ash and William G. Miller. 7th ed. New York: R. R. Bowker, 1993. 2 vols. Index. ISBN 0-8352-3141-0.
This is a guide to special book collections

reported by libraries in North America. Most of the important North American newspaper collections are listed here under the heading "Newspapers." Inverted subject headings like "Newspapers, Armenian" guide the researcher to important collections on specialized topics.

GUIDES TO INDEXED NEWSPAPERS

348. *Checklist of Indexes to Canadian Newspapers Held by the National Library of Canada.* Compiled by the Reference and Information Services Unit of the National Library of Canada. http://www.nlc-bnc. ca/8/12/index-e.html

The Checklist of Indexes to Canadian Newspapers comprises indexes to Canadian newspaper titles received by the library's reference collection. The coverage of these indexes span from the 18th century to the present. The checklist also provides online and Internet sources for indexes to Canadian newspapers. The checklist can be searched by province, index title, or newspaper title. See also Sandra Burrows and Franceen Gaudet's earlier *Checklist of Indexes to Canadian Newspapers* (National Library of Canada, 1987). It was based on a survey of 4,000 institutes across Canada including libraries, newspaper offices, archives, and genealogical and historical societies.

349. *U.S. Newspaper Indexes at the Library of Congress.* Compiled by John Pluge Jr. Library of Congress Serial and Government Publications Division. http://lcweb.gov/rr/newsind.html

Online Newspaper Indexes Available in the Newspaper and Current Periodical Reading Room. http://www.loc.gov/rr/news/ npindex2.html

These two online lists provide one of the most complete lists of indexes for U.S. and foreign newspapers. Pluge's guide to print indexes focuses exclusively on the United States and is searchable by state. He offers the wise advice that few indexes are complete, and many errors and omissions can be expected. The online guide provides lists of domestic titles arranged alphabetically or by state and foreign titles arranged alphabetically and by country. There are even lists of titles for online vendors.

350. *Indexes and Databases: Reference and Current Affairs.* National Library of Australia. http://www.nla.gov.au/ pathways/jnls/newsite/browse/refca. html

This attractive Web site with colorful symbols lists newspaper indexes by nation and state. It notes whether they are Web accessible, CD-ROM, or print.

351. *UMI Newspapers in Microform Catalog.* Indexed Newspapers. http://www.lib.umi. com/nim/entry

The ProQuest Company, UMI division, has published this comprehensive list of newspaper indexes they have been involved in producing. Two of these cover papers have now ceased:

Washington Star-News Index, 1894–1973
New York Times Tribune Index, 1875–1906

Others cover major American dailies in cities ranging from Los Angeles to Nashville.

NEWSPAPER INDEXES: INDIVIDUAL PAPERS

United States (prior to 1900)

352. *Arkansas Gazette Index: An Arkansas Index*. Russellville, AK: Arkansas Tech University Library, 1970s–.
One of the more innovative local indexing projects is the ongoing *Arkansas Gazette Index*. This newspaper was founded in 1819 at Arkansas Post. Two years later it moved to Little Rock, where it remains today as part of the Gannett chain. Two new volumes are currently appearing each year, one in the retrospective series and one in the current. The index is a selective subject index to Arkansas news and personalities appearing in the newspaper. So far 20 volumes have been published in the retrospective series covering the period of 1819 to 1894, and 27 volumes have been produced in the current series covering from 1964 to 1991.

353. *New York Daily Tribune Index, 1875–1906*. New York: Tribune Association. 32 vols. Reprinted as the *New York Tribune Index* on three reels of microfilm by UMI. The *New York Tribune* was founded in 1841 by Horace Greeley and came to be one of the most important of the 19th-century New York dailies. It later merged with the *New York Herald* to become the *Herald-Tribune* in 1924, which ceased publication in 1966. A brief annual subject index was issued for the years 1875 to 1906. Because of the scarceness of this index it was reprinted by UMI on microfilm.

354. *New York Times Index*. New York: New York Times Company, 1913–. Semimonthly with quarterly and annual cumulations.

The most important U.S. newspaper index was launched in 1913 with monthly issues and quarterly, but no annual, cumulations. In 1930, annual cumulations were added and in 1948 it assumed its current format, semimonthly with quarterly and annual cumulations. A detailed subject index giving exact references to dates, pages, and columns, with numerous cross references, it offers the most detailed indexing of any newspaper in the world and is frequently consulted for ready reference. The index is a guide to the late city edition, not the national edition sold in many parts of the country. Articles are coded for length. In 1983 the heading structure and indexing vocabulary was simplified and the number of subheadings reduced. The lag time in distributing this index has grown in recent years and was running almost 8 months behind in 2003. For example, the October 16–31, 2002, issue was not received in most libraries until May 2003.

355. *New York Times Index*. Prior Series. *Sept. 1851–1912*. New York: R. R. Bowker, 1966–1976. 15 vols.
In 1976 Bowker completed a 15-volume set of retrospective indexes to the *New York Times* resulting in a complete run of indexing for the *Times* from its inception in September 1851. The first volume covering the years 1851 to 1858 is a facsimile reprint of the original handwritten volume. The rest of the volumes were based on in-house files except for the years 1905 to 1912, which represent new indexing.

356. *New York Times Obituaries Indexes*. Vol. 1, 1858–1968. Vol. 2, 1969–1978. New York: New York Times Company, 1970, 1980. 1,136pp. and 131pp.
These two volumes of obituaries are partic-

ularly helpful for historians. The first contains more than 350,000 entries while the second added 40,000 more. The second also reprints in full 50 obituaries of prominent individuals for those years.

357. Personal Name Index to the New York Times Index, 1851–1974. Compiled by Byron A. Falk and Valerie R. Falk. Succasunna, NJ: Roxbury Data Interface, 1976–1983. 22 vols. 1975–1993 Supplement. Verdi, NV: Roxbury Data Interface, 1995–1998. 6 vols. ISBN 0-89902-093-3.
This impressive set does much to unlock the riches of the *New York Times* by providing an alphabetical listing of more than 3 million names appearing in the *New York Times Index*. Listings provide complete names and years, but the page references are to the *New York Times Index*, not the newspaper itself. Since the prior series of the *New York Times Index* [see 355] was not complete for the years 1905–1912 when this project began, there are few references to those years. The 1975–1993 supplement continues the indexing through 1993 and includes the names missed from the prior series.

358. Sun (Baltimore) and Evening Sun Index, 1891–1951. Ann Arbor, MI: UMI, n.d. 209 reels of microfilm.
UMI distributes a retrospective index to the Baltimore *Sun* and *Evening Sun* that was originally produced by Bell & Howell. The *Sun* was founded in 1837 and the *Evening Sun* in 1910, and long viewed as one of the most important American dailies, with a notable foreign news bureau. This retrospective subject index provides researchers with additional access to information on the first half of the 20th century. It is based on typed index cards maintained by the

newspapers and by the Enoch Pratt Free Library of Baltimore.

359. Virginia Gazette Index, 1736–1780. By Lester J. Cappon and Stella F. Duff. Williamsburg, VA: Institute of Early American History and Culture, 1950. 2 vols.
The *Virginia Gazette* was actually the name of five different colonial weeklies published in Williamsburg between 1736 and 1780. The last of these moved to Richmond in April 1780. The index is arranged alphabetically with some subject headings. The first of the *Gazettes* was the second newspaper to be published in the South.

360. Washington Star-News Index, 1852–1973. Ann Arbor, MI: UMI, n.d.
The *Washington Star* was founded in 1852 as an evening daily and included the *Sunday Star*. In 1972 it merged with the *Washington Daily News*. A valuable source for its coverage of congressional news, it ceased publication in early 1981. For the period from 1852 to 1906, the indexing is uneven with some years having no index, notably the period of the Civil War. Beginning in 1906, there is a comprehensive index up to 1973.

United States (since 1900)

No new indexes of newspapers were begun in the first half of the 20th century. Then in 1959 Dow Jones began producing the *Wall Street Journal Index* beginning with the year 1958. It was issued monthly with an annual cumulation. Later, UMI provided retrospective coverage back to 1955. In 1960 the *Christian Science Monitor* began issuing a monthly index to the *Monitor* with semiannual and annual cumulations. This index was taken over by UMI and retrospective coverage was provided back to 1945. In 1972 the Bell & Howell Company of Wooster, Ohio, launched the first of its newspaper indexes. Beginning with four newspapers—the *Chicago Tribune*, the *Los Angeles Times*, the *New Orleans Times-Picayune*, and the *Washington Post*—the company now dominates newspaper indexing through its subsidiaries UMI and Data Courier. The indexes themselves are produced by Data Courier in Louisville, Kentucky. Generally, they are published in eight softbound monthly installments with four quarterly cumulations and a hardbound annual. The quality of the indexing has improved dramatically in recent years. All indexes are strictly subject based. In earlier issues personalities and subjects appeared in separate sections. The following indexes were being produced in 2003:

361. *Atlanta Constitution and Journal Index*, 1983–. The *Atlanta Constitution Index: A Georgia Index* was published from 1971 to 1979 by Georgia State University but limited to state coverage.

362. *Boston Globe Index*, 1983–.

363. *Chicago Tribune Index*, 1972–.

364. *Christian Science Monitor Index*, 1949–.

365. *Denver Post Index*, 1999–.

366. *Detroit News Index*, 1976–.

367. *Houston Chronicle Index*, 1993–.

368. *Los Angeles Times Index*, 1972–.

369. *St. Louis Post-Dispatch Index*, 1975–.

370. *San Francisco Chronicle Index*, 1976–. [see 374].

371. *Times-Picayune (New Orleans) Index*, 1972–.

372. *USA Today Index*, 1982–.

373. *Washington Post Index*, 1971–. While this was one of the original Bell & Howell indexes produced from 1971 to 1981, a second index call the *Official Index to the Washington Post* was published by Research Publications from 1979 to 1988. UMI reacquired the indexing rights in 1989.

374. *San Francisco Newspapers Index. San Francisco Chronicle Index*. California Section, California State library, 1986. Compiled from files maintained by the California State Library, the *San Francisco Newspapers Index* covers the period 1904–1949. It indexes the *San Francisco Call* (1904–1913), the *San Francisco Examiner* (1913–1928), and the *San Francisco Chronicle* (1913–1949). The *San Francisco Newspapers Index* is continued by the *San Francisco Chronicle Index,* which covers the period 1950–1980 [for coverage after 1980, see 370]. The *San Francisco Newspapers Index* consists of 699 microfiches containing 1.8 million citations on approximately 922,000 cards. The *Chronicle Index* adds 277 microfiches with 720,000 citations from 363,000 cards. Subject headings are listed on the first four fiches although they are not always used in the index. Citations include the month, day, year, page, and column for each entry.

375. *Wall Street Journal Index*. New York: Dow Jones, 1955–. Monthly with annual cumulations. ISSN 0083-7075.

The *Wall Street Journal Index* is produced by Dow Jones and distributed by UMI. Since 1981 the annual cumulation has also provided indexing to *Barron's*. Unlike UMI, produced indexes, this index is divided into two sections: corporate news (indexed by company name) and general news. Recent annuals have also included an almanac of the closing Dow Jones averages on Wall Street.

Canada

No commercial indexes to individual newspapers are currently being produced.

Great Britain

Indexes to *The Times (London)*.

376. *Palmer's Index to the Times Newspaper* (1790–June 1941). London: Palmer, 1868–1943. Reprint, New York: Kraus, 1965. Quarterly.
The first successful regular index to *The Times* was initiated by London bookseller Samuel Palmer in 1868. In 1891 he began retrospective indexing and eventually extended his index back to 1790. Neither he nor his successors were able to interest the newspaper in providing financial support for the index and it ceased publication in 1941. Using *Palmer's Index* can be a difficult task for the beginner since it indexes items under the first word of a heading rather than by subject. A useful guide to this style of indexing is Doreen Morrison, "Indexes to *The Times of London*," *The Serials Librarian*, September 1987, 89–104. *Palmer's Index* also indexed *The Times Literary Supplement* from 1907 to 1941 and *The Times Educational Supplement* from 1910 to 1941.

377. *The Times Index* (1785–1790 and 1906–). Woodbridge, CT: Primary Source Microfilm, 1906–. Monthly with annual cumulations.
In competition with *Palmer's Index* [see 376], *The Times* decided to publish its own index in 1906, calling it the *Official Index to The Times*. Initially it appeared monthly with an annual cumulation. In 1914 it shifted to quarterly publication. The title changed to the *Index to The Times* in 1957, and it also began bimonthly publication. It was renamed *The Times Index* in 1972 and switched back to quarterly volumes. At this time coverage of the *Sunday Times* (a separate paper), *The Times Literary Supplement*, *The Times Educational Supplement*, and *The Times Higher Educational Supplement* were added to the index. Yet another shift occurred in 1977 when the index returned to a monthly format with an annual cumulation. Retrospective indexing for the period 1785–1790, which was not covered by *Palmer's Index*, was completed in 1978. Primary Source Microfilm, a Thomson/Gale imprint, is the current publisher. Easy to use, *The Times Index* uses a standard list of subject headings that are frequently updated. Despite recent changes in ownership of both the paper and the index, it remains the index of record for the United Kingdom. Unlike the *New York Times Index* [see 354] the lag time is less than two months behind current. For example, the February 2003 issue was distributed in the United States the second week of April.

378. *The Times Literary Supplement Indexes.* I, 1902–1939. II, 1940–1980. Woodbridge,

CT: Research Publications, 1978–1982.
5 vols. ISBN 0-907514-74X.
Since the original *Times Index* did not
include indexing to *The Times Literary Sup-plement*, retrospective cumulative indexes
have been published that serve as a guide to
more than a million items that have
appeared in this weekly publication. The
indexes provide quick access to authors,
books, subjects, translators, illustrators,
poems, or periodicals discussed.

379. *Obituaries From the Times*. I, 1951–1960.
II, 1961–1970. III, 1971–1975. Westport, CT:
Newspaper Archive Developments (now
Primary Source Microfilm), 1975–1979.
This publication reprints approximately
4,000 obituaries that appeared in *The Times*
and provides an index to all other obituar-ies and tributes that appeared during those
years.

Other British Newspapers

380. *Guardian Index*. Ann Arbor, MI: UMI,
1986–. Monthly with annual cumulations.
The Manchester Guardian was founded in
1819 by a group of Manchester liberals. It
has been published continuously since then.
In 1919 the *Guardian Weekly* was intro-duced. *The Guardian* maintains an extensive
staff of foreign correspondents and is noted
for its objective coverage of the news. This
index covers both the daily and weekly edi-tions and uses the standard UMI style.

Other Countries

381. *Le Monde Index*. Reading, U.K.:
Primary Source Microfilm, 1987–. Indexes
are available for 1944–1951, 1965–1968,
and 1979–1999.

The influential Paris daily *Le Monde* was
established in 1944, becoming the first
independent postwar newspaper in France.
Viewed as one of Europe's most intellectual
papers, it publishes no photographs. The
early volumes of the index were published
by the paper beginning in 1965, with retro-spective indexing starting with 1944. This
index was subject based and gives a refer-ence to the date of the issue only. Research
Publications revived the indexing begin-ning with the year 1987 and planned to
publish the current index and one retro-spective volume each year until the retro-spective coverage is complete. Volumes are
currently available from Primary Source
Microfilm, a Thomson/Gale imprint. The
future of this index is uncertain.

382. *El Pais Index*. Reading, U.K.: Primary
Source Microfilm, 1988–1995. Selected
volumes for 1977–1995 are available.
Since its founding in 1976, six months after
the death of the dictator Francisco Franco,
the Madrid daily *El Pais* has gained a repu-tation as Spain's most important national
newspaper. Its Sunday supplement provides
excellent features on politics, culture, litera-ture, and economics. A weekly international
edition is also published. With the takeover
of Research Publications by Thomson/Gale
the index has apparently ceased.

NEWSPAPER INDEXES: COLLECTIVE

United States

383. *Black Newspapers Index*. Ann Arbor,
MI: UMI, 1977–. Quarterly.
This subject-based index covers nine black

newspapers in the United States: *Afro-American*, Capitol edition (Washington, DC), *Amsterdam News* (New York), *Call and Post* (Cleveland), *Chicago Defender, Los Angeles Sentinel, Michigan Chronicle* (Detroit), *Muslim Journal* (Chicago), and the *Journal and Guide* (Norfolk, VA).

384. *National Newspaper Index*. **Detroit, MI: Gale Group. Online via InfoTrac Web.**
The *National Newspaper Index* was launched in 1979 by the Information Access Company (IAC). Extremely innovative for its time, it was issued on microfilm suitable for loading on ROM (record output microform) readers. Initially it indexed the *Christian Science Monitor*, the *New York Times* (both late city and national editions), and the *Wall Street Journal* (both the eastern and western editions). Indexing for the *Los Angeles Times* and the *Washington Post* was added in 1982. The continuously cumulating index provided four years of indexing at the push of a button. After four years of cumulation, the first year was removed to microfiche. In July of 1988 the IAC began issuing the index on compact disc on its InfoTrac system. This version covered the previous four years and was updated monthly. IAC used modified Library of Congress subject headings. In November 1994 IAC was acquired by the Thomson Corporation and in October 1998 Gale Research, IAC, and Primary Source Media were merged to form a new Company, the Gale Group. Presently five newspapers are indexed: *Christian Science Monitor* (national edition); *Los Angeles Times* (home edition); *New York Times* (late and national editions); *Wall Street Journal* (eastern and western editions) and *Washington Post* (final edition). A subscription includes the current year plus three years of back files.

385. *InfoTrac Custom Newspapers*. **Detroit, MI: Gale Group. Online via InfoTrac Web.**
With Custom Newspapers, libraries can select two or more titles from a list of more than 100 newspapers from around the world ranging from the *Arizona Republic* to the *Times* (London). Libraries can customize the product name, screen layout, search parameters, and results. For example, the Walter Clinton Jackson Library at UNC-Greensboro provides selected full text of the *Atlanta Citizen Times, Los Angeles Times, New York Times, Greensboro News & Record,* and *Winston-Salem Journal*. Searches can be limited to one or more newspapers.

386. *NewsBank NewsFile Collection*. *Global NewsBank. NewsBank Full-Text Newspapers.* **Naples, FL: NewsBank.**
NewsBank is one of the world's largest information providers. It is presently marketing a number of different products to libraries. One of the most popular is the NewsBank NewsFile Collection. It is a comprehensive, full-text news source consisting of regional, national, and international sources. Approximately 500,000 articles are selected from over 500 newspapers, news wires, and media transcripts. Seventy thousand articles are added per year with back files to 1992. NewsBank Full-Text Newspapers, which is widely available in academic libraries, provides complete full-text content of local and regional news, including community events, cultural activities, local companies, state industries, and people in the community for more than 400 newspapers. Individual papers need to be selected before searching. Global NewsBank provides access to some 400,000 fully indexed articles from 1,000 sources, including radio and television broadcasts, wire services, and newspaper

and magazine articles. Retrospective coverage is available back to 1996.

387. *ProQuest Newspaper Abstracts.* **Ann Arbor, MI: ProQuest Information and Learning Company.**
This product was first developed by UMI as a CD-ROM index in 1989. Initially it provided indexing and brief abstracts for eight major U.S. dailies. Today a number of different products are available in academic and public libraries. *Newspaper Abstracts Complete* covers 27 primary and secondary newspapers worldwide. It's available online. *Newspaper Abstracts National* includes indexing and abstracting for nine major U.S. papers. It's also available online. *Newspaper Abstracts Major Papers* covers the top five U.S. publications. It's available online and on CD-ROM. Editorials, editorial cartoons, obituaries, and letters to the editor from well-known people are indexed. For each item in the database an abstract of up to 75 words is provided. Updated several times a day, archival coverage dates from 1989. Back files are available from 1985 to 1988. ProQuest also covers international newspapers in their *ProQuest International Selectable Newspapers,* which allows libraries to develop a custom database from some 60 papers published worldwide, from the *Bangkok Post* to the *Waikato Times.* Citations, abstracts, and full-text articles are available back to 1991.

Canada

388. *Canadian Newsstand.* **Toronto: Micromedia ProQuest Online database.**
Micromedia, founded in 1972, has partnered with ProQuest to provide Canadian Newstand through the ProQuest Web interface. Subscribers can choose from a selection of national papers, customized regional packages, or single newspapers. The core of the database is the Major Canadian Dailies collection, which includes *National Post, Calgary Herald, Edmonton Journal, Montreal Gazette, Ottawa Citizen, Regina Leader Post, Vancouver Sun,* and the *Victoria Times Colonist.* Data are updated daily following a seven-day embargo.

ONLINE NEWS SERVICES

389. *Dialog Web.* **Gary, NC: Thomson/ Dialog. http://www.dialog.com/products. dialogweb**
One of the oldest providers of online databases, Dialog is now part of the Thomson family. Dozens of newspapers can be searched full-text online for a fee. Among the most important are:

- *Africa News* File 606, January 1999– and File 806, July 1996–May 1999
- Albuquerque Newspapers (including the *Albuquerque Journal* and the *Albuquerque Tribune*) File 929, January 1995–
- Asia-Pacific News (articles from 11 major dailies including *Bangkok Post, Cambodia Times, Daily Yomjuri, The Hindu, The Jakarta Post, Mainichi Daily News, New Straits Times, The Nikkei Weekly,* and *Straits Times* File 728
- *Atlanta Journal-Constitution* File 713, January 1989–
- *Baltimore Sun* File 714, September 1990–
- *Boston Globe* File 631, January 1980–

- Canadian Newspapers File 727, January 1990–
- *Charlotte Observer* File 642, January 1988–
- *Cincinnati Post/Kentucky Post* File 722, April, 1990–
- Daily and Sunday *Telegraph* (London) File 756, September 19, 2000–
- *Denver Post* File 387, January 1994–
- *Detroit Free Press* File 498, January 1987–
- *Irish Times* File 477, February 1999–
- *Kansas City Star* File 147, September 1997–
- *Miami Herald* File 702, January 1983–
- *Memphis Commercial Appeal* File 740, July 1990–
- *Milwaukee Journal Sentinel* File 979, April 1998–
- (New Orleans) *Times Picayune* File 706, January 1989–
- *Newsday* File 638, January 1987–
- *Philadelphia Inquirer* File 633, January 1983–.
- (Phoenix) *Arizona Republic* File 492, April 1986–
- *Pittsburgh Post Gazette* File 718, June 1990–
- *San Francisco Chronicle* File 640, January 1988–
- *St. Louis Post-Dispatch* File 494, January 1988–
- *USA Today* File 703, January 1989–

To search the complete text of all local, national, and international news articles, use "papers" and "papers nu" categories. To scan the entire collection of U.S. full-text newspaper databases, use "papers U.S." in Dial index. In May 2003 Dialog announced that *Le Monde,* the leading French newspaper, was now available for searching. Dialog's online services now provide access to 1.4 billion unique records.

390. *LexisNexis Academic.* **Bethesda, MD: LexisNexis Academic and Library Solutions. Online database. http://www. lexisnexis.com/academic/1univ/ or http://web.nexis.com/universe**
LexisNexis, a division of Reed Elsevier, is one of the world's largest online news networks. From its "Academic Universe" you can access full-text documents from over 5,600 news, business, legal, medical, and reference publications, including national and regional newspapers, wire services, broadcast transcripts, international newspapers, business news journals, industry and market news, and non–English language sources; 4,451 general news sources, including 3,011 newspapers, are searchable. There is a free searchable directory of online sources at http://web.nexis.com.sources. Sources can be located by title. Directory information includes coverage, frequency, publisher, data format, and description. Other LexisNexis databases available in many libraries include LexisNexis Statistical (including the online version of the *American Statistics Index*) and LexisNexis Government Periodicals Index (indexing 170 magazines and newsletters published by the U.S. government). In March 2003 LexisNexis announced it was adding transcripts from *Al Jazeera,* the only Arabic news channel in the Middle East offering news coverage 24 hours a day.

391. *Data Times Newspaper Abstracts and Index.* **Ann Arbor, MI: ProQuest Information and Learning.**
The Oklahoma City–based Data Times became a wholly owned subsidiary of UMI in 1996. Data Times Newspaper Index

covers articles in 126 U.S. and international newspapers. Emphasis is on current events: 92 papers are from major cities and regions across the United States; 34 are international and include publications from Canada, Europe, the Middle East, Asia, and the Pacific Rim. Items indexed include news articles, reviews, editorials, and commentaries. Data Times is frequently searched through OCLC FirstSearch interface and is available on subscription. [See: 081] http://www.oclc.org/firstsearch/databases/details/dbinformation_DataTimes.html. The number of records exceeds 6 million with coverage since 1996.

392. *Infomart.ca.* http://www.infomart.ca InfoMart, a member of the CanWest Global group of companies, is Canada's largest media concern. It provides same-day and archival access to 200 national and regional sources including daily/weekly newspapers, magazines, trade publications, broadcast transcripts, and news wires, all full-text. Full subscribers have access to over 180 full-text sources. Pay-per-view clients have access to the same day *National Post* plus 15 key full-text sources ranging from the *Calgary Herald* to the *Windsor Star.*

ance of the first full-text and full-image articles for newspapers dating back to the 19th century. For most titles, the collection includes digital reproductions of every page from every issue in downloadable PDF files. The following papers are available:

> *New York Times:* 1851–1999
> *Wall St. Journal:* 1889–1985
> *Washington Post:* 1877–1987
> *Christian Science Monitor:* 1908–1990

The last two were completed in May 2003. Future plans call for digitization of the *Chicago Tribune* and the *Los Angeles Times.* The vast scale of this project can be appreciated by noting that digitizing just the *New York Times* involved scanning, digitizing, zoning, and editing 3.4 million pages from microfilm into digital files, while the *Washington Post* involved more than 2.6 million pages of articles. Researchers with access to these files can now find not only news, editorials, letters to the editor, obituaries, and birth and marriage announcements but also historical photos, stock photos, and advertisements. In some cases the images are more readable than the original film. To make effective use of these newspapers many libraries have developed search guides.

DIGITAL HISTORICAL NEWSPAPERS

United States

393. *ProQuest Historical Newspapers.* **Ann Arbor, MI: ProQuest Information and Learning. Online Database.**
One of the most exciting developments in newspaper research has been the appear-

Canada

394. *The Globe and Mail On-line Historical Newspaper Archive* and *Toronto Star On-line Historical Newspaper Archive.* **Toronto: Micromedia ProQuest.**
Founded in 1972, Micromedia was Canada's largest developer, publisher, and distributor of reference information, with particular expertise in CD-ROMs and

microform. On January 31, 2002, it joined ProQuest's Information and Learning Unit. Widely respected as Canada's leading newspaper, Toronto's *Globe and Mail* dates to 1844. The 1.4 million-page online archive covers over 150 years of Canadian history. Available as an annual subscription product through Micromedia ProQuest's popular Web portal, information can be searched by key word(s), phrase, date, and subject. Coverage includes every news story, photograph, map, advertisement, classified ad, political cartoon, and birth and death notice. Also available is the *Toronto Star* from 1894 to 2000. It brings over a century of news and information from Canada's largest daily newspaper and involved scanning 30,000 back issues of the *Toronto Star*—almost 2 million pages.

Great Britain

395. *The Times Digital Archive.* **Detroit: Thomson/Gale. http://www.gale.com/ Times/about.htm**
The most ambitious undertaking of them all is *The Times* Digital Archive, which promises to deliver a digital database of 200 years of *The Times*. Every page, headline, feature, photo, editorial, and advertisement can be viewed in its original published context. When completed, an estimated 8 million individual articles will be available. A customizable interface with full-text searching and hit-term highlighting is available. A unique browse feature lets you select a specific date and then browse the pages from that issue via thumbnail images. The initial release covered 1936–1946. The current version covers 1880–1985. More data will be added monthly until the entire

period 1785–1985 is available at the end of 2003.

Other

396. *Tiden: A Nordic Digital Newspaper Library.* **http://tiden.Kb.se**
The first historical digital newspaper library in the world to provide full-text access to newspapers in Gothic script is the product of TIDEN—the Nordic Digital Newspaper Project. It is a collaborative effort of libraries in Denmark, Finland, Norway, and Sweden. The Finnish Historical Newspaper Library will include all newspapers published in Finland between 1771 and 1860, some 44 titles. By the end of 2002 more than 191,034 pages had been scanned. The Swedish archive is concentrated on a collection of newspapers called Posttidningar. Two periods covered include 1645–1721 and 1808–1813. The Norwegian archive consists of three major newspapers while the Danish archive contains one major newspaper called *Adresseavisen*.

397. *Paper of Record.* **Ottawa: Cold North Wind (CNW). http://www. paperofrecord.com**
CNW was established in September 1999 with the mission of bringing historical newspapers to life on the Internet for both the consumer and library market. A private company based in Ottawa, they provide expertise in digitizing and publishing newspaper archives. They are building the world's largest searchable archive of historical newspapers with over 6 million pages digitized. Newspapers in Australia, Canada, France, Ireland, Mexico, Spain, United Kingdom, and the United States are available. The

database is particularly strong in Canadian and Mexican newspapers.

GUIDES TO NEWSPAPERS ON THE WEB

398. *American Journalism Review.* http://www.ajr.org
American Journalism Review (AJR) is a national magazine that covers all aspects of print, television, radio, and online media. They maintain an extensive list of links to U.S. newspapers: dailies (1,024), nondailies (1,184), campus (327), major metro (70), national (4), alternative (163), specialty (72), and business (6).

399. *Australian Newspaper Online.* http://www.nla.gov.au/npapers. Maintained by the National Library of Australia, this list is arranged by title, state, and town.

400. *News and Newspapers Online.* http://library.uncg.edu/news
This award-winning site is maintained by the Walter Clinton Jackson Library at the University of North Carolina at Greensboro. Unlike many other purported guides, it limits titles listed to current, up-to-date, freely available full-text papers. These are organized geographically beginning with the United States and Canada and ending with Africa. You can search by individual country or click on an interactive map.

401. *U.S. News Archives on the Web.* http://www.ibiblio.org/slanews/internet/archives.html

News division volunteers of the Special Libraries Association maintain this excellent guide to U.S. Newspaper Archives. Frequently updated, it's arranged alphabetically by region. Papers are listed alphabetically by state and town or city within a state and then by individual paper within a city or state. They provide links to the paper and its archive, and give dates of coverage and costs of searches. For the *Boston Globe* we learn it has searchable archives back to 1992. A search is free; retrievals cost $2.95 Monday-Friday 6:00 A.M.–6:00 P.M., otherwise they're available for $1.50. The *New York Times* has a searchable archive back to 1996 and charges $2.50 per article. You need a free password to search the archives. This is a very helpful site.

SPECIAL NEWSPAPER PROJECTS

402. *The Newsplan 2000 Project.* http://www.newsplan2000.org
The NEWSPLAN 2000 Project, supported by the Heritage Lottery fund and the U.K. Newspaper Industry, seeks to preserve unique and fragile collections of local newspapers held in libraries throughout the United Kingdom. The project will involve 1,700 local newspaper titles, 100,000 reels of microfilm, 33,000 volumes of newspapers, and 65 million pages of newsprint. The project is a £7.8 million initiative.

7

DISSERTATIONS AND THESES

Prior to 1940, bibliographical access to U.S. dissertations was largely confined to searching specialized lists published by the major doctorate-granting institutions on an irregular basis. These were generally confined to listing authors and titles. Access has dramatically improved since then largely through the pioneering efforts of one company, University Microfilms International. They have been abstracting dissertations since 1938 and making these available for purchase as a microfilm or a paper copy. Starting with a few institutions, this endeavor has grown to include over 99 percent of the accredited institutions of higher education in North America along with a growing number of universities throughout Europe and Asia. In 1997, UMI published nearly 55,000 doctoral dissertations and master's theses. The collection of dissertations in the UMI database, which includes the first U.S. dissertation published in 1861, has been indexed, abstracted, and archived. In 2002 UMI added its 1.5 millionth doctoral dissertation to its Dissertation Abstracts database. It also launched ProQuest Digital Dissertations on the World Wide Web [see 412]. Another promising development is the Networked Digital Library of Theses and Dissertations (NDLTD), which has grown

from a pilot program at Virginia Tech in 1996 to include 179 members [see 416].

GUIDES
AND REPOSITORIES

403. *The Center for Research Libraries (CRL).* 6050 South Kenwood Ave., Chicago, IL, 60637. Tel. (312) 955-4545. This nonprofit library was established in 1949 by 10 Midwestern universities in the United States and now has more than 100 members. With more than 750,000 uncataloged foreign doctoral dissertations, CRL maintains the largest collection of foreign dissertations in the world. Through various exchange or deposit arrangements with major western European universities, the CRL endeavors to provide access to virtually all dissertations produced outside of the United States and Canada. In addition to a basically complete collection of French dissertations since 1952, the CRL receives dissertations from 97 universities in Denmark, Finland, Germany, the Netherlands, Norway, Sweden, and Switzerland. It can also obtain abstracts of doctoral dissertations from Russia. The CRL Dissertations

Database may be searched from the online
Web site at http://www.crl.uchicago.edu/
dbdissertations/search:asp. To find additional
dissertations, search the CRLCATALOG at
http://catalog.crl.edu.

404. *Guide to the Availability of Theses.*
Compiled by D. H. Borchard and J. D.
Thawley. Munich: K. G. Saur, 1981. 444pp.
ISBN 3-598-20378-0.

405. *Guide to the Availability of Theses II,
Non-University Institutions.* Compiled by
G. G. Allen and K. Deubert. Munich: K. G.
Saur, 1984. 124pp. ISBN 3-598-20394-2.
Part 1 is an early printed guide to foreign
dissertations based on a survey of 698
institutions in 85 countries. The guide is
arranged alphabetically by country. Part 2
provides information on sources of dissertations from nonuniversity institutions such
as institutes of technology (outside of the
U.S.) and schools of theology, health, and
art. Since this survey was conducted in the
pre-Internet era, much of the information
it reports is no longer accurate. Regrettably,
no newer survey has been conducted.

406. *Guide to Theses and Dissertations: An
International Bibliography.* By Michael M.
Reynolds. Rev. and enl. ed. Phoenix, AZ:
Oryx, 1985. 263pp. ISBN 0-89774-149-8.
Surprisingly, this is the most recent print list
of dissertation and thesis bibliographies.
Reynolds has arranged his guide alphabetically by country and topically by subject.
The most useful sections for historians are
the chapters on universal sources and history sources. Of the some 3,000 titles listed,
180 deal specifically with history. Some of
the information is now dated.

GENERAL

International

407. *UMI Dissertation Services.* http://www.
umi.com/hp/support/Dservices
UMI publishes and archives dissertations
and theses, sells copies on demand, and
maintains the definitive bibliographic record for over 1.4 million doctoral dissertations and master's theses. Libraries provide
access to UMI's Dissertation Abstracts database through various reference products. In
2003 the following were being produced
and distributed:

Printed

408. *Dissertation Abstracts International
(DAI).*
DAI is the most current of the printed
sources and the only one to include abstracts for doctoral dissertations. Published
monthly and cumulated annually, it's available both in softcover and microfiche.

409. *Comprehensive Dissertation Index*
(CDI). Ann Arbor, MI: University
Microfilms International. (UMI), 1973–.
Annual. ISSN 0361-6657.
In 1973 University Microfilms International (UMI) published its landmark *Comprehensive Dissertation Index, 1861–1972*
(CDI) in 37 volumes. This edition, which
UMI refers to as the "main set," listed
417,000 dissertations from U.S. and Canadian institutions. Its sources of information
were *Dissertation Abstracts International, American Doctoral Dissertations* [see 417], lists from
the Library of Congress, and lists supplied
by graduate schools throughout North

America. This main set provides subject and key word access in the first 32 volumes and author access in the last five. Volume 28 is devoted to history. In 1984, UMI published a 10-year cumulative supplement for the years 1973–1982 in 38 volumes, listing an additional 351,000 dissertations. A five-year cumulation for the years 1983–1987 was issued in 22 volumes in 1988. Beginning with the 1988 annual supplement, the CDI began listing British dissertations along with the North American dissertations. As of 1999, *Comprehensive Dissertation Index* listed dissertations and theses from over 250 institutions outside of the United States and Canada.

410. *American Doctoral Dissertations (ADD).* Citations to virtually all U.S. dissertations for the academic year.

411. *Subject Catalogs for Dissertations and Theses.* On an irregular basis UMI has prepared catalogs of dissertations and theses in selected subjects. Copies are available for free from UMI by using their electronic order form at http://www.umi.com/hp/support/DServices/products/catalogs.htm.

Electronic Reference Tools

412. *ProQuest Digital Dissertations.* Online subscription service.
Provides access to more than 1.6 million entries. The Dissertation Abstracts database is the most comprehensive source for information about doctoral dissertations and master's theses. It includes works from over 1,000 graduate schools and universities. Each year they add 47,000 new disserta-

tions and 12,000 new theses to the database. For dissertations completed prior to 1980, only citations are available. From 1980 on, entries include 350-word abstracts written by the author. Citations to master's theses from 1988 forward include 150-word abstracts. The full text of more than 1 million titles is available in paper and microform for a fee ranging from $34 for unbound paper to $53 for hardcover paper. Free 24-page previews of dissertations and theses submitted from 1997 forward are available.

413. *Dissertation Abstracts Ondisc.*
A CD-ROM edition of the Dissertation Abstracts database (DAO) including both dissertations and theses. When paired with ProQuest Search Software, you can search each word in each citation since 1861 plus each word in the abstract for records after July 1980.

414. *Dissertation Abstracts Online.* Online database access is also available from a number of commercial online services.

415. *Master's Abstracts International.* Ann Arbor, MI: UMI, 1962–. Monthly. ISSN 0025-5106.
Bibliographic control for master's theses has been far less successful than that for doctoral dissertations. Coverage is far from complete. Currently, some 94 institutions provide abstracts of their theses to UMI. The arrangement is by the same subject classifications followed by *Dissertation Abstracts International* with an author index. A 15-year cumulative index to the first fifteen volumes was published in 1978 and listed 10,500 theses. In 1986 its name was

changed to *Master's Abstracts International,* which reflects the increased participation of European institutions. It is available online in machine-readable versions of *Dissertation Abstracts International* and is accessible through OCLC FirstSearch, Dialog, and BRS. More than 12,000 citations and abstracts are published each year.

416. *NDLTD: Networked Digital Library of Theses and Dissertations.* http://www.ndltd.org

The objectives of NDLTD are to improve graduate education by allowing students to produce electronic documents, use digital libraries, and understand issues in publishing. It also seeks to expand access, lower the cost of submitting and handling theses and dissertations, and advance digital library technology. The concept of electronic theses and dissertations (ETDs) was first discussed in 1987. In 1996 Virginia Tech piloted a project to enable students to submit ETDs both as SGML and PDF documents. Since that time the NDLTD has expanded to include 179 NDLTD members: 157 member universities (including 6 consortia and 22 institutions worldwide). Individual universities use NDLTD software and formats to mount their own Electronic Theses and Dissertation Files. At the University of Florida, for example, students have been able to submit theses electronically since 1998. It became a requirement for graduate students entering after fall 2001. In early 2003, 456 theses or dissertations were accessible at http://web.Uflib.ufl.edu/etd.html.

National

United States

417. *American Doctoral Dissertations (ADD).* Ann Arbor, MI: UMI, 1933–1934–. Annual. ISSN 0065-809X.

This annual list is compiled for the Association of Research Libraries (ARL) by UMI. It began as a successor to *List of American Doctoral Dissertations* (1912–1938) issued by the Library of Congress. The new annual list includes dissertations accepted for the Ph.D. by American and Canadian institutions and is compiled from corresponding issues of the *Dissertation Abstracts International* as well as from commencement programs and information gathered directly from the institutions. Organization is by broad subject categories going from "Agriculture" to "Zoology" and within these categories is arranged alphabetically by the name of the university granting the degree. There is also an author index. The dissertations listed in this source are also searchable through Dissertation Abstracts Online [see 414]. ADD lists virtually all dissertations written in the United States during the academic year, whether or not UMI published them.

Canada

418. *Theses Canada.* http://www.nlc-bnc.ca/6/4/index-e.html

The mission of Theses Canada is to acquire and preserve a comprehensive collection of Canadian theses at the National Library of Canada, to provide access to this valuable research within Canada and throughout the world, and to provide for their dissemination by interlibrary loan and sale. The "theses service" was launched in 1965 at the request of the deans of Canadian graduate schools. All theses processed were cataloged for listing in the national bibliography, *Canadiana*. The first theses microfilmed and published by the National Library were listed in the 1966 edition of *Canadiana: The National Bibliography*. In 1975, 28 universities were submitting theses to the program. By 2003 that number had grown to 55. On April 1, 2003, the Canadian Theses Service changed its name to Theses Canada. Chronology:

1965–1974 In-house service at NLC. Theses available only in microfilm.
1974–1990 NLC contracted with the National Archives for microfilming. Theses available on microfiche.
1990–1997 NLC had contracts with Micromedia Canada who filmed and acted as sales agent for Canadian theses, and with UMI Dissertations Publishing, which listed the theses in its databases.
1997–Present NLC has contracted with UMI to provide most services.

By 2002 there were over 220,000 theses and dissertations in the NLC collection, with 10,000 being added annually.

To locate a specific thesis in the NLC collection, you can search its free online catalog, AMICUS Web. To access AMICUS Web from the National Library home page, click on AMICUS, the Canadian National Catalogue at http://www.nlc-bnc.ca/amicus/index-e.html, then on AMICUS Web. Be sure to select National Library Collections as the database. You can do either a basic or an advanced search using a variety of indexes, including title, name, or subject key word, or ISBN. Theses can be borrowed from the NLC or purchased from ProQuest Information (parent of UMI).

419. *Doctoral Research on Canada and Canadians, 1884–1983.* By Jesse J. Dossick. Ottawa: Minister of Supply and Services Canada, 1986.

420. *Theses in Canada: A Bibliographic Guide.* 2nd ed. Ottawa: Minister of Supply and Services Canada, 1986. These older printed guides are still helpful for theses completed prior to the early 1980s.

Great Britain

421. *British Thesis Service.* London: British Library Document Supply Centre. http://www.bl.uk/services/document/brittheses.html
The British Thesis Service provides access to more than 165,000 theses submitted for doctorates from almost all U.K. universities. Subject indexed information may be found in the SIGLE (System for Information on Gray Literature in Europe) database available from GEM STN, International and Silver Platter. Records are also included in the document supply books file on the British Library Public Catalogue (BLPC), http://www.bl.uk. Another useful source of info on British theses is the *Index to Theses* [see 423].

422. *The Brits Index.* Ann Arbor, MI: UMI, 1989. 3 vols. ISBN 0-576-40018-1.
This publication was prepared by the British Library in association with UMI

and lists 68,000 dissertations completed at British universities between 1971 and 1987. Theses were microfilmed by the British Library but were never included in the UMI dissertations database. These volumes are a large subject index divided into eight broad categories with further subdivision into 79 disciplines. There are also accompanying author and subject indexes. Most of the titles listed in these volumes are available from the British Library Document Supply Centre. After July 1988, UMI began adding British dissertations to the UMI dissertation database, in association with the British Library, and now they appear in *Dissertation Abstracts International* [see 408].

423. *Index to Theses with Abstracts Accepted for Higher Degrees by the Universities of Great Britain and Ireland and the Council for National Academic Awards.* **London: Aslib, 1953–. Vol. 1 (for 1950–1951)–. Quarterly. ISSN 0073-6066.**

Generally referred to as simply the *Index to Theses*, this is the British equivalent of *Dissertation Abstracts International*. It has gone through a number of changes in format and frequency of publication. In November 1986 with volume 35, part 1, it assumed its present structure with the addition of abstracts and an enhanced subject index. Entries for dissertations are divided into eight broad categories which are then further arranged under detailed subject headings. In the case of history, it is listed in section A for the arts and humanities and given the numerical designation of 9. There are an additional sixteen subdivisions for history ranging from historiography (A9a) to military studies (A9s). Additional access is provided by author and subject indexes. Each calendar year volume lists about 9,000

dissertations awarded by some 50 universities. *Index to Theses* is now available online for subscribers at http://www.theses.com and is searchable by key word, title, author, degree, class, year, and university in both quick and advanced searches. This database covers theses accepted from 1970 on, and the file is updated approximately eight times a year.

424. *Retrospective Index to Theses of Great Britain and Ireland, 1716–1950.* **Edited by Roger R. Bilboul and Francis L. Kent. Santa Barbara, CA: ABC-CLIO, 1975. 5 vols. ISBN 0-903450-02-X.**

The purpose of this five-volume retrospective set is to provide information to scholars on the existence of theses completed for higher degrees in Great Britain and Ireland up to 1950, when Aslib began publishing its *Index to Theses*. The first volume focuses on the social sciences and humanities while the following four volumes cover the sciences. More than 13,000 doctoral dissertations and master's theses issued by 21 universities are listed in Volume 1. Coverage for most universities begins around 1900. Information supplied for the theses includes title, author, institution, degree, and date. The arrangement is alphabetical by title under specific subject headings borrowed from the *British Humanities Index* [see 312] with frequent cross references. There is also an author index.

Australia

425. *Australian Theses.*
Generally master's theses and dissertations are deposited at the library of the institution where the thesis or dissertation was granted. The National Library of Australia

does not receive a copy of every thesis presented to an Australian university. Their catalog, http://www.nla.gov.au, has entries for the theses held in the library's collections. Most of these are on microfiche or microfilm. If you are looking for a known thesis, search under the headings "Personal Author Keywords," "Title Keywords," or "Subject Keywords" and enter the term "Dissertation." The Australian Digital Theses Program is searchable online at http://adt.caul.edu.au. The National Bibliographic Database, accessible through Kinetica, lists materials held in the major libraries in Australia. The online catalogs of many Australian libraries are accessible through the Australian Libraries Gateway at http://www.nla.gov.au/libraries.

France

ThesesNet has now closed. To locate theses granted by French universities, check the "catalogue du Système Universitaire de Documentation" at http://www.sudoc.abes.fr. SuDoc enables you to search the collections of French university libraries and other schools of higher education. You can search by subject and sort by relevance. For example, a search for "Louisana" "theses" locates a dissertation done at Paris's Ett.E.S.S. in 1993.

Germany

426. *Deutsche National Bibliografie (ddb).* http://www.ddb.de/produkte/dnb.htm
German dissertations are listed in Reihe H, Hochschulschriften Verzeichnis, of the German National Bibliography. Previously the information was found in Reihe C, Dissertationen und Habilitationsschriften, and the

Hochschulscriften Verzeichnis. This is available in many research libraries. German theses are also listed in the online Deutsche Bibliothek Database available through RLIN.

Spain

427. *Bases de Datos de Tesis Doctorales (TESEO).* http://www.mcu.es/TESEO/index.html
La Secretaria del Consejo de Universidades has, among others, the function of publishing an annual list of doctorates awarded in Spanish universities. In April 1998 a special commission to review the granting of doctorates established guidelines for university studies leading to the granting of the title "Dr." The Base de Datos TESEO was established for bibliographic access to Spanish dissertations. You can search by author, title, institution, or key word "descriptores." Each entry lists the thesis director, tribunal, and an abstract in addition to the usual bibliographic information.

HISTORICAL

There are literally dozens of specialized lists of dissertations completed or in progress that are of interest to historians. These print lists are particularly useful for students and scholars seeking older history-related dissertations. A major development growing from the emergence of the World Wide Web is the improved access to recently completed dissertations and those in progress. Theses and dissertations may also be searched through the online databases *America: History and Life* and *Historical*

Abstracts. Several of the guides listed below are available online. In addition, many historical journals devoted to various countries, regions, states, or topics regularly list relevant theses and doctoral dissertations. For example, the *Journal of American History* [see 266] lists completed dissertations in its "Recent Scholarship" section. The items listed below are the main guides—both print and electronic—for historical dissertations written in English.

North America

428. *Directory of Dissertations in Progress.* Washington, DC: American Historical Association, 1976–. Annual. ISSN 0145-9929. http://www.theaha. org/pubs/dissertations
Published under various titles and formats, the American Historical Association has sponsored this list of completed dissertations and dissertations in progress since 1901. The primary purpose of these lists has been to register dissertation topics and so avoid duplicate research. The 2002–2003 directory available online contains 4,363 dissertations in progress at 171 academic departments in Canada and the United States. These dissertations in progress are submitted each summer by departments updating the *Directory of History Departments and Organizations in the United States and Canada.* The online file can be searched by author's last name, by school, or by key words in the title.

429. *Dissertations in History: An Index to Dissertations Completed in History Departments of the United States and Canadian Universities.* By Warren F. Kuehl.

Vol. 1, *1873–1960.* Lexington, KY: University of Kentucky Press, 1965. 249pp. Vol. 2, *1961–1970.* Lexington, KY: University of Kentucky Press, 1972. 237pp. ISBN 0-8131-1264-8; Vol. 3, *1970–June 1980.* Santa Barbara, CA: ABC-CLIO, 1985. 465pp. ISBN 0-87436-356-X.
The most useful and complete guide to historical dissertations completed at American and Canadian universities up to mid-1980, it lists almost 25,000 dissertations. Some 7,695 dissertations completed before 1960 appear in the first volume. The second volume has 5,891 awarded during the 1960s, and the third volume contains 10,077 dissertations finished in the 1970s. Superior subject indexing makes it easy to locate dissertations on specific topics. Both author and subject indexes are keyed to the entry numbers assigned to each individual dissertation.

430. *Canadian Historical Association (CHA) Register of Dissertations.* http://www. cha-sch.ca/english/rod.html
For more than 30 years, the Canadian Historical Association made available the *Register of Post-Graduate Dissertations in Progress in History and Related Subjects* (1966–1998). From 1927 to 1965 the list was published in the *Canadian Historical Review* [see 243]. Since 1999 the *Register* has been available online. The new version contains the same information as the previous printed versions with enhanced search capabilities. The primary purpose of the *Register* is to provide an inventory of all Ph.D. and M.A. theses in Canadian universities dealing with any aspect of history. The *Register* also lists theses in Canadian history undertaken in non-Canadian universities. In contrast to the annual printed *Register*, completed or

abandoned theses will not be removed from the online *Register*. The CHA hopes, in future, to be able to add completed theses cataloged in previous issues of the *Register* but subsequently removed.

Great Britain

431. *Historical Research for Higher Degrees in the United Kingdom*. Pt. 1, *Theses Completed*. Pt. 2, *Theses in Progress*. London: University of London, Institute of Historical Research, 1931–. Annual. ISSNs 0268-6716; 0268-6724. http://ihr.sas.ac.uk/ihr/Resources/Theses/tp01.html
Published under various titles since 1931, this publication has recorded theses awarded the B. Litt., B. Phil., and various master's degrees as well as the Ph.D. The entries listed in part 2 are arranged under broad subject headings ranging from Historiography to Australia and are also listed chronologically. There is an author index. This publication is issued annually in May based on information received from all of the universities in the United Kingdom. Recent lists have noted about 750 theses completed annually with over 3,400 in progress. Theses completed and theses in progress can be accessed electronically from IHR's History On-Line Web site. In mid-2003 theses completed from 1995 to 2000 and theses in progress for 2001 were available for browsing.

432. *History Theses, 1901–1970: Historical Research for Higher Degrees in the Universities of the United Kingdom*. By Phyllis M. Jacobs. London: University of London, Institute of Historical Research, 1976. 456pp. ISBN 0-901-17934-5.

433. *History Theses, 1971–1980: Historical Research for Higher Education in the Universities of the United Kingdom*. By Joyce M. Horn. London: University of London, Institute of Historical Research, 1984. 294pp. ISBN 0-901-17981-7.
The British equivalent of Kuehl's *Dissertations in History*, the first volume lists 7,633 B. Litt., master's, and doctoral theses in chronological order under broad subject categories ranging from the Philosophy of History to the Pacific Ocean and Islands. The second volume lists an additional 4,400 theses. Both volumes contain author and analytical subject indexes.

Australia

Postgraduate history theses currently in progress in Australian Universities are listed in the *Melbourne Historical Journal*. Founded in 1961 and published by postgraduate students in the University of Melbourne's Department of History, the *MHJ* is one of the longest running academic journals of its kind in Australia.

SPECIAL

434. *American Studies Dissertations Abstracts, 1986–2002*. http://www.georgetown.edu/crossroads/dis/dissertations_alphabetic.html
This list includes abstracts of dissertations completed in American studies programs that originally appeared in the December issue of *American Quarterly*. The online file is arranged alphabetically by author.

435. *African (IGBO) Scholarship: A Bibliography of Doctoral Dissertations and Some Masters Degree Theses at American, Canadian, and Australian Universities, 1945–1999.* By Uju Nkwocha Afulezi and Ijeoma Ogwogo Afulezi. Vol. 1. Lanham, MD: University Press of America, 2000. 336pp. ISBN 0-7618-1851-0.
This book is the first volume of what the authors hope will be an ongoing bibliography of African-related doctoral and master's work conducted by African American scholars. They describe it as an educational audit and note there is presently no separate database for African and African-related dissertations and theses.

436. *Asian Studies in Hawaii: A Guide to Theses and Dissertations.* Edited by Laurianne Chun. Honolulu: University of Hawaii Press, 1998. 576pp. ISBN 0-8248-2049-5.
This is a fully annotated bibliography of more than 2,000 Asia-related master's theses and doctoral dissertations completed at the University of Hawaii from 1925 to 1994.

437. *Doctoral Dissertations on China and on Inner Asia, 1976–1990.* Vol. 2, *An Annotated Bibliography of Studies in Western Languages.* By Frank Shulman, Patricia Pulansky, and Anna Leon Shulman. Westport, CT: Greenwood, 1998. 1,088pp. ISBN 0-313-29111-X.
The development of Chinese, Mongolian, and Tibetan studies in the West since World War II has been accompanied by a tremendous expansion in the number of doctoral degrees awarded. This bibliography lists more than 10,000 dissertations in all fields.

More than half do not appear in the *DAI* database. Entries are classified and grouped together in topical chapters. See also *Doctoral Dissertations on Hong Kong, 1900–1997: An Annotated Bibliography of Worldwide Research,* by Frank J. Schulman and Anna L. Schulman (Hong Kong University Press, 2002), which summarizes 2,395 dissertations accepted at 415 universities in 29 countries. Three appendixes bring coverage up to 1999. The bibliographical journal *Doctoral Dissertations on Asia (1975–1993)* ceased after volume 16 for 1993 was published in 1996.

438. *Theses on Africa Accepted by Universities and Polytechnics in the United Kingdom and Ireland, 1976–1988.* By Colin Hewson, Helen C. Price, and David Blake. Munich: Hans Zell, 1993. 350pp. ISBN 1-873836-35-X.
Published on behalf of the Standing Conference on Library Materials on Africa (SCOLMA), this book describes 4,000 theses accepted by universities in the United Kingdom and Ireland between 1976 and 1988. It is a continuation of SCOLMA's *Theses on Africa, 1963–1975.* All fields are covered. Contents are arranged by country, region, and subject. There are also author and subject indexes. For similar coverage of North American institutions, see *American and Canadian Doctoral Dissertations and Master's Theses on Africa, 1974–1987.* Compiled by Alfred Kagan, Gregory Larkin, and Joseph J. Lauer for the African Studies Association. Atlanta, GA: Crossroads Press, Emory University, 1989. 377pp. ISBN 0-918456-63-0.

8

GOVERNMENT PUBLICATIONS AND LEGAL SOURCES

Historical researchers often neglect government publications, even though they provide a wealth of primary information. This chapter's purpose is to introduce the major guides, indexes, bibliographies, and electronic and Internet resources used for locating government publications, both in the United States and other countries. It is not meant to be totally comprehensive and tries to provide guidance to the beginning researcher. By the nature of government publications, this chapter will emphasize the 20th century, although there are indexes covering 18th- and 19th-century documents. A distinction is also made between official government publications and archival and manuscript sources, which will be covered in a separate chapter.

It is important to understand how the U.S. government publishes and distributes its publications in order to understand the associated guides and indexes. Most U.S. documents are published by the U.S. Government Printing Office and distributed by the Superintendent of Documents to libraries participating in the Depository Library Program. These documents are divided into three main groups—congressional or legislative, judicial, and executive. They are classified by the Superintendent

of Documents, or SuDoc, classification system. It is a complex system, and this chapter will discuss the introductory guides and some of the specialized indexes that support it. Increasingly, U.S. government publications are available only through accessing the World Wide Web. Internet access to U.S. government documents will also be discussed.

Guides and bibliographies for Canadian, British, European, Soviet, Japanese, United Nations, and other international organizations' official publications will also be listed in this chapter. Another section will selectively cover guides to legal sources such as constitutions, treaties, and other international agreements, laws, and court decisions. There will be a separate section on electronic and Internet law resources at the end of the chapter.

GOVERNMENT PUBLICATIONS

General

439. *Guide to Official Publications of Foreign Countries.* **By American Library**

Association, Government Documents Round Table. 2nd ed. Bethesda, MD: Congressional Information Service, 1997. 494pp.

Under the guidance of Gloria Westfall as editor in chief, this work is a revised edition of the original guide, which was published in 1990. Its purpose is to provide an overview of the official publications of 178 countries. Categories of publications covered include guides to official publications, bibliographies and catalogs, sources of general information on the country, government directories and organization manuals, statistical yearbooks, laws, regulations, and constitutions, legislative proceedings, statements of the head of government, economic affairs, central bank publications, development plans, budget, census, health, labor, education, court reports, environment, and human rights and status of women. The work is arranged alphabetically by country, and the publications for that country are selected by a number of contributing editors, who are librarians specializing in those materials. Emphasis is on recent material published during the 1990s, and there is an index of titles arranged by country. This is an excellent starting point for locating key official publications of particular countries.

United States

Guides

440. *Guide to U.S. Government Publications.* Edited by Donna Andriot. Manassas, VA: Documents Index, 1973–. Annual.

Formerly known as *Guide to U.S. Government Serials and Periodicals*, this annual work includes over 35,000 entries. Often referred to by documents librarians as "Andriot," this guide is the best source for locating the Superintendent of Documents (SuDoc) classification number, the number assigned to U.S. government documents and serial publications. It has an agency, title, and key word in title index, as well as a complete list of SuDoc classification numbers, including the way agency numbers have changed over the years. This historical section is valuable for locating earlier SuDoc numbers for particular agency serials that have changed classification numbers. Andriot also has the advantage over the *Periodicals Supplement* to the *Monthly Catalog of United States Government Publications*, in that it lists serials that have ceased as well as current ones.

441. *Government Information on the Internet.* Edited by Peggy Garvin. 5th ed. Lanham, MD: Bernan, 2002. 990pp. ISBN 0-89059-587-9.

The major change in locating government information in recent years has been the growing amount of material that can be found on the Internet. Garvin's book, which continues the original work of Greg R. Notess, covers over 4,800 government Web sites, including U.S. government, as well as state, foreign, and international sites. In addition, there are detailed descriptions of many of these sites and material on over 1,400 online publications found on government Web sites. Government Internet resources are arranged by topics such as agriculture, business and economics, census and other statistical sources, Congress, education, environment, general reference sources, health sciences, legal information, libraries, military, science, social services, technology and engineering, and the

White House. Emphasis is on the U.S. federal government but there are extensive chapters on state, local, and international sites. Each chapter begins with a listing of featured sites and then divides into subcategories of a specific topic. Individual entries include title, primary and alternate URL (Internet address), sponsors, a brief description, subjects covered by the site, and publications available at that site. Bernan has recently come out with an online version of Garvin's work, which will allow for more frequent updates, and is making it available on a subscription basis. A sixth edition will be published in 2003, with updated material on the new Department of Homeland Security. Internet addresses are constantly changing, but this work serves as an excellent beginning guide for the researcher exploring the wealth of government information on the Internet.

442. *Locating United States Government Information: A Guide to Sources.* **By Edward Herman. 2nd ed. Buffalo, NY: William S. Hein, 1997. 580pp. ISBN 1-57588-203-5. Internet supplement, 2001. 228pp. ISBN 1-57588-683-9.**

This work, written by an experienced documents librarian, is the most comprehensive printed guide to U.S. government documents currently available. Wide-ranging in its coverage, it begins with an introduction to the Superintendent of Documents classification system and includes chapters on indexes to historical documents, Congressional publications, statistical resources, federal regulations, and census information. Recently added was a separate Internet supplement volume, which links Internet resources to the chapters in the main volume. The supplement contains detailed abstracts for each entry, as well as the URL for reaching the location on the World Wide Web. Herman's work can be supplemented by several other volumes, including the latest edition of Joe Morehead, *Introduction to United States Government Information Sources,* 6th ed. (Englewood, CO: Libraries Unlimited, 1999); Gayle J. Hardy and Judith Schiek Robinson, *Subject Guide to U.S. Government Reference Sources* (Englewood, CO: Libraries Unlimited, 1996); and Judith Schiek Robinson, *Tapping the Government Grapevine* (Phoenix, AZ: Oryx, 1998).

Indexes

443. *Catalog of the Public Documents of the Congress and of All Departments of the Government of the United States, March 4, 1893–December 31, 1940.* **Washington, DC: Government Printing Office, 1896–1945. 25 vols.**

Intended to be a "comprehensive index" to both congressional and departmental documents, the *Document Catalog* starts where Ames's *Comprehensive Index* (see 452) ends in 1893 (53rd Congress). The work, each volume of which generally covers a single congressional session, is arranged in an alphabetical sequence, with detailed entries under author, subject, and, in some cases, title. Entries are quite detailed and in many cases the *Serial Set* volume number for individual documents is given. An essential index for locating early 20th-century historical documents that parallels the coverage of the *Monthly Catalog* until 1940, this index's main drawback is that it does not provide Superintendent of Documents classification numbers for locating individual documents.

444. *Checklist of United States Public Documents, 1789–1909.* 3rd ed., rev. and enl. Washington, DC: Government Printing Office, 1911. Reprint, Kraus, 1962. 1,707pp. One of the standard sources for locating historical U.S. documents, this massive volume, as its title indicates, is a checklist, containing information on congressional publications through the close of the 60th Congress and departmental publications to the end of the calendar year 1909. Within the *Checklist* congressional publications are arranged by congressional session, and departmental publications are arranged by Superintendent of Documents classification number. Not very easy to use for someone unfamiliar with the Superintendent of Documents classification system, the *Checklist* is particularly valuable because it lists the Congressional Serial Set number for many documents, which is the volume number for locating a copy of that document.

445. *CIS Annual Index to Congressional Publications and Public Laws.* Bethesda, MD: Congressional Information Service, 1970–. ISBN 0-88692-464-2 (set).

Lexis Nexis Congressional, 1970–. www.lexisnexis.com
This index, the standard CIS index to recent congressional documents on which all the other CIS retrospective indexes are based, is available in print form and electronically on LexisNexis Congressional. Both cover from 1970 to the present and provide access to House and Senate reports, documents, hearings, and committee prints from 1970 to the present. Detailed indexing provides access to Congressional publications by subject, name, title, bill number, document number, hearing number, print

number, and Superintendent of Documents call number. There is information about witnesses who testified at a hearing and separate legislative histories for all the public laws passed during this period. The major difference between the CIS Index and LexisNexis Congressional is that the electronic source also provides the researcher access to the full text of a wide variety of legislative materials, most from the late 1980s to the present. These include congressional hearings, committee reports, bills, committee prints, congressional documents, Federal Register, U.S. Code, and public laws. Full-text coverage varies depending on the item. There is also access to the recent text of the *Congressional Record*, individual voting records, and material from the *National Journal* and *Congress Daily*.

LexisNexis Congressional is an excellent source for recent in-depth information on the Congress and any legislation introduced during the period from 1970 to the present.

446. *CIS Index to U.S. Senate Executive Documents and Reports: Covering Documents Not Printed in the U.S. Serial Set, 1817–1969.* 2 vols. Bethesda, MD: Congressional Information Service, 1987. ISBN 0-8869-2130-9.
This CIS index provides access to over 4,000 Senate executive documents and reports from 1817–1969 not published in the Serial Set and not included in CIS *U.S. Serial Set Index* [see 450]. These documents are on microfiche, and the first volume of the index helps locate them by subject, name, place, title, document, and report numbers. A second reference bibliography volume contains information about each document's title, collation, official number,

and date, and gives a summary of its subject matter.

447. *CIS Index to Unpublished U.S. House of Representatives Committee Hearings, 1833–1968.* 12 vols. Bethesda, MD: Congressional Information Service, 1988–. ISBN 0-8869-2152-X (set).

448. *CIS Index to Unpublished U.S. Senate Committee Hearings, 1823–1980.* Bethesda, MD: Congressional Information Service, 1986–. 9 vols. ISBN 0-8869-2089-2.

These two Congressional Information Service (CIS) publications provide access to a wealth of previously unpublished Congressional hearings. They index thousands of hearings not included in the original set of CIS hearings covering 1833–1969 (see 449). The index to House hearings provides access to over 20,000 unpublished hearings on microfiche covering 1833 to 1968. The index to Senate hearings provides access to over 9,000 hearings on microfiche from 1823 to 1980, with future hearings still being published. The House index is divided into six parts and the Senate index into five parts by time period. Each index volume accesses the hearings by subject and organization, personal name, bill number, and title. Separate reference bibliography volumes provide more detailed bibliographic information including title, date, issuing committee and subcommittee, witnesses, page locations of testimony, subject descriptors, and bill numbers.

449. *CIS U.S. Congressional Committee Hearings Index, 1833–1969.* Washington, DC: Congressional Information Service, 1981–1985. 42 vols. ISBN 0-88692-050-7 (set).

This excellent index from the Congressional Information Services (CIS), a major publisher of reference aids for locating U.S. government documents, is the definitive retrospective index to congressional committee hearings. Covering from the 23rd Congress (December 1833) through the 91st Congress, 1st Session (1969), the index provides detailed indexing of committee hearings for the period before the CIS annual congressional indexes began. Divided into eight parts, each covering several congresses, the index provides access to over 30,000 publications available for purchase on microfiche. Each index part consists of several sections, including reference bibliography volumes, listing detailed bibliographic data on individual hearings, as well as indexes by subject, organization, personal names, title, bill number, Superintendent of Documents classification number, and report or document number.

450. *CIS U.S. Serial Set Index, 1789–1969.* Washington, DC: Congressional Information Service, 1975–1979, 1995–1998. 56 vols. ISBN 0-912380-26-8. LC 75-27448.

Another CIS index that has greatly simplified searching for historical material is the *U.S. Serial Set*, which consists of thousands of volumes containing congressional and executive documents and reports dating back to the 1st Congress (1789). Divided into fourteen parts, each covering a number of congressional sessions, the index is arranged chronologically, covering from the *American State Papers* (1789) through the 91st Congress, 1st session (1969), after which the CIS annual indexes begin. Each of the first 12 parts consists of a detailed alphabetical subject index, a numerical list of reports and documents arranged by congress and session, a schedule of serial volumes, and an index of names of individuals and organizations covered by private relief and related actions. The last two parts, which were published from 1995 to 1998, provide more detailed indexing to bill numbers and maps. They are also arranged chronologically by Congress and session. This multivolume set makes it extremely easy to locate historical material by subject in the original *Serial Set* volumes.

451. *Congressional Indexes, 1789–1969.*
www.lexisnexis.com
All the material in the CIS *U.S. Congressional Committee Hearings Index, CIS U.S. Serial Set Index, CIS Index to Unpublished U.S. Senate Committee Hearings, CIS Index to Unpublished U.S. House of Representatives Committee Hearings, CIS Index to U.S. Senate Executive Documents and Reports*, along with that in the *CIS U.S. Congressional Committee Prints Index*, from 1789 to 1969, is accessible electronically on a Web-based product from LexisNexis called Congressional Indexes. Researchers can search hundreds of thousands of records and almost 200 years of material in these indexes in one search and locate the actual document on microfiche or in hard copy.

452. *Comprehensive Index to the Publications of the United States Government, 1881–1893.* Compiled by John G. Ames. Washington, DC: Government Printing Office, 1905. 2 vols. 1,590pp. House Document no. 754, 58th Congress, 2nd session, Serial Set no. 4745-46.
Although not totally comprehensive, as its title implies, Ames's work fills the gap between Poore's *Descriptive Catalogue* [see

454], which stops in 1881, and the first volumes of the *Document Catalog* [see 443], whose coverage begins in 1893. The work is basically an alphabetical key word list of documents, with documents being listed by congressional session and document number. Under a separate heading, "Congressional documents," the Serial Set volume numbers for individual documents are listed. There is also a personal name index at the end of the volumes, referring the user to a page where an individual is mentioned. Not as detailed an index as the *Document Catalog*, Ames is still useful for finding documents published during this period.

453. *Cumulative Title Index to United States Public Documents, 1789–1976.* Compiled by Daniel W. Lester, Sandra K. Faull, and Lorraine E. Lester. Arlington, VA: United States Historical Documents Institute, 1979–1982. 16 vols.
This multivolume work is basically an alphabetical title list to the U.S. documents contained in the Public Documents Library of the Government Printing Office, now known as the Printed Archives Branch of the National Archives. The entries include the following information: title, publication date, and, most importantly, Superintendent of Documents classification number. A key advantage of this work is that it indexes an extensive collection of documents by title, serving as a quick source for the researcher searching for the government call number for an item, without having to search several other indexes.

454. *A Descriptive Catalogue of the Government Publications of the United States, September 5, 1774–March 4, 1881.* Compiled by Ben Perley Poore. Washington, DC: Government Printing Office, 1885. 1,392pp. Senate Miscellaneous Document no. 67, 48th Congress, 2nd Session, Serial Set no. 2268.

Poore's work marks the earliest attempt at publishing a complete list of all government publications, including executive, congressional, and judicial documents. Covering from 1774 to 1881, the work is divided into two parts: (1) the catalog, where the entries are arranged chronologically, and (2) the index, which refers the user to a page number where the entry is found. Poore has its drawbacks; it is not complete in its coverage, the index is not the most comprehensive, and the entries do not include the Serial Set volume number. Despite these drawbacks and the fact that much of Poore's coverage has been superseded by the *U.S. Serial Set Index*, it can still be a useful guide to 19th-century documents.

455. *Monthly Catalog of United States Government Publications.* Washington, DC: Government Printing Office, 1895–.

This is the major index to U.S. government documents, serving as a bibliography of congressional, departmental, and agency publications. Published monthly since 1895, *Monthly Catalog* entries are arranged alphabetically by issuing agency, and it is indexed on a monthly and annual basis. Entries include the full bibliographic citation as well as the Superintendent of Documents classification number. Since 1941, there have been decennial cumulative indexes to the *Monthly Catalog*, covering 1941 to 1960, and five-year indexes covering 1961 to 1985. In addition, Pierian Press has published several cumulative personal author indexes, covering 1941 to 1970. Also, Car-

rollton Press has published a massive 15-volume *Cumulative Subject Index to the Monthly Catalog of United States Government Publications, 1900–1971*, which indexes 70 years of *Monthly Catalog* volumes in one source.

In more recent years the *Monthly Catalog* has moved away from the print format, which is still published in an abridged version, and toward electronic access. It began to be published first on CD-ROM and currently on the World Wide Web. The official version is available on the World Wide Web through GPO Access, which is the Superintendent of Documents gateway to a number of government electronic indexes, from 1994 to the present. It is also available on OCLC First Search service as GPO, starting from 1976. The *Monthly Catalog* today indexes both electronic and print government documents. It remains the standard index to U.S. government publications, but electronic access through sources such as GPO and GPO Access has opened up a number of other ways for locating recent titles.

456. *Monthly Checklist of State Publications.* By U.S. Library of Congress. Washington, DC: Government Printing Office, 1910–1994.

Although not totally comprehensive in its coverage and no longer being published, this is the most complete retrospective bibliographic guide available for locating state government publications. *Monthly Checklist* lists state publications, both monographs and periodicals, received by the Library of Congress. Monographs in each monthly issue are arranged alphabetically by state and issuing agency; periodicals are listed semiannually in June and December, with the December list being the cumulative list for the year. The entries list full bibliographic information, including price and availability if known. With coverage going back to 1910, this is the best place to start for the historian looking for 20th-century state publications. For more access to current state publications, check the World Wide Web and the state government home pages of each of the 50 states.

457. Public Documents of the First Fourteen Congresses, 1789–1817: Papers Relating to Early Congressional Documents. Compiled by A. W. Greely. Washington, DC: Government Printing Office, 1900. 903pp. Senate Document no. 428, 56th Congress, 1st Session, Serial Set no. 3879.
Covering congressional documents from 1789 to 1817, Greely's work focuses on the period before the *Tables and Index* [see 458] volume begins. Arranged chronologically by Congress and by type of document, this work parallels Poore's *Descriptive Catalogue* in its coverage, but the documents listed do not contain the Serial Set volume numbers. A supplement, also prepared by Greely, was published in volume 1 of the *Annual Report of the American Historical Association, 1903.* Greely is basically a chronological catalog that has largely been superseded by the *U.S. Serial Set Index.* However, it can still be useful because it may be necessary to check several indexes for this period to locate a specific document.

458. Tables of and Annotated Index to the Congressional Series of United States Public Documents. Washington, DC: Government Printing Office, 1902. 769pp.
This one-volume work indexes congressional and executive documents published in the *Serial Set* from the 15th through the

52nd Congresses, 1817–1893. Covering roughly the same period as Poore's *Descriptive Catalogue* and Ames's *Comprehensive Index*, the *Tables and Index* is divided into two parts: (1) tables listing the *American State Papers* and documents from the 15th through 52nd Congresses by *Serial Set* volume number, and (2) a detailed subject and name index to these documents. Although the tables portion has been superseded by the *Checklist,* and the *CIS Serial Set Index* provides more detailed subject searching, this work can still prove useful for finding obscure documents published during this period.

Internet Sources

459. GPO Access. Washington, DC: U.S. Government Printing Office. http://www.gpoaccess.gov
GPO Access, which grew out of the Government Printing Office Electronic Information Enhancement Act of 1993, provides free electronic access to a wealth of information produced by the U.S. government. This includes access to over 1,500 databases of federal information, including the *Federal Register, Code of Federal Regulations, Congressional Record, Congressional Bills, Public Laws, U.S. Code, Supreme Court Decisions,* and *Commerce Business Daily.* Users can also search more than 1,350 official U.S. federal agency and military Internet sites and download over 7,500 individual agency files. Much of the material is available full text. There are also topical links to a number of government Web sites and subject bibliographies, including the Library of Congress American Memory site. This site contains a collection called "A Century of Lawmaking for a New Nation: U.S. Congressional Documents and Debates, 1774–

1873," which includes the full text of the *Journals of the Continental Congress*, volumes of the *U.S. Statutes at Large* from 1789–1873, *House* and *Senate Journals*, and complete coverage of the *Annals of Congress*, *Register of Debates*, and *Congressional Globe*, forerunners of today's *Congressional Record*. More and more material is regularly being added to GPO Access as the government focuses on putting out more information in electronic format.

460. *Thomas: Legislative information on the Internet*. Washington, DC: Library of Congress. http://thomas.loc.gov
Thomas, named after Thomas Jefferson, is the main Library of Congress Web site for accessing recent legislative information for the U.S. Congress. It provides current access to legislative information, such as public laws, bills, *Congressional Record,* committee reports, and committee home pages. The full text of bills and laws goes back to 1989, although there are summaries and legislative histories of House and Senate bills dating back to 1973. There are links to historical documents and a link to the same part of the Library of Congress American Memory Project available through GPO Access. Thomas also provides access to a number of links to other federal agencies' Web sites through the Library of Congress.

461. *University of Michigan Documents Center*. Ann Arbor, MI: University of Michigan Libraries. http://www.lib. umich.edu/govdocs
This University of Michigan libraries site is an excellent place to start for any type of documents information, whether local, state, federal, foreign, or international. There are extensive separate links to U.S. government sites, as well as state, country, and international Web sites. The federal government links are broken down into areas such as directories and Web sites, bibliographies, budget, civil service, copyright, executive branch, judicial branch, legislative branch, president, and many others. Clicking on any main topic gets you to a page where there are further subject links to other resources on the Internet. Regularly updated, this is a good site to bookmark for U.S. government information on the World Wide Web.

Canada

Guides

462. *Canadian Official Publications*. By Olga B. Bishop. New York: Pergamon, 1981. Guides to Official Publications, vol. 9. 291pp. ISBN 0-08-024697-4. LC 80-41572.
Written by Professor Bishop, who for many years taught government documents at the University of Toronto, this work, while dated, remains the best single introductory guide to Canadian publications. It focuses on Canadian federal government documents, including publications of the Canadian Parliament. Other topical chapters cover reference sources, statistics, the Public Archives of Canada, and federal-provincial relations; there is also a chapter explaining the classification and indexing schemes for Canadian documents. Bishop's work focuses only on federal publications; for an introduction to the publications of the provinces and territories, consult Catherine A. Pross, *Guide to the Identification and Acquisition of Canadian Government Publications: Provinces and Territories* (Halifax, Nova Scotia: Dalhousie University School of Library Service, 1983).

Bibliographies

463. *Federal Royal Commissions in Canada, 1867–1966: A Checklist.* By George Fletcher Henderson. Toronto: University of Toronto Press, 1967. 212pp. LC 68-91146.
Henderson's work is important for researchers in Canadian history because it provides a guide to the wealth of primary document material published by the federal royal commissions. Covering a 100-year period from 1867 to 1966, *Checklist* is arranged chronologically and includes information on almost 400 of these bodies and their reports. Entries include information on the appointment of each royal commission, the names of the commissioners, whether or not its report has been printed, and where the report is located. There is a detailed index for locating commissioners, titles, and authors of special studies, and the main subjects of commissions and special studies. More recently, Henderson's work has been updated by two titles: Susan Krywolt and Evelyn Piush, *Federal Royal Commissions in Canada, 1966–1977: An Update* (Edmonton, Alberta, 1977); and Anna Bombak, *Canadian Royal Commissions, 1978–1988: An Update* (Guelph, Ontario: University of Guelph Library, 1989).

464. *Canadian Government Publications: Catalogue; Government of Canada Publications. Quarterly Catalogue.* Ottawa, Canada: Canadian Government Publishing Centre, 1909–1992.
For the history student, this was, until recently, the most comprehensive guide to 20th-century Canadian documents. The Canadian equivalent of the U.S. *Monthly Catalog*, it was the major bibliography of Canadian government publications. Issued quarterly, this periodical has changed title and frequency several times over the years; it began publication during the first decade of the 20th century. Most recently each issue of *Government of Canada Publications* was divided into three parts: (1) Parliamentary publications, (2) departmental publications, and (3) index, which cumulates at the end of each year. The Parliamentary publications are arranged by type of document and the departmental documents are listed alphabetically by issuing agency. Since 1993 recent Canadian government publications are available on the World Wide Web through the *Weekly Checklist Catalogue*, the Canadian Depository Service Program's searchable catalog of information about Canadian government documents. Searching back issues of the *Weekly Checklist* from 1995 is available at the Government of Canada Depository Services Program Web site at http://dsp-psd.communication.gc.ca/index-e.html. The *Quarterly Catalogue* and *Weekly Checklist* are supplemented by a private publication: *Canadian Research Index: Microlog* (Toronto: Micromedia, 1982–). It is available both on CD-ROM and Internet access and includes hundreds of titles not included in the official government lists.

Great Britain

Guides

465. *A Guide to British Government Publications.* By Frank Rodgers. New York: H. W. Wilson, 1980. 750pp. ISBN 0-8242-0617-7. LC 80-322.
Although dated, this work remains an

excellent introductory guide to British official publications up to the late 1970s, covering Parliament as well as individual government departments. The volume is divided into three parts: (1) general, (2) Parliamentary, and (3) executive agencies. Part 1 serves as a general introduction, covering the British Constitution and government and how British government publications are organized. Part 2 covers Parliamentary publications, including the sessional papers, reports of debates, and Parliamentary committees. Part 3 is the largest section, covering the government departments arranged by subject chapters that include material on each department's origins, history, major changes in function, and publications. There is a glossary of terms and a general index at the end. Two more recent guides supplement Rodgers's work. They are Stephen Richard, *Directory of British Official Publications: A Guide to Sources* (London: Mansell, 1984); and David Butcher, *Official Publications in Britain* (London: Library Association, 1991).

Indexes and Bibliographies

466. BOPCRIS (British Official Publications Collaborative Reader Information Service). http://www.bopcris.org.uk
BOPCRIS is an excellent example of what can be done to provide access to historical documents through the power of the Internet. This is a joint project of a number of British libraries, including those at the University of Leeds, Cambridge University, Edinburgh University, University of Southampton, Glasgow University, Queen's University Belfast, University of Wales, University of London, University of Newcastle upon Tyne, University of Warwick,

and the British Library. It provides researchers detailed Web access to information from 23,279 British official publications from 1688 to 1995. The entire database or parts of it can be searched. Abstracts and detailed subject indexing are available for some of the documents and a small portion are available full-text. Researchers can do a simple search, which searches for words in parts or all of a record, a more detailed advanced search using Boolean search terms, or browse by broad subject categories. Abstracts are constantly being added to individual records and more full text of documents continues to appear. BOPCRIS is wonderful for researchers because they can freely search thousands of British documents, learn the nearest location of a particular document, and read the full text of some of the documents online. There are many more British documents than will appear in BOPCRIS, but this is an excellent beginning in terms of revolutionizing access to materials previously only accessible through print or microform sources.

467. *Catalogue of British Official Publications Not Published by TSO*. Cambridge, U.K.: Chadwyck-Healey (ProQuest), 1980–. Bimonthly; annual cumulations.
More than 50 percent of British government publications are not published by the Stationery Office (TSO), the official publishing agency of the British government. This reference source, published by Chadwyck-Healey, which is owned by ProQuest, fills a need by providing access to these publications. The *Catalogue* appears six times a year and covers publications since 1980 from more than 500 official organizations. Publications listed include monographs,

periodicals, pamphlets, technical reports, and audiovisual material. Many of the items listed in the *Catalogue* are available on microfiche from Chadwyck-Healey.

468. *General Alphabetical Index to the Bills, Reports, Estimates, Accounts, and Papers Printed by Order of the House of Commons, and to the Papers Presented by Command, 1801-1948/49.* London: Her Majesty's Stationery Office, 1853-1960.

This work is the major cumulative index to all publications printed by the House of Commons or presented to the House. It presently consists of three 50-year cumulative indexes, 1801–1852, 1852–1899, and 1900–1949, which are cumulated from the earlier annual and decennial indexes. Each cumulative index is arranged alphabetically by broad subject area and the entries give detailed location information. These index volumes do not contain information on the papers of the House of Lords, unless they are duplicated in the House of Commons papers. They also do not index publications of the various government bureaus and departments. The first two of these 50-year indexes are reprinted in the eight-volume *Irish University Press Series of British Parliamentary Papers* (Shannon, Ireland: Irish University Press, 1968). Until the publication of the *Subject Catalogue of the House of Commons Parliamentary Papers, 1801–1900* [see 474], these indexes were the best source for finding 19th century British documents.

469. *Hansard's Catalogue and Breviate of Parliamentary Papers, 1696–1834.* **Reprinted in facsimile with an introduction by Percy Ford and Grace Ford. Oxford: Basil Blackwell, 1953. 220pp.**

For the period of 1696 to 1834 an indispensable aid is this reprint of the *Catalogue of Parliamentary Reports, and a Breviate of Their Contents.* It was originally issued by the House of Commons in 1836 and indexes what is known as the First Series of Parliamentary Reports (15 volumes), the reports that appeared in the *Journals of the House of Commons*, and the reports located in the *Sessional Papers* from 1801 to 1834. These publications are classified under 26 broad subject categories, such as education and charities, trade and manufactures, agriculture, and public works. Each entry lists the location of the document and the subjects it covers. This reprint also includes a select list of House of Lords Papers not found in the original *Catalogue.*

470. *HMSO Annual Catalogue, 1922–1995.* **London: Her Majesty's Stationery Office, 1923–1995.**

471. *Stationery Office Annual Catalogue, 1996–.* **London: Stationery Office, 1997–.**

Until 1996 British government publications were published and distributed by Her Majesty's Stationery Office (HMSO) and the guide to these publications was the *HMSO Annual Catalogue,* published since 1836 and in its most recent form since 1922. In 1996 HMSO was privatized and its publications are currently being published and distributed by The Stationery Office (TSO). These annual cumulative volumes are the British equivalent of the U.S. Government Printing Office's *Monthly Catalog.* They cumulate the monthly issues published by TSO and serve as an index to all British government publications printed by the agency. Each annual volume is divided into sections listing Parliamentary publications, non-Parliamentary publications, and Northern Ireland publications, with an alphabetical index at the end. A private publisher, Carrollton Press, has made it easier for the researcher trying to track down 20th-century British publications by publishing a *Cumulative Index to the Annual Catalogue of Her Majesty's Stationery Office Publications, 1922–1972.* This two-volume work covers a 50-year period and gives references to the original catalogues. The latest official British government publications are accessible at The Stationery Office's Web site at http://www.tso.co.uk/bookshop/bookstore.asp.

472. *Index to Current House of Commons Parliamentary Papers.* CD-ROM. Alexandria, VA: Chadwyck-Healey (ProQuest), 1991–. Quarterly.

This CD-ROM provides electronic access to locating recent House of Commons Parliamentary Papers from late 1991 to the present. It indexes three categories of Parliamentary Papers: Bills, Command Papers, and House of Commons Papers by title, subject, key word, session, paper number, and date. The index gives the number for locating the Parliamentary Papers in the microfiche collection of these documents published by Chadwyck-Healey.

473. *Index to the House of Commons Parliamentary Papers on CD-ROM, 1801–1999.* Cambridge, U.K.: Chadwyck-Healey (ProQuest), 1996–.

This is the only index providing subject access to 200 years of British Parliamentary Papers in one location. The material from the nineteenth century is taken from Chadwyck-Healey's *Subject Catalogue of the House of Commons Parliamentary Papers, 1801–1900* [see 474]. More recent material is taken from *HMSO General Alphabetical Indexes,* which cover from 1900 to 1979, and the *Parliamentary Online Indexing Service* (POLIS), which covers from 1979 to the present. The index can be searched a number of different ways, including subject, title, paper type, paper number, key word, session, and chairmen of committees. Material found in the index can be located on the accompanying Chadwyck-Healey microfiche.

474. *Subject Catalogue of the House of Commons Parliamentary Papers, 1801–1900.* Compiled by Peter Cockton. Cambridge, U.K.: Chadwyck-Healey (ProQuest), 1988. 4,800pp. 5 vols. ISBN 0-85964-133-3 (set). LC 87-5128.

This massive index set, compiled by Peter Cockton, is a companion volume to the microfiche set of 19th-century Parliamentary Papers published by Chadwyck-Healey. The *Subject Catalogue* provides detailed indexing for the Parliamentary Papers by dividing them into 19 broad subject groups, similar to those found in *Hansard,* including central government and administration, agriculture and rural society, trade and commerce, and poverty and social administration. Also within each subject group there are additional subdivisions. Entries include the citation to the volume and page number of the Sessional Papers and the Chadwyck-Healey microfiche number. At the end of the fifth volume there is a subject index to the set. This set provides more detailed indexing to 19th-century Parliamentary Papers than those published by the House of Commons and other privately published sources.

475. *UKOP: A Catalogue of United Kingdom Official Publications on CD-ROM.* Chadwyck-Healey (ProQuest) and TSO. UKOP is a subscription database founded as a joint project of Chadwyck-Healey and The Stationery Office (TSO). It provides searchable access to all British official publications, including those of both the TSO and the departmental, or "Non-TSO," publications, from 1980 to the present. The database includes all Parliamentary publications as well as publications from more than 200 government departments, totaling more than 447,000 records. There is also archival access to the full text of recent documents, with 12,000 full-text documents being added annually.

European Communities and European Union: Guides and Indexes

476. *The Documentation of the European Communities: A Guide.* By Ian Thompson. London: Mansell, 1989. 382pp. ISBN 0-7201-2022-5.
This is the best general introductory guide to the publications of the European Communities (EC). Thompson's guide begins with a brief introduction and then focuses its chapters on the publications of the decision-making institutions of the European Communities: European Commission, Council of Ministers, European Parliament, Economic and Social Committee, European Court of Justice, and the Court of Auditors. There is also coverage of the publications of other EC organizations and appendices covering EC series/periodicals/reports, online services, information offices, non-EC information sources, and

information centers, documentation centers, and depository libraries.

Thompson's work needs to be supplemented by accessing Europa, the European Union's site on the World Wide Web, maintained by EUR-OP, the Union's official publisher, at http://europa.eu.int/index_en.htm. This site serves as a gateway to accessing the sites for the individual organizations, such as the European Parliament. Also important for searching recent European Union publications is ECLAS (European Commission Libraries Catalog) at http://europa.eu.int/eclas. It provides access to references from over 137,000 periodical articles.

477. *Index to the Official Journal of the European Communities.* Luxembourg: Office for Official Publications of the European Communities, 1973–. Monthly, with annual cumulations. The index has changed title and form over the years: *Index to the Official Journal of the European Communities; Alphabetical Index and Methodological Table,* 1978–1979; *Supplement to the Official Journal of the European Communities, Annual Alphabetical and Methodological Index,* 1973–1977.
This is the most detailed index to European Communities and European Union documents published in the *Official Journal.* Since 1980 the *Index* has been published in two parts—an alphabetical index and a methodological table. The alphabetical index is based on Community terminology and is arranged by subject. Entries give references to the issue of the *Official Journal* where the document appears and the page number. The methodological table is arranged by type of document; these documents fall into two categories: legislation and infor-

mation and notices. References are given to the number, page, and date of issues of the *Official Journal*. Documents covered include regulations, decisions, directives, orders, and removals. The *Official Journal* is also searchable on CD-ROM and electronically through two online databases. One online database, CELEX, is available through subscription and one, EUR-Lex, is free but only contains the most recent years of the journal. Information on these indexes is available at the Europa Web site mentioned earlier. The index provides a good starting point for tracing recent European Communities documents on particular issues.

478. *Official Publications of Western Europe. Vol. 1, Denmark, Finland, France, Ireland, Italy, Luxembourg, Netherlands, Spain, and Turkey. Vol. 2, Austria, Belgium, Federal Republic of Germany, Greece, Norway, Portugal, Sweden, Switzerland, and United Kingdom.* Edited by Eve Johansson. London: Mansell. Distributed in the United States by H. W. Wilson, 1984–1988. 2 vols. ISBN 0-7201-1623-6 (vol. 1); ISBN 0-7201-1662-7 (vol. 2).
This two-volume set provides an excellent introduction to the official publications of 17 western European nations, as well as Turkey. Each volume is organized into country chapters written by experts in the publications of each of these nations, which include an introduction to the political system and constitution, as well as material on major publications, publications practices, bibliographic control, and library collections and availability. There is a bibliography at the end of each country chapter, which includes guides to official publications. The first volume contains a good introductory chapter on the acquisition of foreign official

publications and each volume is indexed by subject, organization, and title. See the government Web sites of each of these countries for more recent material on their official publications.

United Nations and International Organizations

Guides

479. *International Information: Documents, Publications, and Electronic Information of International Governmental Organizations.* Edited by Peter I. Hajnal. 2nd ed. Englewood, CO: Libraries Unlimited, 1997–2001. 2 vols. ISBN 1-56308-147-4 (vol. 1); ISBN 1-56308-808-8 (vol. 2).
This work, edited by Hajnal, who is a research associate and a specialist in international documents at the University of Toronto, is a new edition of the original title first published in 1988. It greatly expands the coverage of the first edition to include detailed discussion of electronic information along with the traditional print sources. In volume 1, which was published in 1997, each of the chapters is written by a specialist in the area of international documentation. The focus of the work is on the United Nations, with separate chapters on the agency's electronic resources, the United Nations Library, and the United Nations Scholar's Workstation at Yale University. There are also chapters on the European Union, the G-7, the League of Nations, the Organization for Economic Co-operation and Development, and the International Development Center. The role of private publishers in providing access to international information is examined,

particularly the efforts of publishers such as Chadwyck-Healey, Congressional Information Service, Oxford University Press, Public Affairs Information Service, and Readex. Concluding chapters focus on collection development and reference. A detailed bibliography contains many Internet addresses for locating additional material.

Volume 2 focuses on information published by intergovernmental and non-governmental organizations and how rapid changes in technology have impacted this information. It covers agencies such as the World Bank, International Monetary Fund, the General Agreement on Tariffs and Trade, and the World Trade Organization. Hajnal covers cartographic resources available from the International Civil Aviation Organizations, archives of international organizations, and the wide range of United Nations resources. He covers print, microform, and electronic material.

This work is an excellent starting point for the researcher beginning to work with international agency documents and electronic information sources.

Indexes

480. *Checklist of United Nations Documents, 1946–1949.* **New York: United Nations, 1949–1953.**
The original United Nations index, covering documents from 1946 through 1949, the *Checklist* fills the indexing gap from the earliest U.N. publications until the beginning of the next indexing source, the *United Nations Documents Index*, which began in 1950. Originally, the *Checklist* was scheduled to be published in nine parts, each part listing the publications of a particular U.N. agency or commission. However, only parts 2–8 were ever published, with part 1 (General Assembly) and part 9 (secretariat) never completed. Each part is cumulated for the four-year period, listing documents for each agency, and there is a detailed subject index for each part.

481. *International Bibliography: Publications of Intergovernmental Organizations.* **New York: UNIPUB, 1973–1991. Quarterly.**
Until 1983 this index was known as the *International Bibliography, Information Documentation*, usually referred to by the acronym *IBID*. From 1973 to 1991 the index served as the major index to the publications of over 80 intergovernmental organizations, such as the International Monetary Fund and the Food and Agriculture Organization. Published quarterly with annual cumulative title and subject indexes, each issue was divided into two parts: a bibliographic record (documents), and a periodicals record (serials). Many of the documents listed contain abstracts and, for locating key U.N. documents, this index was easier to use than the standard U.N. printed sources. Historians will find this a useful source for finding publications of intergovernmental organizations issued during the 1970s and 1980s. For more recent coverage the historian needs to turn to the World Wide Web. The University of Michigan Libraries Documents Center [see 461] is a good place for locating links to the Web sites of the major international organizations. There is an extensive list at this site under the heading "International Agencies and Information on the Web."

482. *League of Nations Documents, 1919–1946: A Descriptive Guide and Key to the Microfilm Collection.* **Edited by Edward**

A. Reno Jr. New Haven, CT: Research
Publications, 1973–1975. 3 vols.
LC 73-3061.
This is the major guide to the publications
of the League of Nations, the predecessor
of the United Nations. Covering the period
from 1919 to 1946, this three-volume work
indexes material in the most comprehensive
set of League of Nations documents, that
published by Research Publications. The
documents are divided into 18 broad subject categories, including administrative
commissions, minorities, social questions,
legal questions, and refugees. For each document, the document number is given, as
well as an abstract; reel numbers are interspersed among the entries. There is a consolidated document number index at the
end of each volume. The one drawback of
this index is that there is no specific subject
index, beyond the broad subject categories.
Also useful for locating material on the
League of Nations is George W. Baer, ed.,
*International Organizations, 1918–1945: A
Guide to Research and Materials* (Wilmington, DE: Scholarly Resources, 1991).

483. *Ten Years of United Nations Publications,
1945 to 1955: A Complete Catalogue.* **New
York: United Nations, 1955. 271pp.**
Although certainly not the "comprehensive
guide to Official Records and publications
and periodicals" of the United Nations
from the 1945 San Francisco Conference to
the end of 1954 that it claims to be, this
volume does index many of the publications of the Secretariat and General Assembly from 1946 to 1949 that were not
included in the *Checklist of United Nations
Documents.* The main part of the work consists of a listing of Secretariat and Official
Record documents. There are author, title,

and subject indexes to guide the user. For
the researcher this work does provide access
to early United Nations publications and
fills in the gaps until the *United Nations
Documents Index* begins in 1950.

484. *UNDEX: United Nations Documents
Index, 1974–1978.* **New York: United
Nations, 1974–1980. Series C, Cumulative
Edition, 1974–1978, was also published by
UNIFO, Pleasantville, NY, 1979–1980.**
The predecessor of the *UNDOC: Current
Index,* the *UNDEX* continues the indexing
to United Nations documents begun with
the *United Nations Documents Index.* Different in arrangement from the earlier and
later U.N. indexes, the *UNDEX* was issued
in three series: Series A, Subject Index;
Series B, Country Index; and Series C, List
of Documents Issued. Series B, Country
Index, incorporates some unique features
not found in the *UNDOC.* For example,
documents are arranged under each country by "type of action." Among the types of
action identified are "Statements in
debates" and "Voting: Abst" (Abstaining),
"Voting: No," and "Voting: Yes." This unique
country arrangement helps easily locate a
particular nation's position on various
issues.

485. *UNDOC: Current Index; United Nations
Documents.* **New York: United Nations,
1979–1996. Quarterly, with annual
cumulations. Until 1987, 10 issues per year.
Since 1984, annual cumulations are only
available on microfiche.**
Intended to be the most comprehensive
index to recent United Nations publications, the *UNDOC* started in 1979 and
ceased publication in 1996. It was succeeded by the *United Nations Documents*

Checklist (October 1996–December 1997) and the current *United Nations Documents Index* (1998–). [see 486] Each quarterly issue of the *UNDOC* contained a list of documents and publications arranged by U.N. classification number, a list of official records, sales publications, documents republished, new document series symbols, United Nations maps included in documents, United Nations sheet maps, and author, subject, and title indexes. There are annual author, title, subject, and checklist cumulations. A detailed user's guide at the beginning of each volume aids the researcher using this index for the first time. The *UNDOC* and its successors are the major printed indexes for researchers looking for recent U.N. documents, giving the United Nations classification number for locating the document in many library collections.

486. *United Nations Documents Index.* **New York: United Nations, Dag Hammarskjöld Library, 1998–. Quarterly.**
This is the current printed index to U.N. documents indexed by the Dag Hammarskjöld Library. It continues the work done by the *UNDOC: Current Index* (1979–1996) and the United Nations Documents Checklist (October 1996–December 1997). Issued quarterly, it continues the indexing arrangement provided by the *UNDOC* and provides access to locating a large number of recent U.N. documents. For more detailed access to the most recent U.N. documents, check electronic indexes such as Readex's Index to United Nations Documents and Publications, Access UN, and the U.N. UNBISnet, referred to in the next section.

487. *United Nations Documents Index: United Nations and Specialized Agencies Documents and Publications, 1950–1973.* **New York: United Nations, 1950–1975. Monthly, with annual cumulations beginning in 1963.**
The United Nations Documents Index is the second of the major U.N. print indexes and the longest running, beginning with the end of the *Checklist* in 1950 and continuing until the end of 1973, when it was replaced by the *UNDEX*. This index was arranged into two parts: a subject index and a checklist. Prior to 1963 only the subject index cumulated; from 1963 through 1973 both the subject index and checklist were cumulated annually. Until 1962 the index listed the publications of the specialized agencies, such as the Food and Agriculture Organization. A four-volume cumulated index to the *United Nations Documents Index*, covering the period from 1950–1962, was published by Kraus-Thomson in 1974. This makes it considerably easier to search that period without having to look through each individual index volume. A useful supplement to the official United Nations indexes, especially for the time period it covers, is Mary Eva Birchfield's *The Complete Reference Guide to United Nations Sales Publications, 1946–1978* (Pleasantville, NY: UNIFO, 1982).

Electronic Sources

488. *Access UN.* **Newsbank/Readex, 1946–.**
Readex, the major publisher of United Nations documents on microfiche, provides World Wide Web access to indexing for United Nations documents from 1946 to the present. This includes documents from the six main bodies of the United Nations:

General Assembly, Security Council, Economic and Social Council, Trusteeship Council, Secretariat, and International Court of Justice. The types of documents include masthead documents (formerly called mimeographed documents), official records, sales publications, limited and restricted documents, and documents put out by sessional and standing committees, commissions, conferences, and regional bodies. Also included are the full text of resolutions from the General Assembly (1981–), Security Council (1974–), and Economic and Social Council (1982–), as well as the full text of selected other documents (1990–). The database provides citations to more than 419,000 documents and publications.

489. Index to United Nations Documents and Publications. New Canaan, CT: Newsbank/Readex, 1948–. Monthly. CD-ROM.

Readex also provides access to U.N. documents with this CD-ROM index, which is currently cumulated back to 1948. The CD-ROM indexes the same agencies as Access UN and also contains selective full text of resolutions of the General Assembly, Security Council, and Economic and Social Council, as well as selected provisional verbatim and summary record documents that contain voting records. This index can be searched by subject, session, author, title, text, document date, document number, U.N. sales number, document type (official record or masthead document), date of meeting, and country. The index lists the U.N. call number for each document, making it easy to locate in the Readex microfiche set. Subscribers to the Readex

microfiche receive the CD-ROM as part of the subscription and the most recent years of Access UN. It costs extra to purchase Access UN farther back.

490. UNBISnet. New York: Dag Hammarskjöld Library, United Nations. http://unbisnet.un.org

491. UNBIS Plus on CD-ROM. Alexandria, VA: Chadwyck-Healey (ProQuest). CD-ROM. ISSN 1075-3877.

UNBISnet and UNBIS Plus (United Nations Bibliographic Information System) both provide access to U.N. documents. UNBISnet, produced by the United Nations, provides access on the World Wide Web and has largely superseded UNBIS Plus, although the coverage varies between the two sources. UNBISnet is a subscription database that can be searched by author, title, subject, UN number, and multi-index formats for UN publications indexed by the Dag Hammarskjöld Library, the Library of the United Nations in Geneva, and non-U.N. publications held by the Dag Hammarskjöld Library. It covers from 1979 to the present, although it indexes resolutions of the General Assembly, Economic and Social Council, Security Council, and Trusteeship Council back to 1946. In addition, it provides citations to speeches from the General Assembly, Security Council, and Economic and Social Council (1983–) and the Trusteeship Council (1982–). UNBISnet's main advantage over UNBIS Plus is that it is updated daily, while the CD-ROM is updated quarterly. Also, researchers can access it from other locations, unlike the CD-ROM, which is often limited to the library where it is located.

UNBIS Plus accesses much of the same material as UNBISnet, including full-text documents, including full text of Security Council resolutions (1974–), General Assembly resolutions (1981–), and Economic and Social Council resolutions (1982–). It also has the same voting records and speech citation information as UNBISnet. Both UNBISnet and UNBIS Plus, as well as Readex's Access UN and Index to United Nations Documents and Publications provide detailed indexing and, in some cases, the full text of United Nations documents not found in the printed indexes, making it much easier for the researcher to locate a recent United Nations document on a particular subject.

since the end of World War II. The main part of each chapter consists of the bibliographic entries arranged by type of document, including general bibliographies and reference works, constitutional documents, law codes, other legislative documents, party documents, and general statistics. Brief annotations give information about many individual documents, and there is a name and title index. Walker's work is a starting point for federal official publications. See also the recent publications listed in the *Guide to Official Publications of Foreign Countries* [see 439] and the University of Michigan Libraries' Documents Center's "Foreign Government Resources on the Web" for links to recent country publications.

Russia and the Soviet Union

492. *Official Publications of the Soviet Union and Eastern Europe, 1945–1980: A Select Annotated Bibliography.* Edited by Gregory Walker. London: Mansell, 1982. 620pp. ISBN 0-7201-1641-4.
Although not current since 1980 for material on Russia and other states of the former Soviet Union, this work still remains the most recent general guide to the official publications of these countries. The chapter on the Union of Soviet Socialist Republics covers publications of the separate republics created by the breakup of the Soviet Union in 1991. Covering the period from 1945 to 1980, this work is an excellent guide to the post-war official documents of the Soviet Union and the countries of Eastern Europe. Divided into chapters alphabetically by country, each chapter begins with an introductory section giving a brief outline of political and administrative developments

Japan

493. *Japanese National Government Publications in the Library of Congress: A Bibliography.* Compiled by Thaddeus Y. Ohta. Washington, DC: Library of Congress, 1981. 402pp.
ISBN 0-8444-0326-1. LC 80-607001.
Compiled by the head of the Japanese section of the Asian division of the Library of Congress, this work serves as a guide to Japanese government publications, mainly from the post–World War II period through the end of 1977. Containing 3,376 titles, the document entries are arranged under four major sections: Legislative Branch, Executive Branch, Judicial Branch, and Public Corporations and Research Institutes. Most of the publications listed in this bibliography are serials, but it also includes other publications such as catalogs, directories, guidebooks, handbooks, statistical sur-

veys, census reports, and white papers. Entries include romanized Japanese title or non-Japanese title in the absence of a Japanese title, frequency of publication, and a holdings statement. Another helpful guide to 20th-century Japanese government publications in the Library of Congress is the work compiled by Yoshiko Yoshimura, *Japanese Government Documents and Censored Publications: A Checklist of the Microfilm Collection* (Washington, DC: Library of Congress, 1992).

LEGAL SOURCES

Constitutions

494. *Constitution Finder.* http://confinder.richmond.edu
This Web site, maintained by a law professor at the University of Richmond, lists the full text of drafts, as well as the current text, of constitutions, charters, amendments, and other related documents from countries all over the world. Each nation is listed alphabetically and each is linked to its constitutional text posted somewhere on the Internet. The countries covered range from Afghanistan to Zimbabwe and the text of the constitution is in English translation. For Internet links to other sites containing the text of constitutions, check the University of Michigan Documents Center [see 461].

495. *Constitutions of the Countries of the World.* Edited by Albert P. Blaustein and Gisbert H. Flanz. Dobbs Ferry, NY: Oceana, 1971–.
This multivolume loose-leaf set provides the current text in English of the constitu-

tions of all the nations of the world. Numbering over 50 binder volumes, the set is divided into two parts: the current volumes and the historic constitutions volumes, which cumulate the earlier superseded constitutions, dating back to the 1970s. The volumes are arranged alphabetically by country, from Afghanistan through Zimbabwe, and contain the complete text of the constitution currently in effect, plus a summary of significant events in each country's history and a bibliography of sources. Because of its updating, this set is the best single print source for current world constitutions.

496. *Sources and Documents of United States Constitutions.* Edited by William F. Swindler. Dobbs Ferry, NY: Oceana, 1973–1979, 1988. 13 vols.
ISBN 0-379-16175-3 (set);
ISBN 0-379-16193-1 (bibliography).
This multivolume set reprints the complete text of the constitutions of every U.S. state, including those in effect during the territorial period. The constitutions are arranged alphabetically by state and contain detailed annotations by Professor Swindler, a recognized authority on constitutional law, which provide excellent analysis of the historical background. Each of the state constitutions is also indexed by subject, and in 1988 a bibliography volume was added, citing law journal articles on each state constitution. This work is excellent for constitutional history on each state. For the text of the current state constitutions and those of the U.S. possessions and territories, the historian should consult another loose-leaf Oceana publication, *Constitutions of the United States, National and State* (Dobbs Ferry, NY: Oceana, 1974–). A good site for

state constitutions on the web is Constitutions, Statutes, and Codes at the Cornell University Law School at http://www.law.cornell.edu/statutes.html. This site alphabetically links to each state's constitution and other state government information.

Treaties and Other International Agreements

United States

Texts of Treaties

497. *Treaties and International Agreements Online: U.S. Treaties Researcher.* Dobbs Ferry, NY: Oceana. http://www.oceanalaw.com. Updated monthly.
The advent of the World Wide Web has opened up access to the full text of U.S. and international treaties for researchers. Treaties and International Agreements Online: U.S. Treaties Researcher is the most comprehensive source for locating the text of U.S. treaties on the World Wide Web. It is a subscription database, mainly available in law libraries, that provides access to the texts of over 11,500 treaties and agreements from 1783 to the present. The database also includes recent Senate treaty documents and U.S. State Department documents. This massive collection can be searched in three different ways—table of contents, full text search, and guided field search, which allows the researcher to search 12 index fields, including country, subject, and treaty name. Treaties to which the United States is a party from 1776 to the present are also available online through the original version of the database LexisNexis, not the current LexisNexis Academic, and Westlaw. Each of the three—Treaties and International Agreements Online: U.S. Treaties Researcher, LexisNexis, and Westlaw—contain the texts of treaties that have not yet appeared in the U.S. government's *Treaties and Other International Agreements* series.

498. *Treaties and Other International Agreements of the United States of America, 1776–1949.* Compiled by Charles I. Bevans. Washington, DC: Government Printing Office, 1968–1976. 13 vols.
This multivolume work is the major retrospective index and compilation of U.S. treaties and other international agreements, covering from 1776 to 1949, when the *United States Treaties and Other International Agreements* series began publication. Bevans is divided into three parts: (1) multilateral treaties involving the United States; (2) bilateral treaties, arranged alphabetically by country; and (3) general index. It prints in English or in translation the full text of each treaty involving the United States. The full text of U.S. treaties and agreements from 1776 to 1949 are also printed in the *United States Statutes at Large* [see 510]. Volume 8 of the *Statutes* contains U.S. treaties from 1776 to 1845, and each annual volume through 1950–1951 includes treaties. Since 1950 the texts of all U.S. treaties are published in the annual *United States Treaties and Other International Agreements* (Washington, DC: U.S. Department of State, 1950–). For the texts of more recent U.S. treaties, researchers should check Treaties and International Agreements Online, LexisNexis, or a microfiche set, *United States Treaties and Other International Agreements: Current Service* (Buffalo, NY: William S. Hein, 1990–).

Indexes

499. *Hein's U.S. Treaty Index on CD-ROM.*
Edited by Igor Kavass. Buffalo, NY:
William S. Hein. Semiannual.

**500. *United States Treaty Index, 1776–1990
Consolidation.*** Buffalo, NY: William S.
Hein, 1991. 13 vols. Kept up-to-date by
supplements and revised volumes.
For researchers seeking indexing information about U.S. treaties, the indexes produced by William S. Hein have greatly
simplified the process of locating information. Hein's U.S. Treaty Index on CD-
ROM provides full indexing information
for locating over 17,000 U.S. treaties and
other international agreements from 1776
to the present. Specific parts of the text can
be searched to locate a particular treaty. The
*United States Treaty Index, 1776–1990 Con-
solidation*, was originally published replacing
and updating the earlier *United States
Treaties Cumulative Indexes*, previously published by Hein, which had updated Bevans's
work on the *Treaties and Other International
Agreements*. These volumes, which are regularly updated and revised, contain separate
sections that index treaties by number, date,
country, and subject. The *United States Treaty
Index* volumes are currently being updated
by Hein's loose-leaf United States *Current
Treaty Index*, which provides access to
recent treaty information.

**501. *Treaties and International Agreements
Online: U.S. Treaties Researcher.***

Treaties Index Online. **Dobbs Ferry, NY:
Oceana. http://www.oceanalaw.com**
These two electronic indexes, published by

Oceana, provide access to over 11,500 U.S.
treaties from 1783 to the present. Treaties
and International Agreements Online, mentioned earlier [see 497], also provides the
full text of all the treaties indexed. The
Treaties Index Online is a less expensive
subscription service that provides indexing
information on U.S. treaties by searching a
number of fields, including country, subject,
treaty name, and others, but not the full
text of the treaty. It gives the researcher a
citation to locate the treaty in another
online source or in print form.

International

Texts of Treaties

502. *Consolidated Treaty Series.* **Edited and
annotated by Clive Parry. Dobbs Ferry,
NY: Oceana Publications, 1969–1981.
231 vols.**
This huge set, published by Oceana, contains the texts of treaties from 1648 to
1919. Each volume contains reprints of
treaty texts in the language of one of the
countries who signed the treaty. Many
times this is followed by a French or
English translation or summary. *The Consolidated Treaty Series* is indexed by the *Index-
Guide to Treaties: Based on the Consolidated
Treaty Series* [see 504]. Also useful for the
texts of a number of international treaties,
beginning with the eighteenth century and
focusing on treaties ending individual wars,
is the Avalon Project at the Yale Law School
at http://www.yale.edu/lawweb/avalon/
avalon.htm. For a good collection of key
20th-century international treaties, the
researcher should consult J. A. S. Grenville
and Bernard Wasserstein, *The Major Interna-*

tional Treaties of the Twentieth Century: A History and Guide With Texts (London: Routledge, 2001).

503. *United Nations Treaty Collection.* New York: United Nations. http://untreaty.un.org

United Nations Treaty Series. **New York: United Nations, 1947–.**
The largest collection of international treaties on the World Wide Web is the United Nations Treaty Collection. This huge, ongoing set, which is also available in print form as the *United Nations Treaty Series* (*UNTS*), numbers over 2,000 volumes and is currently available on the Internet only on a subscription basis. A description of this collection is available at the United Nations Web site but it is not accessible unless the library where it is being used has a subscription to the database. The set covers over 40,000 treaties and related actions from 1946 to the present already published in the *UNTS*. It includes the text of all treaties registered or filed with the United Nations by member states or international organizations, as well as some filed by nonmember nations. The texts of the treaties are given in the original language and English and French. Treaties on the Web site can be located by type of agreement, date of signature, entry into force, names of parties, and popular names. The printed *UNTS* also contains index volumes, but they are less current than searching the online version. Researchers should also be aware of the forerunner to this series, the League of Nations Treaty Series, which contains the text of treaties registered by League members from 1920 to 1945.

Another useful Internet site, particularly for the text of multilateral treaties, is the Multilaterals Project located at the Fletcher School of Law and Diplomacy at Tufts University at http://fletcher.tufts.edu/multilaterals.html. This site organizes multilateral treaties chronologically and by subject. It includes treaties covering the entire 20th century. Some recent international treaties are also available for searching and full text electronically through the original version of LexisNexis.

Indexes

504. *Index-Guide to Treaties: Based on the Consolidated Treaty Series.* Dobbs Ferry, NY: Oceana, 1979–1986. 12 vols.
This is the major index to the texts of treaties from 1648 to 1919 between countries worldwide found in the 231-volume *Consolidated Treaty Series,* edited and annotated by Clive Parry (Dobbs Ferry, NY: Oceana Publications, 1969–1981). The first five volumes of the *Index-Guide* are a general chronological list, covering from 1648 to 1919, listing treaties year by year. Volumes 6–10 are a party index, arranged alphabetically by country from Afghanistan to Zanzibar. The last two volumes list colonial, postal, and telegraph treaties chronologically from 1648 to 1920. All the volumes of the *Index-Guide* give the volume and page number of the *Consolidated Treaty Series* where the text is actually located.

505. *Index to Multilateral Treaties.* Edited by Vaclav Mostecky. Cambridge, MA: Harvard Law School Library, 1965. 301pp.
This slim one-volume index deserves separate mention because it is an excellent start-

ing point for locating obscure historical treaties. The major part of the volume is a chronological list of 3,859 items from 1596 through 1963. This volume is also particularly useful because it gives a source that has the text of the treaty. These sources include official gazettes, collections of statutes, treaty series, conference protocols and proceedings, documents of international organizations, unofficial collections, periodicals, and books. There is a regional and subject index at the end of the volume.

506. *United Nations Treaty Index on CD-ROM*. Edited by Igor I. Kavass. Buffalo, NY: William S. Hein, 1995–.
This CD-ROM index, edited by Igor Kavass, a well-known authority on treaties who has edited other U.S. treaty indexes published by Hein, has made it considerably easier to locate United Nations treaties. It is a cumulative index to citations for all the international treaties and agreements in the *United Nations Treaty Series* (*UNTS*). If the researcher does not have access to the United Nations Treaty Collection on the World Wide Web, this is an excellent alternative and far better than the printed index volumes of the *UNTS* for locating information. The software on the CD-ROM makes it easy to locate a citation in the printed U.N. series and it also indexes recent treaties that have not yet been indexed in the U.N. printed indexes.

507. *World Treaty Index*. By Peter H. Rohn. 2nd ed. Santa Barbara, CA: ABC-CLIO, 1984. 5 vols. ISBN 0-87436-141-9 (set).
This is an excellent index to 20th-century national and international treaties, covering treaties from 1900 to 1980. The second edition has been extensively revised and pro-

vides access to a total of 44,000 treaties, twice the number in the original work. Volume 1 contains a detailed introduction to the set, including an excellent user's guide. The major part of the first volume, however, consists of "Treaty Profiles," which provide an extensive array of national, regional, and global treaty statistics. Following this introductory volume is the main part of the work, the listing of all the treaties covered, arranged in chronological order by date of signature. This is included in volumes 2 (covering 1900–1960) and 3 (covering 1960–1980). The detailed entries include information such as a signature date and citation, treaty number, name and title, date on which the treaty entered into force, languages of the treaty, main theme, parties to the treaty, and an annex providing postsignature treaty history. Rohn's final two volumes provide extensive indexing to the main entry listings by party, including countries as well as international organizations (volume 4) and key word (volume 5).

Laws and Courts

Handbooks

508. *Fundamentals of Legal Research*. By Roy M. Mersky and Donald J. Dunn. 8th ed. New York, NY: Foundation, 2002. 821pp. Index. ISBN 1-58778-064-X.
The Internet has revolutionized finding and accessing legal materials, and this book stands out as a basic guide to legal research. Written by two law professors and in its eighth edition, this work is particularly useful for the historical researcher seeking to become familiar with legal sources.

It begins with a glossary of terms used in legal research, and includes chapters on locating and using federal and state court decisions, constitutions, legislation, administrative law, loose-leaf services, Shepards's citations, legal encyclopedias, and legal periodicals. Other chapters cover international law and computer-assisted legal research, including LexisNexis, Westlaw, CD-ROM products, and Internet sites. There are a number of appendixes containing information on legal abbreviations, state guides to legal research, selected law-related Internet sources, and a chart on legal research procedure. The work is indexed for quickly locating material and is available in an abridged paperback edition. Two other works are also useful for an overview on electronic legal research: Diana Botluk's annual volume, *The Legal List: Research on the Internet* (St. Paul, MN: West Group, 1997–); and Stephen Elias and Susan Levinkind, *Legal Research Online and in the Library* (Berkeley, CA: Nolo, 1999).

Indexes and Compilations

509. International Court of Justice. *Reports of Judgments, Advisory Opinions, and Orders*. Leyden, Netherlands: A. W. Sijthoff, 1947–. This ongoing multivolume work publishes the judgments, advisory opinions, and orders of the International Court of Justice, the key decision-making body for international law. Each of the annual volumes, covering from 1947 to the present, contains the full text of the Court's decisions in both English and French. There are also English and French subject indexes at the end of each volume. Prior to World War II, the current court's predecessor was the Permanent Court of International Justice. Its *Judg-*

ments, Orders, and Advisory Opinions were also published (Leyden: A. W. Sijthoff, 1931–1940). Earlier there were separate *Collection of Advisory Opinions, 1922–1930* and *Collection of Judgments, 1923–1930* volumes. There have also been separate collections of the decisions of the Permanent Court, including the four-volume *World Court Reports, 1922–1942* (Washington, DC: Carnegie Endowment for International Peace, 1934–1943). There is a lag time in the appearance of print volumes of the Reports of Judgments, so the researcher should check for recent decisions on the International Court of Justice's Web site located at http://www.icj-cij.org/icjwww/icj002.htm. This site has links to all the cases and advisory opinions referred to the court since 1946. Divided into contentious cases and advisory cases, the recent cases are presented in full overview; the older cases contain a summary of the judgments and orders. The site also has links to other information about and basic documents of the International Court.

510. *United States Statutes at Large*. Boston: Little, Brown, 1845–1873; Washington, DC: Government Printing Office, 1873–. This ongoing series of volumes is the major compilation of the text of U.S. laws, as passed by Congress from 1789 to the present. The *Statutes at Large* volumes are arranged by session of Congress and then chronologically by the date a law was passed. Included in the volumes are the complete texts of public laws, private laws, concurrent resolutions, and presidential proclamations. Also, the *Statutes* were the place where treaties were originally published until the end of 1949, when they were published separately in the *United*

States Treaties and Other International Agreements volumes. Since 1975, the *Statutes* have contained legislative histories of each public law. The more recent volumes also contain subject and individual indexes and citations to the appropriate sections of the *United States Code*. For the official text of legislation since the beginning of Congress, the *Statutes* are the best source. However, with the emergence of electronic sources and the Internet, there are a number of sources the researcher can go to for indexing and the text of recent legislation such as Lexis-Nexis, LexisNexis Congressional, GPO Access, and Thomas.

The full run of the *Statutes at Large* is available to subscribers of the original version of LexisNexis and the volumes of the *Statutes* from 1789 to 1875 are available full text through the Century of Lawmaking part of the Library of Congress American Memory Web site.

511. *United States Supreme Court Digest, 1754 to Date: Covering Every Decision of the United States From Earliest Times to Date.* **St. Paul, MN: West, 1943–. 33 vols.**
For those who do not have access to Lexis-Nexis or Westlaw, this digest is the major index to U.S. Supreme Court decisions and opinions found in the *United States Reports* volumes, covering from 1754 to the present. The first four volumes of the *Digest* serve as a descriptive word index for locating subject headings and key numbers in the main *Digest* volumes. In the main volumes the arrangement is alphabetical, with a brief summary of the case and the citations for locating the case in the *United States Reports*, *Lawyers Edition of the United States Reports*, and the *Supreme Court Reporter*. Pocket parts update each of the

main volumes, and two Table of Cases volumes help locate individual cases if the researcher already knows the name of the case. The digest has made it easy to locate individual Supreme Court cases or a series of cases on a particular legal topic.

Electronic Sources

512. *Findlaw.* **www.findlaw.com**
For researchers who do not have easy access to the major subscription databases, Lexis-Nexis or Westlaw, Findlaw offers a free alternative on the Internet. While not as comprehensive as the two subscription databases, Findlaw does offer a wide range of full text access to opinions in Supreme Court cases, as well as those in federal district court and state court. It provides access to the full text of U.S. Supreme Court decisions since 1893 and recent years (1990s forward) of federal and state court cases. Researchers can search broadly or by specific types of law, such as constitutional law or environmental law. There are also links to other law-related sites, as well as law schools, legal organizations, law firms, and legal news. The big advantage of Find-law is that it is free and does not have to be accessed through a library or private subscription. A major disadvantage is that it does not provide the complete coverage of Supreme Court and lower court decisions found in LexisNexis, Westlaw, or library print copies.

513. *LexisNexis.* **Dayton, OH: Reed Elsevier. http://www.lexisnexis.com**

Westlaw. **St. Paul, MN: West Group (Thomson). http://www.thomson.com**
The emergence of these two online data-

bases has revolutionized outside access to the full text of legal materials, particularly court cases at the Supreme Court, federal district court, and state supreme court level. Researchers have access to one or both of these systems through a large number of research and law libraries, who subscribe to these services on the web. Both of these databases provide similar access to the complete full text of many of the same legal materials, including court cases (Supreme Court, federal court, and state court), legal briefs, law review articles, federal and state legal codes, and federal and state administrative regulations. All of these can be searched by broad topic or by a citation to a specific case. There is also coverage of current legal news and tax material, all full text. Lexis is the legal part of the overall LexisNexis database, which also provides business, newspaper, and medical coverage. It is offered in many libraries through LexisNexis Academic, which provides World Wide Web access to law and business materials in a more user-friendly format than the original LexisNexis. One of the problems with LexisNexis Academic is that this version of LexisNexis only contains legal and business material. It does not contain all the material in the original database, which can still be accessed separately. For example, all the Congressional material, such as federal laws and legislative histories, are in the original version of LexisNexis but are no longer in LexisNexis Academic. They can be found in LexisNexis Congressional, for which libraries must pay a separate subscription.

9

DICTIONARIES AND ENCYCLOPEDIAS

Dictionaries and encyclopedias of history are useful for clarifying points of discussion, determining dates of events, and providing usually standard interpretations of historical events such as battles, wars, treaties, alliances, policies, and people. Before 1970, these types of works were generally confined to a few standard, frequently reissued, general texts covering large spans of time. The past three decades, however, have seen the publication of increasing numbers of specialized topical historical dictionaries and encyclopedias. Because of this proliferation the list that follows is of necessity selective. Emphasis has been given to recent works published since 1970.

A number of classic multivolume general histories have considerable reference value. In earlier decades they often functioned as encyclopedias, reflecting the state of historical scholarship of that time. Of particular note is the *Cambridge Ancient History*, the first edition of which was completed in 12 volumes, with five additional volumes of plates between 1923 and 1939. This series has been thoroughly revised, with some volumes being in their second edition and some volumes being in their third edition.

The latest volume, *The Late Empire, AD 337–425*, appeared in 1998 and completes the current revision of the entire work. Undoubtedly, a fourth edition of certain volumes is already being contemplated.

The *Cambridge Medieval History* appeared in eight volumes between 1911 and 1936 with only volume 4 on the Eastern Roman Empire having been revised (in two parts, 1966–1967). But advances in scholarship dealing with the Middle Ages have resulted in the planning of the *New Cambridge Medieval History* in seven volumes. Since 1995 several volumes have been published, including one in 1998 and two in 1999. Starting to show its age is the *New Cambridge Modern History*, published in 14 volumes between 1957 and 1979, with second editions of the first and second volumes planned or published. This work is the successor to the earlier *Cambridge Modern History*, the original multivolume Cambridge history masterminded by Lord Acton, published in 13 volumes, with an atlas, between 1902 and 1926. The success of these works has inspired more specialized multivolume histories from the Cambridge University Press on various topics and regions such as

Africa, China, economic history, Greek philosophy, India, Islam, Japan, and Latin America.

GENERAL

514. *Blackwell Encyclopaedia of Political Institutions.* **Edited by Vernon Boddanor. New York: Basil Blackwell, 1987. Index. 667pp. ISBN 0-631-13841-2.**

515. *Blackwell Encyclopaedia of Political Thought.* **Edited by David Miller. New York: Basil Blackwell, 1987. Index. 600pp. ISBN 0-631-14011-5.**
These two volumes are a companion set. *The Blackwell Encyclopaedia of Political Institutions* describes the key terms and concepts employed in the study of politics. It analyzes the ideas used in the study of political institutions, important forms of political organizations, and major political families. 250 contributors from 13 countries wrote the 600 entries. Individual entries are followed by short lists of additional readings and are fully cross-referenced and indexed. The *Blackwell Encyclopaedia of Political Thought* encompasses the whole spectrum of the history and theory of politics from Socrates to John Rawls. Some 300 entries written by 120 specialists (mostly British), include a combination of full-length survey articles with shorter definitions. Major concepts in political thought are defined and analyzed. There are brief lists of further readings accompanying the survey articles. All articles are cross-referenced and indexed. Both Blackwell encyclopedias appeared on several "Best Reference Books of the Year" lists in 1988.

516. *The Christopher Columbus Encyclopedia.* **Edited by Silvio A. Bendini. New York: Simon & Schuster, 1992. 2 vols. Index. ISBN 0-13-142662-1.**
Although it is a product of the quincentenary of Columbus's first voyage to the Americas, this reference book is about far more than Columbus; it provides an excellent overview of the European explorations and their background during the 15th and 16th centuries. Containing over 350 entries, written by 131 contributors, this encyclopedia covers such diverse topics as Roger Bacon, dead reckoning, the legend of Prester John, and syphilis. Individual entries range from 250 to 10,000 words and also supply bibliographies for further reading. Cross- and see-references and the index help the reader to explore topics thoroughly.

517. *Dictionary of the History of Science.* **Edited by W. F. Bynum, E. J. Browne, and Roy Porter. Princeton, NJ: Princeton University Press, 1981. 494pp. Index. ISBN 0-691-08287-1.**
The goal of this excellent and unique dictionary is to provide historical explanations of the fundamental concepts of science that can be understood by both laypeople and specialists. It contains no biographical entries. Instead, its 700 signed and alphabetically arranged entries deal with ideas such as evolution, quantum, and technological determinism or related topics like the Copernican Revolution or Mayan Astronomy, including obsolete ideas such as aether or phlogiston. The larger entries provide lists of additional readings. Further aid is given to readers by the provision of a general bibliography, an analytical table of contents, and a detailed biographical index. The

subject of the history of science has really come of age in recent decades. The *Reader's Guide to the History of Science* edited by Arne Hessenbruch (Chicago: Fitzroy Dearborn, 2000) provides a series of essays that assess and describe books on some 500 different topics—some specialized and very specific, others much broader and more general. For a work providing more extended essays, see Ian McNeil, ed., *An Encyclopedia of the History of Technology* (New York: Routledge, 1989). Other more specialized works include the three-volume *Encyclopedia of the History of Arabic Science,* edited by Roshdi Rashed with Regis Morelon (New York: Routledge, 1996); and *Encyclopedia of the Scientific Revolution From Copernicus to Newton,* edited by Wilbur Applebaum (New York: Garland, 2000). Applebaum taught the history of science for 25 years at the Illinois Institute of Technology.

518. *Encyclopedia Judaica.* Jerusalem: Encyclopedia Judaica; New York: Macmillan, 1972. 16 vols. Index. CD-ROM version from Torah Educational Software.
Consisting of 25,000 entries and 8,000 illustrations from 2,200 authors and 250 editors, this is a work of monumental scope that describes the legacy of the Jewish people. Frequently searched now in the CD-ROM version, it integrates the original volumes into a unified text and adds new feature articles, powerful search capabilities, an interactive timeline, plus many new media elements including videos, slide shows, music, maps, charts, tables, and a Hebrew pronunciation bibliography. The best single-volume dictionary is the award-winning *The New Encyclopedia of Judaism,* edited by Geoffrey Wigoder et al. (New York: NYU Press, 2002). The original 1989

edition of this scholarly reference was named an Outstanding Reference Source by ALA. The update includes 250 new entries and 1,200 extensively revised ones. Special features include maps, charts, excerpts of Jewish writing, and illustrations, along with an annotated bibliography of current works. More specialized is the extraordinary *The Encyclopedia of Jewish Life* edited by Shmuel Spector (New York: NYU Press, 2001). Said to be the most expensive project ever undertaken by NYU Press, it involved translation of the original 30-volume Hebrew edition into an abridged English-language edition. It chronicles the lives of 6,500 communities prior to and after the Holocaust in Europe, North Africa, and the Middle East. Other titles describing that horrendous event include *Encyclopedia of the Holocaust,* edited by Israel Gutman (New York: Macmillan, 1990); the *Columbia Guide to the Holocaust,* by Donald Niewyk and Francis Nicosia (New York: Columbia University Press, 2000); and *The Holocaust Encyclopedia,* edited by Walter Lacquer and Judith T. Baumel (New Haven, CT: Yale University Press, 2001).

519. *The Harper Encyclopedia of Military History.* By R. Ernest Dupuy and Trevor N. Dupuy. 4th ed. New York: HarperCollins, 1993. 1,654pp. Index. ISBN 0-06-270056-1.
Originally published in 1970 and revised in 1977, 1986, and 1993, the fourth edition brings this classic work up to date through 1991. It is organized in a series of 21 chronological and geographical chapters. Each chapter begins with a brief introductory essay on the principal military trends of the period, including its outstanding

leaders and the general development of tactics, strategy, weaponry, and organization. There is a short bibliography and an excellent general index, as well as separate indexes of battles and sieges and wars. Some 200 maps complement this outstanding work. The new edition is also physically and topographically bigger than previous editions, making it easier to read. Also useful is the *Reader's Companion to Military History,* edited by Robert Cowley and Geoffrey Parker (Boston: Houghton Mifflin, 1996), which takes a global perspective. It contains almost 600 signed articles by 150 expert contributors on subjects ranging from Aztecs to Zulus and all that lies in between. Individual entries include battles, wars, people, and such broad topics as doctrine, geography, and peace. Only a minority of the articles supply suggestions for further study. Helpful maps and illustrations are provided throughout the volume, which concludes with a general index. For individual battles see the recently updated George Kohn, *Dictionary of Wars,* rev. ed. (New York: Facts on File, 1999); along with David Eggenberger, *An Encyclopedia of Battles: Accounts of over 1,560 Battles from 1479 to the Present* (New York: Dover, 1989), which uses a broad definition of the term "battle."

520. *Air Warfare: An International Encyclopedia.* **Edited by Walter J. Boyne. Santa Barbara, CA: ABC-CLIO Press, 2002. 2 vols. Maps. Index. ISBN 1-57607-345-9.**

521. *Ground Warfare: An International Encyclopedia.* **Edited by Stanley L. Sandler. Santa Barbara, CA: ABC-CLIO Press, 2003. 3 vols. Maps. Index. ISBN 1-57607-344-0.**

522. *Naval Warfare: An International Encyclopedia.* **Edited by Spencer C. Tucker. Santa Barbara, CA: ABC-CLIO Press, 2002. 3 vols. Maps. Index. ISBN 1-57607-213-3.**

These three sets chronicle the history of warfare. *Air Warfare,* edited by Walter Boyne, a former career air force officer, draws on the expertise of 100 top international scholars to describe in 900 entries the history of aerial combat. Sandler, a former command historian with the U.S. Army's Special Operations Command at Fort Bragg, North Carolina, uses 200 international scholars to describe more than 700 wars and battles from the Aryan conquest of India to the Russian War in Chechnya, and includes 600 biographies and 100 survey essays on topics such as weapons, tactics, home front issues, etc. Tucker, a well-known military historian at the Virginia Military Institute, uses a team of international scholars to create the most comprehensive reference work on combat at sea.

523. *An Encyclopedia of World History: Ancient, Medieval, and Modern, Chronologically Arranged.* **Peter N. Stearns, general editor. 6th ed. Boston: Houghton Mifflin, 2001. 1,243pp. Index. ISBN 0-395-65237-5.**

As the title page describes it, this book is "a completely revised and updated edition of the classic reference work originally compiled and edited by William L. Langer." Langer, a Harvard history professor, published the first edition of this classic work in 1940 using the German work of Karl Ploetz as a model. Besides updating the chronological coverage to the year 2000, Stearns's new edition preserves much of what was good in Langer's volume while adding substantial improvements. Langer's basic format has been retained but the various chronological sections begin with broad thematic overviews that introduce the traditional chronological presentation. Whereas the focus of Langer's editions of the *Encyclopedia* had been the West and political history, Stearns's new edition greatly increases the coverage of non-European regions, social history, and popular culture. The coverage of Africa from 500 to 1500 has increased from a single page in Langer's fifth edition to eight and a half pages in Stearns's new edition. To accomplish this transformation, Stearns had to reduce the coverage of Western history. The problematic impact of this change can be readily seen by comparing Langer's version of "England, Scotland, and Ireland, 1485–1649" with Stearns's. When pursuing a question about European history before 1970, it would be a good idea to check an older edition of Langer as well as Stearns. The print version of Stearns is also accompanied by a CD-ROM version that may be used on the CD drive or downloaded to a computer's hard drive. The electronic version can be searched via key words and has files of the maps and the genealogical charts. It is wonderful to have this updated version of a classic available, but don't throw away your Langer. The latest edition of the traditional Langer is the fifth, *An Encyclopedia of World History: Ancient, Medieval, and Modern Chronologically Arranged,* compiled and edited by William L. Langer, 5th ed., rev. and enl. (London: Harrap, 1987), but the most recent American edition is dated 1970.

524. *Der Grosse Ploetz: Die Daten-Enzyklopädie der Weltgeschichte: Daten, Fakten, Zusammenhänge.* **32nd ed. Freiburg:** Verlag Ploetz, 1998. 2,046pp. Index. ISBN 3-87640-384-7.

The single most valuable one-volume historical dictionary in a foreign language, *Der Gross Ploetz* has been almost continuously in print since 1863 when Karl Ploetz, a teacher of the German language, published the first edition. That original edition later served as the inspiration for William Langer's *Encyclopedia of World History* [see 523]. Since Ploetz's original work was translated into English the organization of the later German editions has evolved considerably. The 32nd edition of *Der Gross Ploetz* has the advantage of currency up to 1995. It is divided into six sections: prehistory (60 pages), ancient history (257 pages), the Middle Ages (277 pages), Europe 1500–1945 (411 pages), the rest of the world 1500–1945 (217 pages), and recent history (607 pages). Approximately 75 German scholars authored various subsections of this work. Coverage is balanced and current. Each section has a brief introduction followed by chronological outlines. Fifty-five dynastic charts, numerous timelines, and hundreds of charts complement the text, and there is a detailed 100-page index.

525. *The Oxford Dictionary of the Christian Church.* **3rd ed. Edited by F. L. Cross and E. A. Livingstone. Oxford: Oxford University Press, 1997. 1,786pp.**

There are many reference works dealing with aspects of the history of the Christian Church, but the best general work in one volume is *The Oxford Dictionary of the Christian Church.* The updated and expanded third edition consists of over 6,000 alphabetically arranged, unsigned entries written by some 480 specialists. All of the entries contain some additional bibliography and many provide extensive listings. A large proportion of the entries are biographical, while others deal with events, concepts and institutions (e.g., Synod of Dort, supralapsarianism, and World Council of Churches). Eastern Orthodoxy, Evangelicals, and Third World countries and religious movements have received increased coverage in the third edition. Based on the second edition, *The Concise Oxford Dictionary of the Church* (1989) is available in paperback. Somewhat more detailed articles can be found in *The Encyclopedia of Christianity*, edited by Erwin Fahlbusch et al. (Grand Rapids, MI: Eerdmans-Brill, 1999–), which will eventually consist of five volumes and is partially based on the German work *Evangelisches Kirchenlexikon: Internationale Theologische Enzyklopädie*. Considerable historical information on all religions can also be found in the massive *Encyclopedia of Religion*, edited by Mircea Eliade, 16 vols. (New York: Macmillan, 1987). Many of the individual religious denominations have their own dictionaries or encyclopedias. Among the best are the 15-volume *New Catholic Encyclopedia,* 2nd ed. (Washington, DC: Thomson/Gale in association with The Catholic University of America, 2003). The revised edition represents a third generation in the evolution of the text that traces its lineage back to the *Catholic Encyclopedia* published from 1907 to 1912. The first "New" Catholic Encyclopedia was published in 1967 with numerous supplements. The 2003 edition includes 12,000 entries on theology, philosophy, history, literary figures, saints, musicians, etc. These are supplemented by biographies of contemporary religious figures, photographs, maps, and illustrations. The 15th volume is a cumulative index to the entire encyclopedia.

526. *Oxford Companion to World War II.* **Edited by I. C. B. Dear. Oxford: Oxford University Press, 1995. 1,343pp. ISBN 0-19-866225-4.**
Published to commemorate the 50th anniversary of the end of World War II, this excellent volume assumes pride of place among several one-volume reference works on World War II. It consists of 1,700 entries by over 160 contributors. The entries are arranged alphabetically and range from brief definitions of 50 words to narrative essays of tens of thousands of words covering the important countries participating in the war. This reference book deals with more than traditional military history topics such as battles, campaigns, and generals; it also looks at the social and domestic impact of the war in such topics as "Children" and "Religion." There are also many tables, charts, and photos along with 111 line drawn and color maps. Also worth consulting are *The Simon and Schuster Encyclopedia of World War II*, edited by Thomas Parrish (New York: Simon & Schuster, 1978); Louis Snyder, *Historical Guide to World War II* (Westport, CT: Greenwood, 1982); and Ian Hogg and Bryan Perrett, *Encyclopedia of the Second World War* (Norato, CA: Presidio, 1989), which is heavily illustrated. For an excellent work on World War I, see Stephen Pope and Elizabeth-Anne Wheal, *The Dictionary of the First World War* (New York: St. Martin's, 1995).

527. *The Oxford Encyclopedia of Economic History.* **Edited by Joel Mokyr. Oxford: Oxford University Press, 2003. 5 vols. 2,560pp. ISBN 0-19-510507-9.**
This comprehensive reference work is unique in its worldwide geographical scope and its broad chronological scope, which

ranges from prehistory to the present. It consists of some 900 signed articles from a group of distinguished international scholars. Economic history is broadly defined as including agricultural history, demographic history, business history, technological history, the history of migrations, and transportation history. Individual entries include individual countries, regions, concepts, institutions, events, and brief biographies of important individuals.

528. *World History: A Dictionary of Important People, Places, and Events, from Ancient Times to the Present.* By Bruce Wetterau. New York: Henry Holt, 1994. 1,173pp. ISBN 0-8050-2350-X.

This one-volume dictionary of world history is a revised and updated edition of the author's *Macmillan Concise Dictionary of World History* (1983). Thus, unlike Langer or *Der Gross Ploetz* [see 523 and 524], it is arranged alphabetically rather than chronologically and so is more useful for checking particular incidents, events, or personages than for reviewing the history of a region or a country. Its overall coverage is far less detailed than those two works. Besides the standard textual entries, however, Wetterau's dictionary does include chronologies. The textual entries provide essential information about a particular topic, while the chronologies cover broader topics such as individual countries or major wars. In all there are 10,000 entries and another 7,000 chronologically arranged items covering world history from the beginnings of civilization to 1982. For another excellent one-volume dictionary of world history, see *The Hutchinson Dictionary of World History* (Santa Barbara, CA: ABC-CLIO, 1993), which complements Wetterau's. More recent, but

only containing 4,000 brief entries, is the *Oxford Encyclopedia of World History* (New York: Oxford University Press, 1998), which is available in paperback as *A Dictionary of World History* (2000).

UNITED STATES

General

529. *Dictionary of American History.* Edited by Stanley I. Kutler. 3d ed. New York: Scribner's, 2003. 10 vols. Index (vol. 10). ISBN 0-684-80533-2.

Scribner's published the first *Dictionary of American History* (DAH) in five volumes in 1940. As originally conceived by its first editor, James Truslow Adams, it was intended to bring together in a convenient format thousands of facts about American history and to serve as a complement to the *Dictionary of American Biography* [see 657]. The first edition included 6,425 entries, and it quickly became a core reference source in most libraries. An eight-volume revision was published in 1976 to mark America's bicentennial. The new edition expands the *Dictionary* to over 3 million words, updates and increases bibliographies, and provides illustrations for the first time with the inclusion of 1,200 photographs and 252 maps. A substantial number of single entries have been consolidated into the new 4,434 entries. Of these 1,785 were retained from the original, 448 were revised, 1,360 were replaced, and 841 new articles were commissioned. Volume 9 contains archival maps and primary source documents while volume 10 includes the index and a research guide to major events and themes. Certain to become a classic. Similar in scope but with more of a high school audience in mind is the 11-volume *Encyclopedia of American History,* edited by Gary B. Nash (New York: Facts on File, 2003).

530. *Encyclopedia of the American Constitution.* **Edited by Leonard Levy, Kenneth L. Karst, and Dennis Mahoney. 2nd ed. New York: Macmillan, 2000. 6 vols. Index. ISBN 0-02-8648800-3.**

531. *Encyclopedia of the American Presidency.* **Edited by Leonard W. Levy and Louis Fisher. New York: Simon & Schuster, 1994. 4 vols. Index. ISBN 0-13-275983-7.**

532. *Encyclopedia of the United States Congress.* **Edited by Donald C. Bacon, Roger H. Davidson, and Morton Keller. New York: Simon & Schuster, 1995. 4 vols. Index. ISBN 0-13-276361-3.**

These three multivolume reference works provide a comprehensive, scholarly guide to major components of the U.S. government's history and workings. The first edition of the *Encyclopedia of the American Constitution* appeared in 1984 and won the Dartmouth Medal as the outstanding reference work of 1987. The second edition includes 2,750 signed original articles by some 300 leading constitutional scholars in an alphabetical arrangement. Each has a short bibliography, and cross-references are indicated in boldface. Topics cover constitutional history, people, Supreme Court cases, concepts and terms, and public acts. Volume 1 contains alphabetical lists of all the articles and of the contributors and their contributions. A variety of appendixes complement the text and include the Articles of Confederation, the Constitution, a chronology of

the framing of the Constitution, a list of important events in the development of American constitutional law, and a glossary of legal terms. Indexes include a case index, a personal name index, and a subject index. The other two volumes are very similar in conception and coverage. The *Encyclopedia of the American Presidency* consists of 1,011 signed articles, written by 335 expert contributors with suggestions for further reading; 550 specialists wrote the 1,056 entries comprising the *Encyclopedia of the United States Congress.* A useful collection of reference essays on the presidency is found in the two volumes of the *Guide to the Presidency,* edited by Michael Nelson (Washington, DC: Congressional Quarterly, 1996). G. K. Hall is also publishing an excellent series of one-volume presidential encyclopedias which so far includes *Franklin D. Roosevelt, His Life and Times: An Encyclopedic View,* edited by Otis L. Graham Jr. (Boston: G. K. Hall, 1985); and *The Harry S. Truman Encyclopedia,* edited by Richard S. Kirkendall (Boston: G. K. Hall, 1989). For the Supreme Court see the excellent *Oxford Companion to the Supreme Court of the United States,* edited by Kermit L. Hall (New York: Oxford University Press, 1992).

533. *Encyclopedia of American Cultural and Intellectual History.* **Edited by Mary Kupiec Cayton and Peter W. Williams. New York: Scribner's/Gale, 2001. 3 vols. Index. ISBN 0-684-80561-8.**

These excellent volumes provide a wonderful overview of the intellectual and cultural history of America from the colonial era to the present. Consisting of 200 substantial essays of several thousand words each, the encyclopedia includes copious cross-referencing along with bibliographies for further study. Individual essays deal with such diverse topics as "Abolitionism," "Festivals," "Library of Congress," "Patriotism," "Romanticism," "Stereotypes," "Webpages," and "Zoot Suit Riots." There are no biographical essays, but brief biographical information is provided for selected individuals in sidebars. The entries are arranged into eight chronological sections and nine thematic sections. Photos, illustrations, and graphs are included throughout the work. Two more specialized works with a literary bias are the *Cultural Encyclopedia of the 1850s in America,* by Robert L. Gale (Westport, CT: Greenwood, 1993); and *The Gay Nineties in America: A Cultural Dictionary of the 1890s,* by Robert L. Gale (Westport, CT: Greenwood, 1992).

534. *Encyclopedia of American History.* Edited by Richard B. Morris and Jeffrey B. Morris. 7th ed. New York: HarperCollins, 1996. 1,278pp. Index. ISBN 0-06-181605-1. First published in 1953, this classic work is widely viewed as the best one-volume reference book on American history. The 7th edition covers events from the age of discovery to December 1994. Comprehensive in scope, the encyclopedia is divided into four sections. Part 1 is a basic chronology of major political and military events. Social, economic, constitutional, and cultural events are dealt with in part 2. Part 3 is a mini-biographical dictionary of 500 notable Americans, while the structure of the federal government forms the focus of part 4. Lists of presidents and their cabinets, party strengths in Congress, the text of the Declaration of Independence, and a detailed index complete this enduring reference work.

535. *Encyclopedia of American Military History.* Edited by Spencer C. Tucker. New York: Facts on File, 2003. 3 vols. Index. ISBN 0-8160-4355-8. This three-volume encyclopedia of 600,000 words covers the period from the colonial wars to the events of September 11, 2001. The entries, written by a distinguished cast of military historians, focus on key individuals, give overviews of the causes, courses, and effects of America's wars, describe key technological developments, and discuss weapons systems. There is a helpful glossary and a selective bibliography divided into general reference works, monographs, encyclopedias, and atlases.

536. *Encyclopedia of American Political History: Studies of the Principal Movements and Ideas.* Edited by Jack P. Greene. New York: Scribner's, 1984. 3 vols. Index. ISBN 0-684-17003-5. Unlike other historical encyclopedias, which strive for comprehensive coverage, the intent of the editors of this set was to provide detailed coverage of a selected list of important topics in American political history. Some 90 topics are described in lengthy essays by some 90 scholars. Following a 25-page review of the historiography of American political history by Richard Jensen, the essays are arranged alphabetically, proceeding from agricultural policy to women's rights. Each essay includes a lengthy bibliography and numerous cross-references. Volume 3 contains a detailed index. Similar in arrangement and conception are Glenn Porter, ed., *Encyclopedia of American Economic History: Studies of Principle Movements and Ideas,* 3 vols. (New York: Scribner's, 1980); and Alexander DeConde, ed., *Encyclopedia of American Foreign Policy:*

Studies of the Principal Movements and Ideas, 3 vols., 2nd ed. (New York: Scribner, 2001). A useful single-volume work is *The Encyclopedia of American Political History,* edited by Paul Finkelman and Peter Wallenstein (CQ Press, 2001).

537. *The Encyclopedia of American Religious History.* **By Edward L. Queen, Stephen R. Prothero, and Gardiner H. Shattuck. Rev. ed. New York: Facts on File, 2001. 2 vols. Indexes. ISBN 0-8160-4335-3.**
This alphabetically arranged work contains articles on concepts, denominations, places, events, and persons. Each entry includes a bibliography, and the contributors are experts in their subjects. This excellent encyclopedia fills a unique and needed position in the reference literature and is well worth consulting or merely browsing. For a large and more specialized work on one group see the five-volume *Encyclopedia of Mormonism: The History, Scripture, Doctrine, and Procedure of the Church of Jesus Christ of Latter-Day Saints,* edited by Daniel H. Ludlow (New York: Macmillan, 1992). Also useful is *The Encyclopedia of American Catholic History,* edited by Michael Glazier and Thomas J. Shelley (Collegeville, MN: Liturgical, 1998).

538. *Encyclopedia of American Social History.* **Edited by Mary Kupiec Cayton, Elliot J. Gorn, and Peter W. Williams. New York: Scribner's, 1993. 3 vols. Index. ISBN 0-684-19246-2.**
This reference work consists of 180 comprehensive essays, written by 200 specialists, which are organized into the three volumes. Volume 1 contains the broad chronological essays and such topics as race, class, and gender; volume 2 deals with ethnicity, regionalism, and aspects of everyday life;

and volume 3 looks at popular culture, science and technology, and education. Each essay provides cross-referencing to related material in other essays. A detailed index of persons, places, and subjects is included in volume 3. While not organized as a work of ready-reference, the contents of these volumes are still valuable and easy to use. For a work focusing on the counterculture of the 1960s see *The ABC-CLIO Companion to the 1960s: Counterculture in America* (Santa Barbara, CA: ABC-CLIO, 1997).

539. *Encyclopedia of U.S. Foreign Relations.* **Edited by Bruce W. Jentleson and Thomas G. Patterson. 4 vols. Oxford: Oxford University Press, 1997. Index. ISBN 0-19-511055-2.**
United States foreign policy, foreign relations, diplomacy, and treaties from 1776 to the 1990s form the focus of this excellent, multivolume set. Consisting of 1,024 articles, alphabetically arranged and ranging in length from 150 to 10,000 words written by specialists in the field, this work is up-to-date, authoritative, and comprehensive. Individual entries cover events, concepts, and treaties along with numerous biographical entries. Similar in scope is the three-volume *Encyclopedia of American Foreign Policy,* edited by Alexander DeConde et al., 2nd ed. (New York: Scribner's, 2001). Also worth consulting is *Chronological History of U.S. Foreign Relations,* edited by Lester H. Brune and Richard D. Burns, 2nd ed. (New York: Routledge, Taylor & Francis, 2003), a three-volume reference work that updates the 1985 set. Following a brief introductory section on the colonial period up to 1775, the set describes every event concerning U.S. foreign affairs on a year-by-year basis through 2000. A select bibliography plus

an appendix describing the careers of secretaries of state 1781–2001 complement the set.

540. *The Reader's Companion to American History*. **Edited by Eric Foner and John A. Garraty. Boston: Houghton Mifflin, 1991. 1,226pp. Index. ISBN 0-395-51372-3.**
Sponsored by the Society of American Historians, this reference book strives for and succeeds in making history accessible to the broad public. It consists of over 1,000 entries, written by 400 scholars, on all aspects of American history from the beginning to 1990. The three types of entries—short subjects, interpretive essays, and biographies—are well written and linked together by generous cross-referencing to aid the reader in finding more about a subject. There is a detailed subject index along with helpful maps and charts. This volume does a particularly good job of integrating the results of new research in social history into the main fabric of American history. Very appropriate for addition to one's personal library, as is the similar *American Heritage Encyclopedia of American History,* edited by John Mack Faragher (New York: Holt, 1998), with its 3,000 brief entries, and the excellent *Oxford Companion to United States History,* edited by Paul S. Boyer et al. (New York: Oxford University Press, 2001).

Regions, States, and Cities

541. *Encyclopedia of the American West*. **Edited by Charles Phillips and Alan Axelrod. New York: Macmillan/Simon & Schuster, 1996. 4 vols. Index. ISBN 0-02-897495-6.**
Because both the West and the South have long been distinctive regions in the con-sciousness of popular culture and professional history, it is not surprising that they should lead the way in being represented by reference encyclopedias for specific regions. This set covers the history of the West, defined as the 23 states west of the Missouri River, during the 18th and 19th centuries. The four volumes contain 1,700 entries written by 400 contributors. About half the entries are biographical, but the subject entries tend to be longer and cover such topics as disease, Ghost Dance, and Virginia City. Nicely complementing this work is *The New Encyclopedia of the American West,* edited by Howard R. Lamar (New Haven, CT: Yale University Press, 1998), which contains 2,400 up-to-date but generally shorter entries written by 300 experts.

542. *Encyclopedia of Southern Culture*. **Edited by Charles Reagan Wilson and William Ferris. Chapel Hill, NC: University of North Carolina Press, 1989. 1,634pp. Index. ISBN 0-8078-1823-2.**
More than a reference book for history, this impressive reference work deals with the whole range of southern culture, including music, food, geography, politics, and myths. It consists of 1,300 entries, of which 350 are biographical. Individual entries are signed and include a bibliography for further reading. The entries are organized into 20 sections such as media, literature, and environment. Each section opens with a survey essay by the section editor and is followed by a group of longer entries and then a group of shorter entries. The entire volume is linked by the general index. A two-volume paperback edition is available. For a more historically oriented reference work on the South, there is the venerable *Encyclopedia of Southern History,* edited by David C. Poller and Robert W. Twyman

(Baton Rouge: Louisiana State University, 1979). Other regional cultural encyclopedias are in preparation. The *Encyclopedia of New England Culture,* which features 1,200 articles organized in 23 thematic sections, will be published by Yale University Press in 2003. The *Encyclopedia of the Great Plains* is in copyediting at the University of Nebraska Press. Expected publication date is 2004. The *Encyclopedia of Appalachia,* which continues to suffer financial problems, is due out in 2005 from the University of Tennessee Press.

543. *The New Handbook of Texas.* **Edited by Ron Tyler. Austin: Texas State Historical Association, 1996. 6 vols.**
ISBN 0-87611-151-7.
Probably the most elaborate and comprehensive reference book for the history of a single state, the *New Handbook of Texas* is an updating and expansion of the justly famous and beloved *Handbook of Texas* (Austin: Texas State Historical Association, 1952). The *New Handbook* consists of 23,500 entries written by 3,000 contributors. The entries cover counties, cities, towns, physical features, education institutions, railroads, oilfields, businesses, and newspapers, among other categories. There are also 7,200 biographical entries. Individual entries are signed, with a bibliography for further reading, and range from 50 words to some thousands. Black-and-white illustrations and photographs enliven the text. There is no index, but generous cross-referencing is provided. Other reference works on states include the *Dictionary of Oregon History,* edited by Howard McKinley Corning, 2nd ed. (Portland, OR: Binford & Mort, 1989); *The Kentucky Encyclopedia,* edited by John E. Kleber (Lexington: University Press of

Kentucky, 1992) (also available online); and the *Utah History Encyclopedia,* edited by Allan Kent Powell (Salt Lake City, UT: University of Utah Press, 1994). Forthcoming is the *West Virginia Encyclopedia* from the West Virginia Humanities Council. Among the most innovative projects is the *New Georgia Encyclopedia* (NGE), which debuted in late 2003. It will be the first online encyclopedia in the United States to be developed exclusively on the World Wide Web and will be available without charge.

544. *The Encyclopedia of New York City.*
Edited by Kenneth T. Jackson. New Haven, CT: Yale University Press, 1995. 1,350pp. Index. ISBN 0-300-05536-6.
This outstanding reference work takes as its subject the greatest city in the United States. Consisting of 4,300 entries written by 680 scholars, it covers all aspects of the city and its history—people, events, institutions, buildings, parks, and concepts. Individual entries are signed and range from 10 or 20 words to 6,000 words in length. Most include a bibliography for further reading. There are numerous black-and-white illustrations, charts, and maps. This encyclopedia received much attention from the publishing world, but it is actually modeled on the earlier *Encyclopedia of Cleveland History,* first published in 1988 but brought out in a second edition in 1996 by Indiana University Press. There is also an *Encyclopedia of Indianapolis* (Bloomington, IN: Indiana University Press, 1994), as well as a *Dictionary of Cleveland Biography*, edited by David D. Van Tassel and John J. Grabowski (Bloomington, IN: Indiana University Press, 1996), which is a companion volume to the *Encyclopedia. The Encyclopedia of Louisville,* edited by John E. Kleber (Lexington: University

Press of Kentucky, 2000), was an *LJ* Best Reference Book. It includes more than 1,800 entries on Kentucky's largest city. The *Encyclopedia of Chicago History*, edited by James R. Grossman, Ann Durkin Keating, and Janice L. Reiff, is currently in preparation at the Newberry Library. It will contain 1,400 entries when it is published by the University of Chicago Press and will also be available as a hypermedia encyclopedia on the Web site of the Chicago Historical Society.

By Chronological Periods

Colonial and Revolutionary

545. *Encyclopedia of the North American Colonies*. **Edited by Jacob Ernest Cooke. 3 vols. New York: Scribner's, 1993. Index. ISBN 0-684-19269-1.**
Comprehensive, up-to-date scholarship characterizes this impressive three-volume set covering colonial North America from the Norse settlements of c. 1000 to 1820 in New Mexico and 1860 in Alaska. The history of non-English colonies is also dealt with extensively. The three volumes contain 274 topical and thematic essays ranging from 1,000 to 15,000 words, which provide both factual and interpretive information including cross-referencing and bibliography; 193 recognized specialists wrote these essays. A detailed chronology appears in volume 1 and a master index for the entire set is included in volume 3. Those seeking a ready-reference source on this topic should see *The Encyclopedia of Colonial and Revolutionary America*, edited by John Faragher (New York: Facts on File, 1989), with its 1,500 entries focusing on the colonial era

of the United States. Those interested in the military history of this era should consult *Colonial Wars of North America, 1512–1763: An Encyclopedia*, edited by Alan Gallay (New York: Garland, 1996).

546. *The American Revolution, 1775–1783: An Encyclopedia*. **Edited by Richard L. Blanco. New York: Garland, 1993. 2 vols. ISBN 0-8240-5623-X.**
Forming part of Garland's "Wars of the United States" series, this set focuses on the American Revolution, the subject of a number of very good reference works. Over 800 entries, ranging in length from 250 to 25,000 words and written by a team of 125 expert contributors, largely cover the military aspects of the conflict. Broader coverage of social and cultural issues is provided by the *Blackwell Encyclopedia of the American Revolution*, edited by Jack P. Greene and J. R. Pole (Cambridge, MA: Blackwell, 1991), which is mostly a collection of interpretive reference essays and so is not a ready-reference tool. An older but still useful work is Mark Mayo Boatner III's *Encyclopedia of the American Revolution* (New York: David McKay, 1974), which was published in a third edition without any discernible updating in 1994.

19th Century

547. *Encyclopedia of the United States in the 19th Century*. **Edited by Paul Finkelman. Farmington Hills, MI: Scribner's/Gale Group, 2001. 3 vols. Index. ISBN 0-684-80500-6.**
This wonderful three-volume set ably fills in the chronological gap between the *Encyclopedia of the North American Colonies* and the *Encyclopedia of the United States in the*

20th Century. It consists of 599 alphabetically arranged entries, usually two to three pages in length, signed by the contributor, and containing bibliographies for further reading. Among the topics of the individual entries are "Alcoholic Beverages," "Compromise of 1850," "Language," "Panics and Depressions," "Sexual Morality," and "War of 1812." Individual states and important cities also have entries. Ample cross-referencing is provided throughout as well as an extensive index.

548. *Dictionary of Afro-American Slavery.* **Edited by Randall M. Miller and John David Smith. Updated ed. Westport, CT: Praeger/Greenwood, 1997. 892pp. Index. ISBN 0-313-23814-6.**
A skillful update to the excellent 1988 edition, this outstanding reference work remains the best comprehensive reference work on Afro-American slavery. Its alphabetical arrangement contains almost 300 lengthy topical articles written and signed by 230 contributors, many of whom are distinguished historians of slavery. Each article includes a select bibliography. The United States forms the principal focus, although there are articles on African and Afro-American cultures, slave resistance, and religion which transcend national boundaries. Chronological coverage extends from the first English settlements in the 17th century to Reconstruction in the mid-19th century. There is a helpful chronology of Afro-American slavery in an appendix. The updated edition is also available in an inexpensive paperback edition. Two other excellent works that take a global perspective and complement each others' contents are the two-volume *Historical Encyclopedia of World Slavery,* edited by

Junius P. Rodriquez (Santa Barbara, CA: ABC-CLIO, 1997) and the two-volume *Macmillan Encyclopedia of World Slavery,* edited by Paul Finkelman and Joseph Miller (New York: Macmillan, 1998). Taking a more historiographical and geographical approach is *A Historical Guide to World Slavery,* edited by Seymour Drescher and Stanley L. Engerman (New York: Oxford University Press, 1998).

549. *Encyclopedia of the American Civil War: A Political, Social, and Military History.* **Edited by David S. Heidler and Jeanne T. Heidler. Santa Barbara, CA: ABC-CLIO, 2000. 5 vols. Index. ISBN 1-57607-066-2 (print), ISBN 1-57607-382-3 (eBook).**
The American Civil War has been the subject of many fine reference works, but the most comprehensive is this five-volume set. Consisting of 1,600 entries, written by over 300 recognized scholars, it deals with people, institutions, events, groups, laws, and concepts including such diverse topics as: Louisa May Alcott, Antietam, Daniel Butterfield, Cairo [the ironclad], New York Draft Riots, and Zouaves. Each entry is signed by the contributor and includes a brief bibliography for further reading. The entire encyclopedia contains over 500 illustrations and 75 maps. Five appendixes and 250 primary sources are included along with a chronology, a bibliography, and a large general index located in volume 5. This title is also available in a massive, unabridged one-volume edition from W. W. Norton that appeared in 2002. Still useful is Patricia L. Faust, *The Historical Times Illustrated Encyclopedia of the Civil War* (New York: Harper & Row, 1986), with some 2,100 entries. These works are superior to the 1959 classic by Mark Boatner, *The Civil*

War Dictionary, rev. ed. (New York: David McKay, 1988). An excellent biographical complement is the widely praised Stewart Sifakis, *Who Was Who in the Civil War* (New York: Facts on File, 1988). Concentrating on the South is the four-volume *Encyclopedia of the Confederacy,* edited by Richard N. Current (New York: Simon and Schuster, 1993) with its 1,500 entries, some of which are up to 17,000 words long.

550. *The ABC-CLIO Companion to American Reconstruction.* **By William L. Richter. Santa Barbara, CA: ABC-CLIO, 1996. 505pp. Index. ISBN 0-87436-851-0.**
An excellent one-volume historical dictionary dealing the immediate post–Civil War era, it consists of interpretative essays ably written by a single author. These entries are generously cross-referenced, while an index further aids the reader. A useful chronology is also included. Another excellent recent work on the same topic is Hans L. Trefousse, *Historical Dictionary of Reconstruction* (Westport, CT: Greenwood, 1991).

20th Century

551. *Encyclopedia of the Vietnam War.* **Edited by Stanley I. Kutler. New York: Scribner's/ Simon & Schuster/Macmillan, 1996. 711pp. Index. ISBN 0-13-276932-8.**

552. *Encyclopedia of the Vietnam War: A Political, Social, and Military History.* **Edited by Spencer C. Tucker. Santa Barbara, CA: ABC-CLIO, 1998. 3 vols. Index. ISBN 0-87436-983-5.**
These two works represent the latest and the greatest in the busy field of reference works on the Vietnam War. Kutler's work consists of 10 long interpretative essays by leading scholars covering such topics as diplomacy and the antiwar movement, and hundreds of shorter articles dealing with people, events, places, and concepts written by other specialist scholars. Each entry is signed and includes a bibliography. There is also an extensive bibliography for the entire volume. Tucker's three-volume work contains 900 alphabetically arranged entries written by 80 specialist contributors. It also includes timelines, maps, statistical tables, and a bibliography. Unique among reference works, the third volume is made up of primary source materials. These works supersede previous works, although the *Dictionary of the Vietnam War,* edited by James S. Olson (Westport, CT: Greenwood Press, 1988), remains useful and is available in paperback.

553. *Encyclopedia of the United States in the 20th Century.* **Edited by Stanley I. Kutler et al. New York: Scribner's/Simon & Schuster, 1996. 4 vols. Index. ISBN 0-13-210535-7.**
Students and scholars of 20th-century American history will find this reference work to be an invaluable resource. The work is divided into six sections—the American people; politics; global America; science, technology, and medicine; the economy; and culture. Within each of these sections are the 74 interpretive essays written by 80 specialists. These essays cover such topics as bureaucracy, limited wars, and mass culture. While this work is not organized for ready-reference use, its detailed index allows specific information to be located readily and accurately. For a more specialized two-volume work there is the excellent *Encyclopedia of the Great Depression and*

the New Deal, edited by James Ciment (Armonk, NY: M. E. Sharpe, 2001). Among the better one-volume, ready-reference works specializing in various parts of 20th-century U.S. history there are the *Historical Dictionary of the New Deal: From Inauguration to Preparation for War,* edited by James S. Olson (Westport, CT: Greenwood, 1985); *The Historical Dictionary of the 1920s: From World War I to the New Deal, 1919–1933,* by James S. Olson (Westport, CT: Greenwood, 1988); *The Longman Companion to America in the Era of the Two World Wars, 1910–1945,* by Patrick Renshaw (White Plains, NY: Longman, 1996); *The Historical Dictionary of the 1950s,* by James S. Olson (Westport, CT: Greenwood, 2000); *The Columbia Guide to America in the 1960s,* by David Farber and Beth Bailey (New York: Columbia University Press, 2001); the *Historical Dictionary of the 1960s,* edited by James S. Olson and Samuel Freeman (Westport, CT: Greenwood, 1999); and the *Historical Dictionary of the 1970s,* edited by James S. Olson (Westport, CT: Greenwood, 1999).

554. *Historical Dictionary of the Progressive Era, 1890–1920.* **Edited by John D. Buenker and Edward Kantowicz. Westport, CT: Greenwood, 1988. 599pp. Index. ISBN 0-313-24309-3.**
Defining the Progressive Era as a broad-gauged response by Americans to the emergence of the United States as a modern industrial power during 1890–1919, this helpful dictionary includes 800 signed, alphabetically arranged entries from almost 200 contributors. The entries include important persons, events, institutions, and such items as notable films like *Birth of a Nation.* There is a helpful chronology and

three separate indexes to names, publications, and subjects.

555. *The Cold War Encyclopedia.* **By Thomas Parrish. New York: Henry Holt, 1996. 490pp. Index. ISBN 0-8050-2778-5.**
Now that the Cold War has ended, it has become a popular subject for historical scholarship and the focus of several reference works. This one-volume work provides descriptive and analytical entries for the important events, places, people, and concepts of that dangerous era in the history of the United States and the world. Similar in scope is Thomas S. Arms, *Encyclopedia of the Cold War* (New York: Facts on File, 1994). There is also a three-volume work that is more of a biographical dictionary, *The Cold War, 1945–1991,* edited by Benjamin Frankel (New York: Gale, 1992), and a valuable chronology, Kenneth Hill, *Cold War Chronology: Soviet American Relations, 1945–1991* (Washington, DC: Congressional Quarterly, 1993).

Ethnic

556. *Dictionary of Asian American History.* **Edited by Hyung-Chan Kim. Westport, CT: Greenwood, 1986. 627pp. Index. ISBN 0-313-23760-3.**
This is the first comprehensive reference work to focus exclusively on Asian Americans, one of the most rapidly growing ethnic minorities in the United States. It is divided into two major sections: (1) essays and (2) short entries. The first section consists of seven essays on the historical development of different ethnic groups from Asia and the Pacific Islands and eight essays

on the place of these groups in the American social order. Contributors include historians, sociologists, and Asian studies specialists. Eight hundred short entries written by the editor make up the second section. These focus on the historical experiences of the Chinese, Japanese, Korean, Asian Indians, Filipinos, and the various Southeast Asians. The entries highlight topics such as associations, legislation, companies, and important individuals concerned with the Asian American experience and include suggestions for additional readings. Appendixes include a select bibliography, a chronology, and 1980 census data. *The Asian American Encyclopedia*, edited by Franklin Ng, 6 vols. (New York: Marshall Cavendish, 1995), deals with the same subject.

557. *Dictionary of Mexican American History.* **By Matt S. Meier and Feliciano Rivera. Westport, CT: Greenwood, 1981. 498pp. Index. ISBN 0-313-21203-1.**
Although covering the entire range of the Mexican American experience in the region of the present-day United States, the principal focus is on the period after 1835. Entries for the period 1519–1835 largely concentrate on individuals and events connected with the exploration and settlement of northern New Spain. Alphabetically arranged, the approximately 1,000 entries written by the two editors and 20 contributors highlight virtually every aspect of the Mexican American experience, including prominent individuals, treaties, major migrations, legislation, literature, folklore, and special terms like "braceros" and "undocumented." These are followed by a short bibliography, a chronology, a glossary of Chicano terms, census data (now somewhat dated), a list of Mexican American journals, and a series of maps. This volume is complemented by Meier and Rivera's *Mexican American Biographies: A Historical Dictionary, 1836–1987* [see 704] and the *Encyclopedia of the Mexican American Civil Rights Movement,* which Meier coedited with Margo Gutierrez for Greenwood Press in 2000.

558. *Harvard Encyclopedia of American Ethnic Groups.* **Edited by Stephen Thernstrom. Cambridge, MA: Belknap Press of Harvard University Press, 1980. 1,076pp. ISBN 0-674-37512-2.**
Using a broad definition of "ethnicity," this encyclopedia includes 106 group entries and 29 thematic essays written by 120 contributors. Some of the essays are exhaustive and focus on the following topics concerning the ethnic group: origins, migration, arrival, settlements, economic life, social structure, social organization, family and kinship, behavior, culture, religion, education, politics, intergroup relations, group maintenance, and individual ethnic commitment. Each essay is signed and includes a brief bibliography of reference and secondary studies. An excellent complement is provided by *We the People: An Atlas of America's Ethnic Diversity* [see 771].

559. *Encyclopedia of African-American Culture and History.* **Edited by Jack Salzman, David Lionel Smith, and Cornel West. New York: Macmillan, 1996. 5 vols. Index. ISBN 0-02-897345-3.**
Given the flourishing state of African American history, this volume provides a useful and needed summing up and overview of an important subject. The five

volumes contain some 2,200 entries covering all aspects of the African American
experience from their beginnings in North
America to the present, including demographics, economics, music, art, and sports.
Two-thirds of the articles are biographical,
but most white figures who played a role
in African American history have been
excluded. The articles are arranged alphabetically, include a bibliography for further
reading, and are signed by the specialist
author. There are many large interpretive
essays, and each individual state has its own
entry. For some useful one-volume reference works see the classic *Negro Almanac:
A Reference Work on the African American*,
compiled and edited by Harry A. Ploski
and James Williams, 5th ed. (Detroit: Gale,
1989) and W. August Low, *Encyclopedia of
Black America* (New York: McGraw-Hill,
1981). A more recent volume covering
both African and African American topics is
the excellent *Africana: The Encyclopedia of the
African and African-American Experience*,
edited by Kwame Anthony Appiah and
Henry Louis Gates Jr. (Reading, MA: Basic
Civitas Books/Perseus Books, 1999).

560. *Encyclopedia of Women in American
History*. Edited by Joyce Appleby, Eileen K.
Cheng, and Joanne Goodwin. New York:
M. E. Sharpe, 2002. 3 vols. Index.
ISBN 0-7656-8-38-6.

For a unique and very comprehensive guide
to women's history, one cannot do better
than the *Encyclopedia of Women in American
History*. The three volumes each cover a
specific period of time—1585–1820, 1820–
1900, and 1900 to present. Each volume
contains a timeline and broad essays surveying topics such as "Women and Religion,"
"Women and Western Expansion, 1820–

1900," and "Feminism." There are also over
1,000 briefer articles divided between the
volumes that deal with people (Abigal
Adams), events (Seneca Falls convention),
institutions (Working Women's Clubs), laws
(Equal Pay Acts), and customs (courtship).
These entries are organized alphabetically
within the individual volume. There is also a
section of documents dealing with women's
history in each volume along with a select
bibliography and a biographical index of
women. Sidebars are scattered throughout
the text listing women's firsts, prize winners, and important quotations, along with
illuminating graphs and charts. Two good
single volume reference works are Kathryn
Cullen-DuPont, *The Encyclopedia of Women's
History in America* (New York: Facts on File,
1998) and the *Handbook of American Women's
History*, edited by Angela M. Howard and
Frances M. Kavenik, 2nd ed. (Thousand
Oaks, CA: Sage, 2000).

UNITED KINGDOM
AND IRELAND

561. *The Columbia Companion to British
History*. Edited by Juliet Gardiner and Neil
Wenborn. New York: Columbia University
Press, 1997. 840pp. ISBN 0-231-10792-7.

562. *The Oxford Companion to British
History*. Edited by John Cannon. Oxford:
Oxford University Press, 1997. 1,004pp.
ISBN 0-19-866176-2.

It is impossible to say which of these two
excellent dictionaries of British history is
the best. When possible both should be
consulted. Each contains over 4,000 entries,
ranging in length from 50 to several thou-

sand words and dealing with events, institutions, people, and concepts. First-class scholars contributed to both projects. Both works cover the same core topics of British history, but each has its special strengths. The *Columbia Companion* puts more emphasis on politics while the *Oxford Companion* includes many more entries on places and has more topics relating to America. In Great Britain, the *Columbia Companion* was published as the *History Today Companion to British History*. Also useful are J. P. Kenyon, ed., *A Dictionary of British History* (New York: Stein & Day, 1983), available in an inexpensive Wordsworth paperback; Arthur Marwick, *The Illustrated Dictionary of British History* (New York: Thames & Hudson, 1980); and S. H. Steinberg and I. H. Evans, eds., *Steinberg's Dictionary of British History,* 2nd ed. (New York: St. Martin's, 1970), which is a revision of *A New Dictionary of British History.* An excellent but more specialized volume is Ben Weinreb and Christopher Hibbert, eds., *The London Encyclopedia* (London: Macmillan, 1984). Various historical dictionaries and encyclopedias are available for specific periods of British history such as *The Blackwell Encyclopedia of Anglo-Saxon England,* edited by Michael Lapidge et al. (Malden, MA: Blackwell, 1999); *Medieval England: An Encyclopedia,* edited by Paul F. Szarmach, M. Teresa Tavormina, and Joel T. Rosenthal (New York: Garland, 1998); *The Historical Dictionary of Late Medieval England, 1272–1485,* edited by Ronald H. Fritze and William B. Robison (Westport, CT: Greenwood, 2001); *The Historical Dictionary of Tudor England, 1485–1603,* edited by Ronald H. Fritze (Westport, CT: Greenwood, 1991); *The Historical Dictionary of Stuart England, 1603–1689,* edited by Ronald H. Fritze

and William B. Robison (Westport, CT: Greenwood, 1996); *Britain in the Hanoverian Age, 1714–1837,* edited by Gerald Newman et al. (New York: Garland, 1997); *Victorian Britain: An Encyclopedia,* edited by Sally Mitchell (New York: Garland, 1988); *The Oxford Companion to 20th-Century British Politics,* edited by John Ramsden (Oxford: Oxford University Press, 2002); and *A Companion to Early Twentieth-Century Britain,* edited by Chris Wrigley (London: Blackwell, 2003).

563. *The Oxford Companion to Irish History.* Edited by S. J. Connolly. 2nd ed. Oxford: Oxford University Press, 2002. 672pp. ISBN 0-19-866270-X.

Covering every aspect and era of Irish history, this reference book is a great tool for ready-reference and is also a browser's delight. Eighty-seven experts wrote the 1,800 entries that deal with people, events, institutions, traditions, concepts, and places. Still useful is the first dictionary devoted to Irish history, *A Dictionary of Irish History Since 1800,* by D. J. Hickey and J. E. Doherty (Totowa, NJ: Barnes & Noble, 1981); also see Peter R. Newman, *Companion to Irish History: From the Submission of Tyrone to Partition, 1603–1921* (New York: Facts on File, 1991).

564. *A Dictionary of Scottish History.* By Gordon Donaldson and Robert S. Morpeth. Edinburgh: John Donald, 1977. 234pp. ISBN 0-85976-018-9.

Containing more than 5,000 very brief entries, the book's coverage is comprehensive for events, civil and ecclesiastical institutions, titles, and offices but more selective for other areas. Some entries are almost too brief to be helpful, and no criteria for inclusion is mentioned. There is a brief chronology of Scottish history from 843 to 1707. A companion volume is the same authors' *Who's Who in Scottish History* (New York: Barnes & Noble, 1973). Covering Scottish history from the 16th century to the present is *A Companion to Scottish History: From Reformation to the Present,* by Ian Donnachie and George Hewitt (New York: Facts on File, 1989), while religious history, very broadly defined, is the scope of the very useful *Dictionary of Scottish Church History and Theology,* edited by Nigel M. de S. Cameron et al. (Downers Grove, IL: Inter-Varsity Press, 1993). Also useful for ready-reference is the *Collins Dictionary of Scottish History,* edited by Ian Donnachie and George Hewitt (New York: HarperCollins, 2002).

CANADA

565. *The Canadian Encyclopedia.* 2nd ed. Edmonton, Alberta: Hurtig, 1988. 4 vols. Index. ISBN 0-88830-326-2. CD-ROM Version, 1994–.

Well-known Edmonton publisher Mel Hurtig worked diligently to secure funding for a Canadian encyclopedia that would replace one published by Grolier in 1957. With support from the Alberta government as part of its 75th anniversary celebrations, the first edition was published in 1985 to considerable acclaim. Succeeding print editions sold 220,000 sets. The first CD-ROM version appeared in 1994. The most recent issue provides more powerful searching, allows you to bookmark and take notes, includes 4,000 photos and maps, 100 videos, and hundreds of sounds. With more

than 200,000 copies sold, it's the standard reference on Canada. See also *Encyclopedia of British Columbia* edited by Daniel Francis (Vancouver, B.C.: Heritage House Publishing, 2000) which contains 4,000 articles and over 1,000 historic and color photographs. A full feature CD-ROM edition is also available.

566. *The Collins Dictionary of Canadian History: 1867 to the Present.* By David J. Bercuson and J. L. Granatstein. Toronto: Collins, 1988.

Students of Canadian history since Confederation will be well served by this helpful one-volume dictionary. The combined talents of two of Canada's most prominent historians have produced some 1,600 entries ranging over politics to agriculture with abundant cross-references. There are helpful timelines and many black-and-white illustrations. Various appendixes list the governors general, prime ministers, and all provincial premiers (in chronological order by province), along with lists of principal imports and exports and other economic data.

EUROPE

Multiperiod

567. *Encyclopedia of European Social History: From 1350 to 2000.* Edited by Peter N. Stearns. Farmington Hills, MI: Scribner's/Gale, 2001. 6 vols. Index. ISBN 0-684-80582-0.

Covering some 650 years of history, the *Encyclopedia of European Social History: From 1350 to 2000* ranges from the age of the

Black Death to the beginning of the third millennium. It consists of some 230 essays written by almost 170 international scholars. Individual essays range from 5,000 to 10,000 words in length. The essays in the first five volumes are arranged under broad categories such as "Gender," "Population and Geography," and "Social Protest," with individual entries dealing with such topics as "Animals and Pets," "Rural Revolt," and "Public Health." There are also chronological and geographical sections titled "The Periods of Social History" and "Regions, Nations, and Peoples." The sixth volume includes relevant biographies extracted from other Gale publications and a detailed index for the entire set.

Ancient

568. *Civilization of the Ancient Mediterranean: Greece and Rome.* **Edited by Michael Grant and Rachel Kitzinger. New York: Scribner's, 1988. 3 vols. Index. ISBN 0-684-17594-0.**

Like the similar sets for American history, this publication includes 97 lengthy essays arranged under 14 broad headings such as government and society, private and social life, and history. The latter is the focus of the two historical summaries on Greece and Rome. While it lacks short definitions and brief entries, the useful index makes it easy to locate information on the most frequently discussed topics of Greek and Roman history. Specialized essays describe virtually every topic of historical debate from slavery to attitudes towards birth control. For some useful one-volume ready-reference works, see *A Dictionary of Ancient History*, edited by Graham Speake (Cam-

bridge, MA: Blackwell, 1994); David Sacks, *Encyclopedia of the Ancient Greek World* (New York: Facts on File, 1995); and Matthew Bunson, *Encyclopedia of the Roman Empire*, rev. ed. (New York: Facts on File, 2002).

569. *The Anchor Bible Dictionary.* **Edited by David Noel Freedman. 6 vols. New York: Doubleday, 1992. ISBNs 0-385-19351-3, -19360-2, -19361-0, -19362-9, -19363-7, and -26190-x.**

Although not strictly a historical reference work, the monumental *Anchor Bible Dictionary* will be useful and of great interest to many students of the ancient Near East and the Classical World. Unlike previous multivolume dictionaries of the Bible, this work is more concerned with history, social context, and archaeology than with philology and textual criticism. Consisting of over 6,000 entries by almost 1,000 well-qualified contributors, it is arranged alphabetically. Each entry is signed and all but the smaller entries provide up-to-date bibliographies. Entries range in size from 50 words to several thousand and cover people, places, and topics. Cross- and see-references abound. It is definitely the place to start for topics in biblical history and a good supplement to other reference works on ancient Near Eastern and Classical history.

570. *Late Antiquity: A Guide to the Postclassical World.* **Edited by G. W. Bowersock, Peter Brown, and Oleg Grabar. Cambridge, MA: Harvard University Press, 1999. 780pp. ISBN 0-674-51173-5.**

571. *Encyclopedia of Early Christianity.* **Edited by Everett Ferguson et al. New York: Garland, 1997. 2 vols. ISBN 0-8153-1663-1.**

572. *Encyclopedia of the Early Church.* Edited by Angelo Di Berardino. New York: Oxford University Press, 1992. 2 vols. ISBN 0-19-520892-7.

These three works cover the same basic chronological period and subject but with some important differences. *Late Antiquity* covers the years 250–800 and consists of 11 topical essays and 500 entries covering all aspects of that era. As such it is a unique work that bridges the ancient and medieval worlds in the West. Christianity and the early church are the more specialized focus of the other two works. Almost 1,200 entries by over 130 scholars appear in the Garland work, while 167 scholars wrote the multitudinous articles in the Oxford volumes. Articles in both sets describe doctrines, institutions, events, practices of worship, heresies, and prominent leaders and thinkers of the Church, as well as pagans who had a major impact on the development of Christianity. While the Garland volumes cover only the first six centuries of the Christian faith, the Oxford volumes continue their coverage to 735 in the West and 759 in the East. There are more unique biographical entries in the Oxford volumes, but the Garland volumes include a significant number of important subject entries. The Oxford volumes were originally published in Italy and were updated bibliographically when they were translated into English.

573. *Oxford Classical Dictionary.* Edited by Simon Hornblower and Anthony Spawforth. Rev. 3rd ed. Oxford: Oxford University Press, 2003. 1,704pp. ISBN 0-19-860641-9.

A significantly updated and revised third edition of the *Oxford Classical Dictionary*

(*OCD*) appeared in 1996. It was some 30 percent larger than the second edition with over 6,200 signed entries written by 364 scholars. The 2003 revision is a modest expansion of the third edition. The *OCD* has always been the first stop for anyone with a question about ancient Greek and Roman history. Coverage of women, the Far East, and interdisciplinary topics has been greatly increased in the two most recent editions. The earlier editions of this work can still be useful, but the new edition should be the considered the final authority. Also useful are Simon Hornblower and Anthony Spawforth, *Oxford Companion to Classical Civilization* (Oxford: Oxford University Press, 1998); the second edition of *The Oxford Companion to Classical Literature,* edited by M. C. Howatson (Oxford: Oxford University Press, 1989); Lesley Adkins and Roy A. Adkins, *Handbook to Life in Ancient Greece* (Oxford: Oxford University Press, 1997); and Lesley Adkins and Roy A. Adkins, *Handbook to Life in Ancient Rome* (Oxford: Oxford University Press, 1993).

Medieval/Middle Ages

574. *Dictionary of the Middle Ages.* Edited by Joseph R. Strayer. New York: Scribner's, 1982–1989. 12 vols. ISBN 0-684-16760-3 and *Supplement.* New York: Scribner's, 2003. ISBN 0-684-80642-8.

This magnificent multivolume reference work on the Middle Ages was completed in late 1988, shortly after the death of the editor in 1987. Alphabetically arranged, the 5,000 entries are divided into volumes averaging about 600 pages. While definitions and identifications average less than 100 words in length, some of the major articles extend to 10,000 words. Each article is signed and includes a short list of recent works. The majority of the contributors were American and Canadian academics, although there are also many from European institutions. The chronological scope of this set extends from AD 500 to 1500. Its principal geographical focus is on the Latin West, the Slavic world, Asia Minor, the Islamic Middle East, and Muslim and Christian North Africa. The *Supplement* published in 2003 adds a 13th volume to the set. A four-volume abridgement of this work is available as *The Middle Ages: An Encyclopedia for Students,* edited by William Chester Jordan (New York: Scribner's/ Simon & Schuster/Macmillan, 1996). There is also the two-volume *Encyclopedia of the Middle Ages,* edited by André Vauchez with Barrie Dobson and Michael Lapidge (London: Routledge, 2001), which is based on a French publication but has been expanded and revised for English readers. Other useful one-volume works on the same topic are Matthew Bunson, *Encyclopedia of the Middle Ages* (New York: Facts on File, 1995); and Norman F. Cantor, *The Encyclopedia of the Middle Ages* (New York: Viking, 1999).

575. *The Oxford Dictionary of Byzantium.* Edited by Alexander Kazhdan et al. New York: Oxford University Press, 1991. 3 vols. ISBN 0-19-504652-8.
Providing an impressive complement to the *Dictionary of the Middle Ages,* this impressive encyclopedia covers the frequently neglected topic of the Byzantine Empire. Its 5,000 signed entries were written by over 100 specialists and cover all aspects of Byzantium's history and culture including art, literature, and religion. Individual entries range from 75 to 100 words up to

several thousand, and most include bibliographies for further study.

Renaissance/Reformation/ Early Modern

576. *Encyclopedia of the Renaissance.* Edited by Paul F. Grendler. New York: Scribner's, 1999. 6 vols. ISBN 0-684-80514-6.
The chronological scope of this wonderful multivolume reference work starts with Italy in 1350 and continues with the rest of Europe, along with parts of the rest of the world in 1450 and concludes around 1650. It is multi- and interdisciplinary in its approach as befits an encyclopedia of the Renaissance covering European and world history, literature, art, music, science, and religion as well as other topics. Topics of individual articles are arranged alphabetically and include people, places, events, concepts, and historiographical essays, which range from 250 to 7,000 words in length. There are also hundreds of illustrations, 35 maps, a chronology, and an index. The *Encyclopedia of the Renaissance* is destined to be the premier and classic reference work for its subject. For useful one-volume works on the Renaissance, see the *Encyclopedia of the Renaissance,* edited by Thomas Bergin and Jennifer Speake (New York: Facts on File, 1987) and *The Hutchinson Encyclopedia of the Renaissance,* edited by David Rundle (Boulder, CO: Westview, 1999).

577. *Oxford Encyclopedia of the Reformation.* Edited by Hans J. Hillerbrand. New York: Oxford University Press, 1996. 4 vols. Index. ISBN 0-19-506493-3.
This comprehensive, scholarly work of ref-

erence is the definitive guide to the Reformation of the 16th century, which is broadly defined both topically and chronologically to encompass relevant subjects from the 15th and 17th centuries including art, travel, social problems, and exploration, as well as religion and politics. The 1,200 entries by an international group of over 450 scholars range from 300 to 7,500 words. They cover events, institutions, concepts, groups, and individual people. Cross- and see-references and a detailed index aid readers in finding as much as they can about a topic. This work is complemented by the two-volume *Handbook of European History, 1400–1600,* edited by Thomas Brady Jr., Heiko Oberman, and James D. Tracy (Grand Rapids, MI: Eerdmans, 1994), a collection of topical and chronological essays similar in format to the *New Cambridge Modern History.* Also useful, and available in paperback, is *The Longman Companion to the European Reformation, c. 1500–1618,* by Mark Greengrass (London: Longman, 1998).

578. *The Penguin Dictionary of English and European History, 1485–1789.* By E. N. Williams. New York: Penguin, 1980. 509pp. Index.

Although this dictionary only consists of about 500 entries, it is packed full of information on European history from 1485 to 1789. Individual entries are limited to major subjects and provide detailed accounts of people's careers, wars, institutions, groups, and concepts. Topics of political, military, and diplomatic history predominate. A detailed index allows more specialized topics to be located within larger entries. This inexpensive volume is a useful addition to any ready-reference collection or scholar's study.

579. *A Dictionary of Eighteenth-Century World History.* Edited by Jeremy Black and Roy Porter. Cambridge, MA: Blackwell, 1994. 880pp. ISBN 0-631-18068-0.

Covering the "long" 18th century from the 1690s to the fall of Napoleon in 1815, this handy one-volume reference work contains over 1,000 entries written by more than 100 specialists. Individual entries range from short entries of fewer than 100 words to long ones having over 1,000 words. Each entry is signed and includes a bibliography for further reading. European history is the primary focus of this volume, although the history of other parts of the world is discussed and ably summarized. There are also sections for a master bibliography, a detailed chronology, and maps. This book is available in paperback as *The Penguin Dictionary of Eighteenth-Century History* (1996). For recent useful titles covering the important intellectual history of the 18th century see *The Blackwell Companion to the Enlightenment,* by John W. Yolton et al. (Cambridge, MA: Blackwell, 1992); Peter Hanns Reill and Ellen Judy Wilson, *Encyclopedia of the Enlightenment* (New York: Facts on File, 1996); and the monumental *Encyclopedia of the Enlightenment,* edited by Alan Charles Kors, 4 vols. (Oxford: Oxford University Press, 2002). This latter set includes 700 signed articles by an international team of leading scholars and reflects new theoretical and methodological approaches to Enlightenment Studies.

Modern

General

580. *A Dictionary of Nineteenth-Century World History.* Edited by John Belchem and

Richard Price. Cambridge, MA: Blackwell, 1994. 746pp. Index. ISBN 0-631-18352-3. Focusing on the years 1800–1900, with modest overlap on either end of the chronological scale, this work contains 800 signed entries, ranging from 150 to 400 words in length, covering events, concepts, and persons. There is also a chronology, seven maps, and a personal name index. While the focus is on Europe and North America, other parts of the world receive attention. It has been published in paperback as the *Penguin Dictionary of Nineteenth-Century History*.

581. *The Penguin Dictionary of Modern History, 1789–1945.* By Alan Palmer. 2nd ed. New York: Penguin, 1983. 315pp. ISBN 0-14-051-125-3.

This bargain-priced standard dictionary of recent history is a useful addition to any historian's library. One reviewer called it a sort of mini-encyclopedia of persons, events, and key words. The second edition adds 100 new entries on North America and Australia in an attempt to balance the British and European emphasis of the first edition. Generally the engagingly written entries deal with political and military history. A companion volume is the same author's *Penguin Dictionary of Twentieth-Century History*, 2nd ed. (New York: Penguin, 1983), which originally appeared as *The Facts on File Dictionary of 20th Century History* (New York: Facts on File, 1979). Also useful is Chris Cook and John Stevenson, *The Longman Handbook of Modern European History, 1763–1985* (New York: Longman, 1987).

582. *A Dictionary of Twentieth Century History 1914–1990.* By Peter Teed. New

York: Oxford University Press, 1992. 520pp. ISBN 0-19-211676-2.

Attempts to provide a comprehensive reference work for world history in the 20th century in some 2,000 entries. Individual entries range from a few words to approximately 500 words. Events, people, politics, military, economics, culture, society, and technology are all discussed, but with an emphasis on politics. Inevitable gaps exist in this volume's coverage, which means that while it can readily serve as the first stop in someone's search for information on the 20th century, it will probably not be the last stop. Other useful and sometimes more specialized one-volume reference works on the history of the 20th century are Chris Cook and John Stevenson, *The Longman Handbook of World History since 1914* (New York: Longman, 1991); *The Columbia Dictionary of European Political History since 1914*, edited by John Stevenson (New York: Columbia University Press, 1992); Derek W. Urwin, *A Dictionary of European History and Politics, 1945–1995* (White Plains, NY: Longman, 1996); and Jan Palmowski, *A Dictionary of Twentieth Century World History* (New York: Oxford University Press, 1997).

By Region/Country

France

583. *Critical Dictionary of the French Revolution.* Edited by François Furet and Mona Ozouf. Cambridge, MA: Harvard University Press, 1989. 1,604pp. Index. ISBN 0-674-17728-2.

Two leading members of the revisionist school on the history of the French Revolution, both professors at the Ecole des Hautes Etudes in Paris, have put together this very provocative reference work. Published in France in 1988, it became something of an academic bestseller. Neither exhaustive nor encyclopedic, its entries are divided into five sections: Events, Actors, Institutions and Creations, Ideas, and Historians. Each lengthy entry corresponds to an important event or ideal of the Revolution. The entries are well-written, discuss controversial aspects of the subject, include sources for further reading, and provide cross-references to related topics. Of the 99 entries, the editors wrote 43, while the remaining 46 were written by 22 other historians and philosophers, many from the Ecole des Hautes Etudes. Beautiful color illustrations and name and subject indexes complement the volume. Two other works on the same subject are John Paxton, *Companion to the French Revolution* (New York: Facts on File, 1988) and the particularly helpful Colin Jones, *Longman Companion to the French Revolution* (New York: Longman, 1988).

584. *Historical Dictionary of the French Revolution, 1789–1799.* Edited by Samuel F. Scott and Barry Rothaus. Westport, CT: Greenwood, 1985. 2 vols. ISBN 0-313-21141-8.

585. *Historical Dictionary of Napoleonic France, 1799–1815.* Edited by Owen Connelly. Westport, CT: Greenwood, 1985. 586pp. ISBN 0-313-21321-6.

586. *Historical Dictionary of France from the 1815 Restoration to the Second Empire.* Edited by Edgar L. Newman and Robert L. Simpson. Westport, CT: Greenwood, 1987. 2 vols. ISBN 0-313-22751-9.

587. *Historical Dictionary of the French Second Empire, 1852–1870.* Edited by William E.

Echard. Westport, CT: Greenwood, 1985. 829pp. ISBN 0-313-21136-1.

588. *Historical Dictionary of the Third French Republic, 1870–1940.* Edited by Patrick H. Hutton, Amanda S. Bourque, and Amy J. Staples. Westport, CT: Greenwood, 1986. 2 vols. ISBN 0-313-22080-8.

589. *Historical Dictionary of World War II France: Occupation, Vichy, and the Resistance, 1938–1946.* Edited by Bertram M. Gordon. Westport, CT: Greenwood, 1998. 432pp. ISBN 0-313-29421-6.

590. *Historical Dictionary of the French Fourth and Fifth Republics, 1946–1991.* Edited by Wayne Northcutt. Westport, CT: Greenwood, 1992. 527pp. Index. ISBN 0-313-26356-6.

This outstanding series contains articles on a vast number of topics concerning French history from the outbreak of the Revolution in 1789 to the Fifth Republic in 1991. Entries within each set are arranged alphabetically, signed by the contributor, and include a brief, up-to-date bibliography. There are numerous cross-references with each set having a separate index and a chronology of events. Contributors include both well-known scholars and younger professors from North America and Europe. Unlike many historical dictionaries, political and military affairs do not predominate so there is broad coverage of social history, literature, education, journalism, religion, and labor. For France during the Middle Ages, see *Medieval France: An Encyclopedia* edited by William M. Kibler and Grover A. Zinn (New York: Garland, 1995), which covers from the early fifth century to the late 15th century. Early modern France awaits its lexicographer.

Germany

591. *Modern Germany: An Encyclopedia of History, People, and Culture, 1871–1990.* Edited by Dieter K. Buse and Jürgen C. Doerr. New York: Garland, 1998. 2 vols. Index. ISBN 0-8153-0503-6.

Germany's important role in the history of the 20th century makes it a fitting topic for a scholarly and comprehensive work of reference. Some 400 contributors wrote the 1,300 entries found in this two-volume work. All aspects of German history, society, and culture are included. Individual entries are signed by the specialist author, thoroughly cross-referenced to related articles, and include bibliographies to guide further study. An older and shorter one-volume work covering a somewhat longer chronological period is Wilfred Fest, *Dictionary of German History, 1806–1945* (New York: St. Martin's, 1978). For a more general work in German, there is the *Lexikon der Deutschen Geschichte: Personen, Ereignisse, Institutionen,* edited by Gerhard Taddy (Stuttgart: Alfred Kröner Verlag, 1977).

592. *The Encyclopedia of the Third Reich.* Edited by Christian Zentner and Friedemann Bedurftig. New York: Macmillan, 1991. 2 vols. Index. ISBN 0-02-897500-6.

Nazi Germany is a subject of perennial interest among scholars, students, and the general public; this two-volume set is the best of a group of generally excellent works of reference. It is an updated and expanded English translation of the German work *Das grosse Lexicon des Dritten Reiches,* published in 1985. It contains over 3,000 entries, some of which are quite long treatments of their subject, and includes well over 1,000 illustrations and graphics. Events, groups, laws, and places all have their place in the entries along with biographies of important individuals. There is a useful master index and the bibliography has been updated to include English works. An older one-volume English work is Louis L. Snyder, *Encyclopedia of the Third Reich* (New York: McGraw-Hill, 1976). For a much needed work on a neglected topic, see the related *Historical Dictionary of Germany's Weimar Republic, 1918–1933,* by Vincent C. Paul (Westport, CT: Greenwood, 1997).

593. *The Holy Roman Empire: A Dictionary Handbook.* Edited by Jonathan W. Zophy. Westport, CT: Greenwood, 1980. 551pp. Index. ISBN 0-313-21457-3.

Voltaire is said to have quipped that the Holy Roman Empire was "neither Holy, nor Roman, nor an Empire," but it did endure from 800 to 1806 and encompassed much of central and southern Europe. Zophy, a historian at the University of Houston at Clear Lake, and some 30 American contributors have compiled approximately 500 entries on the important people and events of that Empire. While the emphasis is on the biographical, there are 10 histories of cities, along with essays on women, Jews, witchcraft, and wars. Entries average a page or more and include lists of works about and, in some cases, by the biographee. Appendixes include a list of Emperors and their predecessor kings, a chronology, and a list of the rulers of the Hohenzollern dynasty. There is a short bibliography. For a more specialized work covering the years 500 to 1500, there is *Medieval Germany: An Encyclopedia,* edited by John M. Jeep (New York: Garland, 2001).

Italy

594. *Dictionary of Modern Italian History.*
Edited by Frank J. Coppa. Westport, CT:
Greenwood, 1985. 496pp. Index.
ISBN 0-313-22983-X.

Dictionaries of modern Italian history are
not common, but this one is excellent.
Coppa, a historian at St. John's University,
organized a notable group of American
academics as consultants and contributors
to create this volume. Coverage includes
18th-century Italy, the Risorgimento
(1796–1861), Liberal Italy (1861–1922),
Fascist Italy (1922–1945), and post–World
War II Italy. Following brief introductions
for these periods, the signed entries are
arranged alphabetically. They range from
100 to 900 words in length and occasionally include lists of further readings. There
are chronologies of important events, a long
list of ministries since 1848, a list of presidents of the Italian Republic, a list of kings
of Piedmont and Italy, and a short list of
popes since 1700. More detailed and narrower in scope is Philip V. Cannistraro, *Historical Dictionary of Fascist Italy* (Westport,
CT: Greenwood, 1982).

Russia/Soviet Union

595. *Dictionary of the Russian Revolution.*
Edited by George Jackson and Robert
Devlin. Westport, CT: Greenwood, 1989.
704pp. Index. ISBN 0-313-21131-0.

Although narrow in focus, this alphabetically arranged dictionary provides a wealth
of information about the institutions,
events, and personalities that influenced the
course of the Russian Revolution of 1917.
More than 100 contributors from the
United States, Canada, Great Britain,

France, Holland, and Australia wrote some
300 in-depth articles on social forces; political parties; prominent individuals; institutions, groups, and associations; significant
events; regional and ethnic studies; and
other important themes. Most articles are
signed and include short bibliographies
of monographs in English and Russian.
Appendixes include a chronology of the
Revolution from 1898 to the death of
Lenin in 1924, a series of maps, and census
statistics for 1897 and 1926. See also Harold
Shukman, ed., *The Blackwell Encyclopedia of
the Russian Revolution* (New York: Basil
Blackwell, 1988) and the *Critical Companion
to the Russian Revolution 1914–1921,* edited
by Edward Acton, Vladimir Iu. Cherniaev,
and William G. Rosenberg (Bloomington,
IN: Indiana University Press, 1997).

596. *Modern Encyclopedia of Russian, Soviet,
and Eurasian History.* Edited by Joseph
Wieczynski and George N. Rhyne. Gulf
Breeze, FL: Academic International,
1976–2000. 60 vols. ISBN 0-87569-064-5.

597. *The Supplement to The Modern
Encyclopedia of Russian, Soviet, and Eurasian
History.* Edited by and Edward J. Lazzerini
and George N. Rhyne. Gulf Breeze, FL:
Academic International, 1995–. 2 vols.
ISBN 0-87569-142-0.

Formerly known as *The Modern Encyclopedia of Russian and Soviet History*, this work
makes available for the first time, in English,
articles from a variety of Russian and Soviet
reference works, including the *Soviet Historical Encyclopedia*, the *Great and Small Soviet
Encyclopedias*, the *Brockhaus-Efron* and *Granat
Encyclopedias*, the *Siberian Soviet Encyclopedia*,
and the *Russian Biographical Dictionary*.
While the majority of the articles are sim-

ply translations from the Russian, others are original contributions from North American scholars. Articles vary in length and quality. Some are signed and include lengthy bibliographies. Others are short, unsigned, and without additional sources. Individual entries can be found in volumes 1 through 55. Volume 56 is an index of authors, volume 57 is a topical index of the entries, and volume 58 is an index of entries by time periods. Volumes 59–60 index respectively volumes 1–10 and 11–20 of the encyclopedia. They will eventually be joined by three or four more volumes. The volumes of the supplement consist of new articles that are intended to update material in the original and bring greater objectivity, especially in light of the fall of the Soviet Union and the opening of many archives. Other valuable sources for Russian and Soviet history are the magnificent translation of the third edition of the *Great Soviet Encyclopedia* (New York: Macmillan, 1973–1983), which must be used with the index volume and the *Cambridge Encyclopedia of Russia and the Soviet Union* (New York: Cambridge University Press, 1982). John Paxton's *Encyclopedia of Russian History: From the Christianization of Kiev to the Break-Up of the U.S.S.R.* (Santa Barbara, CA: ABC-CLIO, 1993) is a rather disappointing attempt at a comprehensive, one-volume alphabetical reference work.

Scandinavia

598. *Dictionary of Scandinavian History.* Edited by Byron J. Nordstrom. Westport, CT: Greenwood, 1986. 703pp. Index. ISBN 0-313-22887-6.
This is the only English-language historical dictionary to focus on the entire history of the countries of Denmark, Norway, Iceland, Sweden, and Finland. It includes some 400 signed, alphabetically arranged entries from some 70 contributors. Articles range in length from half a page to 12 pages, depending on the topic. Each is accompanied by a short list of additional readings. Appendixes include a bibliography of works in English, lists of monarchs, presidents, and prime ministers, and a chronology. Coverage is up-to-date through 1983. For an excellent but more specialized work, see *Medieval Scandinavia: An Encyclopedia*, edited by Phillip Pulsiano et al. (New York: Garland, 1993).

Spain

599. *Historical Dictionary of Modern Spain, 1700–1988.* Edited by Robert W. Kern and Meredith D. Dodge. Westport, CT: Greenwood, 1990. 688pp. Index. ISBN 0-313-25971-2.
Kern and Dodge, professors at the University of New Mexico, have assembled a cast of 70 scholars from the United States, Canada, Great Britain, Spain, and Latin America to provide the first modern comprehensive reference work on Spanish history. The focus is on seven major areas: political, governmental, institutional, cultural, social, military, and diplomatic. Maps, illustrations, tables, an index, and a selected bibliography enhance the utility of the volume. Narrower in focus are James W. Cortada, *Historical Dictionary of the Spanish Civil War, 1936–1939* (Westport, CT: Greenwood, 1982); *Historical Dictionary of the Spanish Empire, 1402–1975,* edited by James S. Olson et al. (Westport, CT: Greenwood, 1992); and Robert W. Kern, *The Regions of Spain: A Reference Guide to History*

and Culture (Westport, CT: Greenwood, 1995), which describe key persons, places, organizations, and events. For a comprehensive Spanish-language source, see *Diccionario de Historia de España*, edited by Germán Bleiberg, 2nd ed., 3 vols. (Madrid: Revista de Occidente, 1968–1969).

ASIA

General

600. *Asian/Oceanian Historical Dictionaries Series.* Metuchen, NJ: Scarecrow, 1989–.
In 1989 Scarecrow Press launched another series of historical dictionaries on Asia as a successor to its earlier Historical and Cultural Dictionaries of Asia series. Like its predecessor, it consists of one-volume, general, historical dictionaries on individual countries prepared by a specialist. The first volume in the series is William J. Duiker, *Historical Dictionary of Vietnam,* with one or more new volumes appearing most years. The *Historical Dictionary of Nepal* by Nanda R. Shrestna and Keshav Bhattari appeared in late 2003, the 46th volume in the series.

601. *Encyclopedia of Asian History.* Edited by Ainslie T. Embree. New York: Scribner's, 1988. 4 vols. Index. ISBN 0-684-18619-5.
Designed as an authoritative encyclopedia for nonspecialists, this acclaimed set focuses on Iran and Central Asia, China, Japan, Korea, South Asia, and Southeast Asia. It excludes the USSR except for the Central Asian republics. Entries discuss people (living and dead), places, events, geographic features, ethnic groups, the arts, historical periods, and a variety of other subjects.

Articles are signed with lists of additional readings and arranged alphabetically. The text is accompanied by more than 160 black-and-white illustrations and 60 maps. The fourth volume contains a detailed subject index, various special lists, and a topical outline of subjects. Since this publication uses the Pinyin rather than the Wade-Giles system of transliterating Chinese characters, a conversion table is included. With contributions from an international cast of scholars, this is the best general encyclopedia on Asian history. For a useful complement and compilation of chronologies see the *Columbia Chronologies of Asian History and Culture,* edited by John S. Bowman (New York: Columbia University Press, 2000).

602. *Encyclopedia of Modern Asia.* Edited by David Levinson and Karen Christensen. New York: Scribner's, 2002. 6 vols. Index. ISBN 0-684-31245-X.
This extraordinarily rich reference source profiling 33 Asian nations took four years to complete and involved more than 900 editors from 60 countries. Geographical coverage extends from Japan in the east to Turkey in the west, and from Kazakhstan in the north to Indonesia in the south. One of the aims of the set is to give an Asian perspective to Asian topics.

By Country/Region

China

603. *Cambridge Encyclopedia of China.* Edited by Brian Hook. 2nd ed. New York: Cambridge University Press, 1991. 502pp. Index. ISBN 0-521-35594-X.
Like similar Cambridge encyclopedias

focusing on a specific country or region, this volume is intended as a general introduction to the geography, history, and culture of China. About a third of the book is devoted to history from prehistoric times to 1980. Articles are generally short; initialed by the author; and often complemented by illustrations, maps, and dynastic charts. The 70 contributors largely come from universities in Great Britain and the United States. Peculiarly, the index is placed at the beginning of the volume rather than the end. Sources for further reading are presented in a topical index at the end of the volume. A more specialized work is the three-volume *Information China: The Comprehensive and Authoritative Reference Source of New China and Its Historical Background*, compiled and translated by the Chinese Academy of Social Sciences; edited for Pergamon Press by C. V. James (Oxford and New York: Pergamon, 1988).

604. *Companion to Chinese History.* **By Hugh B. O'Neill. New York: Facts on File, 1987. 397pp. ISBN 0-87196-841-X.**
With about 1,000 entries arranged in alphabetical order, this handbook is intended as a general reference work on the most popular topics in Chinese civilization from prehistory to the mid-1980s. Since traditional Chinese names are presented surname first and the given name last, all Chinese surnames are printed in upper-case letters to avoid confusion. Most names are rendered in the Wade-Giles system of transliteration. Some articles list sources for further reading. Appendixes include a short chronology from 1506 to 1985 and 12 maps. Also useful is Michael Dillon, *Dictionary of Chinese History* (Totowa, NJ: Frank Cass, 1979), which is similar in its coverage but does include

some unique terms. More recent, and also covering the entire span of China's history, is Dorothy Perkins, *Encyclopedia of China: The Essential Reference to China, Its History and Culture* (New York: Facts on File, 1999). For a specialized work on a crucial period in modern Chinese history, see the *Historical Dictionary of Revolutionary China, 1839–1976*, edited by Edwin Pak-wah Leung (Westport, CT: Greenwood Press, 1992). Also covering the modern period with 1,000 entries is *Modern China: An Encyclopedia of History, Culture, and Nationalism*, edited by Wang Ke-wen (New York: Garland, 1998) and *The Columbia Guide to Modern Chinese History*, by R. Keith Schoppa (New York: Columbia University Press, 2000).

India

605. *The Cambridge Encyclopedia of India, Pakistan, Bangladesh, Sri Lanka, Nepal, Bhutan, and the Maldives.* **Edited by Francis Robinson. New York: Cambridge University Press, 1989. 520pp. Index. ISBN 0-521-33451-9.**
This regional encyclopedia is intended as a general reference work on South Asia and includes chapters on such topics as land, peoples, history, politics, economies, religions, and culture. History is well covered from prehistoric times to the present with numerous short signed articles by specialists. Dozens of black-and-white and color maps, numerous illustrations, and lists of major states and rulers supplement the text. Longer articles include lists of books for further reading. Smaller countries or regions like Sri Lanka, Nepal, Sikkim, Bhutan, and the Maldives are separately treated. This volume is one of the best of the Cambridge encyclopedias.

606. *A Dictionary of Modern Indian History, 1707–1947.* By Parshotam Mehra. New York: Oxford University Press, 1987. 823pp. Index. ISBN 0-19-561552-2.

As the first historical dictionary to focus on modern Indian history, it covers the period from the death of the Mogul ruler Aurangzeb in 1707 to Indian independence in 1947. The some 400 alphabetically arranged entries focus on people, places, battles, movements, societies, treaties, political parties, and other important topics. Numerous historical maps and complete lists of British governors, governors-general, and viceroys of India complement this useful reference work. For an older work that covers the entire span of Indian history, there is Sachchidananda Bhattacharya, *A Dictionary of Indian History* (New York: George Braziller, 1967).

Japan

607. *Concise Dictionary of Modern Japanese History.* By Janet Hunter. Berkeley: University of California Press, 1984. 347pp. ISBN 0-520-04390-1.

The focus of this brief dictionary is on the period from 1853, when Commodore Matthew Perry sailed into Uraga Bay, to 1980. Entries are arranged alphabetically with short lists of additional readings. Appendixes list era names (from Tenpo to Showa), emperors since 1817, population from 1872 to 1977, a timeline on Japanese political parties, and Japanese cabinets since 1885. There is a glossary of Japanese words which commonly appear in English-language texts and a Japanese-English index (not a general index), arranged according to the number of strokes in the first character of the entry. Also worth consulting is *The*

Columbia Guide to Modern Japanese History, by Gary D. Allinson (New York: Columbia University Press, 1999). Allinson treats each facet of Japanese history, includes an encyclopedia style compendium, provides excerpts from historical documents, and has a chronology and list of prime ministers.

Focusing on the nationalistic aspects of post-Mejii Japanese history is *Modern Japan: An Encyclopedia of History, Culture, and Nationalism,* edited by James L. Huffman (New York: Garland, 1998).

608. *Kodansha Encyclopedia of Japan.* Tokyo: Kodansha, 1983. 9 vols. and supplement. Index. ISBN 0-87011-620-7.

Responding to the need for a general reference work on Japan in English, this encyclopedia was a collaborative effort between 680 Japanese scholars and 527 scholars from 27 other countries. It contains more than 9,000 articles, including 123 major articles of more than 3,500 words, 1,429 medium-length articles of 750 to 2,500 words, and 7,865 short entries of 50 to 500 words. Approximately 40 percent of the work was written in Japanese and then translated into English. Although intended as a general rather than a historical encyclopedia, history and biography are exceptionally well covered. The article on the history of Japan (almost 70,000 words) is the longest in the set. There are numerous charts, maps, genealogical charts, and black-and-white illustrations. All articles are signed and the longer ones include lists of additional readings. Volume 9 is the index for the set. This work is also available by subscription on the World Wide Web. For a single volume ready-reference work, Dorothy Perkins, *Encyclopedia of Japan: Japanese History and Culture, from Abacus to Zori* (New York: Facts on File, 1991), is very useful and should be consulted in addition to the *Kodansha*.

Middle East

609. *Civilizations of the Ancient Near East*. Edited by Jack M. Sasson et al. New York: Scribner's, 1995. 4 vols. Index. ISBN 0-684-19279-9.
This volume consists of 189 interpretative essays organized into 11 sections: the ancient Near East in Western thought; environment; population; social institutions; history and culture; economy and trade; technology and artistic production; religion and science; language, writing, and literature; visual and performing arts; and retrospective essays. Cross-referencing and a detailed index allow readers to locate specific topics quickly, even though the work is not organized in a traditional ready-reference manner. A good overview of the state of scholarly knowledge is provided for specialists, students, and general readers.

610. *Encyclopedia of the Modern Middle East*. Edited by Reeva S. Simon, Philip Mattar, and Richard W. Bulliett. New York: Macmillan, 1996. 4 vols. Index. ISBN 0-02-896011-4.
Covers the 19th and 20th centuries for the area stretching from Afghanistan in the east to Morocco in the west, including Israel. The four volumes contain almost 4,000 alphabetically arranged articles written and signed by specialists, including bibliographies for further study. More than a historical encyclopedia of politics and military affairs, this work also covers such topics as religion, economics, literature, and the arts, among others. Definitely the premier reference work for the modern era in this

region. For useful one-volume works, see the *Cambridge Encyclopedia of the Middle East and North Africa,* edited by Trevor Mostyn and Albert Hourani (New York: Cambridge University Press, 1988) and Robin Bidwell, *Dictionary of Modern Arab History: An A to Z of Over 2,000 Entries from 1798 to the Present Day* (New York: Columbia University Press, 1998).

611. *The Encyclopedia of Islam. New Edition*. Edited by E. Van Donzel, B. Lewis, and Ch. Pellat. Leiden: Brill, 1954–2002. 11 vols. ISBN 90-04-05745-5.
Encompassing the old Arabo-Islamic empire; the Islamic states of Iran, Central Asia, the Indian subcontinent, and Indonesia; the Ottoman Empire; and the various Islamic states throughout the world, this is an entirely new edition of the most important English-language reference set on Islam. Contributors include some of the world's leading Orientalists. Articles are signed with bibliographies and describe key people, events, places, institutions, religious beliefs, manners and customs, and the industries and sciences connected with various Islamic groups. There are many black-and-white maps done to scale including some large fold outs, various genealogical and dynastic charts, and some black-and-white illustrations. Delays have caused some of the material in this set to be dated. The first nine volumes (A–U) of *The Encyclopedia of Islam* appeared on CD-ROM in 2002 with searchable indexes for "Glossary and Index of Terms," "Index of Proper Names," and "Index of Subjects." Index volumes are available for proper names and terms for most of the set but indexes for all 11 volumes have not yet been published. Still useful is the *Encyclopedia of Islam: A Dictionary*

of the *Geography, Ethnography, and Biography of the Muhammadan Peoples,* originally published between 1913 and 1936 in four volumes with supplements. It has been reprinted as the *First Encyclopaedia of Islam* (Leiden: E. J. Brill, 1987) in nine volumes. See also Cyril Glasse, *The New Encyclopedia of Islam* (Walnut Creek, CA: AltaMira, 2001), which is a revised edition of Glasse, *The Concise Encyclopedia of Islam.*

AFRICA

612. *African Historical Dictionaries Series.* **Edited by Jon Woronoff. Metuchen, NJ: Scarecrow, 1974–.**
Each of these historical dictionaries treats an individual African country and provides in dictionary form the basic information on its geography, history, economy, prominent people, significant events, and institutions. All volumes contain bibliographies. Individual volumes in this series have been widely praised. Several new titles or new editions of existing titles are published annually with some volumes having gone through third editions.

613. *Encyclopedia of Africa South of the Sahara.* **Edited by John Middleton. New York: Scribner's, 1997. 4 vols. Index. ISBN 0–684–80466–2.**
Knowledge and awareness of the noncolonial aspects of Africa has grown impressively among scholars in recent years. An impressive fruit of those labors is this reference work, consisting of 896 signed articles dealing with the entire range of African history and culture. Each includes a bibliography for guiding further study. Because such

overlap was both unavoidable and desirable, some 6 percent of the contents deals with North Africa. Another smaller but still useful work is the *Encyclopedia of Precolonial Africa: Archaeology, History, Languages, Cultures, and Environment,* edited by Joseph O. Vogel and Jean Vogel (Walnut Creek, CA: AltaMira, 1997). It consists of topical chapters written by experts in the field and so is not a ready reference work. Also see the three-volume *Encyclopedia of African History and Culture,* by Willie F. Page (New York: Facts on File, 2001); the *Encyclopedia of 20th Century African History,* by Tiyambe Zeleza and Dichson Eyoh (Routledge, 2003); and the one-volume *Cambridge Encyclopedia of Africa,* edited by Roland Oliver and Michael Crowder (New York: Cambridge University Press, 1981).

614. *The Oxford Encyclopedia of Ancient Egypt.* **Edited by Donald B. Redford. Oxford: Oxford University Press, 1999. 3 vols. Index. ISBN 0–19–510234–7.**
Ancient Egypt has been an object of avid interest throughout the ages, such curiosity has at times even degenerated into Egyptomania. Oxford's new encyclopedia should become a standard readable guide for scholars and students of ancient Egypt as well as the interested educated public. It contains 600 articles written by an international and interdisciplinary team of 300 scholars. The chronological scope ranges over 5,000 years from the predynastic era to the period of Roman rule. Political, religious, economic, social, and intellectual topics are included along with numerous entries for people and places. Some 400 illustrations, maps, and helpful bibliographies enhance the text. There is also extensive cross-referencing and a massive index. For a useful one-

volume work intended for students and the general reader, there is Margaret R. Bunson, *Encyclopedia of Ancient Egypt,* rev. ed. (New York: Facts on File, 2002).

LATIN AMERICA

615. *Encyclopedia of Latin American History and Culture.* Edited by Barbara A. Tenenbaum. New York: Scribner's, 1996. 5 vols. Index. ISBN 0-684-19253-5. Although fine reference works dealing with Latin America have been published before, this excellent new encyclopedia supersedes them all. It consists of 5,287 signed entries written by 832 specialists, each with a bibliography and cross-referencing. These range from 100 words to extended essays of several thousand words. Almost 3,000 of the entries are biographical, while the rest cover events, institutions, groups, literature, arts, economies, and many other topics. Geographically, the scope of the encyclopedia covers not just the Latin American nations from Mexico southward, it also deals with the Spanish-speaking borderlands of the United States. Also of interest is the *Cambridge Encyclopedia of Latin America and the Caribbean*, edited by Simon Collier, Harold Blake, and Thomas E. Skidmore, 2nd ed. (New York: Cambridge University Press, 1992) and *A Reference Guide to Latin American History,* by James D. Henderson et al. (New York: M. E. Sharpe, 2000).

616. *Latin American Historical Dictionaries Series.* Edited by A. Curtis Wilgus, Karna S. Wilgus, and Laurence Hallewell. Metuchen, NJ: Scarecrow, 1970–. Designed as convenient source books of historical and contemporary facts and statistics for the various nations of Latin America, each book deals with a single country. The first 21 volumes in the series were edited by A. Curtis Wilgus. Volumes vary in quality and completeness. Updated second editions of existing titles are in progress or have been published. *The Historical Dictionary of Chile,* 3rd ed., the 28th in the series, by Salvatore Bizzaro, was published in December 2003.

617. *Encyclopedia of Mexico: History, Society, and Culture.* Edited by Michael S. Werner. Chicago: Fitzroy Dearborn, 1997. 2 vols. Index. ISBN 1-884964-31-1. This excellent work consists of 600 lengthy entries written by 350 scholars of Mexican history from around the world. Concepts, people, events, and places are all covered with up-to-date bibliographies being supplied. The encyclopedia is good for both ready-reference and as a starting place for more detailed research. Also useful is the massive 14-volume *Enciclopedia de Mexico,* 2nd ed. (Mexico: Secretaria de Education Publica, 1987–1988), which was intended as a general Spanish-language encyclopedia devoted to Mexico. More than 5,000 biographical sketches of notable Mexicans from the colonial period to the present are included. Several detailed indexes in volume 14 provide easy access to the text. For the history of pre-Columbian Mexico and Central America see Margaret R. Bunson and Stephen M. Bunson, *Encyclopedia of Ancient Mesoamerica* (New York: Facts on File, 1996) and the outstanding *Oxford Encyclopedia of Mesoamerican Cultures: The Civilizations of Mexico and Central America,* edited by David Carrasco, 3 vols. (Oxford: Oxford University Press, 2001).

AUSTRALIA,
NEW ZEALAND, AND
OCEANIA

618. *Australians: A Historical Library.* Fairfax, Syme, and Weldon Associates; Distributed by Cambridge University Press, 1988. 11 vols. Index. ISBN 0-521-34073-X.
Some 400 of Australia's leading historians, economists, archaeologists, geographers, librarians, and journalists contributed to this major historical work published in honor of the bicentennial of European settlement in Australia. The set consists of five historical volumes, which examine Australian history in 50-year intervals, beginning with 1788 followed by six reference volumes. The reference volumes include *A Guide to Sources, Events and Places, A Historical Dictionary, Historical Statistics,* and an index volume. The most useful for general historical reference are volume 8, *Events and People,* and volume 9, *A Historical Dictionary.* The former is a combination chronology and gazetteer, which provides a guide to the most important and interesting happenings in Australian history, along with a summary history of more than 700 cities, towns, and geographical features. The latter has over 1,000 entries on people, movements, ideas, and institutions that have shaped Australia's past. For a one-volume work, see the *Concise Oxford Dictionary of Australian History,* by Jan Bassett (New York: Oxford University Press, 1994). Two recent reference works bring Australian history up-to-date. *The Australian People: An Encyclopedia of the Nation, Its People and Their Origins,* by James Jupp, 2d ed. (New York: Cambridge University Press, 2002), uses 250 contributors and almost 1 million words to describe the history of Australian settlement. The second edition incorporates data from the 1996 census. *Australia: The Complete Encyclopedia,* by Pat O'Shane and Peter Cosgrove (Toronto: Firefly, 2001), Print and CD-ROM edition, is a comprehensive encyclopedia edited by Australian-based academics. Two thousand color photographs make this one of the most visually attractive references on Australia.

619. *The Illustrated Encyclopedia of New Zealand.* Edited by Gordon McLauchlan. Auckland: David Bateman, 1989. 1,448pp. Index. ISBN 1-86953-007-1.
An updated version of a multipart edition first published in 1986, this work was updated in 1989 and designed to be an authoritative one-volume country reference work. Its arrangement is alphabetical and all articles are written by the editor. Many include illustrations. There are no bibliographies or lists of additional readings and no historical maps. The brief subject index lists entries by topic but without page numbers. A selective chronology of New Zealand history is included in the appendix. There is a list of prime ministers under that name in the regular dictionary sequence. It is considerably larger and more detailed than its companion volume by the same author, *The Bateman New Zealand Encyclopedia,* 5th ed. (Auckland, NZ: Bateman, 2000).

620. *The Pacific Islands: An Encyclopedia.* Edited by Brij V. Lal and Kate Fortune. Honolulu: University of Hawaii Press, 2001. 664pp. CD-ROM.
Winner of numerous accolades, this authoritative encyclopedia draws on leading scholars from the Pacific, the United States, Canada, Europe, and Japan to provide infor-

mation on the major aspects of Pacific Island life (the physical environment, peoples, history, politics, economy, society, and culture). 200 brief biographies of important figures are included. The accompanying CD-ROM version of the encyclopedia provides enhanced searching and numerous hyperlinks between sections.

621. *Historical Dictionary of Oceania.* **Edited by Robert D. Craig and Frank P. King. Westport, CT: Greenwood, 1981. 392pp. Index. ISBN 0-313-21060-8.**

Despite the general title, the focus of this historical dictionary is mainly on the European penetration of the islands. Some 500 signed entries from 200 scholars are alphabetically arranged and vary in length from 250 to 4,000 words. It provides broad coverage of geographical features, personalities, politics, and education. There are the usual Greenwood appendixes, along with a bibliography and a name and subject index.

ANTARCTICA

622. *Antarctica: An Encyclopedia from Abbott Ice Shelf to Zooplankton.* **By Mary Trewby. Toronto: Firefly, 2002. 208pp. Index. ISBN 1-55297-590-8.**

623. *Antarctica and the Arctic: The Complete Encyclopedia.* **Edited by David McGonigal, Lynn Woodworth, and Edmund Hillary. Toronto: Firefly, 2001. 608pp. Index. 1-55297-545-2.**

624. *Antarctica: An Encyclopedia.* **By John Stewart. Jefferson, N.C.: McFarlan, 1990. 2 vols. Index. ISBN 0-89950-470-5.**

In 1990 John Stewart published the first encyclopedia on Antarctica, which he defined as ranging from 60 degrees south latitude to the South Pole at 90 degrees south. He described geographical features, expeditions, people, and scientific subjects, as well as describing stamps, shipwrecks, and expeditions.

The McGonigal and Woodworth volume with its spectacular illustrations describes climatology, geophysics, ecology, exploration, flora and fauna, and adaptations for human life in frigid environments. Though there is an emphasis on Antarctica there are numerous comparisons to the Arctic. A fully searchable CD-ROM with even more stunning illustrations is included.

The most recent work by Mary Trewby provides nearly 1,000 entries and numerous stunning photographs and maps. Together these three complimentary reference sources shed new light on what someone has called the largest research station in the world.

10

BIOGRAPHICAL SOURCES

Biographical information is particularly useful and important to students of history. Not surprisingly, some of the of the most heavily used reference works are those supplying details about the lives of people. Collective works of biography can be current, containing only living persons; retrospective, containing only lives of deceased persons; or a combination of the two. It is also worth noting that some older editions of biographical reference works, like many of the *Who's Who* type of publications, can be quite valuable to historians, even though they are out of date for current usage. This chapter lists those biographical reference works that are essential aids to students of history, along with a selection of more specialized works selected for their outstanding quality or their unique approach, or because they represent a common type of work.

BIBLIOGRAPHIES

625. *ARBA Guide to Biographical Dictionaries*. Edited by Bohdan S. Wynar. Littleton, CO: Libraries Unlimited, 1986. 444pp. Index. ISBN 0-87287-492-3. LC 86-2851.

626. *ARBA Guide to Biographical Resources, 1986–1997*. Edited by Robert L. Wick and Terry Ann Mood. Littleton, CO: Libraries Unlimited, 1998. 603pp. Indexes. ISBN 1-56308-453-8.

American Reference Books Annual (ARBA) is well-known as a source for short, authoritative reviews of current reference books of all types for some 30 years. These two one-volume works contain entries for 718 and 1,180 biographical dictionaries, largely taken from previous volumes of *ARBA*. Each guide is divided into chapters covering various types and subjects of biographical reference works ranging from "Universal Sources" to various specialized chapters covering biographical dictionaries in the fields of "Literature," "Performing Arts," and "Sports." Each chapter begins with a short introduction that outlines some of the older biographical works, as well as important current reference works. The individual entries include detailed annotations, which describe and evaluate the work, along with useful comparisons to similar reference works. There is an author-title index and a detailed subject index. Although these works largely deal only with biographical reference works published in the past 27 years, the value is that they highlight the best. A similar work that includes the most important older works is *Biographical Sources: A Guide to Dictionaries and Reference Works,* compiled by Diane J. Cimbala, Jennifer Cargill, and Brian Alley (Phoenix, Arizona: Oryx, 1986), which has 687 entries with detailed annotations.

627. *Biographical Books, 1876–1949.* New York: Bowker, [1983]. 1,768pp.

628. *Biographical Books, 1950–1980: Vocation Index; Name/Subject Index; Author Index; Biographical Books in Print Index.* New York: Bowker, [1980]. 1,557pp. ISBN 0-8352-1315-3.

These two volumes basically can be characterized as a "books that were in print" in the United States on biographical subjects, since most of the listings can no longer be purchased. Compiled out of the database used in the publication of *American Book Publishing Record,* the two volumes list any book of a biographical or autobiographical nature. Individual entries supply the same type of biographical information found in *Books in Print,* along with additional subject classifications. The main listing is a name-subject index in which most of the entries are found under personal name. There are also separate vocation, author, and title indexes. The large number of works listed in these volumes make them worth consulting for exhaustive searches.

629. *Biographical Dictionaries and Related Works: An International Bibliography of More Than 16,000 Collective Biographies, Bio-Bibliographies, Collections of Epitaphs, Selected Genealogical Works, Dictionaries of Antonyms and Pseudonyms, Historical and Specialized Dictionaries, Biographical Materials in Government Manuals, Bibliographies of*

Biography, Biographical Indexes, and Selected Portrait Catalogs. **Edited by Robert B. Slocum, 2nd ed. Detroit: Gale, 1986. 2 vols. Index. LC 85-8163. ISBN 0-8103-0234-8.**

The second edition of the eminently useful *Biographical Dictionaries* substantially cumulates and updates the first edition. It contains 4,000 new items in its total listings of 16,000. As the title indicates, it is more than an annotated bibliography of biographical dictionaries. Large numbers of related materials are also listed, making it very comprehensive in its coverage. Generally, a work has to contain 100 or more biographies to be included, and the entries must be more than a simple listing of names.

The entries are arranged in three major sections: Universal Biography, including general works having wide range and scope of chronology, geography, or subject; National or Area Biography, covering specific countries or regions; and Biographies by Vocation, listing materials on specific professions and occupations. Within these broad categories many subheadings further divide the work. Entries are listed alphabetically by author or sometimes by title, if that is applicable. They contain full bibliographical information, and the annotations are kept as brief as possible while still providing an accurate and useful description. There are separate, detailed indexes for authors, titles, and subjects.

Biographical Dictionaries is well worth consulting both by beginning and advanced researchers in history. Obviously the updated second edition is to be preferred, but the first edition and its two supplements (1972 and 1978) are still useful.

630. *Who's Who: An International Guide to Sources of Current Biographical Information.*

By Mary A. Farrell. METRO Miscellaneous Publication no. 21. New York: New York Metropolitan Reference and Research Library Agency, 1979. 102pp. The classic *Who's Who* of Great Britain has been widely imitated and, due to its great usefulness, that imitation continues. Mary Farrell's guide lists the numerous existing *Who's Who*–type publications in many parts of the world as they existed in 1979, excluding the familiar publications for Canada, Great Britain, and the United States. The compilation is divided into two sections: regional biographical dictionaries and individual country biographical dictionaries. The individual entries list author, title, and standard publishing information, followed by a description and evaluation of the work including the type of biographical information, coverage, arrangement, and special features. This useful list needs to be updated since new current biographical works and new editions of existing works are continually being published.

INDEXES

631. *Biography Index: A Cumulative Index to Biographical Materials in Books and Magazines.* New York: H. W. Wilson, 1947–. vol. 1–.
Biography Index is part of the H. W. Wilson Company's series of indexes but, besides indexing some 2,600 periodicals, it also indexes monographs for biographical information along with works of collective biography. The main index is arranged alphabetically by surname with vital dates, nationality, and occupation, followed by citations to relevant periodicals and books.

There is an additional detailed index to professions and occupations and separate listings of the periodicals and books covered by the index. Since it is published quarterly, it is a source of up-to-date biographical indexing. Annual and three-year cumulations help to ease the task of retrospective searching and, beginning in 1984, the index has been available on compact disc through WilsonDISC and online through Wilsonline. It is also available on OCLC's First Search. This is an excellent source to use when beginning a biographical research project.

632. *Biography and Genealogy Master Index: A Consolidated Index to More Than 3,200,000 Biographical Sketches.* Edited by Miranda C. Herbert and Barbara McNeil. 2nd ed. Detroit: Gale, 1980. 8 vols. ISBN 0-8103-1094-5. With annual supplements.

633. *Biography and Genealogy Master Index: 1981–85 Cumulation.* Edited by Barbara McNeil. Detroit: Gale, 1985. 5 vols. ISBN 0-8103-1506-8.

634. *Biography and Genealogy Master Index: 1986–90 Cumulation.* Edited by Barbara McNeil. Detroit: Gale, 1990. 3 vols. ISBN 0-8108-4803-9.

635. *Biography and Genealogy Master Index: 1991–95 Cumulation.* Edited by Barbara McNeil. Detroit: Gale, 1995. 3 vols. ISBN 0-8103-5516-7.

636. *Biography and Genealogy Master Index: 1996–2000 Cumulation.* Edited by Barbara McNeil. Detroit: Gale, 2000. 4 vols. ISSN 0730-1316.
The most useful reference work for biogra-

phical research is the *Biography and Genealogy Master Index*. It should be the first work consulted. Basically the set is an index to the contents of hundreds of current and retrospective biographical reference works. Instead of guessing which specific works contain needed information, the *BGMI* supplies the researcher with an exact location or locations. Furthermore, if it does not contain a listing, there is a good chance that no such listing exists. Names are listed alphabetically and often include the dates of birth and death. Each entry then lists, in abbreviated form, those books of biographical reference that contain information on the individual. Unfortunately, some entries do not supply birth and death dates, making it hard to differentiate between different individuals sharing a common name. In addition, some people may be listed in several locations if their name was not listed in the same form by different reference works. These problems are minor, however, when compared with the usefulness of this reference book. This work is available for online searching as Biography Master Index on Dialog files 287 and Galenet. There is also an annual *Biography and Genealogy Master Index* CD-ROM that contains the entire collection. Some libraries may only hold the much smaller *Biography Almanac*, edited by Annie Brewer (Detroit: Gale, 1981). Other more specialized publications in the Gale Biographical Index Series simply draw their information from the larger *BGMI* database. Similar, but focusing on African Americans, is *Black Biography 1790–1950: A Cumulative Index*, edited by Randall K. Burkett, Nancy Hall Burkett, and Henry Louis Gates Jr., 3 vols. (Alexandria, VA: Chadwyck-Healey, 1991).

637. *Biography and Genealogy Master Index (BGMI).* **Online database available on subscription from Gale Group.**
For almost 30 years the BGMI has been the first place to begin a search for information about people. The online version incorporates data from the several print editions published in 1980, 1985, 1990 and 1995. It indexes current, readily available reference sources. Sources indexed in BGMI include: biographical dictionaries and who's whos, subject encyclopedias that have biographical entries, volumes of literary criticism, and indexes. BGMI indexes only reference works containing multiple biographies. It does not index periodical articles or books of biography about a single individual. Basic, advanced, and expert search modes can be used. Approximately 300,000 new citations are added twice a year. These are drawn from 100–150 volumes and editions of 60–90 biographical dictionaries, including new titles and new editions of previously indexed sources. The total number of biographical sketches exceeds 13.6 million.

638. *The New York Times Obituaries Index, 1858–1968.* **New York: New York Times, 1970. 1,135pp.**

639. *The New York Times Obituaries Index II, 1969–1978.* **New York: New York Times, 1980. 131pp.**
These two volumes respectively list 353,000 and 36,000 obituaries, including those of many non-Americans, that appeared in the *New York Times* from September 1858 to December 1978. Since obituaries are an important source of biographical information of well-known, as well as of lesser known, people, this is an extremely valuable

source. The second volume actually reprints 50 obituaries of certain well-known individuals. Volume I simply lists the name and the newspaper citation for the obituary; in volume II there is an additional notation whether the death occurred as a result of natural causes or otherwise, as for instance by violence. Another convenient source for obituaries from the late 1940s through 1978 is *Obituaries on File*, edited by Felice D. Levy (New York: Facts on File, [1979]) in two volumes. For another source of original obituaries, see Patricia Burgess, ed., *The Annual Obituary* (Chicago: St. James, 1980–).

640. *People in History: An Index to U.S. and Canadian Biographies in History Journals and Dissertations.* Edited by Susan K. Kinnell. Santa Barbara, CA: ABC-CLIO, 1988. 2 vols. ISBN 0-87436-493-0.

641. *People in World History: An Index to Biographies in History Journals and Dissertations Covering the Countries of the World Except Canada and the U.S.* Edited by Susan K. Kinnell. Santa Barbara, CA: ABC-CLIO, 1989. 2 vols. ISBN 0-87436-550-3 (set).

These two titles are bibliographies of biographical information on some 6,000 Americans and Canadians and almost 8,000 people from the rest of the world. The previous ten years of ABC-CLIO's databases for *Historical Abstracts* [see 320] and *America: History and Life* [see 318] are the sources for this information. Entries are arranged alphabetically by the biographee's name. Individual entries supply a complete citation, an abstract, and the item's chronological coverage. Extensive indexing by subject, geography, occupation, and authors,

along with other useful categories, is provided. Both titles are now updated by the electronic versions of *America: History and Life* and *Historical Abstracts*.

UNIVERSAL (INTERNATIONAL): CURRENT AND RETROSPECTIVE

642. *Biographie universelle: Ancienne et moderne.* Edited by M. Michaud. Paris: Mme. C. Desplaces, 1845–1865. 45 vols.

643. *Nouvelle biographie generale.* Edited by M. le Dr. Hoefer. Paris: Firmin Didot, 1853–1866. 46 vols. Reprint, Copenhagen: Rosenkilde & Bagger, 1963–1966.

These two massive French works represent classic 19th-century projects to produce multivolume works of international biography. National biographies, pioneered by the *Dictionary of National Biography* and the *All-gemeine Deutsche Biographie*, are now the norm [see 663, 669]. *Biographie universelle* is commonly cited as Michaud after its editor, while *Nouvelle biographie generale* is often referred to as Hoefer. Publication of both sets was delayed because some of the earlier Hoefer volumes plagiarized from Michaud, which resulted in a lawsuit. Articles in both sets are signed and include a bibliography. Originally, Hoefer was planned to be more comprehensive than Michaud, and for the letters A-M it lists more minor figures. However, Hoefer's N-Z coverage is definitely less extensive. Generally Michaud's articles are longer and have better bibliographies. Hoefer's typography is superior.

644. *Biography Reference Bank.* Online database available on subscription from H. W. Wilson.

Biography Reference Bank includes biographical information on approximately half a million people, from ancient times to the present, along with thousands of images. It contains the full text of the articles from more than 100 volumes of biographical reference books published by Wilson, including *Current Biography,* the World Authors series, *Nobel Prize Winners, World Artists, World Film Directors,* and many others. It also includes biographies from other publishers like Greenwood Press, Harvard University Press, Houghton Mifflin, and so on. You can search by name, profession, title, place of origin, gender, race/ethnicity, titles of works, date of birth/death, key word, and availability of images.

645. *Current Biography.* New York: H. W. Wilson, 1940–. Vol. 1–.

This biographical periodical is published monthly except for December and is cumulated annually into the more familiar *Current Biography Yearbook.* It is a standard part of most reference collections. About 150 biographies are brought out each year for newsworthy people from all countries and professions. Individual entries include the person's full name, date of birth, occupation, address, a biographical sketch of approximately 2,500 words, and a list of references. The information is well presented, but the relatively small number of people covered limits the value of this source. Each annual volume contains a 10-year cumulated index, and there is also *Current Biography Cumulated Index, 1940–1970* (New York: H. W. Wilson, 1973).

646. *Merriam-Webster's Biographical Dictionary.* Springfield, MA: Merriam-Webster, 1995. 1,170pp. ISBN 0-87779-743-9.

A revision of the classic *Webster's New Biographical Dictionary*, this one-volume work is the place to go for quick access to the basic biographical facts. The dictionary lists some 30,000 names from all periods of time and all parts of the world. This revised edition, unlike previous editions, only lists persons who are deceased. Entries are arranged alphabetically and supply pronunciation, titles, vital dates, nationality, occupation, and other pertinent biographical information. Besides being a standard item in any library's reference collection, this work is easily affordable for the personal library. An equivalent British publication is *Chambers' Biographical Dictionary*, edited by J. O. Thorne and T. C. Collocott, centenary ed. (London: Chambers, 1999).

647. *New Century Cyclopedia of Names.* Edited by Clarence L. Barnhart. New York: Appleton-Century-Crofts, 1954. 3 vols.

While this fascinating and well-produced work is not solely a biographical dictionary, that is where its primary utility lies. Containing entries for over 100,000 proper names from all ages and areas, its scope includes, "persons, places, historical events, plays and operas, works of fiction, literary characters, works of art, mythological and legendary persons and places, and any other class of proper names of interest or importance today." Still, most of the entries are biographical and provide the basic information of vital dates, nationality, and career. Generally, they are somewhat more detailed than the entries in *Webster's Biographical Dictionary* and *Chambers Biographical Dictionary* [see 646]. Its age greatly diminishes the *New Century Cyclopedia's* usefulness for modern topics.

648. *New York Times Biographical Service: A Compilation of Current Biographical Information of General Interest.* **New York: New York Times, 1970–. Vol. 1–. Monthly.** Originally titled *New York Times Biographical Edition*, this publication reproduces major obituaries and biographical articles appearing in the *New York Times*. People, living or dead, from all nations and all forms of endeavor can appear in this collection. Articles will be journalistic and not academic in style. Each annual volume has a cumulative index, but there is no master index.

649. *Obituaries from The Times 1951–1960; including an index to all obituaries and tributes appearing in The Times during the years 1951–1960.* **[Reading, U.K.]: Newspaper Archive Developments; Westport, CT: Meckler, [1979]. 896pp.**

650. *Obituaries from The Times 1961–1970; including an index to all obituaries and tributes appearing in The Times during the years 1961–1970.* **Reading, U.K.: Newspaper Archive Developments [1975]. 952pp.**

651. *Obituaries from The Times 1971–1975; including an index to all obituaries and tributes appearing in The Times during the years 1971–1975.* **[Reading, U.K.]: Newspaper Archive Developments; [Westport, CT]: Meckler, [1978]. 647pp.**
The obituaries appearing in *The Times* of London are well-written and well researched and so have great value to the historian. What these three volumes do is index all obituaries appearing in *The Times* from 1951 to 1975. In addition, they also print in full about 4,000 of those obituaries. Sixty percent of the entries are British. While many of these will ultimately appear in the *Oxford Dictionary of National Biography* [see 664], some will not. Therefore, these entries and indexes form an important resource for biographical information on 20th-century figures.

652. *Research Guide to American Historical Biography.* **Edited by Robert Muccigrosso. Washington, DC: Beacham, 1988. 5 vols. ISBN 0-933833-09-1.**

653. *Research Guide to European Historical Biography, 1450–Present.* **Edited by James A. Moncure. Washington, DC: Beacham, 1992. 8 vols. ISBN 0-933833-28-8.**
These two sets are especially helpful for students writing term papers in colleges and universities. The *Research Guide to American Historical Biography* contains bibliographical information and other reference aids on 278 prominent men and women who helped shape American history. Each entry includes a detailed chronology and describes activities of historical significance. This is followed by an overview of current biographical sources, an evaluation of principal biographical sources, an overview and evaluation of primary sources, a list of fiction and adaptations about the individual, a list of museums, historical landmarks and societies concerning the individual, and a list of other sources. The lives of 400 prominent men and women who shaped European history since 1450 are described in the European history set. The first four volumes cover explorers, monarchs, heads

of state, diplomats, political and military leaders, and social reformers. The second four volumes cover scientists, philosophers, political theorists, theologians, popes, artists, writers, and musicians.

NATIONAL AND REGIONAL BIOGRAPHICAL DICTIONARIES

United States and North America

654. *American National Biography*. Edited by John A. Garraty and Mark C. Carnes. Oxford: Oxford University Press, 1999. 24 vols. ISBN 0-19-520635-5.

655. *American National Biography: Supplement I*. Edited by Paul Betz and Mark C. Carnes. Oxford University Press, 2002. 936pp. ISBN 0-19-515063-5.
Designed to take the place of the classic but aging *Dictionary of American Biography* [see 657], the *ANB* contains 17,500 signed articles written by 6,000 specialists. Entries range in length from 100 words to several thousand and provide a bibliography for further reading. The *ANB* not only covers more people than the *DAB*, it also updates the scholarship that underpins the articles. Important people from all aspects of American life who died before 1995 are included—politics, the military, literature, the arts, social reformers, business people, and scientists. Definitely the new first stop for someone needing concise but authoritative biography information concerning American history. The *ANB* is also available on a Web-based site that was established

one year after its publication in book form and is regularly updated. The first supplement adds 400 new entries to the print version.

656. *Appleton's Cyclopedia of American Biography*. Edited by James Grant Wilson and John Fiske. New York: Appleton, 1887–1900. 7 vols. Reprint, Detroit: Gale, 1968.
Although *Appleton's* has been superseded first by the *Dictionary of American Biography* [see 657], and, more recently, by *American National Biography*, it is still an interesting work that is well worth consulting. Not only native and naturalized citizens of the United States appeared in these volumes; also included are important individuals from Canada, Mexico, and other Latin American countries, and those foreigners closely associated with American history. Some of the people in *Appleton's* were still living at the time of its publication. Articles are arranged in alphabetical order by surname, although articles for families are arranged chronologically. Individual entries, written in a narrative fashion, are fairly detailed, include little or no bibliography, and are unsigned. Scattered throughout the volumes are small black-and-white inset portraits. This work should be used with caution as some articles contain errors, while others deal with totally fictitious individuals. A further six-volume supplement titled *Cyclopedia of American Biography* was published from 1918–1931.

657. *Dictionary of American Biography*. Published under the Auspices of the American Council of Learned Societies. New York: Scribner's, 1928–1937. 20 vols. Index. Reprint, 1943. 21 vols. with 10

supplements and comprehensive index, 1944–1996.

The *Dictionary of American Biography* (commonly known as the *DAB*) is the most authoritative of the major biographical dictionaries of American history, although it is not the most comprehensive. It was designed to be the American equivalent of the British *Dictionary of National Biography* [see 663]. When the original set was completed, it contained over 13,600 entries written by professional historians. With the addition of the eight supplements, the *DAB* now consists of about 20,000 entries. Each entry is signed and includes a bibliography. From the very beginning, the editors of the *DAB* sought to provide a broad coverage of significant Americans. Besides the traditional politicians, soldiers, and religious leaders, they have added scientists, businessmen, artists, musicians, and any others who have made a significant contribution to American life. The *DAB* has also been liberal in its definition of an American. Its major restrictions are that no living persons and no persons who have not resided in the present territory of the United States are included. Beginning with the fifth supplement, the individual entries have omitted some facts, if they are not directly relevant to the subject's career, which had previously been included. These facts include detailed information about siblings, religious affiliations of the parents and spouses, and children's names and dates of birth. In 1989 a comprehensive index for the base set and the supplements was published, which was comprehensively updated in 1996 to include the most recently published supplements. In 1997 a CD-ROM of the *Dictionary of American Biography* appeared. The *Concise Dictionary of American Biography* 5th ed. (New York: Scribner's, 1997) is a one-volume abridgement of the original *DAB* and the first six supplements. The *Scribner Encyclopedia of American Lives*, which so far has five volumes, picks up where the supplements to the *Dictionary of American Biography* end. It currently covers Americans who died between 1981 and 1999. Salem Press, *Great Lives from History: American Series* (Englewood Cliffs, NJ, 1986), contains 500 biographies that overlap heavily with the coverage of the *DAB*.

658. *Dictionary of Canadian Biography / Dictionnaire biographique du Canada.* Toronto: University of Toronto Press, 1966–. 14 vols. In progress. Vol. 1, AD 1000–1700; Vol. 2, 1701–1740; Vol. 2, 1741–1770; Vol. 4, 1771–1800; Vol. 5, 1801–1820; Vol. 6, 1821–1835; Vol. 7, 1836–1850; Vol. 8, 1851–1960; Vol. 9, 1861–1870; Vol. 10, 1871–1880; Vol. 11, 1881–1890; Vol. 12, 1891–1900; Vol. 13, 1901–1910; Vol. 14, 1911–1920.

The *DCB/DBC* was founded in 1959 after the University of Toronto received a bequest from James Nicholson for the purpose of developing a Canadian equivalent of the British *Dictionary of National Biography*. The original plan was for a dictionary of 15–20 volumes that would provide critical biographies of important figures in Canadian history from the 16th century to the middle of the 20th century. Since 1961, when the Universite Laval joined the project, all work has been carried on in English and French and the volumes published simultaneously in both languages. The first volume, which presents the biographies of individuals whose death or last known activity occurred in the years 1000–1700, was published in 1966. By

1990 twelve volumes had been published, taking the project through the 19th century. Of the four volumes planned for the period 1901–1940, two have already been published: volume 13, for individuals who died between 1901 and 1910 (1994), and volume 14, for individuals who died between 1911 and 1920 (1998). An index covering volumes 1-12 was published in 1991 and a CD-ROM covering volumes 1–14 was published in 2000. Individual biographical entries start with the listing of the individual's occupation, vital dates, places of birth and death, and parentage. A biographical essay follows and the entry concludes with a detailed bibliography of primary and secondary sources. Each entry is signed by the author, an expert in Canadian history. Indexes of identifications (professions and occupations), geographical places, and personal names conclude each volume. Unlike the *DNB* and the *DAB* [see 663, 657], each volume of the *DCB* covers the people who died in a certain span of years (several centuries in the first volume but only a decade in later volumes). There are between 500 and 600 entries per volume. For ready reference and 20th-century Canadian biographies, there is the *Macmillan Dictionary of Canadian Biography*, 4th ed. (1978), containing 5,000 entries.

659. *Encyclopedia of American Biography.* Edited by John A. Garraty and Jerome L. Sternstein. 2nd ed. New York: HarperCollins, 1995. 1,263pp. ISBN 0-06-270017-0.

660. *Webster's American Biographies.* Edited by Charles Van Doren and Robert McHenry. Springfield, MA: Merriam, 1975. 1,233pp. Indexes. ISBN 0-87779-053-1.

These two single-volume biographical dictionaries of American history cover fewer people than the *Concise Dictionary of American Biography* [see 657], but they provide more detailed information and evaluation. Garraty consists of over 1,000 signed entries on individuals, both living and dead. The first part of each entry supplies a factual summary of the person's life, while the second part gives a historical evaluation of the individual's significance. One or two suggestions for further reading are usually provided. The 3,000 entries found in *Webster's* are unsigned and shorter, averaging 350 words with no bibliography.

661. *National Cyclopedia of American Biography.* New York: James T. White, 1892–1984. 62 vols. plus vols. labeled A–N63. Index.

The *National Cyclopedia of American Biography* in its permanent (numbered) volumes and current (lettered) volumes contains over 66,500 biographical entries. Only deceased persons appear in the permanent series and only living persons are found in the current series. Volume N–63, which may be the last volume of the set to be published, is an exception, as it contains both living and dead individuals. Each entry provides information on vital dates, parentage, education, family, outline of career, and historical significance. The information found in the entries is based on answers given to questionnaires, which the publisher sent to the individual or the family of the deceased. Basically, the entries read like *Who's Who* [see 662] entries written as a narrative. The entries are unsigned and include no bibliography. A very useful feature of the set is the inclusion of portraits. Since the individual entries do not appear in any organized fashion, it is essential to use the *Index: National Cyclopedia of American Biography* (1984), which supersedes all previous indexes and covers both the permanent and current sets. It is a detailed index that includes not only the main biographical entries but also other persons and subjects. Although it is not nearly as scholarly and authoritative as the *Dictionary of American Biography*, the broad coverage of the *National Cyclopedia* makes it a good source for finding information on lesser figures from American history.

662. *Who's Who in America*. Wilmette, IL: Marquis, 1899–. vol. 1–. Biennial.
The 57th edition of *Who's Who in America: 2003* contains some 120,000 biographical entries. Beginning publication in 1899, this venerable mainstay of current American biography followed the revised format of the British *Who's Who* [see 668]. Admission to *Who's Who in America* is limited to living persons of widespread reference interest, including government and religious officials and well-known people in private life. Not strictly limited to Americans, this work includes Canadian and Mexican government officials. Most biographical sketches are based on questionnaires filled out by the biographees, although some sketches are compiled by the Marquis staff. Individual entries provide date and place of birth, family information, an outline of the career, a list of major publications (if any), personal interests, and an address. There is an online version of this publication, which includes *Who's Who in Science and Technology,* on Dialog file 234 with over 100,000 entries, updated quarterly. *Who Was Who in America* contains selected biographies of deceased individuals beginning with 1897, who orig-

inally appeared in the current volumes. There is also a *Who Was Who in America: Historical Volume, 1607–1896* (Chicago: Marquis, 1963; rev. 1967), which consists of more than 13,000 entries. Marquis publishes numerous other specialized *Who's Who* publications for various regions, professions, and ethnic and religious groups. There is a master index to all of these, *Marquis Who's Who Publications: An Index to All Books* (Chicago: Marquis, 1974–), published biennially. Most nations and regions are covered by some sort of Who's Who publication, for which see Mary A. Farrell's guide [see 630].

British Isles

663. *Dictionary of National Biography.* Edited by Sir Leslie Stephen and Sir Sidney Lee. London: Smith, Elder, 1885–1901. 63 vols. Reprinted with minor revisions, 1908–1909, in 22 vols. Published by the Oxford University Press since 1917. 11 supplements cover the years 1901–1990.

664. *Oxford Dictionary of National Biography.* Edited by H. C. G. Matthew and Brian Harrison. Oxford: Oxford University Press, 2004. 60 vols.
The *Dictionary of National Biography*, or *DNB* as it is commonly abbreviated, was the largest and oldest scholarly biographical dictionary in the English language. It was superseded in 2004 by the *Oxford Dictionary of National Biography*, possibly the largest collaborative research project in the history of the humanities.

The *Dictionary of National Biography,* including its most recent supplement, contains 36,500 biographies of significant people in all forms of activity from the British Isles and their colonies. No living persons are listed. Each entry is signed by its author, an expert on the subject. These entries are generally concise, well-written, provide a bibliography of writings by the biographee (if any exist), and list primary and secondary works for further study. In spite of its age, the information in the old *DNB* remains quite useful for researchers. The greatest surprise is often who can be found in the *DNB* rather than who cannot. This work is one of the most important reference works available to students of English history and literature. It has served as the model for most other national collective biographies.

Originally titled the *New Dictionary of National Biography,* the *Oxford Dictionary of National Biography* is a completely rewritten and revised version of the *DNB*. It contains biographies of 50,000 people, spanning the years from ancient Britain to 31 December 2000 in some 60 volumes. Besides including the 36,500 people in the *DNB*, the *ODNB* contains 13,500 new entries. The format of the individual articles remains the same as in the *DNB,* but the *ODNB* includes 10,000 illustrations and it is in electronic format. The project publication date is 2004. Oxford University Press has an excellent Web site for the *ODNB* at http://www.oup.com.uk/newdnb. For a less comprehensive but still useful work, there is *Great Lives from History: British Series* (Englewood, NJ: Salem, 1987) in five volumes, which contains 500 biographies from all periods of British history and which overlaps heavily with the *ODNB*.

665. *A Dictionary of Irish Biography.* **By Henry Boylan. 3rd ed. New York:**

R. Reinhart, 1998. 462pp. ISBN 1-57098-236-8.
Approximately 1,700 biographical entries make up the contents of this work. Its scope consists of famous Irish and people significantly associated with Ireland, from all ages up to December 1997. No living persons are included. Figures of dubious authenticity from the early history of Ireland have been left out. All entries are written by Boylan, and they provide a brief basic summary of the person's life. They include no bibliography, although there is a select bibliography for the entire volume. While this work does not rank at the forefront of collective biography, it is still useful for ready reference. It supersedes J. S. Crone, *A Concise Dictionary of Irish Biography* (1937), which, however, remains worth consulting.

666. *The Dictionary of Welsh Biography down to 1940.* **By the Honourable Society of Cymmrodorion. Oxford: Blackwell, 1959. 1,157pp.**
Originally published in Welsh in 1953, this volume later appeared in this revised English translation. It consists of approximately 3,500 signed biographical articles, 180 of which deal with families, so that almost 5,000 individuals actually are discussed in the dictionary. Each article includes a bibliography. Planned as a Welsh version of the *Dictionary of National Biography*, it includes Welsh who led significant lives, as well as non-Welsh who played an important part in the history of Wales. No living people are included. Considering its age, it is not useful for recent Welsh history.

667. *The Scottish Nation: Or, the Surnames, Families, Literature, Honours, and Biographical History of the People of Scotland.* **By William**

Anderson. Edinburgh: A. Fullerton, 1878–1880. 3 vols.

No relatively modern and satisfactory collective biographical work for Scotland exists, although there are several recent historical dictionaries of Scotland that contain biographical entries [see 564]. Therefore, this 19th-century work is the best biographical work available. It is arranged alphabetically and includes Scottish men and women from all endeavors, although political, military, and aristocratic figures predominate. Individual entries are unsigned and supply a portrait. No bibliography for further study is supplied, although works written by the biographee are listed. There is much overlap with its contemporary, the far superior *Dictionary of National Biography.* The *Chambers Scottish Biographical Dictionary,* edited by R. Goring (Edinburgh: Chambers, 1992), contains 2,400 entries, but their shallowness has not been viewed favorably by reviewers and readers.

668. *Who's Who: An Annual Biographical Dictionary.* London: Black/New York: St. Martin's, 1849–. Vol. 1–. Annual.

Although this venerable patriarch of the Who's Who genre was founded in 1849, it did not assume its present form as a biographical dictionary until 1897. Prior to that date, *Who's Who* was a list of prominent officeholders in the British government, the Church of England, and certain prominent businesses. Afterwards, it started providing biographical sketches of prominent living people from all forms of activity, whose achievements have significantly affected British life. Thousands of such entries make up *Who's Who* and are based on questionnaires filled out by the biographee. The entries emphasize details of the individual's career but also include family information and recreations. *Who Was Who* is a publication that consists of a selection of biographies of deceased individuals up to 1980, who originally appeared in *Who's Who.* It has a separate index for 1897–1980. A complete back file of old *Who's Whos* is more comprehensive for use in historical research rather than relying on *Who Was Who. Who's Who in America* is almost identical in its format [see 662].

Western and Eastern Europe

669. *Allgemeine Deutsche Biographie.* Leipzig: Drucker, 1875–1912. Reprint, 1967–1971. 56 vols.

For those who can read German, this massive set is an outstanding resource for biographical information. As the German equivalent of the *DNB,* it contains articles on significant Germans from earliest times to the end of the 19th century. Each article is signed and includes a bibliography. Their length ranges from about 200 words for minor persons to over 30 pages for Martin Luther. Later volumes contain supplementary material on people in earlier volumes. Therefore, it is important to consult the index in volume 56 in order to find all the available information. Twentieth-century material can be found in *Neu Deutsche Biographie* (Berlin, 1953–1982), vols. 1–13 in progress. This set also adds some earlier figures not included in the *ADB,* although it also omits many that can be found there. The index for each volume in the *NDB* includes references to the appropriate volumes in the *ADB,* so that the two sets complement each other. Also see the *Biographisches Wörterbuch zur Deutschen*

Geschichte, edited by Hellmuth Rössler and
Günther Franz , 3 vols. (Munich: Francke
Verlag, 1973–1976). For those who do not
read German, the new *Dictionary of German
Biography*, edited by Walther Killy and
Rudolf Vierhaus, 10 vols. (Munich: K. G.
Saur, 2001) provides biographies for 60,000
German-speaking people. Translated from
the German, it is the first multivolume
biographical dictionary dealing with
Germans.

670. *A Biographical Dictionary of the Soviet
Union, 1917–1988*. By Jeanne Vronskaya,
with Vladimir Chuguev. New York:
K. G. Saur, 1989. 525pp.
ISBN 0-86291-470-1.
Tsarist Russia and the Soviet Union are
poorly served by biographical reference
works in English when compared with
other major countries. Therefore, this volume, containing biographies of 5,000 people in all walks of life from during the
post-1917 Soviet period through December 1988, is a welcome addition. The
Library of Congress system of transliteration is used to list all Russian names, except
where the person is far better known under
a different spelling. Alternate spellings are
also supplied and are followed by the individual's vital dates and his occupation.
Although major figures like Stalin and Trot-
sky, respectively, have 1,700 and 700 words
in their entries, most entries are about 100
words long. They usually provide the place
of birth, family background, education,
main career events, and the place and manner of death (which is not always easy to
determine if the individual was a victim of
Stalin's purges). There is an index of occupations. Similar works are Archie Brown,
The Soviet Union: A Biographical Dictionary

(New York: Macmillan, 1991) and Martin
McCauley, *Who's Who in Russia Since 1900*
(New York: Routledge, 1997).

671. *Biographisches Lexicon zur Geschichte
Sudosteuropas*. Edited by Mathias Bernath
and Fleix von Schroder. Munich: R.
Oldenourg, 1974–1981. 4 vols.
The 1,500 entries in this German work
deal with important figures from the history of Hungary, Romania, Yugoslavia,
Bulgaria, Albania, Greece, Turkey, and the
former Ottoman Empire for all periods up
to 1945. There are also a large number of
Germans and Austrians among the entries.
Each entry is signed and includes a bibliography for further study. This is a very well-
done work of scholarly reference.

672. *Dictionnaire de Biographie Française*.
Paris: Letouzey et Ane, 1933–. In progress.
It is this set, rather that the *Biographie Universelle* or *Nouvelle Biographie Generale,* that
provides a collective national biography for
France. Coverage extends from antiquity to
recent times. Geographically, the limits are
somewhat hard to fix. Overseas territories
and former colonies are covered only during their relationship with France. French
Flanders, the Franche-Comte, Lorraine,
Provence, Savoy, and Comtat Venaissin are
covered completely. Foreign born individuals prominent in French history are also
included. Under way for a long time, the
Dictionnaire is being published in facsicles
(booklets) of approximately 128 pages in
length. Six of those are combined in a volume. Fascicle 115 of T20 (vol. 20) covering
"Lavallee-Leblois" was published in 2003.
Biographies of major figures include bibliographies. The dictionary was originally
edited by J. Balteau, M. Bamux, and M.

Prevost. It is currently being edited by J. C. Roman d'Amat, an archivist/conservator from the Bibliotheque Nationale, R. Limouzin-Lamothe, H. Tribout de Morembert, and historian Jean-Pierre Lobies.

Africa

673. *Dictionary of African Historical Biography.* By Martin R. Lipschutz and R. Kent Rasmussen. 2nd ed. Berkeley: University of California Press, 1986. 328pp. Indexes. ISBN 0-520-05179-3.

In spite of its title, the geographical scope of this volume is restricted to sub-Saharan or black African history. The 850 entries are largely biographical, although some supply lists of rulers or explanations of titles. While this volume attempts to be evenhanded in its coverage, the paucity of research into some aspects and time periods of African history has resulted in some areas being relatively under-represented. Native Africans and foreigners who played a significant role in African history are included, along with some living persons. The year 1960 was chosen as the cutoff date for the original edition, which the second edition has updated to 1980. This volume includes a useful general bibliography and a subject index. Students of African history will find this book to be a useful introductory work of reference and it is available in paperback. Similar in scope is Norbert C. Brockman, *An African Biographical Dictionary* (Santa Barbara, CA: ABC-CLIO, 1994), which contains 549 entries from all eras of African history. Still slowly in progress is the *Encyclopedia Africana: Dictionary of African Biography* (New York, 1977–). Scarecrow Press's series of historical dictionaries covering

individual African nations, however, contain many biographical articles.

Asia and Oceania

674. *The Australian Dictionary of Biography.* Melbourne: Melbourne, 1966–. In progress. Vols. 1–2, 1788–1850; vols. 3–6, 1851–1890; vols. 7–12, 1891–1939; vols. 13–16, 1940–1980.

Considered one of the most important publication ventures in Australia, the *ADB* begun in 1957 reached volume 16 in November 2002, completing the series (vols. 13–16) for people who died between 1940 and 1980. Work has commenced on volumes 17–18 (1981–1990). Although the format follows that established by the *DNB* [see 663], the arrangement of the volumes is most similar to the *Dictionary of Canadian Biography.* One reviewer has noted that "for consistency, interest, fluency, accuracy, and sheer pleasure, the *ADB* may be the best English-language biographical dictionary in the world." Volume 16 includes biographies of 673 individuals, with surnames from Pike to Zinnbauer, who died between 1940 and 1980. Major figures are profiled in articles of 2,000 to 6,000 words. Less prominent individuals receive shorter sketches. In 2002 it was resolved that the *ADB* should be made freely available electronically to scholars, students, and the general public.

675. *Biographical Dictionary of Japanese History.* Edited by Seiichi Iwao. New York: Kodansha International, 1978. 655pp. Index. ISBN 0-87011-274-0.

Translated from Japanese, this volume is intended to increase Western understanding of Japanese history. Its over 500 biographical entries have been prepared by a panel of Japanese historians. The chronological scope is from the earliest period of Japanese history to 1978. A few living persons have been included among the biographees. For the most part, the people in this volume are natives of Japan who have contributed to that nation's political, military, economic, and social development, together with a few significant foreigners. Companion volumes are *Biographical Dictionary of Japanese Literature,* edited by Seachi Hisamatsu (1976), for writers, and *Biographical Dictionary of Japanese Art,* edited by Yukata Tazawa (1982), for artists.

676. *Dictionary of Ming Biography, 1348–1644.* **Edited by L. Carrington Goodrich for the Association for Asian Studies Ming Biographical History Project. New York: Columbia University Press, 1976. 2 vols. Index. LC 75-26938.**

677. *Eminent Chinese of the Ch'ing Period (1644–1912).* **Edited by Arthur W. Hummel. Washington, DC: U.S. Government Printing Office, 1943–1944. 2 vols.**

678. *Biographical Dictionary of Republican China.* **Edited by Howard L. Boorman. New York: Columbia University Press, 1967–1979. 5 vols.**

679. *Biographical Dictionary of Chinese Communism, 1921–1965.* **Edited by Donald W. Klein and Anne B. Clark. Cambridge, MA: Harvard University Press, 1971. 2 vols.** China is well served by specialized biographical dictionaries. These four multivolume sets all together contain about 2,500 biographical articles covering individuals from the period 1368–1965. The very scholarly Ming era volumes consist of 650 signed

entries from the years 1368–1644, including extensive bibliography and detailed indexing. Some 800 signed biographical articles with bibliography make up the volumes for the Ch'ing period, 1644–1912. They include considerable information on figures who lived after 1912. The period 1911–1949, however, is most authoritatively covered by the 600 essays on significant people for Republican China, both living and dead. An extensive bibliography is contained in the fourth volume, while the fifth volume is an extensive personal name index. There are 433 biographical sketches for significant people from the People's Republic of China up to 1965. These sketches were largely written by the editors. Because of the current nature of their subject, these last volumes do not contain the depth of documentation found in the earlier volumes. Current information on living persons in the People's Republic of China can be found in *Who's Who in the People's Republic of China* (Munich: K. G. Saur, 1997). Chinese women have finally received their due in the *Biographical Dictionary of Chinese Women: the Qing Period, 1644–1911*, edited by Clara Wing-chung Ho et al. (New York: M.E. Sharpe, 1998) and in Barbara Bennett Peterson's *Notable Women of China: Shang Dynasty to Early Twentieth Century* (New York: M. E. Sharpe, 2000). Although it is quite old, the standard single-volume biographical dictionary of Chinese history remains *A Chinese Dictionary of Biography,* by Herbert A. Giles (London: Quaritch, 1898; reprint 1968).

680. *Dictionary of National Biography* [India]. **Edited by S. P. Sem. Calcutta: Institute of Historical Studies, 1972–1974. 4 vols.** Consciously modeled on its namesake, the British *Dictionary of National Biography*, this

Indian biographical project contains nearly 1,400 signed articles. Unlike its namesake, this work includes living persons. The chronological scope is 1800–1947 and geographically it covers present-day India, Pakistan, and Bangladesh. Each article includes a bibliography. Although people from all backgrounds and pursuits appear on its pages, selection is heavily based on political and nationalistic considerations. For a shorter work containing 2,500 entries, including many British and going back to 1750, see Charles Edward Buckland, *Dictionary of Indian Biography* (London: Sonnschien, 1906; reprint, 1968). More recent but highly selective with only 157 entries is *The Biographical Dictionary of Greater India,* edited by Henry Scholberg (Promilla, 1998). For biographical information on earlier periods of the Indian subcontinent's history, along with the Middle East, see Henry George Keene, *An Oriental Biographical Dictionary* [see 681].

681. *An Oriental Biographical Dictionary: Founded on Materials Collected by the Late Thomas William Beale.* **By Henry George Keene. Rev. ed. 1894. Reprint, New York: Kraus, 1965. 431pp. ISBN 0-527-06250-7.**
Written and revised in the later 19th century, this biographical dictionary is not a work of modern scholarship, although it is still quite useful. Its title is somewhat misleading since it is largely concerned with Islamic Asia and excludes Chinese, Japanese, and Europeans active in Asian history. Hundreds of difficult to locate persons are identified. Individual entries are brief descriptions ranging from one sentence to 150–200 words. Each begins with an English transliteration of the name followed by the Persian character version. Dates are given according to both the Christian and Islamic calendars. Cross-references are provided from the more familar European version of names to the proper transliteration, (e.g., Averroes see Ibn Rashid). This volume is a good complement to the Indian *Dictionary of National Biography* [see 680].

682. *Political Leaders of Modern China: A Biographical Dictionary.* **Edited by Edwin Pak-Wah Leung. An Oryx Book. Westport, CT: Greenwood, 2002. 278pp. Index. ISBN 0-313-30216-2.**
Leung is a professor of Asian studies at Seton Hall University and the author of six other reference works on China. This dictionary focuses exclusively on political leaders of modern China from the Opium War (1839–1842) to the 21st century. About 30 international scholars have contributed signed sketches with suggested references. Coverage includes leaders of the imperial government, republican government, communist government, and local governments. There is a comprehensive chronology and an introductory essay on the nature and characteristics of modern Chinese history.

Latin America

683. *Biographical Dictionary of Latin American and Caribbean Political Leaders.* **Edited by Robert J. Alexander. Westport, CT: Greenwood, 1988. 507pp. Index. ISBN 0-313-24353-0.**
Latin American history has been poorly served by biographical dictionaries in the English language. This volume somewhat redresses that gap by its coverage of some 450 people of political significance from the 19th and 20th centuries. Living persons have been included. Each signed entry focuses on

the political significance of the individual's career and includes a bibliography for further study. The contributors are experts on Latin America and Caribbean studies. It is unfortunate that individuals who were not politicians or statesmen and persons from the colonial period of Latin America remain neglected. The *Encyclopedia of Latin American Politics* (Westport, CT: Greenwood, 2002) lists heads of state (from independence to the present) and provides brief biographical sketches at the end of each country's profile.

684. *Notable Caribbeans and Caribbean Americans.* **By Serafin Mendez and Gail Cueto. Westport, CT: Greenwood, 2003. 488pp. Index. ISBN 0-313-31443-8-1.**
The authors wrote the award-winning *Puerto Rico Past and Present: An Encyclopedia* for Greenwood Press in 1998. The present volume claims to be the first major biographical dictionary devoted exclusively to celebrating Caribbeans and Caribbean Americans who have made significant contributions to their society and beyond. More than 160 profiles describe historical and contemporary figures from every Caribbean island, the United States, the United Kingdom, and Canada. Coverage ranges from singer/activist Harry Belafonte to poet Derek Walcott. Individual narratives discuss family background, education, challenges, and notable achievements. Some entries include photographs.

CHRONOLOGICAL PERIODS

685. *Contemporaries of Erasmus: A Biographical Register of the Renaissance and Reformation.* **Edited by Peter G. Bietenholz and Thomas**

B. Deutscher. Toronto: University of Toronto Press, 1985–. 3 vols.
This impressive biographical collection contains 1,900 entries for those individuals mentioned in the correspondence of the famous humanist scholar Erasmus (1466?–1536). Although it was primarily compiled to supplement the *Collected Works of Erasmus*, this work also provides a valuable biographical guide to the important political, religious, and intellectual figures of the late Renaissance (particularly northern) and the early Reformation. A number of obscure individuals are also included. Entries are listed in alphabetical order according to the vernacular spellings, except those people whose Latin or Greek names are by far the most familiar. The size of the entries varies from 3,500 words to fewer than 50, depending on the fame of the individual and the availability of information. Besides providing basic biographical information, entries include bibliography and are signed by the contributor. *Contemporaries of Erasmus* is an excellent example of recent collective biographical scholarship.

686. *Great Lives from History: Ancient and Medieval.* **Edited by Frank N. Magill. Englewood Cliffs, NJ: Salem, 1988. 5 vols. ISBN 0-89356-545-8.**

687. *Great Lives from History: Renaissance to 1900.* **Edited by Frank N. Magill. Englewood Cliffs, NJ: Salem, 1989. 5 vols. ISBN 0-89356-551-2.**

688. *Great Lives from History: Twentieth Century.* **Edited by Frank N. Magill. Englewood Cliffs, NJ: Salem, 1990. 5 vols. ISBN 0-89356-565-2.**
Each of these three biographical reference sets consists of five volumes and contain

almost 500 alphabetically arranged biographical essays. Chronologically, they range from the ancient world through the 20th century. All areas of the world are represented except for the English speaking nations, which have their own separate *Great Lives from History* sets. Significant individuals from all aspects of human activity (politicians, rulers, religious leaders, scholars, explorers, scientists, etc.) are represented. The signed essays are written by experts on their subjects to a uniform format of 2,000 words. A ready-reference section providing vital information is followed by a biographical sketch and analysis and concludes with an annotated bibliography of readily available works for further reading. These volumes are particularly valuable since they cover many individuals not readily found in other standard reference sources or draw together information that has previously been scattered through various sources. The same judgment does not apply to the publisher's American (1986) and British (1987) sets, which basically consist of material readily found in other reference works of high quality.

689. *Makers of Nineteenth Century Culture, 1800–1914.* **Edited by Justin Wintle. London: Routledge & Kegan Paul, 1982. 709pp. Index. ISBN 0-7100-9295-4.**
Part of the series *Makers of Culture*, this volume contains 493 signed biographical entries written by 190 contributors. Essays are interpretive, in that they concentrate on the individual's contribution to modern culture, and include a bibliography. Although the geographical scope of this work is worldwide, the biographees largely come from Europe and the United States. Political and military leaders are ignored for the most part. Instead, this work focuses on

artists, writers, scholars, musicians, and religious figures. There is a companion volume for the 20th century, also edited by Justin Wintle, *Makers of Modern Culture* (London: Routledge & Kegan Paul, 1981).

690. *Twentieth-Century Culture: A Biographical Companion.* **Edited by Alan Bullock and R. B. Woodings. New York: Harper & Row, 1983. 865pp. Index. ISBN 0-06-015248-6.**
In spite of its misleading title, *Twentieth-Century Culture* is a quite useful biographical dictionary of almost 2,000 individuals who, with a few exceptions, were born or active after 1900. Although it was conceived as a companion volume to the *Harper Dictionary of Modern Thought* (New York: Harper & Row, 1977), this work easily stands on its own. The idea of this work is to provide ready reference information for the various people from all fields (e.g., arts, business, philosophy, politics, and religion), who have shaped modern western culture. Some 300 contributors wrote the entries, which are signed with initials. Each entry provides vital dates and a summary account of the individual's career and significance. Some entries include a brief bibliography for further reading, normally no more than two items. The British title for this work is the *Fontana Biographical Companion to Modern Thought*. For a similar work, see *Thinkers of the Twentieth Century*, edited by Roland Turner, 2nd ed. (Chicago: St. James, 1987). Its approximately 450 signed essays are more detailed and include more extensive bibliographies. For an excellent ready-reference work containing 5,000 biographies, with less detail and including more figures from popular culture, there is *The International Dictionary of 20th-Century Biography* by Edward Vernoff and Rima Shore (New

York: New American Library, 1987). It is available in paperback.

691. *Who Was Who in the Greek World: 776 B.C.–30 B.C.* **Edited by Diana Bowder. Ithaca, NY: Phaidon Book/Cornell University Press, 1982. 227pp. Index. ISBN 0-8014-1538-1.**

692. *Who Was Who in the Roman World, 753 B.C.–A.D. 476.* **Edited by Diana Bowder. Ithaca, NY: Cornell University Press, 1980. 256pp. Index. ISBN 0-8014-1358-3.**
These two volumes contain, respectively, some 750 and 900 biographical entries for important individuals in the Classical era. Biographical sketches tend to be brief and descriptive, although they also supply at least one citation for further reading. The Greek volume includes a series of essays on various periods of Greek history as its introduction. Both volumes provide helpful maps, genealogies, glossaries of terms, and bibliographies. They were both available in inexpensive paperback editions, but both hardback and paperback edition are out of print. Similar in scope and approach are John Hazel, *Who's Who in the Greek World* (New York: Routledge, 2000) and *Who's Who in the Roman World* (New York: Routledge, 2001), which are in print.

BIOGRAPHICAL COLLECTIONS FOR SPECIFIC GROUPS AND SUBJECTS

693. *American Men and Women of Science: A Biographical Directory of Today's Leaders in Physical, Biological, and Related Sciences.* **21st ed. Detroit, MI: Thompson/Gale, 2003. 8 vols. ISBN 0-7876-6523-1.**

694. *Directory of American Scholars.* **10th ed. Detroit, MI: Gale Group, 2002. 6 vols. ISBN 0-7876-5013-7.**
Originally published triennially, these two current biographical collections basically serve as *Who's Whos* for scholars and scientists active in the United States, although social scientists are slighted. *American Men and Women of Science* began publication in 1901 and now lists some 140,000 persons in one alphabetical sequence. The *Directory of American Scholars* first appeared in 1942. The *Directory's* five volumes are organized by subject: volume 1, history; volume 2, English, speech, and drama; volume 3, foreign languages, linguistics, and philology; volume 4, philosophy, religion, and law; volume 5, psychology, sociology, and education; and volume 6, indexes. The individual entries in both sets use a *Who's Who* style format giving name, date and place of birth, family information, education, career outline, memberships, publications, and address. These volumes are an outstanding source for current biographical information because earlier editions can be used retrospectively. For this purpose *American Men and Women of Science Cumulative Index, Editions 1–14* (New York: R. R. Bowker, 1983) is a good research aide, while the more recent editions have been available online on Dialog file 236 starting in 1979. A similar British publication that is badly in need of updating is *Academic Who's Who, 1975–1976: University Teachers in the British Isles in the Arts, Education, and Social Sciences,* 2nd ed. (New York: Gale, 1975).

695. *Biographical Dictionary of American Business Leaders.* **By John N. Ingham. Westport, CT: Greenwood, 1983. 4 vols. ISBN 0-313-21363-3.**

The focus of this reference work is the "historically most significant business leaders" in American history. There are 835 biographical entries covering some 1,159 people (some entries discuss families such as the Vanderbilts and the Rockefellers). The author chose his subjects with the aid of a panel of historians of business. All entries were written solely by the author and include a bibliography. They average 750 words in length, although entries for particularly important individuals and families run much longer. Although most of the people included in this collection are deceased, it includes some living people (e.g., Lee Iacocca). Furthermore, this work includes many individuals not found in other historical works of biography such as Harland Sanders and Bernard H. Kroger. There is a similar work for Great Britain, *Dictionary of Business Biography: A Biographical Dictionary of Business Leaders Active in Britain in the Period 1860–1980,* edited by David J. Jeremy, 5 vols. (London: Buttersworths, 1984).

696. *Biographical Dictionary of American Labor.* Gary M. Fink, editor in chief. Rev. ed. Westport, CT: Greenwood, 1984. 767pp. Index. ISBN 0-313-22865-5.
As an example of a single-volume biographical dictionary on a specialized group, this book is outstanding. Each of more than 700 signed biographical entries were written by an expert in labor history. Individual entries give vital dates, an outline of the career, and a bibliography for further reading. The biographees come from all aspects and periods of American labor history and include some persons still living. A lengthy introduction provides a useful quantitative and qualitative portrait of 20th century labor leaders including numerous tables.

Six appendixes organize the biographees by union affiliation, religion, place of birth, education, political preference, and public officeholding. Anyone doing research in American labor history will want to consult this book frequently. The seven-volume *Dictionary of Labour Biography,* edited by Joyce M. Bellamy and John Saville (London: Macmillan, 1972–1984), does the same thing for British labor history in much more detail.

697. *Biographical Dictionary of American Sports: Baseball.* Edited by David L. Porter. Westport, CT: Greenwood, 1987. 730pp. Index. ISBN 0-313-23771-9.

698. *Biographical Dictionary of American Sports: Basketball and Other Indoor Sports.* Edited by David L. Porter. Westport, CT: Greenwood, 1989. 776pp. Index. ISBN 0-313-26261-6.

699. *Biographical Dictionary of American Sports: Football.* Edited by David L. Porter. Westport, CT: Greenwood, 1987. 763pp. Index. ISBN 0-313-25771-X.

700. *Biographical Dictionary of American Sports: Outdoor Sports.* Edited by David L. Porter. Westport, CT: Greenwood, 1988. 776pp. Index. ISBN 0-313-26260-8.

701. *Biographical Dictionary of American Sports: 1989–1992 Supplement for Baseball, Football, Basketball, and Other Sports.* Edited by David L. Porter. Westport, CT: Greenwood, 1992. 784pp. Index. ISBN 0-313-26706-5.

702. *Biographical Dictionary of American Sports: 1992–1995 Supplement for Baseball, Football, Basketball, and Other Sports.*

Edited by David L. Porter. Westport, CT: Greenwood, 1995. 848pp. Index. ISBN 0-313-28431-8.

703. *Biographical Dictionary of American Sports: Baseball.* **Edited by David L. Porter. Rev. and exp. ed. Westport, CT: Greenwood, 2000. 3 vols. ISBN 0-313-29884-X.**

For students of American sports history and sports buffs in general, these seven volumes will form a useful and fascinating resource. The scope of the baseball and football volumes is obvious, including professionals and amateurs. Besides basketball, the figures in the indoor sports volume come from bowling, boxing, gymnastics, wrestling, skating, and weightlifting. Outdoor sports are defined as golf, horse racing, skiing, tennis, and track and field. Each volume contains over 500 signed biographical essays, which include a helpful bibliography. In all, over 4,000 individuals, both living and dead, appear in these volumes, as long as they played a prominent role in some aspect of sports. Coverage is not limited just to athletes; sports writers, owners, and managers also are included. There are numerous appendixes found in each volume, which supply information on topics such as the birthplaces of the biographees and lists of sports leagues with their duration.

704. *Biographical Dictionary of Hispanic Americans.* **Edited by Nicholas E. Meyer. 2nd ed. New York: Facts on File, 2001. 324pp. Index. ISBN 0-8160-4330-2.**

This biographical dictionary seeks to supply information on Hispanic notables while highlighting the significance, richness, and variety of the Hispanic participation in U.S. history. It includes profiles of 250 outstanding Hispanics from every field of activity from the discovery of the United States to the present day. Indexes of year of birth and subject and a bibliography enhance this easy to read dictionary. Similar in nature is Matt S. Meier, *Mexican American Biographies: A Historical Dictionary, 1836–1987* (Westport, CT: Greenwood, 1988), which includes 270 alphabetically arranged entries for contemporary Mexican Americans.

705. *Contemporary Authors: A Bio-Bibliographical Guide to Current Authors and Their Works.* **Detroit: Gale, 1962–. Vol. 1–. Annual. 1st Revision Series (1967–1979) 44 vols. in 11 vols. New Revision Series (1981-) vol. 1–, irregular. Permanent Series (1975-) vol. 1–, irregular.**

As a source for biographical and bibliographical information on recent authors, both living and dead, *Contemporary Authors* is unmatched. Basically, the scope of *CA* includes anyone who has published a book in North America. The individual biographical sketches contain *Who's Who* type information along with a bibliography of the author's works. This information is largely derived from a standard questionnaire and includes the author's current projects. In the case of some more famous authors, the entry will include a bibliography of secondary writings about the author. These entries also usually include biographical sketches that attempt some analysis of the author's work. The two revision series represent an updating of earlier entries in the annual series for authors who are still active. The permanent series contains the final updated entries for authors who have died or definitely retired. This is available on CD-ROM from Gale and electronically through GaleNet. Each annual volume contains a cumulative index for all the current, revision, and permanent series volumes.

706. *Dictionary of American Negro Biography.* **Edited by Rayford W. Logan and Michael R. Winston. New York: Norton, 1982. 680pp. ISBN 0-393-01513-0.**
Although numerous works of collective biography for black Americans had been published before the *Dictionary of American Negro Biography*, it is the first work whose primary purpose was scholarly and not apologetic. Its some 800 signed entries were elegantly and concisely written by some 280 scholars. No living person was included and the cut-off date was January 1, 1970. The chief criteria for inclusion was historical significance rather than fame or merely being the "first" black to do something. Many of the people included in this volume had little impact on the mainstream of American history but were very influential in the development of the largely segregated African American community. Walter L. Hawkins's *African American Biographies: Profiles of 558 Current Men and Women* (Jefferson, NC: McFarland, 1992) and *African American Biographies 2: Profiles of 332 Current Men and Women* (Jefferson, NC: McFarland, 1994) provide a large number of contemporary biographies.

707. *Dictionary of American Religious Biography.* **Edited by Henry Warner Bowden. Westport, CT: Greenwood, 1977. 572pp. Index. ISBN 08371-8906-3.**
The primary purpose of this volume is to illustrate the religious diversity of the United States. It consists of 425 biographical entries all written by Henry Warner Bowden. Each entry supplies vital dates, a narrative survey of the life, a selected bibliography of the subject's writings, and a selected bibliography of primary and secondary sources. Persons from all denominations and faiths are represented. A special effort was made to include individuals outside of the mainstream of institutional religion. Two appendixes organize the biographees by denomination and birthplace. This work both complements and supplements the *American National Biography*. It is also important to keep in mind that many Christian denominations have their own biographical dictionaries.

708. *Dictionary of Jewish Biography.* **By Geoffrey Wigoder. New York: Simon & Schuster, 1991. 567pp. ISBN 0-13-210105-X.**
This first-class work of reference comprehensively takes the entire span of Jewish history and Jews anywhere on the globe as its chronological and geographical scope. A good place to begin research, its hundreds of entries range from ancient times through the Middle Ages and into the 20th century. Living persons are excluded. Individual entries include at least one bibliographical reference, and when available, entries are often accompanied by a photograph. *Who's Who in Jewish History* by Joan Comay and Lavinia Cohn-Sherbok, 3rd ed. (London: Routledge, 2002) is similar in scope. Another useful source is *The Concise Dictionary of American Jewish Biography,* 2 vols. (Brooklyn, N.Y.: Carlson Publishing, Inc. 1994) which contains 24,000 brief biographies of American Jews. It is by far the largest such biographical dictionary ever undertaken. Entries have been taken from standard sources for American Jewish biography and include brief entries coded to a bibliography of sources.

709. *Dictionary of Literary Biography.* **Detroit, MI: Gale Research, 1978–. Vols. 1–.**
Originally the *DLB* was limited to American literary figures but in 1982 the scope was broadened to include British, Commonwealth, and modern European writers. The definition of writers and literary figures was not limited to fiction and includes historians, journalists, and other authors of works of non-fiction. By 1988, the main *DLB* reached 79 volumes. There are also separate documentary and yearbook volumes. Individual volumes are devoted to specific topics (e.g., *American Newspaper Journalists, 1873–1900* or *Jacobean and Caroline Dramatists*). The biographical essays are signed and focus on the individual's literary career. They include pictures, a bibliography of the biographee's works, and a list of references. Each new volume provides a cumulative index to all the previous volumes. Although primarily a tool of literary reference, the *DLB* deals with many topics of potential interest to students of history.

710. *Dictionary of Saints.* **By John J. Delaney. Garden City, NY: Doubleday, 1980. 647pp. ISBN 0-385-13594-7.**

711. *The Oxford Dictionary of Saints.* **By David Hugh Farmer. 4th ed. New York: Oxford University Press, 1997. 547pp. Index. ISBN 0-19-280058-2.**
Hagiography, the study of the lives of saints, is a complex subject. Truly exhaustive works on saints of Latin Christianity, Greek Christianity, or even simply Ireland, require many volumes. But for most students of history, these brief but comprehensive, one-volume works will be sufficient. The 5,000 entries in John J. Delaney's dictionary make it the most comprehensive. In comparison,

the *Oxford Dictionary of Saints* only contains 1,000 biographies and leans strongly toward British saints, although its entries are more detailed and include bibliography. It is available in paperback, as is Donald Attwater and Catherine Rachel John's *Penguin Dictionary of Saints,* 3rd ed. (New York: Penguin, 1995). Delaney is also available in an abridged paperback edition containing 1,500 entries (New York: Doubleday, 1983).

712. *Dictionary of Scientific Biography.* **Charles Coulston Gillespie, editor in chief. New York: Scribner's, 1970–1990. 18 vols. including Supplement II.**
The *DSB* was envisioned as the scientific counterpart of the *Dictionary of National Biography* and the *Dictionary of American Biography* [see 663, 657]. This very scholarly work consists of some 5,300 entries written by over 1,200 expert contributors. Each entry is signed, surveys the individual's career, and supplies a bibliography for further study. The scope of the set is international and it includes all periods of history. No living persons were included nor were individuals in technology, medicine, behavioral sciences, and philosophy whose work was not closely connected with scientific research. Two areas where coverage is weak are 20th-century scientists and those from India, China, and Japan. This situation reflects gaps in the available western scholarship. Volume 16 is a detailed index to the dictionary. *Supplement II* adds entries for 600 scientists who died in the late 20th century and were not included in the original set. For anyone doing research in the history of science, the *DSB* is a fundamental reference work. It is supplemented by the excellent *Women in Science, Antiquity through the Nineteenth Century: A Biographical*

Dictionary with Annotated Bibliography by
Marilyn Bailey Ogilvie (Cambridge, MA:
MIT Press, 1986). Four useful, recent works
are the *Biographical Dictionary of the History
of Technology,* edited by Lance Day and Ian
McNeil (New York: Routledge, 1996); the
two-volume *Biographical Encyclopedia of
Scientists,* by John Daintith et al., 2nd ed.
(Institute of Physics Publishing, 1994); the
Biographical Dictionary of Scientists, edited by
Roy Porter and Marilyn Ogilvie, 3rd ed.
(Oxford: Oxford University Press, 2000);
and *The Cambridge Dictionary of Scientists,*
by David Millar, 2nd ed. (Cambridge:
Cambridge University Press, 2002).

713. *The Discoverers: An Encyclopedia of
Explorers and Exploration.* Edited by Helen
Delpar. New York: McGraw-Hill, 1980.
471pp. Index. ISBN 0-07-016264-6.

714. *Who Was Who in World Exploration.*
By Carl Waldman and Alan Wexler.
New York: Facts on File, 1992. 712pp.
ISBN 0-8160-2172-4.

715. *World Explorers and Discoverers.* Edited
by Richard E. Bohlander. New York:
Macmillan, 1992. 532pp. Index.
ISBN 0-02-897445-X.

These three dictionaries provide a wealth of
information on some of the most significant men and women in the history of
exploration. *The Discoverers* includes signed
articles from 28 historians, geographers and
librarians. The focus is worldwide with
emphasis on the discoveries of Western
European explorers. Articles are either short
biographical sketches or longer articles on
regional exploration. There are numerous
cross-references and each article includes a
short bibliography. *Who Was Who in World*

Exploration is organized alphabetically by
explorer's name and provides capsule information at the beginning of each explorer's
entry, a brief chronology for that individual,
and then a description of his or her career
in exploration and travel. *World Explorers
and Discoverers* is a biographical dictionary
containing profiles of 313 men and women
who were prominent in the history of world
exploration. More specialized is *The Encyclopedia of Women's Travel and Exploration,* by
Patricia D. Netzley (Westport, CT: Oryx,
2001), whose 315 entries emphasize
women who have been the first to accomplish a travel or exploration related feat.

716. *Encyclopedia of Frontier Biography.* By
Dan L. Thrapp. Glendale, CA: Arthur H.
Clark, 1988. 3 vols. ISBN 0-87062-191-2.

717. *Encyclopedia of Frontier Biography.* Vol. 4,
Supplemental Volume. By Dan L. Thrapp.
Spokane, WA: Arthur H. Clark, 1994.
610pp. ISBN 0-87062-222-6.

718. *Encyclopedia of Frontier Biography on
CD-ROM.* Lincoln, NE: University of
Nebraska Press, 1995. IBM or compatible
format.

The original three-volume set covered
4,500 men and women associated with
frontier America. Chronologically, the scope
of these volumes starts with the frontier of
colonial North America in the 17th century
and continues up to the closing of the frontier. Geographically they cover all of North
America. A detailed index greatly enhances
the utility of these volumes. The fourth supplemental volume adds over 1,000 new
people and greatly increases the coverage of
Russian Alaska, Hispanics in general, and
the Old Northwest. Another useful feature

is the inclusion of Western writers. The
CD-ROM version contains the material in
all four volumes and provides a compact
and easily searchable body of biographical
information. The more specialized *Encyclopedia of Women in the American West,* edited
by Gordon Morris Bakken and Brenda Farrington (Thousand Oaks, CA: Sage, 2003),
uses a multidisciplinary and multicultural
approach which describes the lives of cow-
girls, ranchers, authors, poets, artists, judges,
doctors, educators, and reformers. All told,
it includes sketches of the lives of more
than 150 women who made their mark
from the mid-1800s to the present.

719. *Great Historians from Antiquity to 1800:
An International Dictionary.* **Edited by
Lucian Boia et al. Westport, CT:
Greenwood, 1989. 417pp. Index.
ISBN 0-313-24517-7.**

720. *Great Historians of the Modern Age: An
International Dictionary.* **Edited by Lucian
Boia et al. Westport, CT: Greenwood,
1991. 841pp. Index. ISBN 0-313-27328-6.**
Information about the people who write
the histories is frequently essential for
obtaining a truer understanding of the
process of how history is written. These
two volumes provide convenient and reliable information on some 1,300 historians
from ancient times to 1987. Entries are
500–2,000 words in length, include a helpful bibliography, and are written by experts
in the subject. They are organized geographically by country or region. Many
neglected figures are included in these volumes, although others unfortunately continue to be neglected. No living historians,
as of 1987, were included, which means
that many well-known 20th-century histo-

rians will not be found in these pages.
Hopefully, a supplemental volume will
appear at some time in the near future. Also
useful is *The Blackwell Dictionary of Historians,* edited by John Cannon, R. H. C.
Davis, William Doyle, and Jack P. Greene
(New York: Blackwell Reference, 1988),
which includes some 450 biographical
entries, including some living persons, as
well as 19 brief essays on the various types
of history (e.g., social, legal), 25 essays on
the historiography of various nations and
regions, and entries for specialized terms
commonly used in historical writing (e.g.,
historicism, positivism). For more detailed
information on various American historians, the *Dictionary of Literary Biography* [see
709] includes these three volumes: *American
Historians, 1607–1865,* (1984); *American
Historians, 1866–1912,* (1986); and *Twentieth-Century American Historians* (1983), all
edited by Clyde N. Wilson. Two other useful, specialized biographical dictionaries of
historians are John R. Wunder, *Historians of
the American Frontier: A Bio-Bibliographical
Sourcebook* (Westport, CT: Greenwood,
1988) and Jennifer Scanlon and Shaaron
Cosner, *American Women Historians,
1700s–1990s: A Biographical Dictionary*
(Westport, CT: Greenwood, 1996).

721. *Jewish Women in America: An Historical
Encyclopedia.* **Edited by Paula E. Hyman
and Deborah Dash Moore. New York:
Routledge, 1997. 2 vols. 1,770pp. Index.
ISBN 0-415-91936-3.**
Winner of the 1998 Dartmouth Medal, this
encyclopedia was a collaboration between
the Jewish Historical Society and Ralph
Carlson, the publisher of *Black Women in
America.* It includes 800 biographical entries
and 110 topical entries covering the period

1654 to the present. While primary emphasis is given to the deceased, women over 60 and those in special fields (sports, entertainment, and politics) are also included. The set concludes with an annotated bibliography of major writings on Jewish women and a massive index.

722. *Notable Asian Americans.* **Edited by Helen Zia and Susan B. Gall. Detroit: Gale Research, 1994. 468pp. Index. ISBN 0-8103-9623-8.**

Helen Zia is a second-generation Chinese American who is a contributing editor to *Ms. Magazine.* Gall is a partner in Eastwood Publications Development, which develops reference books. The book is designed as a reference source on the fastest growing ethnic group in the United States. It includes 250 biographical sketches of noteworthy Asian Americans both living and dead from all fields of endeavor. There are over 220 photographs, and subject, occupation, and ethnicity indexes.

723. *Notable Black American Women.* **Edited by Jessie Carney Smith. Detroit: Gale Research, 1992. 1,334pp. Index. ISBN 0-8103-4747-0.**

724. *Notable Black American Women.* **Vol. 2. Edited by Jessie Carney Smith. Detroit: Gale Research, 1996. 775pp. Index. ISBN 0-8103-4749-0.**

Winner of the 1994 Dartmouth Medal, this outstanding reference source includes 500 alphabetically arranged entries which illustrate a wide range and diversity of experiences and accomplishments. The earliest birth entry dates from 1730 and the most recent from 1956. Photographs accompany a third of the essays. Entries vary in length and style. Volume 2 includes an additional 300 sketches written by over 100 writers. All include lists of references and many include photographs, personal names, place-names, events, and institutions; other subject areas are indexed. See also *Facts on File Encyclopedia of Black Women in America,* 11 vols. (New York: Facts on File, 1997). Edited by Darlene Clark Hine, the John A. Hannah Professor of American History at Michigan State University, this encyclopedia spans three centuries and profiles more than 1,000 African American women and the institutions that influenced them.

725. *Notable Black American Men.* **Edited by Jessie Carney Smith. Detroit: Gale Research, 1999. 1,365pp. Index. ISBN 0-7876-0763-0.**

Notable Black American Men is designed to serve as a companion to *Notable Black American Women* (1992, 1996). It profiles the lives of 500 men both living and dead over the past three centuries. The earliest known birthdate is 1711, when poet Jupiter Hammon was born. The most recent entry is for Tiger Woods, born in 1975. Entries vary in length and style and are accompanied by 400 photographs, as well as geographic, occupation, and subject indexes.

726. *Notable Native Americans.* **Edited by Sharon Malinowski. Detroit: Gale Research, 1995. 492pp. Index. ISBN 0-8103-9638-6.**

Following the familiar "Notable" formula, an advisory board selected 165 notable Native American men and women throughout history from a list of more than 1,400 names. Approximately 30 percent of the entries focus on historical figures and 70 percent on contemporary or 20th-century individuals. Signed narrative essays of one to three pages include Indian names and their English translations, list reference sources, and often include photographs or illustrations. See also *Biographical Dictionary of American Indian History,* by Carl Waldman, rev. ed. (New York: Facts on File, 2001). This book covers Native American history from early contacts between Indians and non-Indians through the end of the 19th Century.

727. *The Oxford Dictionary of the Popes.* By J. N. D. Kelly. Oxford: Oxford University Press, 1986. 346pp. Index. ISBN 0-19-213964-9.

Prior to the publication of this volume, no convenient and scholarly one-volume biographical work on the papacy existed. The purpose of this dictionary is to provide summary biographies of all the popes and antipopes (those persons who claimed to be pope but were not officially recognized by the Roman Catholic Church), and also to include introductory bibliographies to the relevant primary and secondary sources. Entries are arranged in chronological order and the datings generally follow those found in the *Annuario Pontifico* of 1984. John Paul II is obviously the last pope listed. A separate alphabetical list of popes and antipopes, along with their dates and page locations, allows the reader to find entries for individual popes. The detailed index allows important topics to be followed throughout the volume. In addition, certain unfamiliar terms and concepts are marked by asterisks, which refer the reader to the index. There the page reference printed in italics indicates where a definition of the term or concept can be found. This dictionary is well-written and well-researched and is available in paperback.

Almost identical in its scope is *Lives of the Popes: The Pontiffs from St. Peter to John Paul II,* by Richard P. McBrien (San Francisco: Harper, 1997). Another new reference work on the topic of the papacy is the French work *Dictionnaire historique de la papauté,* edited by Philippe Levillain and translated into English as *The Papacy: An Encyclopedia,* 3 vols. (New York: Routledge, 2001).

728. *Women in World History: A Biographical Encyclopedia.* Edited by Anne Commire and Deborah Klezmer. Farmington Hills, MI: Gale Group, 1999–2002. 17 vols. Index. ISBN 0-7876-3736-X.

Impressive, comprehensive, and authoritative are all words that accurately describe this new reference work, which contains some 10,000 biographical entries. Chronologically the entries range from ancient times through to people born before 1926. Geographically the scope is international and the types of women selected include artists, politicians, athletes, saints, and prostitutes, among many others. Some biographees are treated in a full, signed entry while others are only given a brief entry or sidebar. The full entries include bibliographies for further reading. Volume 16 will be an index for the entire set. *Women in World History* is the best and most comprehensive work on its subject. It is not exhaustive and the many more specialized biographical works dealing with women should also be consulted. One such set is the excellent *Notable American Women 1607–1950: A Biographical Dictionary,* edited by Edward T. James, 3 vols. (Cambridge, MA: Harvard University Press, 1971) and *Notable American Women, the Modern Period: A Biographical Dictionary,* edited by Barbara Sicherman and Carol Hurd Green (Cambridge, MA: Harvard University Press, 1980), which contain almost 2,000 detailed biographical entries covering from the colonial era up to 1975. It is also available in paperback. For a one-volume work containing 1,000 biographies, see Robert McHenry, *Famous American Women: A Biographical Dictionary from Colonial Times to the Present* (New York: Dover, 1983), which is a reprint of a work originally titled *Liberty's Women* (1980). Information on famous women from outside the United States can be found in Jennifer S. Uglow, *International Dictionary of Women's Biography* (New York: Continuum, 1982), and Erika A. Kuhlman, *A to Z of Women in World History* (New York: Facts on File, 2002). British women are covered in 1,000 entries by Anne Crawford, ed., *The Europa Biographical Dictionary of British Women* (Detroit: Gale, 1983).

11

GEOGRAPHICAL SOURCES
AND ATLASES

In his book *Cosmographie* (1652), the ecclesiastical historian Peter Heylyn observed, "If joined together, [history and geography] crown our reading with delight and profit; if parted, [they] threaten both with a certain shipwreck." And it is true. Geography has had a big impact on the unfolding of historical events. Maps are, therefore, an essential component of many history books. To further aid historical research, many excellent historical atlases have been published and more are being added all the time. This chapter lists some of the main geographical reference works and atlases of interest to historians, along with a representative selection of specialized historical atlases.

DICTIONARIES, DIRECTORIES, AND GUIDES

729. *Guide to U.S. Map Resources*. Compiled by David A. Cobb. 2nd ed. Chicago: American Library Association, 1990. 495pp. Index. ISBN 0-8389-0547-1. Basically this publication is a directory of map collections in the United States arranged alphabetically by state and then by

city. Each entry provides the name of the institution, address, telephone number, hours of opening, and a detailed description of the collection: special strengths (if any), size of the collection, classification system used, the state of its cataloging, staff, and copying facilities. It is important to keep in mind that the map collections listed in this guide are basically those of large public libraries, state libraries, historical society libraries, and various colleges and universities. A map collection does not have to be of research quality to have been included in this list, and that makes it useful for the local researcher simply looking for the nearest basic map collection. Following the main directory are several lists of useful addresses: U.S. Geological Survey Depositories, Defense Mapping Agency Depositories, National Cartographic Information Centers, State Information Resources, State Mapping Advisory Committees, and Map Societies. *Guide to U.S. Map Resources* overlaps heavily with the 804 entries of David Carrington and Richard Stephenson, *Map Collections in the United States and Canada: A Directory*, 4th ed. (New York: Special Libraries Association, 1985), going beyond it in the breadth and depth of its coverage, although omitting Canadian map collections. For map collections in the rest of the world consult Olivier Loiseaux, ed. *World Directory of Map Collections,* 4th ed. (Munich: K. G. Saur, 2000). The work and products of the U.S. Geological Survey are described by Morris M. Thompson, *Maps for America: Cartographic Products of the U.S. Geological Survey and Others,* 3rd ed. (Washington, DC: Government Printing Office, 1987).

730. *Historical Geography of the United States: A Guide to Information Sources.* **By Ronald E. Grim. Detroit: Gale, 1982. 291pp. Index. ISBN 0-8103-1471-1.**
Historians interested in geographical approaches to their subject will find Grim's guide invaluable if they are studying the United States. It consists of 686 annotated entries divided into 20 chapters. Subjects of the individual chapters include "Historical Atlases," "Land Records," and "Historical Cultural Geography." These chapters are arranged under three broad headings: "Cartographic Sources," "Archival and Other Historical Sources," and "Selected Literature in Historical Geography." The third section on secondary literature covers the years 1965–1980, which is where Douglas R. Manis, *Historical Geography of the United States: A Bibliography* (Eastern Michigan University, Division of Field Services, 1965), stops. Another more recent work is *A Scholar's Guide to Geographical Writing on the American and Canadian Past,* by Michael P. Conzen, Thomas A. Mumney, and Graeme Wynn (Chicago: University of Chicago Press, 1993). The entire discipline of geography is covered by Stephen Goddard, ed., *A Guide to Information Sources in the Geographical Sciences* (Totowa, NJ: Barnes & Noble, 1983), and Chauncey Dennison

Harris, *A Geographical Bibliography for American Libraries* (Washington, DC: Association of American Geographers, 1985).

731. *Longman Dictionary of Geography: Human and Physical.* **By Audrey N. Clark. White Plains, NY: Longman, 1985. 724pp. ISBN 0-582-35261-4.**
Containing over 10,500 entries, this dictionary is a convenient, accurate, and concise reference work for both the specialist and the nonspecialist. The terms defined include plants, animals, topographical features, geographical techniques, and concepts. Many of the entries are relevant to historians investigating the geographical aspects of their subject. Unlike Sir Dudley Stamp, *Longman's Dictionary of Geography* (London: Longman, 1966), Clark's dictionary does not have entries for specific people or places. For more detailed dictionaries of human geography, see R. J. Johnson, ed., *Dictionary of Human Geography,* 4th ed. (Oxford: Blackwell, 2000) and Robert P. Larkin and Gary L. Peters, *Dictionary of Concepts in Human Geography* (Westport, CT: Greenwood, 1983).

732. *The World Through Maps: A History of Cartography.* **By John Rennie Short. Toronto: Firefly, 2003. 224pp. ISBN 1-55297-811-7. Index.**
This wonderful new illustrated history of mapping, from prehistoric to present times, is a great place to review the history of cartography. It's important to remember that while maps are plentiful today and generally accurate this was not always the case. The *World Through Maps* tells the history of mapping through text, photographs, diagrams, and historical examples. Some of the latter includes: Aboriginal dream time

maps, Ptolemy's map, the Hereford Mappa Mundi, the Ortelius Atlas, Mercator's World map, and Lewis and Clark's maps of exploration. Short is a professor of geography at the University of Maryland.

GAZETTEERS AND PLACE-NAME DICTIONARIES

733. *The Cambridge Dictionary of English Place-Names.* **By Victor Watts. Cambridge: Cambridge University Press, 2003. 1,000pp. ISBN 0-521-36209-1.**
Although it is only a single volume, this new guide to English place-names is neither concise nor superficial in its coverage. Based on the archives of the English Place-Name Society and the latest research, the entries are arranged alphabetically. Every name—whether city, town, village, river, hill, or other geographic feature—found in the *Ordnance Survey Road Atlas of Great Britain* (1983) is included in this work, along with many other additional place-names. Contemporary as well as historical names are included, and each entry supplies an etymology for the name along with variant spellings and pronunciations. The value of a reference work of this nature is that it helps the researcher to identify unfamiliar places that are mentioned in primary sources. Similar in scope is A. D. Mills, *A Dictionary of English Place-Names*, 2nd ed. (New York: Oxford University Press, 1998). For more detailed information on English place-names, the work to consult is the English Place-Name Society's multivolume *Survey of English Place-Names* (Cambridge: Cambridge University Press, 1924–). Similar works also exist for many other coun-

tries since place-names studies are an important aspect of history, geography, folklore, and linguistics.

734. *Canadian Geographical Names.* **http:// geonames.nrcan.gc.ca/index_e.php**
In Canada, names on official federal government maps have been authorized through the Geographical Names Board of Canada (GNBC). This national committee, which dates to 1897, includes representatives from each province and territory and from various federal departments. The CGNDB can be searched online; simply type in the name of a city, town, or geographical feature, specify the type of feature you are searching for, choose a province or a territory, and click "Submit Query." The Government of Canada publishes a *Concise Gazetteer of Canada,* which provides a complete compilation of all provincial and territorial gazetteers and lists the locations and all the approved names of populated places, lakes, rivers, mountains, provincial parks, and Native reserves in individual provinces and territories. *The Gazetteer of Canada* is a serial publication published since 1952.

735. *The Columbia Gazetteer of the World.* **Edited by Saul B. Cohen. 3 vols. New York: Columbia University Press, 1998. ISBN 0-231-11040-5.**
Updates the classic but aging *Columbia Lippincott Gazetteer of the World* (1962) and lists the massive geographical changes that have occurred in the world. At three volumes, it is much larger than its predecessor, containing 165,000 alphabetically arranged entries, of which 30,000 are new. Countries, regions, cities, towns, physical features, parks, prominent public works, and military bases are among the subjects of the entries,

which range from a few lines to several thousand words. Considerable physical, economic, social, and historical information is provided in individual entries when appropriate. Generous cross-referencing is provided. It is also available electronically. A similar work, useful for identifying an obscure place or geographical feature, is an irregular serial publication—the U.S. Board on Geographic Names, *Gazetteer* (Washington, DC: Government Printing Office, 1955–1984), which has so far published well over 100 volumes.

736. *The Encyclopedia of Historic Places.* By Courtlandt Canby. New York: Facts on File, 1984. 2 vols. ISBN 0-87196-126-1.
While the contents of this encyclopedia heavily duplicate other standard geographical dictionaries and gazetteers, its historical focus gives it a special appeal for students and researchers in history. Each of the 100,000 entries provides information on alternative spellings, location, and a brief description of the place's historical significance. Quite often Canby's entries provide little more historical detail than can be found in *Webster's New Geographical Dictionary* or the *Columbia-Lippincott Gazetteer* [see 740 and 735]. However, his entries are always easier to read since they are written in a narrative form with complete sentences rather than as clipped and abbreviated dictionary entries. See- and cross-references are generously provided. Although the *Encyclopedia of Historic Places* has a wide appeal for students of history at many levels, it is sufficiently expensive to prevent it from being purchased by individuals or by many school and college libraries. Far more detailed, but only covering 1,000 places, is the *International Dictionary of Historic Places* (Chicago:

Fitzroy Dearborn, 1995–1996). Joseph Nathan Kane, *The American Counties: Origins of County Names, Dates of Creation and Organization, Area, Population including 1980 Census Figures, Historical Data, and Published Sources,* 4th ed. (Metuchen, NJ: Scarecrow, 1983) is a far more specialized and detailed work. A more recent work on the same topic is Michael A. Beatty, *County Name Origins of the United States.* (Jefferson, NC: McFarland, 2001).

737. *Geoscience Australia.* http://www.ga.gov.au/about
Geoscience Australia is Australia's national agency for geoscience and geospatial information. It forms part of the Industry, Tourism, and Resources portfolio. They provide an online *Place-Name Search,* which is continuously being updated by commonwealth and state government authorities. The gazetteer now includes elevations for 500 mountains, hills, and peaks, and postal codes for 14,652 localities. You can search by place-name, place type, and state or territory.

738. *Getty Thesaurus of Geographic Names Online.* http://www.getty.edu/research/tools/vocabulary/tgn/index.html
The *TGN* and other Getty vocabularies are made available via the Web to support research and cataloging efforts. While not intended to be comprehensive, *TGN* contains more than 1 million names and other information about places. It includes all continents and nations of the modern political world as well as historical places. It includes physical features and administrative entities, such as cities and nations. Each place has a unique numeric ID that links it to a hierarchy. Thus, a search for Belmopan

(inhabited place) gives longitude and latitude, notes its selection as the new capital of Belize, places it in a hierarchy (world, continent, nation, district), notes its role as the national capital, and cites sources of information.

739. *A Guide to the Ancient World: A Dictionary of Classical Place-Names.* By Michael Grant. New York: H. W. Wilson, 1986. 708pp. ISBN 0-8242-0742-4.

Michael Grant is well known as a historian whose prolific writings have made the latest scholarship on ancient history accessible to educated laymen. In *A Guide to the Ancient World* he has provided descriptions of cities and towns along with some physical features such as mountains and rivers. Each of the 900 entries (which are generally 300–800 words in length) discusses the historical, geographical, and archaeological aspects of each place, along with any artistic or mythological aspects when appropriate. The places included in this dictionary range chronologically from the Bronze Age to the late fifth century AD. See-references lead the user to alternative entries, while 15 black-and-white maps help locate the places described by the entries. Information in the individual entries is not documented, although a substantial bibliography of primary and secondary sources has been included. For most undergraduate and ready-reference type questions, this dictionary will be satisfactory and more than sufficient. When there is a need, however, for a more specialized and scholarly reference work, *The Princeton Encyclopedia of Classical Sites* edited by Richard Stillwell (Princeton, NJ: Princeton University Press, 1976), with its 3,000 documented entries on 3,000 places, is the book to consult.

740. *Merriam-Webster's Geographical Dictionary.* 3rd ed. Springfield, MA: Merriam-Webster, 1998. 1,361pp. ISBN 0-87779-546-0.

As a classic of the general reference collection, this frequently revised work continues to retain its value. Its compact size, reasonable price, and comprehensive character (over 48,000 entries with 15,000 cross-references) make it a natural choice for ready-reference collections, the classroom, and the personal study. Each entry briefly provides (when applicable) information about pronunciation, location, population (based on the latest censuses), economy, and history. While not as comprehensive, this work is handier to use and more readily available than the massive *Columbia Gazetteer of the World* [see 735]. *Merriam-Webster's Geographical Dictionary* also contains over 200 black-and-white maps to aid the user. Similar in scope is David Munro, *Chambers World Gazetteer: An A-Z of Geographical Information* (New York: Chambers/Cambridge, 1988) and Frank R. Abate, *The Oxford Desk Dictionary of People and Places* (Oxford: Oxford University Press, 1999).

741. *USGS Geographic Names Information System (GNIS).* http://geonames.usgs.gov/index.html

The *GNIS,* developed by the U.S. Geological Survey in cooperation with the U.S. Board on Geographic Names (BGN), contains information about 2 million physical and cultural geographic features in the United States. The federally recognized name of each feature described in the database is identified, and references are made to a feature's location by state, country, and geographic coordinates. For example, a search for "Reservoir Hill" in Kentucky tells you that it is a summit, in Kentucky, Warren County, Bowling Green South and then gives longitude and latitude.

INDEXES TO MAPS

742. *Index to Maps in Books and Periodicals.* Map Department, American Geographical Society. 10 volumes. Boston: G. K. Hall, 1968, with supplements for 1971, 1976, and 1987.

Many useful and interesting maps are found in other books and articles besides atlases. What this index does is locate many of these maps alphabetically by subject and geographical-political divisions found in various books and approximately eighty international periodicals (mostly geographical). Originally this index was compiled as a card file maintained by the Map Department of the American Geographical Society. It has been made more widely accessible by a photo reproduction of that card file by the publisher, G. K. Hall. This index is definitely worth consulting for the location of maps on subjects not routinely included in most atlases, although it is unfortunate that the latest supplement is no more current than 1986.

GENERAL ATLASES

Any good library will have several up-to-date atlases. Those published by Rand McNally and National Geographic always rank among the best available. The next few atlases are classics that merit special mention.

743. *Oxford Economic Atlas of the World.* 4th ed. Oxford: Oxford University Press, 1972. 239pp. Index.

The Cartographic Department of the Clarendon Press excels in the production of readable topical maps. Their *Oxford Economic Atlas of the World* is an example of and a tribute to their great map-making abilities. Geographical coverage by this atlas is world-wide, with the subjects of the maps ranging from soil types to the distribution of computer usage circa 1970. Furthermore, since the economic specialization of this atlas is broadly defined, it is definitely a valuable work for general reference. A gazetteer lists the map(s) where various place-names appear, while a country by country statistical supplement provides further useful economic information. Unfortunately, the information in the supplement is dated and it is time for a new edition of this fine atlas to be produced. From a historical point of view, however, dated earlier editions of works like this one can be a source of much hard to find and detailed information. There are also smaller regional versions of the *Oxford Economic Atlas.*

744. *Rand McNally 2003 Commercial Atlas and Marketing Guide.* 134th ed. Chicago: Rand McNally, 2003. 577pp. Index. ISBN 0-528-85334-1.

As a source for up-to-date geographical information on population, economic activity, and transportation facilities in the United States and Canada, the *Rand McNally Commercial Atlas and Marketing Guide* is both convenient and reliable. It is arranged into five sections: "Metropolitan Area Maps," "Transportation and Communications Data," "Economy," "Population," and "State Maps and Index Places with

Statistics" (the largest section of the atlas). The maps, tables, and charts contained in this atlas are all well designed and readable.

745. *Times Atlas of the World: Mid-Century Edition.* London: Times Publishing, 1955–1959. 5 vols. 524pp.
As the *Oxford English Dictionary* is to dictionaries, so the *Times Atlas of the World: Mid-Century Edition* is to atlases—the biggest and the best general reference book in its field. The *Times Atlas* has been rightly praised for its balanced coverage of the world's geography. For the most difficult geographical questions, it is the work to consult. Furthermore, this work has spawned two other important geographical reference works. One is the *Times Atlas of the World,* 10th ed. (New York: Harper-Collins, 1999), which continues to be widely regarded by many as the best one-volume general atlas available. The other is the *Times Index-Gazetteer of the World,* containing 345,000 locations. These entries are listed with latitude and longitude so that the *Times Index-Gazetteer* can be used with any map indicating latitude and longitude with sufficient preciseness.

HISTORICAL ATLASES: WORLD

746. *Atlas Historique Larousse.* Edited by Georges Duby. Paris: Librairie Larousse, 1978. 324pp. Index. ISBN 2-03-053305-X.
The *Atlas Historique Larousse* is a somewhat less ambitious French equivalent of the *Times Atlas of World History* [see 756]. Its chronological coverage ranges from prehistory to 1977 and begins with a large

section of general maps on ancient and medieval history. This section is followed by a section of general European history maps and an alphabetical country by country section of maps. After that come individual sections for Asia, Africa, and the Americas. European history receives the most attention in this atlas. Although it is not specifically a historical atlas of France, it is a good source for French maps. The cartography is very good and the index is detailed.

747. *Atlas of Western Civilization.* By Frederic van der Meer, with English version by T. A. Birrell. 2nd rev. ed. Princeton, NJ: Van Nostrand, 1960. 240pp.
The focus of this excellent atlas is the culture of western civilization from archaic Greece to 1918. There are 52 maps in this collection arranged in chronological order, which are accompanied by an explanatory text and a large number of well-chosen black-and-white illustrations. Except for brief glances at the Byzantine Empire, early Islamic civilization, and the Western Hemisphere, the maps are confined to western Europe once the Classical era has been described. Artistic, intellectual, and religious themes figure as prominently in these maps as political developments. Historians of art and ideas will find this atlas to be of special interest, and browsers will find it a delight.

748. *The Complete Atlas of World History.* Vol. 1., *Prehistory and the Ancient World: 4,000,000 years ago–AD 600.* Vol. 2, *The Medieval and Early Modern World: AD 600–1783;* Vol. 3, *The Modern World: 1783–Present.* Vol. 1 by John Haywood; vol. 2 by Simon Hall and John Haywood; and vol. 3 by Brian Catchpole with Edward

Barratt. Armonk, NY: Sharpe Reference, 1997. 400pp. Index. ISBN 1-56324-854-9. This very attractive historical atlas of the world is truly comprehensive in its coverage. Each of the three volumes contains 56 color maps for a total of 168 maps. Explanatory text accompanies each map. The atlas claims and delivers a chronological series of world maps and time charts depicting the global situation at different points in time and so provides an overview. A series of regional maps follows. These maps are grouped into the regions of Europe, the Middle East, Africa, Central and South Asia, East and Southeast Asia, and the Americas. When deemed of sufficient significance, individual maps focus on a single topic or country, such as the emergence of the Greek city-states or the Tokugawa Shogunate in Japan. Each volume has its own index, and volume 3 includes an index for the set. This atlas compares favorably with the *Times Atlas of World History*.

749. *DK Atlas of World History.* **Edited by Jeremy Black. New York: DK Publishing, 2000. 352pp. Index. ISBN 0-7894-4609-X.** Although many so-called historical atlases turn out to be disappointments in terms of the number and quality of their maps, the *DK Atlas of World History* is not one of them. It is a true atlas with many maps of high quality that are a delight to browse or use. The editor, Jeremy Black, is an expert scholar and critic of historical atlases, and this volume is a tribute to his putting his preaching into practice. The many maps are arranged into two big sections. The first is "Eras of World History," in which the maps take a global perspective. As the maps move through time, a world map for a particular era is followed by a specialized map or

maps; for example, a map of "The World 1300–1400" is followed by three maps illustrating the topic of "Trade and Biological Diffusion 700–1500." The second section deals with regional history with sub-sections for North America, South America, Africa, Europe, West Asia, South and Southeast Asia, North and East Asia, and Australia and Oceania. There is also a subject index and glossary, an index-gazetteer, and a bibliography.

750. *Grosser Historischer Weltatlas.* **Munich: Bayerischer Schulbuch-Verlag, 1978–1981. Vol. 1,** *Vorgeschichte und Alterum.* **56pp. 19pp. Index. Vol. 2,** *Mittelalter.* **134pp. 57pp. Index. Vol. 3,** *Neuzeit.* **110pp. 36pp. Index. ISBN 3-7627-6021-7.** The *Grosser Historischer Weltatlas* is one of the more impressive achievements of German cartography. Arranged in three chronological volumes, it is one of the most comprehensive collections of maps available. Although the emphasis is European, with particular attention paid to Germany, many interesting and detailed maps are provided for other areas, for example, a map of Nestorian Christianity in Asia during late antiquity and the early Middle Ages (vol. 2, p. 72). Another outstanding feature of this atlas is its many fine overlay maps, for example, an overlay map of ancient Rome that fits over a map of the city in 1950 (vol. 1, p. 35). The indexing of each volume is extensive. Whenever it is available, this atlas is definitely worth consulting or even simply browsing.

751. *Hammond Atlas of the 20th Century.* **[Maplewood, NJ]: Hammond, 1996. 239pp. Index. ISBN 0-8437-1148-5.** This attractive atlas traces the history of the world in the 20th century cartographically up to the beginning of 1996. 250 color maps, accompanied by explanatory text and plentiful illustrations and pictures, form the bulk of this atlas. Education, religion, leisure, and drugs are among the atlas's non-traditional topics for maps. It also covers the traditional political and military topics. Other useful features are a detailed chronology, glossary, bibliography, and an index. It is available in hardback and paperback versions. Michael Dockrill, *Atlas of 20th Century World History* (New York: Harper, 1991), covers the same territory, although less satisfactorily, and is also available in paperback.

752. *Harper Atlas of World History.* **Rev. ed. New York: HarperCollins, 1992. 355pp. Index. ISBN 0-06-270067-7.**
More than an atlas, the *Harper Atlas of World History* also supplies a succinct narrative, attractive and abundant illustrations, and a running chronology. Based on the French work *Histoire de l'Humanite*, the atlas deals with all parts of the world and all mapable aspects of history from traditional political history to artistic, social, and economic topics. The information presented is arranged in chronological order and is most detailed for Europe and the United States, although Asia and Africa are given more attention than they usually receive in works of similar scope. This atlas is a helpful introductory work for the layman or the student and would be a good addition for the home library. For scholarly reference it is less useful, but that was not the primary purpose for which it was published.

753. *The New Cambridge Modern History Atlas.* **Edited by H. C. Darby and Harold Fullard. Cambridge: Cambridge University Press, 1970. 319pp. Index. LC 57-14935.**
Although this atlas was made to accompany the *New Cambridge Modern History* as volume 14, it can stand on its own as a reference work. Its geographical coverage is worldwide, while its chronological coverage is from the mid-15th century to the late 1960s. About 300 color maps fill the pages of this atlas. Although the volume's size is smaller than normal for an atlas, most of the maps are quite readable thanks to the excellent cartography. The arrangement of the maps is geographic, beginning with world maps showing various changes from the 15th to the 20th century. That section is followed by a large group of maps illustrating wars and treaties of the modern era. From that point onward the maps are grouped by region and country, beginning with Europe and followed by the individual European countries. Numerous maps for the other continents follow. It should be kept in mind that the index for this atlas is for subjects and not place-names. Another important consideration for individuals is that this atlas can be purchased separately from the *New Cambridge Modern History* and is available in paperback for the personal library.

754. *Oxford Atlas of World History: From the Origins of Humanity to the Year 2000.* **Edited by Patrick K. O'Brien. Oxford: Oxford University Press, 1999. 368pp. Index. ISBN 0-19-521567-2.**
Claiming to be the first new historical atlas in 20 years, the *Oxford Atlas of World History* is an excellent addition to the field. It is well researched, attractively produced, and highly usable. Its 450 color maps are divided into five chronological sections: the ancient

world (to AD 500), the medieval world
(500–1500), the early modern world (c.
1500–1770), the age of revolution (c. 1770–
1914), and the 20th century (from 1914). In
terms of geographical coverage, it is truly
an atlas of world history. In terms of the
number and the size of its maps, it is really
an atlas as opposed to a heavily illustrated
coffee table book masquerading as an atlas.
The helpful accompanying text explains the
maps, and 200 illustrations, charts, and photographs add to the atlas's utility. There is
also a 20-page gazetteer and considerable
cross-referencing throughout the text. It is
the equal of the highly respected *Hammond
[Times] Atlas of World History* [see 756]. In
1999 Oxford also published *World Atlas of
the Past,* a four-volume set edited by John
Haywood, which won the 1999 Design
Award from the British Cartographic Society. The *World Atlas of the Past* combines
over 100 newly rendered full-color maps
with art and photographs to illustrate the
history of humankind.

755. *Rand McNally Historical Atlas of the
World.* **Edited by R. I. Moore. Chicago:
Rand McNally, 1992. 192pp. Index.
ISBN 0-528-83499-1.**
This edition is largely the same as the 1981
edition except for updated bibliographies
and revisions of the post-1945 maps. The
approximately 100 maps in this atlas range
from prehistory through the 1990s in their
chronological coverage. They are arranged
into five sections: "The Ancient World,"
prehistory to 500 AD; "Heirs to the Ancient
World," 500 AD to 1500 AD; "The Age of
European Supremacy," 1500–1900; "The
Emergence of the Modern World," 1900–
1990; and "United States Historical Maps."
Europe is the focus of this atlas and receives
the most attention. Political and military

developments are also more commonly
portrayed in the maps than religion, economics, and population. The maps that do
appear for these topics, however, are done
very well. In fact, the overall cartography of
the atlas is attractive and easy to understand,
while the accompanying text enhances the
usefulness of the maps. This atlas definitely
supersedes R. R. Palmer, *Rand McNally
Atlas of World History* (Chicago: Rand
McNally, 1957). Furthermore, although
William R. Shepherd's classic but Eurocentric *Shepherd's Historical Atlas,* 9th ed. (New
York: Barnes & Noble, 1980), has more
maps, the *Rand McNally Historical Atlas of the
World* is more up-to-date and has clearly
superior cartography to the older and mini-
mally revised *Shepherd's.* Another justly
famous and attractive but Eurocentric and
sadly dated historical atlas is *Muir's Historical
Atlas: Ancient, Medieval, and Modern,* by
Ramsey Muir and edited by R. F. Treharne
and Harold Fullard, 10th ed. (New York:
Barnes & Noble, 1964). The many editions
of this atlas testify to its status as a classic,
while the coverage of its maps further
reveals it as the product of an earlier age
when the political and military history of
Europe dominated western education. The
Rand McNally Historical Atlas of the World is
also available in a reasonably priced paperback for addition to the personal library.

756. *The Hammond Atlas of World History.*
**Edited by Richard Overy. 5th ed.
Maplewood, NJ: Hammond, 1999. 375pp.
Index. ISBN 0-7230-0534-6.**
Containing 450 color maps, this volume
represents a significant revision and updat-
ing of the original 1978, 1984, 1989, and
1993 editions of the much acclaimed *Times
Atlas of World History.* Every page spread in
the fifth edition has been revised, and an

even greater effort has been made to assure a global perspective. Therefore, if possible, the newer edition should be consulted since the maps have been changed, sometimes radically. All five editions, however, are masterpieces of the map-maker's art. Well over 100 plates depict the broad sweep of global history from prehistoric times to the 1990s, as arranged in seven chronological sections. As a result of such a wide geographical and chronological scope, some detail, especially at the level of national history, is lost. Maps for military events are also overly generalized; for example, the American Civil War is depicted by one map with an inset. Of course, more specialized atlases exist to supply such details. The *Times Atlas of World History* seeks to present a broad interpretive overview and to avoid Eurocentricism. In those goals it has been quite successful, making it the best and most comprehensive atlas of world history available in English. There is also a *Times Concise Atlas of World History* based on the second edition, which is available in paperback. An excellent recent addition to the Times atlases is *The Times Atlas of the Second World War* (New York: Harper & Row, 1989). The *National Geographic Atlas of World History* by Noel Grove (Washington, DC: National Geographic Society, 1997) is largely a picture book with relatively few maps and they are of disappointing quality.

757. *Westerman Grosser Atlas zur Weltgeschichte.* **By Hans-Erich Stier et al. Munich: Orbis, 1991. 170pp. of maps, 78pp. of summary and index. ISBN 3-572-04755-2.**
German cartography is deservedly famous for its high quality and eye-pleasing appearance. The simple act of browsing through Westerman's historical atlas will be a distinct

pleasure for any map lover. Its over 400 maps are well designed and magnificently produced in full color. They begin with prehistory and proceed through to the world in 1991. Although political maps form the bulk of this atlas, there are also many maps dealing with culture, economics, population, and religion along with numerous maps of cities. There is no explanatory text in the 1991 or the 1981–1982 edition, although the 1968 edition included a narrative introduction to the list of maps at the beginning of the volume. Europe is the main focus of this atlas, although Asia and Africa receive a fair amount of attention. The United States and the rest of the Western Hemisphere, however, are definitely slighted. Except for the last four pages of color maps dealing with 1981, there is no difference between the 1968 edition of this atlas and the 1981–1982 and 1991 editions.

HISTORICAL ATLASES: UNITED STATES

758. *Atlas of African-American History.* **By James Ciment. New York: Facts on File, 2001. 224pp. ISBN 0-8160-3700-0.**

759. *Atlas of Asian-American History.* **By Monique Avakian. New York: Facts on File, 2002. 224pp. ISBN 0-8160-3699-3.**

760. *Atlas of Hispanic-American History.* **By George Ochoa. New York: Facts on File, 2001. 224pp. ISBN 0-8160-3698-5.**
With its large format and attractive design, this trio of atlases, illustrated with maps, original photographs, and drawings, will prove popular with many students. They illustrate the diverse immigrant experiences

in the United States. The volumes on Asian American history and Hispanic American history are exceptionally well done and were on several "best" lists in 2001 and 2002. Avakian uses 69 black-and-white photographs, 28 color photographs, 60 maps, and 34 line illustrations to illuminate the various waves of Asian immigrants to the United States. She even adds a section on Asian history. Ochoa's work on Hispanics includes 63 black-and-white photographs, 45 color photographs, 79 maps, and 29 line illustrations and graphs, all designed to trace the history of Hispanic Americans from the founding of New Spain to the present.

761. *The American Heritage Pictorial Atlas of United States History.* **Edited by Hilde Heun Kagan. New York: American Heritage, 1966. 424pp. Index.**
Beginning with prehistory, this atlas covers U.S. history up to 1965. Clear and attractive cartography accompanied by an informative text and illustrations characterize this impressive production. Although all aspects of history are dealt with, military subjects dominate, including a selection of interesting pictorial maps for the American Revolution and the Civil War. Like all American Heritage books, this volume is a pleasure to browse and to study. A generous index further enhances its value. Unlike the *Atlas of American History* [see 762], this atlas excels in depicting the motion and dynamics of history. It is unfortunate that it has been allowed to go out of print.

762. *Atlas of American History.* **2nd rev. ed. New York: Scribner's, 1984. 306pp. Index. ISBN 0-684-18411-7.**
Originally produced in 1943 as a compan-

ion volume to the *Dictionary of American History*, this newly revised and expanded atlas can also stand on its own as an outstanding reference tool. Unlike many atlases, the Scribner's atlas with its 200 maps does not have any accompanying text. The maps are composed solely in black-and-white with a lucid presentation free of the clutter of unnecessary detail. Chronological coverage ranges from the age of discovery through 1982, with the population figures based on the 1980 census. Many topics such as politics, religion, the economy, and military affairs are dealt with by these maps. The military maps generally only show places and do not depict movements of troops. There are also no individual battlefield maps. For the reader seeking historical place-name maps, the *Atlas of American History* is the best source. If dynamics, change, and color are wanted, however, National Geographic, *Historical Atlas of the United States* [766] or *Mapping America's Past: A Historical Atlas* [769] are better and more attractive atlases. Another classic work is Charles O. Paullin, *Atlas of the Historical Geography of the United States* (Washington, DC: Carnegie Institution, 1932). Also of interest are the updated editions of Robert H. Ferrell and Richard Natkiel, *Atlas of American History* (New York: Facts on File, 1993); and Martin Gilbert, *The Routledge Atlas of American History*, 4th ed. (New York: Routledge, 2003). Many individual states have historical atlases, and the University of Oklahoma Press is publishing a serviceable series of historical atlases for individual states. Of broader interest is *Historical Atlas of the American West,* by Warren A. Beck and Inez D. Haase (Norman, OK: University of Oklahoma Press, 1989). See also John H. Long, ed., *Historical Atlas and Chronology of*

County Boundaries, 1788–1980 (Boston, MA: G. K. Hall, 1984).

763. *Atlas of American Military History.* **Edited by James Bradford. New York: Oxford University Press, 2003. 244pp. ISBN 0-19-521661-X.**
Covers America at war, examining personalities, methods, strategies, and the historical context of each conflict. Following a "loose" chronological arrangement, the book describes virtually every significant military campaign and war in which the United States has engaged, both domestically and internationally, from the Revolutionary War to the Middle East. Maps show troop, ship, and aircraft movements of major campaigns and battles, the theaters of fighting, the balance of forces, and the wider strategic balance.

764. *Atlas of Early American History: The Revolutionary Era, 1760–1790.* **Edited by Lester J. Cappon and others. Princeton: Newberry Library/Institute of Early American History and Culture/Princeton University Press, 1976. 157pp. Index.**
As an example of the heights that historical cartography can reach, the *Atlas of Early American History* is unsurpassed. All aspects of American life from 1760 to 1790 form the subject of its 286 well-conceived and beautifully produced maps. Population, religion, cultural activity, political and legislative distributions, and economic activity all provide topics for the many detailed maps found in this atlas. Where did the various members of the American Philosophical Society live in 1790? What did Detroit look like in 1760? How did the news of Lexington and Concord spread? All of these questions and more are answered by the maps

and text of this atlas. This atlas is the final word for the time period it covers and it is to be hoped that further volumes of similar quality will someday be published. A recent addition to this topic is Ian Barnes and Charles Royster, *The Historical Atlas of the American Revolution* (New York: Routledge, 2000).

765. *New Historical Atlas of Religion in America.* **By Edwin Scott Gaustad and Phil L. Barlow, with Richard Dishko. 3rd ed. Oxford: Oxford University Press, 2001. 464pp. Index. ISBN 0-19-509168-X.**
Replacing Gaustad's classic *Historical Atlas of Religion in America* (1962 and 1976), this volume is a significant improvement and enhancement of the original. It is much larger and is reorganized with 260 maps and 200 graphs in full color as compared to 76 black-and-white maps in the 1976 edition. It remains a convenient and useful reference work for the geographical and statistical history of the various Christian denominations and Judaism from 1650 to 2000. An extensively, if incompletely, rewritten text and many detailed figures and tables supplement and explain the 260 color maps. The material is arranged into four parts. Part 1 deals with "Institutional and Ethnic Religion before 1800" and discusses the establishment of the colonial patterns for the major denominations and groups. "Institutional and Ethnic Religion after 1800" is the subject of part 2 of the atlas. It continues chronological coverage of the groups covered in the first part but includes new Christian groups such as the Adventists and Millenarians, the Jews, Methodists, and Mormons along with non-Christian groups such as Buddhists and Muslims. Parts 3-4 are totally new additions. The third part

consists of three case studies of Lutherans, Mormons, and Roman Catholics in American society. Finally, the fourth part deals with topics that go beyond denominationalism such as camp meetings and belief and unbelief. There are seven appendixes and an index. Whereas Gaustad's early atlases provided denomination snapshots at 100-year intervals (1650, 1750, 1850, and 1950), this new atlas adds maps for 1890 and 1990. Also useful is Bret Carroll, *The Routledge Historical Atlas of Religion in America* (New York: Routledge, 2000), which is available in paperback.

766. *Historical Atlas of the United States.* Rev. ed. Washington, DC: National Geographic Society, 1993. 289pp. Index. ISBN 0-87044-970-2.
Extremely attractive in its presentation and design, the original 1988 edition of this atlas took six years to produce. The maps are accompanied by explanatory text and are organized into the thematic sections of land, people, boundaries, economy, transportation, and communities, with chronological chapters interspersed. A comprehensive index allows topics to be quickly located within the volume. This revised edition differs from the 1988 edition in that a folder with historical maps for 17 regions, along with a reference and a physical map for the entire United States, have been added. Each map is separately indexed.

767. *Historical Atlas of the United States*. By Mark C. Carnes. New York: Routledge, 2002. 240pp. Index. ISBN 0-415-94111-3.
This new atlas provides 350 color maps to illustrate the history of North America and the United States from Mezozoic times to the beginning of the 21st century. The maps are arranged into 22 chronological and thematic sections. There is also an appendix of maps for presidential elections from 1796 to 2000.

768. *The Historical Atlas of United States Congressional Districts, 1789–1983.* By Kenneth C. Martis. New York: Free Press, 1982. 302pp. Index. ISBN 0-02-920150-0.
This important work of reference does several things: it supplies maps of all congressional districts for the United States House of Representatives, it has descriptions of these districts based on the legal documents, and it identifies all the representatives elected to Congress with their proper district. The atlas is divided into three parts: an introduction that explains how the maps were compiled and how they might be used, a section consisting of 97 national congressional district maps and a list of members for each congress, and finally a section tracing the congressional redistricting of each state. It is envisioned that this atlas is the first volume of a three-volume set that will include *The Historical Atlas of Political Representation in the United States Congress: 1789–1987,* and *The Atlas of Critical Votes in the United States Congress.* Martis's atlas supersedes Stanley B. Parsons, William W. Beach, and Dan Hermann, *United States Congressional Districts, 1788–1841* (Westport, CT: Greenwood, 1978). The latter work is much less comprehensive but provides some information on population for each district not included in the Martis volume.

769. *Mapping America's Past: A Historical Atlas*. Edited by Mark C. Carnes and John A. Garraty, with Patrick Williams. New York: Henry Holt, 1996. 288pp. Index. ISBN 0-8050-4927-4.

Containing some 200 color maps, this atlas covers American history from prehistoric times to the present. Its maps reflect much of the recent scholarship in cultural and social history and also give due attention to ethnic groups and women. Unlike many traditional atlases, military history is only given modest coverage. A well-researched text accompanies the maps, along with many attractive and appropriate illustrations. While many maps provide a comprehensive overview of the whole country or large regions, others portray smaller areas in order to illuminate larger points. For example, two maps compare bookstores in Austin, Texas, in 1969 and 1988 to illustrate the rise of chain stores. The index locates subjects in the text but not places on the maps.

770. *The Routledge Atlas of American History.* **By Martin Gilbert. New York: Routledge, 2002. 176pp. ISBN 0-4152-8151-2.**
Published as part of the Routledge Historical Atlases Series, this new atlas, which is also available in an inexpensive paper edition, describes the history of America from its origins to the present in 320 maps. Other helpful atlases in this series include: *The Routledge Atlas of African American History* (2002); *The Historical Atlas of the American Revolution* (2002); and *The Routledge Historical Atlas of Women in America.*

771. *We the People: An Atlas of America's Ethnic Diversity.* **Edited by James P. Allen and Eugene J. Turner. New York: Macmillan, 1988. 315pp. Index. ISBN 0-02-901420-4.**
Students of immigration and ethnic studies will find a useful tool in this most impressive atlas. It consists of 111 color maps with another four in black-and-white, showing the distribution of 67 ethnic groups in the United States. The county is used as the geographical unit of study. There are also numerous appendixes of county by county ethnic census information. A useful complement is John F. Rooney, Jr., Wilbur Zelinsky, and Dean R. Louder, eds., *This Remarkable Continent: An Atlas of United States and Canadian Society and Culture* (College Station, TX: Texas A&M University Press, 1982), which looks at such diverse topics as music, food, house types, and sports.

772. *The West Point Atlas of American Wars.* **Edited by Vincent J. Esposito. 1st rev. and updated ed. New York: Henry Holt, 1995, 1997. 2 vols. Various pagings.**
Published in two handsome volumes, this atlas is one of the finest reference works on military history available. Volume 1 covers the years 1689–1900 and volume 2, 1900–1918. This is a fine revision of a classic work. A detailed text accompanies and explains the maps. Civil War maps are available separately as the *West Point Atlas of the Civil War* (New York: Praeger, 1962). Of related interest is the excellent *Atlas of the Civil War,* edited by James M. McPherson (New York: Macmillan/Simon & Schuster, 1994).

HISTORICAL ATLASES: OTHER NATIONS AND REGIONS

773. *Centennia Historical Atlas Software.* **Chicago: Clockwork Software, 1992–1998.**
This computerized atlas is available in Windows, Macintosh, and DOS formats and is

undoubtedly at the vanguard of a new form of historical mapping. Starting in the 11th century, it traces boundary changes in Europe, North Africa, and the Middle East up to the present. Some 9,000 such changes are depicted. Unlike paper atlases, it is possible either to pause the atlas for a static view or have it run forward or backward and let the changes unfold in rapid succession. For a grasp of the political dynamics of historical change, this atlas is superb. The cartography is simple and undetailed. Aspects of population, economics, or religion are not addressed nor are the movements of armies, trade, or explorers. Computerized atlases attempting to depict such topics will appear in the future.

774. *Historical Atlas of Africa.* **Edited by J. F. Ade Ajayi and Michael Crowder. New York: Cambridge University Press, 1985. IV. Various paging. ISBN 0-521-25353-5.** Africa's history and geography have been beautifully served by the *Historical Atlas of Africa,* published by Cambridge University Press. It contains some 300 maps arranged into 72 sections. An excellent brief introduction tells how to use this atlas and also explains the basic purposes and limitations of any historical atlas. The first few sections of maps deal with questions of physical features, climate, geology, and distribution of flora, fauna, and language groups. After that the maps are arranged in a chronological sequence, starting with prehistory and ending with 1980. The maps are classified into three types by their makers: "event" maps depicting wars and political changes, "process" maps illustrating the spread or movement of things over time such as cattle, religions, or ethnic groups, and "quantitative" maps that supply numerical informa-

tion and allow for comparisons between different areas or the same area over time. An index allows people, places, and geographical features to be located easily on the various maps. Prior to the appearance of this atlas, the best atlas of African history available was J. D. Fage's still useful *An Atlas of African History,* 2nd ed. (New York: Africana, 1978). A recent smaller atlas that is useful and attractive is Samuel Kasule, *The History Atlas of Africa* (New York: Macmillan, 1998). For a useful and comprehensive listing of other atlases and maps dealing with Africa, see *Maps and Mapping of Africa: A Resource Guide,* by John McIlwaine (London: Hans Zell, 1997).

775. *Historical Atlas of Canada.* **Vol. 1,** *From the Beginning to 1800.* **Edited by R. Cole Harris. Toronto: University of Toronto Press, 1987. 198pp. Index. ISBN 0-8020-2495-5. Vol. 2,** *The Land Transformed, 1800–1891.* **Edited by R. Louis Gentilcore et al. Toronto: University of Toronto Press, 1993. 184pp. Index. ISBN 0-8020-2495-5. Vol. 3,** *Addressing the 20th Century, 1891–1961.* **Edited by Donald Kerr and Deryck W. Holdsworth. Toronto: University of Toronto Press, 1990. 197pp. Index. ISBN 0-8020-3448-9.** This handsome three-volume set consists respectively of 69, 58, and 66 color plates dealing with Canadian history starting with the prehistoric era and ending with the situation of Canada in 1961. The cartography is excellent and the topics illustrated by the maps are all based on extensive research. Fifty of the maps in the second volume were computer generated, a cost-saving move that allowed the project to be completed. This three-volume atlas stands as a model of scholarship and presentation for all historical atlases focused on an individual nation. The *Concise Historical Atlas of Canada,* edited by William G. Dean, Conrad E. Heidenreich, Thomas F. McIlwraith, and John Warkentin (Buffalo, NY: University of Toronto Press, 1998), is a simplified version of the three-volume *Historical Atlas of Canada. The Historical Atlas of Canada: Canada's History Illustrated with Original Maps* (Vancouver: Douglas & McIntyre; Seattle: University of Washington Press, 2002), edited by Derek Hayes, includes a beautiful collection of original maps, many never before reproduced. Many of the maps are artistic rather than utilitarian. They include maps by Samuel de Champlain, James Cook, David Thompson, and many other surveyors. There are even maps drawn by Native people such as Beothuk, Blackfoot, and Cree. *The Atlas of U.S. and Canadian Environmental History,* edited by Char Miller (New York: Routledge, 2003), examines the influence of the environment on human behavior and the impact of past environmental issues and policies.

776. *An Historical Atlas of China.*
By Albert Herrmann. New edition by Norton Ginsburg. Chicago: Aldine, 1966. 88pp. Index.
China, like many countries and areas, needs an up-to-date historical atlas based on the latest scholarship and cartographic techniques. In the meantime, however, what is available for China is better than what exists for most countries. Albert Herrmann's atlas first appeared in English in 1935 and was based on the highest standards of scholarship for that time. It was reprinted in 1966 and, as a resource for both Chinese and general Asian history from prehistory to just prior to the 19th

century, it remains quite useful. The cartography is excellent and combines great detail with clear presentation. For the modern period, it is best to consult Caroline Blunden and Mark Elvin, *Cultural Atlas of China* (New York: Checkmark, 1998).

777. *Historical Atlas of East Central Europe.*
By Paul Robert Magocsi. Rev. and exp. Seattle: University of Washington Press, 2002. 274pp. Index. ISBN 0-295-98193-8.
By far the best historical atlas for Eastern Europe, it is part of a 10-volume history of East Central Europe. Geographically, its scope is the area between German and Italian speakers in the west and up to the political boundaries of Russia and the old Soviet Union in the east, including Poland, the Czech Republic, Hungary, Romania, Albania, the lands of the former Yugoslavia, Bulgaria, and Greece. Chronological coverage begins in the late 5th century and goes up to 2000. Its over 100 color maps cover political, military, economic, cultural, and ethnic topics, among others, and include 21 new maps not found in the first edition of 1993. The maps are strongest on the Middle Ages and the early modern era. The index includes place-names. Also worth consulting is Dennis P. Hupchick and Harold Cox, *The Palgrave Concise Historical Atlas of Eastern Europe,* rev. ed. (New York: Palgrave/St. Martin's, 2001), with 52 maps in four colors, and Dennis P. Hupchick and Harold E. Cox, *The Palgrave Concise Historical Atlas of the Balkans* (New York: Palgrave/St. Martin's, 2001), with 50 maps in four colors. There are also the following older works: Arthur E. Adams et al., *An Atlas of Russian and East European History* (New York: Praeger, 1967) and the French work by Pierre Kovalevsky, *Atlas Historique et*

Culturel de la Russie et de Monde Slave (Paris, 1961).

778. *An Historical Atlas of Islam.* **Edited by Hugh Kennedy. Boston: Brill Academic, 2002. 86pp. Index. ISBN 90-04-12235-4. With a CD-ROM.**

The history of Islam is inextricably tied to the history of large parts of Asia and Africa. This revised atlas reflects that fact, as did the first edition, which was compiled as a companion volume to the massive and erudite *Encyclopedia of Islam*, also published by E. J. Brill. The second edition represents a significant revision and expansion. About a third of its maps are new and provide a strengthened coverage of the central Islamic lands of Egypt, the Fertile Crescent, and Iran. These areas were relatively neglected in the first edition. Many other maps from the first edition have been extensively revised and corrected. Coverage of the Ottoman Empire and India has been reduced so scholars interested in those regions should also consult the first edition. City maps for important Islamic metropolises such as Makka (Mecca), Cairo, and Jerusalem are also provided for various historical eras. All of the 82 maps are in color and are excellent examples of the cartographer's art. Eight maps take up two pages while another 29 are full-page spreads. There is a detailed atlas of place-names and ethnic names. Along with the print atlas, there is a CD-ROM version that can be easily searched through its alphabetical index of places and regions. The CD-ROM includes a four-level zooming function. There is no text accompanying the maps, so readers will need to know some Islamic history before they can effectively use this atlas. Once again the 20th century is neglected. Both of these problems can be partially alleviated by consult-

ing G. S. P. Freeman-Grenville and Stuart Christopher Munro-Hay, *Historical Atlas of Islam* (New York: Continuum, 2002), which provides both a detailed explanatory text and coverage of the 20th century. Its black-and-white maps, however, suffer in comparison with the Brill atlas. Additional coverage of the 20th century can be found in G. S. P. Freeman-Grenville, *Historical Atlas of the Middle East* (New York: Simon & Schuster, 1993), with 113 four-color maps. An older color atlas is R. Rookvink, *Historical Atlas of the Muslim Peoples* (Amsterdam: Djambatan, 1957).

779. *A Historical Atlas of South Asia.* **Edited by Joseph E. Schwartzberg et al. Chicago: University of Chicago Press, 1978. 352pp. Index. ISBN 0-226-74221-0.**

780. *A Historical Atlas of South Asia.* **Edited by Joseph E. Schwartzberg et al. 2nd impression. New York: Oxford University Press, 1992. 376pp. Index. ISBN 0-19-506869-6.**

The history of South Asia, which is defined in this case as the area of the present nations of India, Pakistan, Bangladesh, Afghanistan, Nepal, Bhutan, Sri Lanka, and the Maldives, is impressively depicted in this excellent atlas and its second impression. A dedicated team of scholars labored for over a decade to produce its 650 well-researched four-color maps that deal with cultural, social, demographic, and economic topics as well as political ones. Chronologically the maps range from the Old Stone Age to 1977, although more than half of the atlas is concerned with the post–1857 period. Furthermore, the emphasis of the maps in this atlas is to portray periods of time rather than specific points in time, for example, "1526–1707" rather than simply "1526." A text of over 100 pages helps to explain the maps while an index with some 15,000 entries will aid the reader in the location of places and subjects. There is also a bibliography of over 4,000 entries on South Asian history and related topics. Inserts at the back of the volume consist of two transparent overlay maps and three chronological charts. This work is one of the most scholarly atlases available in English and is definitely the best source for the historical geography of South Asia. The second impression contains minimal, although important, new material on prehistory and contemporary history, mostly in the form of text and tables, including the addition of 500 new items to the bibliography. There is also a new transparent overlay map of the new Indian administrative units. Most readers will be able to get by with the first edition. Individuals desiring a less expensive alternative should look at Karl J. Schmidt, *An Atlas and Survey of South Asian History* (Armonk, NY: M. E. Sharpe, 1995), which is available in hardback and paperback. Also of interest is *The Geographical Dictionary: Ancient and Early Medieval India,* by N. N. Bhattacharyya (New Delhi: Munshiram Manoharlal, 1991).

781. *Historical Atlas of South-East Asia.* **By Jan M. Pluvier. E. J. Brill, 1995. 147pp. ISBN 90-04-10238-8.**
Contains over 60 full-color maps with a 45-page historical introduction to explain the maps. This atlas is scholarly and well-produced, and it helps illuminate an area of the world whose history is poorly known in the West. It is not as magnificent as the *Historical Atlas of South Asia,* but it forms a fine complement to it.

782. *Historical Atlas of Central America.* **By Carolyn Hall and Hector Perez Brignoli.**
Norman: University of Oklahoma Press, 2003. ISBN 0-8061-3037-7. Index.
This is the most exciting new historical atlas on Latin America in two decades. It combines the talents of Carolyn Hall, one of central America's leading geographers, with Perez Brignoli, a professor of history at the University of Costa Rica. The first two sections of the atlas review 500 years of territorial organization, demography, and culture. The final three sections focus on the economic, political, and social issues specific to each country, beginning with the colonial period. It is lavishly illustrated with more than 140 color and black-and-white illustrations and 400 original full-color maps with explanatory and interpretive text. Still useful but somewhat dated is *Latin American History: A Teaching Atlas* (Madison: University of Wisconsin Press, 1983). By today's standards the 104 black-and-white maps are not very colorful.

783. *The Penguin Atlas of British and Irish History.* **Edited by Barry Cunliffe et al. London: Penguin, 2002. 320pp. Index. ISBN 0-141-009-152.**
Reflecting the influence of the "New British History," this attractive new atlas avoids the Anglocentric preoccupations of earlier atlases of British history. It is also a true atlas as opposed to a picture book with a few maps masquerading as an atlas. Some sort of map appears on almost every other page; many of them occupy the entire page with a multicolor presentation. The atlas is divided into five chronological sections—ancient, medieval, early modern, 19th century, and modern. Each section contains chronological or topical subsections; for example, the Roman conquest, the medieval church, languages 1500–1800, Britain's overseas trade, and women's suffrage. There

is also an extensive chronological table, a list of rulers, a bibliography, and a simple index. The cartography is well done and the text is authoritative while the volume is an attractive, inexpensive paperback. Still worth a look is the *Historical Atlas of Britain*, edited by Malcolm Falkus and John Gillingham (New York: Continuum/ Crossroad, 1981), which provides good coverage of economic and social history topics such as population, wealth distribution, transportation, and agriculture. For a specialized atlas that uses the Geographical Information Systems technology to display medieval data, there is Bruce M. Campbell and Ken Bartley, *Lay Lordship, Land, and Wealth: A Socio-Economic Atlas of England, 1300–1349* (Manchester: Manchester University Press, 2003).

784. *Routledge Atlas of Russian History.* **By Martin Gilbert. 3rd ed. New York: Routledge, 2003. 216pp. Index. ISBN 0-415281180.**

Atlases in English of non-English speaking countries are rare. Hence the third edition of Martin Gilbert's atlas of Russian history, which ranges from prehistory to the fall of the Soviet Union, is particularly welcome. Its 169 maps are done in black-and-white with no accompanying narrative, although they are heavily annotated. The cartography is clear and serviceable although by no means a work of art. Although the maps are primarily political and military in their subject matter, religion, economics, and culture also appear on some maps. This atlas is particularly useful for its detailed treatment of medieval and early modern Russia, the Russian civil war, and the non-Muscovite ethnic groups. The third edition includes new maps detailing the collapse of communism, the dissolution of the Soviet Union,

and the aftermath. Another useful atlas is Allen F. Chew, *An Atlas of Russian History: Eleven Centuries of Changing Borders* (New Haven, CT: Yale University Press, 1967). It consists of 34 maps in black-and-white accompanied by an explanatory text.

785. *The Times Atlas of European History.* **Edited by Thomas Cussans et al. New York: HarperCollins, 1994. 206pp. Index. ISBN 0-06-270101-0.**

Beginning in 900 BC and concluding in 1993, this atlas takes Europe as its geographical focus and political history as its topical focus. Its over 200 color maps are well produced and easy to read. The atlas is organized in chronological order into four-page sections. The first two pages of a section contain a map of Europe for a year of specific significance to political history. The next two pages consist of three or four maps depicting various more specialized geographical areas that help illuminate the larger map. A large map for 1618 titled "The Eve of the Thirty Years' War" is followed by maps depicting the religious divisions of the Hapsburg and Palatinate lands, the bishoprics and archbishoprics of the Holy Roman Empire, and the political divisions of the Netherlands. An accompanying text explains what the maps are portraying. This excellent atlas presents a lucid narrative of European political history that will be more helpful to its readers.

HISTORICAL ATLASES: SPECIFIC PERIODS AND TOPICS

786. *Atlas of Medieval Europe.* **Edited by Angus MacKay with David Ditchburn.**

London: Routledge, 1997. 272pp. Index. ISBN 0-414-01923-0.

Consists of almost 140 black-and-white maps, with explanatory text, that cover European history from approximately 400 to 1500. The maps are arranged into three chronological sections of the Early Middle Ages (c. 400–1100), the Central Middle Ages (c. 1100–c. 1300), and the Late Middle Ages (c. 1300–c. 1500). Within these chronological sections, the atlas combines the presentation of traditional topics with many maps depicting unique subjects. One map depicts the transfer of saints' relics from France and Rome to Anglo-Saxon monasteries in England for the purpose of maintaining interest among the formerly pagan converts. Of related interest are Nicholas Hooper and Matthew Bennett, *Cambridge Illustrated Atlas of Warfare: The Middle Ages, 768–1487* (Cambridge: Cambridge University Press, 1996); Angus Konstam, *Atlas of Medieval Europe* (New York: Facts on File, 2000); and Jonathan Riley-Smith, *The Atlas of the Crusades* (New York: Facts on File, 1990).

787. *Atlas of Medieval Jewish History.* **By Haim Beinert. New York: Simon & Schuster, 1992. 144pp. Index. ISBN 0-13-050691-5.**

788. *Atlas of Modern Jewish History.* **By Evyatar Friesel. Oxford: Oxford University Press, 1990. 159pp. Index. ISBN 0-19-505393-1.**

Taken together, these two atlases provide excellent coverage of Jewish history from the fifth century well into the 20th century. Beinert's coverage, which goes through the 17th century, is depicted in 120 maps, while Friesel's starts with the 18th century and proceeds up to the 1980s in 185 maps. Nar-

rative accompanies the maps in both volumes. Friesel's work is an updated translation of a Hebrew work published in 1983. Covering all of Jewish history, but not with the same detail and scholarly rigor, are *The Illustrated Atlas of Jewish Civilization: 4,000 Years of Jewish History*, edited by Martin Gilbert (New York: Macmillan, 1990) and the *Historical Atlas of the Jewish People: From the Time of the Patriarchs to the Present,* by Elie Barnavi and Miriam Eliav-Feldon, 3rd ed. (London: Kuperard, 1998).

789. *Atlas of Maritime History.* **By Richard Natkiel and Antony Preston. New York: Facts on File, 1986. 256pp. Index. ISBN 0-8160-1132-X.**

The ancient Phoenicians to oceanic trade in the 1980s forms the chronological scope of this excellent atlas. All maritime topics are covered in this work, although military subjects predominate. There is some bias toward English and European history, which is much more heavily represented than naval episodes from American history. Text, illustrations, and the many detailed maps are nicely integrated. The maps are produced in black, white, and blue, with fine attention to detail, while at the same time remaining clear and uncluttered in their presentation. A small but useful glossary and a simple index conclude this volume. This atlas is far superior to Christopher Lloyd, *Atlas of Maritime History* (New York: Arco, 1975).

790. *Barrington Atlas of the Greek and Roman World.* **Edited by Richard J. A. Talbert. Princeton, NJ: Princeton University Press, 2000. 272pp. ISBN 069103169X.**

This wonderful atlas marks the first attempt to provide a comprehensive historical atlas of the Classical world in over 100 years. Seventy-five scholars developed the 99 full-color maps, most of which are two-page spreads in a 13x19 inch format. The chronological scope is from about 1000 BC to about AD 640. Individual maps cover the British Isles, North Africa, and the Near East, along with all other regions that had strong connections with the Greco-Roman world. The highly detailed maps will allow readers to trace the routes of Hannibal and Alexander the Great and gain an accurate understanding of the topography that they encountered. A map by map directory of place-names is included on a CD-ROM and is also available in print in two volumes, totaling 1,500 pages. Still highly useful is the *Atlas of Classical History*, edited by Richard J. A. Talbert (New York: Macmillan, 1985), which is also available in a reasonably priced paperback.

791. *Historical Atlas of the Religions of the World*. By Isma'il Ragi al-Faruqi. New York: Macmillan, 1974. 346pp. Indexes. ISBN 0-02-336400-9.

As much an encyclopedia as an atlas, the *Historical Atlas of the Religions of the World* is divided into three parts: "Religions of the Past" (e.g., ancient Egyptian and Greco-Roman paganism); "Ethnic Religions of the Present" (e.g., Sikhism and Shinto); and "Universal Religions of the Present" (e.g., Christianity and Islam). There are 65 maps distributed through 20 illustrated chapters that are each written by an expert on the subject. The text is followed by an appendix of chronologies for the various religions. The *Historical Atlas of Religions*, by Karen Farrington (New York: Checkmark, 2002) is a similar title. Another more specialized atlas is Henry Chadwick and Gillian Evans, *Atlas of the Christian Church* (New York: Facts on File, 1987).

792. *The Macmillan Bible Atlas*. By Yohanan Aharoni and Michael Avi-Yonah. Revised by Anson F. Rainey and Ze'ev Safrai. 3rd ed. New York: Macmillan, 1993. 215pp. Index. ISBN 0-02-500605-8.

The almost 300 three-color maps of this atlas range from the prehistoric Near East to the extent of Christianity in the second century AD. Although biblical events form the primary focus of its maps, this atlas also deals extensively with large segments of the history of the ancient Near East. Originally the product of two well-respected Israeli archaeologists with clear and uncluttered cartography and a readable accompanying text, it has been thoroughly revised to reflect new discoveries and research. Presentation and design of the maps has also been improved. The new edition still contains a detailed biblical chronology and an index. When it is relevant, each map is related to the appropriate section of the Bible. Another more recent atlas on the same subject is James B. Pritchard, *The Harper Atlas of the Bible* (New York: Harper & Row, 1987).

793. *The New Penguin Atlas of Ancient History*. Revised by Colin McEvedy. London: Penguin, 2002. Paper. 128pp. ISBN 0140513485.

Now in a revised edition, this popular paperback atlas provides a chronological series of maps and text, which trace the history of Europe, the Mediterranean, and the Near East from 50,000 BC to the fourth century AD. This is a companion volume to the *New Penguin Atlas of Medieval History*, *The Penguin Atlas of Modern History (to 1815)*, and *The New Penguin Atlas of Recent History*.

794. *The Times Atlas of World Exploration: 3,000 Years of Exploring, Explorers, and*

Mapmaking. Edited by Felipe Fernández-Armesto. New York: HarperCollins, 1991. 286pp. Index. ISBN 0-06-270032-4.

The chronological scope of this impressive atlas is from the ancient world (c. 2000 BC) to the late 20th century, while its geographical scope is the entire world. Significant attention is given to non-European travels and discoveries, although the bulk of the volume deals with explorations by Westerners. The first seven chapters deal with explorations up to the 15th century by various ancient and medieval peoples. The remaining 40 chapters are divided into geographical sections covering sections of oceans or a continent (e.g., Central Asia, South America, or the Pacific Ocean). Approximately 200 color maps fill the book's pages. Some are quite small (3x3), while others take up two full pages. An equal number of pictures of historical maps are also included along with many well chosen full color illustrations. An explanatory text, written by a specialist historian, accompanies each chapter. A chronology, a glossary of technical terms, and a biographical dictionary are also included in this useful and attractive atlas. Smaller and less elaborate, but also less expensive and still useful, is the *Oxford Atlas of Exploration* (New York: Oxford University Press, 1997).

795. *The World Atlas of Archaeology.* Boston: G. K. Hall, 1985. 423pp. Index. ISBN 0-8161-8747-9.

Beautiful and impressive are the two adjectives that justly describe this atlas. Its coverage is truly worldwide, with the ancient Near East, Meso-America, China, and other regions of the world all getting their fair share of attention. The 19 sections are organized on a partly chronological and partly geographical basis with further subdivisions within each section. Ninety experts have produced the text, which is well integrated with the many maps and illustrations, most of which are in color. Cartographically, the maps are a pleasure to look at and are easy to read. This work is intended for the layman and the beginner in archaeology, as is the excellent *Hammond Past Worlds: The Times Atlas of Archaeology*, edited by Chris Scarre (New York: Hammond, 1989). More modest but updating both of the larger archaeological atlases is *The Atlas of Archaeology*, by Mick Aston and Tim Taylor (New York: DK Publishing, 1998).

MAP COLLECTIONS AVAILABLE ONLINE

796. *UT Library Online: Perry-Castaneda Map Collection.* http://www.lib.utexas.edu/maps/map_collection_guide.html

The Perry-Castaneda Library Map Collection is a general collection of more than 250,000 maps covering all areas of the world. However, it is known worldwide for its more than 5,000 map images available online, including a collection of historical maps. Online maps are arranged by region with a separate section for historical maps.

797. *David Rumsey Historical Collection.* http://www.davidrumsey.com

The David Rumsey Collection started 20 years ago and focuses primarily on cartography of the Americas in the 18th and 19th centuries but also has maps of the World, Asia, Africa, Europe, and Oceania. Collection categories include antique atlas, globe, school geography, maritime chart, state, country, city, pocket, wall, children's, and manuscript maps. The collection is used to study history, genealogy, and family history. Reproductions can be purchased. In June 2003, 811 maps were added to the online collection, bringing the total to over 8,800 maps online, which may be the largest collection in the world.

798. *Map Collections Home Page.* http://lcweb2.loc.gov/ammem/gmdhtml/gmdhome.html

The Geography and Map Division of the Library of Congress holds more than 4.5 million items, of which Map Collections represents only a small fraction of those converted to digital form. The focus of the online site is American, and Cartographic Treasures of the Library of Congress Map Collections is organized according to seven major categories: cities and towns, conservation and environment, discovery and exploration, cultural landscapes, military battles and campaigns, transportation and communication, and general maps.

12

HISTORICAL
STATISTICAL SOURCES

Statistical sources are of value to the historian, particularly those publications compiling a wide range of statistics over a period of time. Most of the data in these statistical compilations comes from the 19th and 20th centuries, with data on earlier periods being very hard or impossible to obtain in any convenient form. Historical statistics are diverse and include data ranging from population or climate to religion or agriculture. The terminology used in these statistical sources may be unfamiliar to the beginning historical researcher. Time series data, for example, refers to any series of data collected or recorded at regular intervals of time, while the term national accounts is defined as the totaling up of various economic accounts to provide an estimate of national income.

This chapter is designed to make the student of history aware of basic print historical statistical sources and data sources on the Internet. These sources include general bibliographies and indexes, periodicals and time series, as well as international, regional, and country sources of statistical information. Many of these sources are available directly electronically or at sites on the World Wide Web. The chapter does not

attempt to be exhaustive, but seeks to provide a good introduction to the topic.

GENERAL

Guides

799. Finding Statistics Online: How to Locate the Elusive Numbers You Need. By Paula Berinstein. Medford, NJ: Information Today, 1998. 356pp. ISBN 0-910965-25-0. Written by a librarian turned consultant, this volume provides an excellent overview of locating statistics online. It begins with general chapters on basic statistics and searching tips, followed by subject specific chapters including demographics and population statistics; industry, market, and general business statistics; financial and economic statistics; health and medical statistics; historical statistics; and political and government statistics. Each chapter has sections on types of data available, key producers, sources covering the subject, best places to look, and case studies. The appendixes include a section on vendor information and a bibliography. Berinstein's work is full of information and locations for Internet resources, along with a separate Web site that was created to update sources used in the book.

Bibliographies and Indexes

800. *Bibliography of Official Statistical Yearbooks and Bulletins.* By Gloria Westfall. Alexandria, VA: Chadwyck-Healey. 1986. 247pp. ISBN 0-85964-124-4.

This volume provides detailed information on 374 statistical yearbooks and bulletins, covering data published by the national statistical offices of more than 180 countries. The main part of the work is divided into five broad geographical headings: Africa, the Americas, Asia, Europe, and Oceania. Within these headings the material is arranged alphabetically by country. Entries include the title of the yearbook or bulletin, publisher, length and frequency of publication, and detailed information about the subjects covered (e.g., demography and economic affairs). Information on sources of historical statistics for each country is also provided, when available. More recent changes in a country's statistical yearbooks and bulletins can be found in the *Guide to Official Publications of Foreign Countries* [see 439]. Data from many of the statistical yearbooks listed in Westfall's work can also be found in a convenient microfiche set: *Current National Statistical Compendiums* (Bethesda, MD: Congressional Information Service, 1974–). The most recent statistics from these country sources can be found on the World Wide Web at sites such as OFFSTATS: Official Statistics on the Web [see 830] and the University of Michigan Documents Center: Statistical Resources on the Web [see 832].

801. *Index to International Statistics (IIS): A Guide to the Statistical Publications of International Intergovernmental Organizations.* Bethesda, MD: Congressional Information Service, 1983–. ISSN 0737-4461. Monthly, with annual cumulations.

The *Index to International Statistics* (*IIS*) serves as a comprehensive guide to the English-language statistical publications of international organizations, including those of the United Nations, the Organization for Economic Cooperation and Development, the European Union, and the Organization of American States. Covering from 1983 to the present and indexing over 2,200 titles, IIS is arranged similarly to another Congressional Information Service product, the *American Statistics Index* (*ASI*) [see 810]. IIS is divided into two parts—indexes and abstracts. In the index volume, sources are indexed by subject, name, geographic area, category, issuing source, title, and publication number. There are detailed abstracts for each publication, many of which are available on microfiche from *IIS*. It is an excellent index for finding international statistics on a wide variety of subjects. Two other publications that also provide subject access to a large number of U.S. and international statistical publications are *Global Data Locator* (Lanham, MD: Bernan, 1997) and *Instat: International Statistics Sources: Subject Guide to Sources of International Comparative Statistics* (London: Routledge, 1995). The *IIS* is searchable electronically through Lexis-Nexis Statistical [see 802].

802. *LexisNexis Statistical.* www.lexisnexis. com

This electronic database, available through the World Wide Web, allows the user to search federal, state, private, and international statistical sources from the 1970s to the present. It includes all the indexing and abstracting information available through three statistical indexes: American Statistics Index (1974–), Statistical Reference Index (1980–), and Index to International Statistics (1983–). There are many different ways to search this database, including by key word, title, subject, document number, etc., and you can narrow your search further by limiting the time period, as well as limiting it by selecting geographic, demographic, and economic categories. One major feature of this database is the power tables. This pulls together thousands of individually indexed statistical tables from a variety of sources that are searchable through the database. The base edition of LexisNexis Statistical provides access to 30,000 tables and an optional research edition provides access to another 100,000. Having these searchable and then accessible full text greatly enhances access to statistics on every level. Sources such as LexisNexis Statistical have revolutionized access to statistics through increased flexibility in searching and in access to data over time. The researcher no longer has to search through a number of years of printed indexes to find material.

803. *Statistics Sources*. Edited by Steven R. Wasserman. Detroit, MI: Gale Group, 1962–. 2 vols.
This massive two-volume work, which is in its 26th edition, is extremely useful as a subject-finding guide to sources of statistics, including sources of data on industry, business, society, education, finance, and other subjects both for the United States and the rest of the world. It contains nearly 100,000 citations from more than 2,000 sources,

both print and nonprint. *Statistics Sources* covers U.S. government statistical publications, as well as statistical publications from the United Nations, other international organizations, and various national statistical offices. The volumes are arranged alphabetically by issuing organization within a given subject area. Also within the subject categories are headings for U.S. states and individual countries. At the beginning of the work are lists of key statistical sources, including print, online, Internet, and World Wide Web sites, as well as federal statistical databases. Following the main listing by subject there are appendixes that contain the print and nonprint statistical data sources used in compiling this work. *Statistics Sources* is a good starting point for finding country statistical publications on a number of topics. Also useful are related titles such as the *Index to International Statistics*, *Global Data Locator*, and *Instat: International Statistics Sources*. LexisNexis Statistical [see 802] also pulls together a number of country and international statistical sources.

Periodicals and Time Series

804. *Cross-Polity Time Series Data*. By Arthur S. Banks and the Staff of the Center for Comparative Political Research, State University of New York at Binghamton. Cambridge, MA: MIT Press, 1971. 300pp. ISBN 0-262-02071-8.
Although a single volume, this unique work presents a wide range of statistical time series country data drawn from the data archive at the Center for Comparative Political Research at the State University of New York at Binghamton. The data is drawn from a number of sources, including

the *Statesman's Year-Book, Europa Yearbook,* and the U.N. *Statistical Yearbook,* and covers the period from 1815 to 1966. Banks's work is divided into 10 sections, each containing statistical data on particular subjects, such as population, area, national government revenue, transportation, economic data, and domestic conflict. Within each section, the data is arranged alphabetically by country and chronologically. For the historian, this work brings together information on over 100 topics for many different countries, covering a time period of over 100 years, in some cases.

The historian should also be aware that there is an enormous amount of statistical time series data on the United States and other countries available on the World Wide Web through the Inter-university Consortium for Political and Social Research (ICPSR), located in Ann Arbor, Michigan. Many research libraries belong to this organization and have contact people who can help researchers looking for data. For more detailed information on Web access to ICPSR, see 829.

805. *The Statesman's Year-Book.* **London: Macmillan; New York: St. Martin's, 1864–. ISSN 0081-4601. Annual.**
Since its first publication in 1864, this annual volume has contained a wealth of statistical information about the different countries of the world. The most recent volumes are divided into two parts: (1) international organizations and (2) countries of the world, listed alphabetically. Concise information is supplied for each country including its history, area and population, climate, constitution and government, defense, economy, energy and natural

resources, communications, justice, religion, education, and diplomatic representatives. Much of the information is statistical and at the end of each country's profile there is a bibliography of references. Since its first appearance this extremely useful reference source has more than doubled its size. Material in the early volumes is less comprehensive but, for the historian, is a good source of statistical information on various countries dating back to the mid-19th century. Macmillan, which publishes the print *Statesman's Year-Book,* has produced a Web version called SYBWorld, which provides access to detailed information on 192 countries.

UNITED NATIONS

806. *Demographic Yearbook; Annuaire Demographique.* **New York: United Nations, 1948–. Index. ISSN 0082–8041. Annual.**
The United Nations is the major publisher of recent international statistical information, including a number of serial statistical publications. One major statistical reference source it publishes is the *Demographic Yearbook,* prepared by its Statistical Office. Published annually since 1948, this yearbook supplies detailed world and country data on population and vital statistics, such as birth rates, infant and maternal mortality, general mortality, marriage, and divorce. Each volume is divided into two parts: (1) statistical tables and (2) special topics tables, for example, mortality statistics updating earlier tables. In 1979 a special *Historical Supplement* volume of the *Demographic Yearbook* was published, containing time series data on

population, natality, mortality, and nuptiality from 1948 to 1978. The 1948 volume, the first one in the series, also contains annual data for the years 1932–1947. More recently the United Nations published the *Demographic Yearbook CD-ROM Historical Supplement, 1948–1997*, making available 50 years of data on 229 countries. Since the *Yearbook* is not totally current, more up-to-date information can be found in the U.N. quarterly *Population and Vital Statistics Report*, the latest issues of which are available on the Web and update many of the statistical tables found in the main *Yearbook* volumes. Individual country sites on the World Wide Web may also have more current statistics.

807. *Statistical Yearbook; Annuaire Statistique.* **New York: United Nations, 1948–. ISSN 0082-8459. Annual. Latest volumes also available on CD-ROM.**

This is the major statistical compendium of social and economic data published by the Statistical Office of the United Nations. It draws on a number of other more specialized U.N. and international agency publications. Beginning in 1948, the *Yearbook* has been published annually and contains statistics on over 200 countries. Much of the data covers 10-year periods and includes world and country statistics on population and manpower, national accounts, wages, prices, consumption, balance of payments, finance, health, education, agriculture, manufacturing, energy, trade, transportation, and communications. Although the annual volumes of the *Yearbook* are not quite current, they can be updated by the U.N. *Monthly Bulletin of Statistics*, the latest issues of which are in print and on the Web and contain

more recent data. Subject access to U.N. data is available through the *Index to International Statistics* [see 801], which is part of a broader electronic source, LexisNexis Statistical [see 802]. Much of the statistical data published by the United Nations is available through CD-ROM, diskette, and electronically on the World Wide Web. The United Nations has also created a separate electronic database, the United Nations Common Database [see 808], which pulls together U.N. data from a number of sources. A number of U.N. agencies also have their own Web sites for current data, which are linked through the official Web site locator for the U.N. system at http://www.unsystem.org.

808. United Nations Common Database. New York: United Nations.

This U.N. database is available by subscription on the World Wide Web. It provides access to a wide variety of time series data from 30 international sources from 1946 to the present. The database contains access to country statistics on a number of different subjects, including agriculture, economics, health, education, labor, environment, and others. A basic view option allows access to a single type of data for as many as 10 countries for a 20-year period; the database also allows for an advanced search, which allows searching for multiple series, years, and countries. The material found in the advanced search can then be downloaded into a number of different formats to be manipulated by the researcher. The Web site for the database also includes definitions of statistical terms, a topical list of subjects, and a list of sources. The advantage of this database is it pulls together access to a number of U.N. statistical sources in one spot and it provides access to time series data from a number of different sources.

UNITED STATES

809. *A Statistical Portrait of the United States: Social Conditions and Trends.* **By Patricia C. Becker. 2nd ed. Lanham, MD: Bernan, 2002. 450pp. ISBN 0-89059-584-4.**
The advantage of this work is that it pulls together a variety of U.S. government and private statistics for the past 25 years in one volume. Becker's work is intended as an update to the government's social indicators volumes, which were last published in 1980. The first half of the book is divided into 12 chapters focusing on all areas of American society, including population characteristics; households and families; social conditions; labor force and job characteristics; housing; income, wealth, and poverty; education; crime and criminal justice; health; leisure, volunteerism, and religiosity; voting; and government. Each chapter of this work is full of numerous charts and tables containing a wealth of economic and demographic data useful for the 20th-century U.S. historian. At the end of each chapter is a bibliography of additional sources and a list of Web sites. The latter half of the work is the appendix, which is made up of statistical tables, some of them going back to the 1940s and 1950s, corresponding to the earlier chapters. This is an excellent one-volume source on 20th-century U.S. statistics.

810. *American Statistics Index: A Comprehensive Guide to the Statistical Publications of the U.S. Government.* **Bethesda, MD: Congressional Information Service, 1973–. ISSN 0091-1658. Annual, with monthly supplements.**
This Congressional Information Service (CIS) index has greatly simplified locating statistical information published by the federal government. Similar in arrangement to the *Index to International Statistics* [see 801], the *American Statistics Index* (*ASI*) is the most comprehensive index to recent U.S. government statistical publications, covering 5,000 titles, including 450 periodicals. There is a retrospective edition that indexes publications from 1960 to 1973, and the annual cumulative volumes, beginning in 1974. The *ASI* is divided into two parts—index and abstracts. Items are indexed by subject and name, category, title, agency report numbers, and Superintendent of Documents (SuDoc) numbers. Abstracts are extremely detailed, providing the SuDoc number and an extensive description of the statistical material contained in a particular publication. Since 1980 another CIS publication, the *Statistical Reference Index* (*SRI*), has indexed statistics published by private organizations and state agencies. This index, along with *ASI* and *IIS,* is available through LexisNexis on the World Wide Web under the title LexisNexis Statistical [see 802]. A number of research libraries provide access to this service. Almost all the documents indexed on *ASI, SRI,* and *IIS* are available on microfiche from CIS.

811. *Bureau of the Census Catalog of Publications, 1790–1972.* **Washington, DC: Government Printing Office, 1974. 591pp. Index.**
The publications of the U.S. Bureau of the Census are a valuable source of historical

and current statistics about all aspects of American life. For the historian interested in using census publications, this one-volume *Catalog of Publications* is an excellent bibliographic guide. It is in reality a compilation of two catalogs: *The Catalog of United States Census Publications, 1790–1945* (Washington, DC: Government Printing Office, 1950) and the more recent *Bureau of the Census Catalog of Publications, 1946–1972*. Within the volume, publications are arranged by broad census subject areas, such as population, housing, and agriculture. There are detailed descriptions of individual publications and subject indexes to each of the two catalogs. For recent information on current census publications, the researcher should check the annual *Census Catalog and Guide* (Washington, DC: Government Printing Office, 1947–). Recent census information is searchable through the U.S. Census Bureau Web site http://www.census.gov and more of it is being produced in electronic format. Also helpful as a guide to historical census material are three volumes by Suzanne Schulze: *Population Information in Nineteenth Century Census Volumes* (1983), *Population Information in Twentieth Century Census Volumes, 1900–1940* (1985), and *Population Information in Twentieth Century Census Volumes, 1950–1980* (1988), all published by Oryx Press.

812. *Historical Statistics of the States of the United States: Two Centuries of the Census, 1790–1990*. Compiled by Donald B. Dodd. Westport, CT: Greenwood, 1993. 478pp. ISBN 0-313-28309-5.
This recent volume pulls together state-level federal census material on population, agriculture, and manufacturing for the past 200 years. The purpose of this work is to fill in the gap in U.S. historical statistics between material in the *Historical Statistics of the United States* and the more recent county level data compiled by the Inter-University Consortium for Political and Social Research. It includes population data from 1790 to the present and data on agriculture and manufacturing from 1850 to 1990. There is also a table giving the population of cities with 100,000 inhabitants from 1790 to 1990 and a glossary of terms. Dodd's work is significant because it pulls together a wide range of census data from a number of census volumes and prints it in one convenient source.

813. *Historical Statistics of the United States, Colonial Times to 1970*. Bicentennial ed. Washington, DC: Government Printing Office, 1975. 1,200pp. 2 vols. Index. Reprinted by Kraus International in 1989. ISBN 0-527-91756-7 (set). Also available on CD-ROM. New York: Cambridge University Press, 1997.
This volume is the third and most recent in the *Historical Statistics* series published by the Bureau of the Census, which is a supplement to the *Statistical Abstract of the United States* [see 814]. The current two-volume work conveniently compiles federal statistics from the colonial period to 1970, including over 12,500 time series, representing a 50 percent increase over the previous edition. Statistics compiled in these volumes cover every social and economic area, including population, vital statistics, labor, consumer income and expenditures, agriculture, manufactures, transportation, energy, business enterprise, and government. There are extensive notes before each chapter, which list statistical sources and explain the type and reliability of the data.

Data in the tables is mainly annual and there is a chapter at the end on colonial and prefederal statistics. The volumes are indexed by time period and by subject. Most of the current time series tables found in *Historical Statistics* are updated in the annual volumes of the *Statistical Abstract of the United States*, beginning with the 1973 issue.

814. *Statistical Abstract of the United States.* **Washington, DC: Government Printing Office, 1879–. Index. Annual.**
Published annually since 1879, this single volume is the standard ready-reference source of U.S. government political, social, and economic statistics. It contains a wide-ranging selection of statistics drawn from many federal and private statistical publications. Within the volume, the data is arranged into chapters by subject (e.g., population, elections). Usually the tables cover the past several years, although some tables cover 15–20 years. There is a detailed index, and several appendixes include material on guides to sources of statistics, metropolitan statistical areas and their components, and statistical methodology and reliability. In recent years there have been two supplements to the *Statistical Abstract*: the *County and City Data Book* (Washington, DC: Government Printing Office, 1952–) and the *State and Metropolitan Area Data Book* (Washington, DC: Government Printing Office, 1980–). The tabular data published in the *Statistical Abstract* and both of its supplements is also available on CD-ROM and in electronic format on the World Wide Web through the U.S. Census Bureau home page. It is also searchable through LexisNexis Statistical.

CANADA

815. *Historical Statistics of Canada.* **Edited by F. H. Leacy. 2nd ed. Ottawa: Statistics Canada, 1983. ca. 900pp. Index. ISBN 0-660-11259-0. http://www. statcan.ca/english/freepub/11-516-XIE/ sectiona/toc.htm**
The Canadian equivalent to the *Historical Statistics of the United States*, this volume publishes in one location Canadian statistics from 1867 through the mid–1970s. This second edition updates the earlier *Historical Statistics of Canada* (Toronto: Macmillan, 1965). Arranged by broad subjects, like the U.S. volume, chapters include time series data on population and migration, vital statistics and health, price indexes, agriculture, and energy and electric power. At the beginning of each chapter there is a detailed explanation and list of the sources. A subject index ends the volume. For more current Canadian statistics, the researcher should check the annual volumes of the *Canada Year Book* (Ottawa: Statistics Canada, 1906–), which update the historical volume and are the Canadian version of the *Statistical Abstract of the United States* [see 814]. Recent Canadian statistics are available on the World Wide Web through the Statistics Canada home page, http://www.statcan.ca/ start.html.

EUROPE

General

816. *International Historical Statistics: Europe, 1750–1993.* **By B. R. Mitchell. 4th ed.**

New York: Stockton, 1998. 959pp.
ISBN 1-56159-236-6.

This work, one of three by the same author covering historical statistics all over the world, is valuable because it brings together a compendium of statistics for individual European countries from 1750 to 1993. In its fourth edition, Mitchell's volume draws heavily on the official statistical publications of the European governments. The data is presented in 77 tables arranged under 10 broad subject areas. These include population and vital statistics, labor force, agriculture, industry, external trade, transport and communications, finance, prices, education, and national accounts. Some changes have been made in this edition, including the elimination of the section on climate, new tables showing recent money supply statistics, and an effort to handle the problems created by the recent division of the Soviet Union and Yugoslavia. The comprehensiveness of the data varies from country to country. Following a brief introductory chapter covering methodology and boundary and currency changes, each major chapter includes an introduction to the statistical tables. One drawback of this work is the lack of a detailed subject index for quickly locating material. For more recent statistics on Europe, there are the statistical yearbooks of individual countries along with the many statistical publications of the Organization for Economic Cooperation and Development (OECD)—available electronically as *Source OECD*, which includes time series data—as well of those of the United Nations Economic Commission for Europe, and the European Union. There is also a wealth of current statistical data on individual countries available on the World

Wide Web. The University of Michigan Documents Center site provides easy access to this statistical information.

817. *The East European and Soviet Data Handbook: Political, Social, and Developmental Indicators, 1945–1975.* By Paul S. Shoup. New York: Columbia University Press, 1981. 482pp. ISBN 0-231-04252-3.

Shoup's work makes available to researchers a great deal of historical data on the Soviet Union and the countries of Eastern Europe prior to the breakup of the Communist system. Covering 1945 to 1975, it also contains some data from the period before World War II. This volume is structured to provide cross-national and historical comparisons. After a lengthy general introduction describing the types of data collected and the reliability of that data, the *Handbook* is arranged by sections. These include chapters on population, party membership, national and religious affiliation, level of education, classes, background of party leaders, occupations, and developmental indicators and standard of living. Some of this material is not available in other sources. There are a number of appendixes, as well as a bibliography, a summary of sources, and a listing of sources for individual tables. This work is an excellent source for political and social statistics on this region for the post–World War II period.

Great Britain

818. *British Historical Statistics.* By B. R. Mitchell. Cambridge: Cambridge University Press, 1988. 886pp. Index. ISBN 0-521-33008-4.

This volume, which is an updating of two earlier volumes—*Abstract of British Historical Statistics* and the *Second Abstract of British Historical Statistics*—is the best single source for social and economic statistics for the history of Great Britain. The emphasis is on economic statistics, but in this new volume a greater amount of social statistics has been added. Mitchell's work is arranged into 16 chapters, including the broad topics of population and vital statistics, labor force, agriculture, external trade, public finance, and prices. There is a detailed explanatory introduction before each chapter, followed by the tables. These present data from a wide range of years, in some cases dating back to the 14th century. Most of the annual data covers the 19th and 20th centuries, and there is a subject index at the end of the volume. For more recent statistics on Great Britain, see the *Annual Abstract of Statistics* (London: Her Majesty's Stationery Office (now the Stationery Office), 1840/53–) and the Government Statistical Service Web site at http://www.statistics.gov.uk. There is also the Great Britain Historical Database located at the University of Essex, http://hds.essex.ac.uk/gbh.asp. It contains a large amount of 19th and 20th century statistical data from government sources, including census material as well as employment, demographic, marriage, and mortality statistics.

France

819. *Annuaire Statistique de la France.* Paris: Institut National de la Statistique et des Etudes Economiques, 1878–. Index. Annual, with occasional historical volumes.

Written in French, this yearbook is the best statistical source for all aspects of French political, economic, and social life. Published since 1878, these annual volumes are arranged by broad subject categories including climate, environment, population, vital statistics, agriculture and food, commerce and business, education, housing, and labor. Most of the statistical tables give several years of data. There is a subject index at the end of each volume, along with a list of French statistical agencies. Certain volumes in the series provide historical statistical data (e.g., the volumes for 1946, 1951, 1961, and 1966). Furthermore, the volumes from 1881 to 1939 included data for earlier periods. For current statistics on France, see the National Institute of Statistics and Economic Studies Web site, http://www.insee.fr/en/home/home_page.asp.

Germany

820. *Statistisches Jahrbuch für die Bundesrepublik Deutschland.* Wiesbaden: Statistisches Bundesamt, 1952–. Index. Annual.

Published since 1952. Until 1990 this was the statistical yearbook for West Germany. With the unification of Germany it merged with the separate statistical source for East Germany, *Statistisches Jahrbuch der Demokratischen Republik* (Berlin: Staatliche Zentralverwattung für Statistik, 1955–1990), to form a single statistical source for a united Germany. The most recent edition contains statistics on the social and economic life of the country, including population, elections, employment, production, tourism, foreign trade, transportation, communications, education, health, prices, and the environment.

There is a subject index at the end of the volume. For earlier German statistics, there is the *Statistisches Jahrbuch für das Deutsche Reich*, published by the Statistisches Reichsamt, which covers the years 1880 to 1942. The most current statistical data on Germany is available on the World Wide Web at the Federal Statistical Office's Web site, http://www.statistik-bund.de/erg_e.htm.

Russia and the Commonwealth of Independent States

821. *Russia and Eurasia Facts and Figures Annual.* Gulf Breeze, FL: Academic International Press, 1993–. Annual. ISSN 1074-1658.
The best and most reliable English-language annual for recent statistics on Russia and the nations of the former Soviet Union. After the breakup of the Soviet Union, it continues the coverage of the *USSR Facts and Figures Annual*, which began publication in 1977. Each volume in this series contains a wide variety of statistics. After some basic information on the Commonwealth of Independent States, the new name for these countries, the work is divided into individual chapters on Russia and other independent states such as Armenia, Estonia, Kazakstan, Ukraine, and Uzbekistan. All the states of the former Soviet Union are covered. Each chapter begins with basic information and a chronology followed by sections on state and politics; military, security, and crime; health and welfare; economy, industry, and agriculture; energy and environment; and foreign trade, investment, and aid. It is important to note that the latest volume in this series does not cumulate the earlier ones. Each new volume contains

a great deal of material that is not found in the other volumes. Some volumes also index in detail earlier volumes in this series. For earlier statistics on the former Soviet Union, see the work of B. P. Pockney, *Soviet Statistics Since 1950* (Aldershot, U.K.: Dartmouth, 1991) and *The Statistical Handbook of Social and Economic Indicators for the Former Soviet Union* (New York: Norman Ross, 1996). For current statistical data on Russia and the other members of the Commonwealth of Independent States, see the Statistics of the Commonwealth of Independent States Web site, http://www.cisstat.com/eng.

LATIN AMERICA

822. *International Historical Statistics: The Americas, 1750–1993.* By B. R. Mitchell. 4th ed. New York: Stockton, 1998. 830pp. ISBN 1-56159-235-8.
This work is the second in a series of historical statistics volumes compiled by B. R. Mitchell, including *International Historical Statistics: Europe, 1750–1993* and *International Historical Statistics: Africa, Asia, and Oceania, 1750–1993* [see 816, 825]. The main change between this work and the previous edition is that Australasia is included with Africa and Asia in a separate volume. This new volume contains statistical information drawn mainly from the statistical yearbooks of all the countries of North and South America. The data is presented in 85 tables arranged under 10 broad subject areas, including population and vital statistics, labor force, agriculture, industry, external trade, transport and communications, finance, prices, education, and national accounts. As in the earlier volume,

data on climate is omitted and there are new tables covering annual population and the money supply. While most of the tabular data is for the 20th century, there is also statistical information for much of the 19th century. The amount of information supplied by the tables varies according to the topic and the country. More recent data on individual countries can be found by searching the World Wide Web.

823. *Statistical Abstract of Latin America.* Los Angeles: UCLA Latin American Center Publications, 1955–. Index. Annual. ISSN 0081-4687.

This is the best and most detailed annual compilation of social and economic statistical data on the countries of Latin America. Published since 1955, the most recent of these volumes contains data from over 200 sources on 20 South and Central American countries, including Cuba, Haiti, and the Dominican Republic. The arrangement of the latest volume consists of 10 sections with tables on the topics of geography, land, and environment; transportation and communications; population, health, and education; politics, religion, and the military; working conditions and migration; illegal and legal industry; mining, energy, and sea and land production; foreign trade; financial flows; and national accounts, government policy and finance, and prices. Tables contain both recent and time series data. Since 1970 the Latin American Center has published supplements to the *Abstract* containing data on more specialized topics. The *Statistical Yearbook for Latin America and the Caribbean* (Santiago, Chile: Economic Commission for Latin American and the Caribbean, 1985–) also contains recent statistical information on Latin America. More

recent data on individual Latin American countries can be found searching the World Wide Web, particularly at the University of Michigan Documents Center [see 832] or at the OFFSTATS [see 830] site.

AFRICA AND ASIA

General

824. *African Statistical Yearbook.* Addis Ababa: United Nations Economic Commission for Africa, 1974–. Annual. ISSN 0252-5488.

Beginning publication in 1974, this work provides detailed statistical information for 53 African countries. The *Yearbook* is divided geographically into four parts: North Africa, West Africa, East and Southern Africa, and Central Africa. Each volume is arranged alphabetically by country and contains country statistics on such topics as population and employment, national accounts, agriculture, industry, prices, education, and health. This data covers the most recent 10 years available. The *Yearbook* is not completely current and more recent statistical data on African countries can be found in a number of United Nations publications, the most current being the *Monthly Bulletin of Statistics.* The most recent statistics on individual African countries are on the World Wide Web; the University of Michigan Documents Center [see 832] and OFFSTATS: Official Statistics on the Web [see 830] are good starting points for detailed links to country statistical Web sites.

825. *International Historical Statistics: Africa, Asia, and Oceania, 1750–1993.* By B. R.

Mitchell. 3rd ed. New York: Stockton, 1998. 1,113pp. ISBN 1-56159-234-X.

This is a companion to the two *International Historical Statistics* volumes mentioned earlier [see 816, 822]. The main change between this volume and the earlier edition is the incorporation of data from the countries of Oceania, including Australia and New Zealand, and from the People's Republic of China, which was not included in the previous edition. Like the previous volumes in this series, this volume contains statistical data, drawing heavily from the official publications of the countries of Africa, Asia, and Oceania. The data is presented in 81 tables arranged according to the same 10 broad subject categories as the earlier volumes in this series: population, labor force, agriculture, industry, external trade, transport and communication, finance, prices, education, and national accounts. As in the other volumes, data on climate has been omitted and tables on annual population and the money supply have been included. Much of the annual data included in the volume is for the 20th century, although there is coverage for some countries going back to the mid-19th century. This volume contains historical statistics on the countries of the Middle East, including Egypt and Israel. More recent country information can be found in the many statistical yearbooks of the countries covered and in tables on the World Wide Web.

826. *Statistical Yearbook for Asia and the Pacific*. Bangkok, Thailand: United Nations Economic and Social Commission for Asia and the Pacific, 1973–. Annual. ISSN 0252-3655.

Continuing an earlier U.N. publication, *Statistical Yearbook for Asia and the Far East*, this annual volume contains detailed statistics on Asian and Pacific countries, including China, Vietnam, Japan, and Korea. Each statistical volume covers a broad range of topics, including population, manpower, national accounts, agriculture, forestry and fishing, industry, energy, transport and communications, external trade, wages, prices and consumption, and finance and social statistics. The statistics are taken from international and national statistical agencies and generally contain data covering the past ten years. Since the most recent volume of the *Statistical Yearbook* is not totally current, it can be updated by consulting the quarterly *Statistical Indicators for Asia and the Pacific*. Recent statistical data on Asian countries is also available by searching the World Wide Web. The University of Michigan Documents Center Web site [see 832] and OFF-STATS: Official Statistics on the Web [see 830] are good starting points. For historical statistics on many Asian countries, refer to the *International Historical Statistics: Africa, Asia, and Oceania, 1750–1993* [see 825].

China

827. *China Statistical Yearbook*. Compiled by the State Statistical Bureau, People's Republic of China. Beijing: China Statistical Publishing House, 1982–. Annual. ISSN 1052-9225.

This is the official and most detailed volume of social and economic statistics for the People's Republic of China. It currently is divided into a number of chapters that include detailed statistical tables on national accounts; population; employment and wages; investment; production and consumption of energy; government finance;

price indexes; people's livelihood, survey of cities; agriculture; industry; construction; transportation; postal and telecommunications services; domestic trade; foreign trade and economic cooperation; tourism; banking and insurance; education, science and culture; and sports, public health, social welfare, and others. In some tables, data goes back to the 1950s. Appendixes include material on Taiwan and Macao and a comparison of China's economic and social indicators with other countries. Data on Hong Kong, which is part of China, is included. Also useful for statistics on China is the annual *China Facts and Figures Annual* (Gulf Breeze, FL: Academic International Press, 1978–). For the most current statistics, search the World Wide Web, including sites such as the China Data Center, at the University of Michigan, http://www.umich.edu/~iinet/chinadata/index.html.

Japan

828. *Historical Statistics of Japan.* Tokyo: Nikon Tokei Kyokai (Japan Statistical Association), 1987–1988. 5 vols. Also available on CD-ROM (Tokyo: Japan Statistical Association, 1999).
This five-volume work contains statistics on Japan from 1868 to 1985. It includes the major social and economic statistical series on Japan such as climate, population, labor, agriculture, manufacturing, energy, prices, national accounts, health, education, and disasters and accidents. These volumes contain data from the *Statistical Yearbook of the Empire of Japan*, which was published from 1882 to 1941, and are updated by the *Japan Statistical Yearbook* (Tokyo: Statistics Bureau),

which began publication in 1949. The latest volume of the *Japan Statistical Yearbook* has an appendix showing table numbers in the yearbook and similar tables in the *Historical Statistics of Japan* volumes. For the most recent statistics on Japan, go to the Japanese Statistics Bureau Web site at http://www.stat.go.jp/english/index.htm.

INTERNET RESOURCES

829. *ICPSR Home Page.* http://www.icpsr.umich.edu/index.html
This site is available through the auspices of ICPSR, the Inter-university Consortium for Political and Social Research, located within the Institute for Social Research at the University of Michigan. Many universities and colleges are members of this organization, including over 400 institutions all over the world. Through their university's membership in ICPSR, faculty and students have access to the world's largest archive of computerized data in the social sciences, including disciplines such as political science, sociology, demography, economics, history, education, gerontology, criminal justice, public health, foreign policy, and law. ICPSR data sets are mainly accessible online and available for downloading through the World Wide Web, although some are available on CD-ROM and on diskette. Researchers can go to the ICPSR Home Page and view the data sets by subject. Most of the data covers the 20th century, although some census data sets go back to the 18th century. An excellent site for researchers seeking quantitative data on a wide variety of subjects.

830. *OFFSTATS: Official Statistics on the Web.* http://www.auckland.ac.nz/lbr/stats/offstats/OFFSTATSmain.htm This site, which is maintained by the University of Auckland (New Zealand) Library, offers easy access to current data and time series data provided from two sources: (1) the statistical offices, central banks, and government departments and agencies of individual countries, and (2) topical links to statistics compiled by international organizations, associations, and some commercial sites. Links to data are available by country, region, and topic. The data can be downloaded as text or spreadsheet files. This site, like the University of Michigan site, serves as a central place to link to national and international statistical data on a wide variety of subjects.

831. *United States Historical Census Data Browser.* http://fisher.lib.virginia.edu/census This site, located at the Fisher Library at the University of Virginia, contains statistical census data for each U.S. state and county from 1790 to 1960. The data was initially created by the Inter-university Consortium for Political and Social Research (ICPSR). It includes population by state, race, nationality, numbers of families, size of family,

births, deaths, marriages, occupation, religion, and general economic conditions. Users can use the search software to search for up to 15 variables by census and quickly receive a table or graph of results to the county level. Related to this site in its use of historical census information online is *Historical Census Statistics on the Foreign-Born Population of the United States, 1850–1990,* which is accessible through the U.S. Bureau of the Census home page at http://www.census.gov.

832. *University of Michigan Documents Center: Statistical Resources on the Web.* http://www.lib.umich.edu/govdocs/stats/html This is part of a massive government documents site at the University of Michigan. The statistical part links to a huge number of statistical sources by topic, including abortion, banking, capital punishment, defense, education, foreign trade, gambling, health, immigration, and life expectancy. Statistical Resources also links to statistical sites for foreign countries, which are listed alphabetically, and to United Nations and international agency Web sites. The beauty of this site is the links to all the country sites, as well as quick access to statistical data on a wide variety of subjects.

13

ARCHIVES, MANUSCRIPTS, SPECIAL COLLECTIONS, AND DIGITAL SITES

Serious research in history requires the use of primary documents, which include archival, manuscript, and special collection material. The term archives often refers to the official records of a nation, an institution, or an organization. It can also refer to the repository which houses these types of records. Manuscripts usually refer to a collection of primary documents housed in an archive, library, or research institution. Special collection material can include manuscripts but also can contain other types of primary source documents.

In recent years the development of the World Wide Web has changed ways of accessing the collections available in many archives and the ways of accessing the records themselves. By going on the Internet researchers can find out the most recent information about the holdings of an increasing number of archives and special collections. Rapid progress in digitizing records is making more and more of these records accessible online at separate digital sites. Most archival records must still be viewed in person or on microfilm, but digi-

tizing is making some of this material, as well as finding aids, available directly on the researcher's computer.

This chapter will cover guides to archives, manuscripts, and special collections, both print and online. It is not designed to be totally comprehensive but to provide a good introduction to the specialized reference works available to aid researchers in using these primary materials. The main part of the chapter will cover guides to archives and manuscript collections, arranged from more general meta sites and directories to those focusing on archival resources by country. This will be followed by a section on guides for locating special collection and subject resources and a closing section introducing key digital sites, such as the Library of Congress American Memory Project. It is hoped that by using this chapter researchers will have a sound grounding in the major sources available for finding material in these specialized collections and can use this knowledge to locate specific resources in their areas of research interest.

ARCHIVES AND MANUSCRIPT COLLECTIONS

General Sites

833. *Repositories of Primary Sources.* http://www.uidaho.edu/special-collections/Other.Repositories.html
Maintained by the Special Collections Department at the University of Idaho Library, this site is the closest thing to a comprehensive international list for locating links to archival Web sites. It lists over 5,000 archival sites with information on holdings of manuscripts, archives, rare books, and historical photographs. The site is organized geographically by region—western United States and Canada, eastern United States and Canada, Latin America and the Caribbean, Europe, Asia and the Pacific, and Africa and the Near East. Links are regularly checked to make sure the site is working and there are links to other archive sites. This is the most complete list of links to international archival Web sites, both in the United States and in other countries. It is also updated much more quickly than any print directory.

834. *UNESCO Archives Portal: An International Gateway to Information for Archivists and Archives Users.* http://www.unesco.org/webworld/portal_archives/Archives
This site, maintained by the United Nations Educational, Scientific, and Cultural Organization (UNESCO), is another general site, containing 4,830 links to archival sites around the world. The site is mainly arranged by categories of archives, including architectural archives, archives of inter-

national organizations, archives of ministries, audiovisual archives, business and labor archives, diplomatic archives, family archives, literature and art archives, military archives, municipal archives, national archives, parliaments and political parties archives, religious communities archives, state and regional archives, universities and research institutions archives, women archives, and other archives. Each category is arranged by region and then mainly by country. Within each country there are links to individual subject Web sites. Regularly updated, this site is not as comprehensive as the Repositories of Primary Sources site, but it still serves as an excellent gateway to a wide variety of archives. It is a good starting point for the beginning researcher.

United States

835. *Archives USA.* Alexandria, VA: ProQuest (Chadwyck-Healey). Updated periodically.
This electronic database provides Web access to primary source archival and manuscript materials in over 5,480 U.S. repositories, including information on over 132,000 collections. Archives USA integrates and makes fully searchable the entire collection of the *National Union Catalog of Manuscript Collections (NUCMC)* [see 847] from 1959 to the present. It also includes indexing access to over 54,000 collections, whose finding aids are published in ProQuest's *National Inventory of Documentary Sources in the United States (NIDS)* [see 911], as well as links to over 4,700 finding aids. The database is searchable by key word, collection, repository, *NIDS* fiche number, and *NUCMC* number. Individual

records contain detailed information about the collection and repository, including phone and fax numbers, hours of service, materials solicited, and e-mail and Web site links, if they are available. This database is an excellent source because it allows researchers to electronically search a large collection of U.S. archives to initially determine which collections might have material useful for their research needs. If there is a Web site link, it can then lead them to the archive's home page and additional finding aids.

836. *Find Public Records Fast: The Complete State, County, and Courthouse Locator.* **Edited by Michael L. Sankey and Carl R. Ernst. 3rd ed. Tempe, AZ: Facts on Demand Press, 2000. 491pp. ISBN 1-889150-13-4.**

837. *Public Records Online: The National Guide to Private and Government Online Sources of Public Records.* **Edited by Michael L. Sankey and Peter J. Weber. 4th ed. Tempe, AZ: Facts on Demand Press, 2003. 518pp. ISBN 1-889150-37-1.**
These two guides, both produced by Facts on Demand Press, provide a wealth of information for researchers working with state and county public records such as court records, civil and criminal records, real estate records, and other types of local records. The first volume concentrates more on locating county records, while the second volume concentrates more on finding online sources at the state level. The second volume is broader in that it also covers federal and private sites for locating information. Both volumes have excellent introductions defining public records and how to search for them. They also offer a number of hints on how to search for certain

types of records, for example, court records, documents located at county agencies, material located at state agencies, and federal records. The main part of each volume is the state by state detailed listing of Web sites and locations for finding public records. While most of the records covered in these two sources are mainly of value for current research, these guides are valuable for the researcher looking for earlier material in state and county records. It may give them a location for starting their research into these sources.

838. *Guide to Federal Records in the National Archives of the United States.* **Compiled by Robert B. Machette et al. Washington, DC: National Archives and Records Administration, 1995. 3 vols. 2,428pp. ISBN 0-16048312-3. http://www.archives. gov/research_room/federal_records_guide**
The National Archives is the major repository of the government's historical records, and these volumes, both print and electronic, are the key guide to this wealth of information, totaling millions of records. This latest version of the guide supersedes the original 1974 edition, which was reprinted in 1987. The print volumes include descriptions of federal records in the National Archives as of September 1, 1994. These volumes are regularly updated by the Web version, which includes acquisitions since the 1995 edition came out. Both the print and electronic versions of the guide have the same organization. Each chapter covers a record group, which includes the records of an individual agency or department of the federal government. The chapters begin with an administrative history followed by detailed descriptions of the records down to the subgroup level.

Volume 3 of the print guide contains a detailed index, arranged alphabetically by name, agency, and subject. The online version of the guide is searchable by key word and record group number. There is also an alphabetical index, and a list of records by record group number and by broad subject category. This guide is a good overview of the holdings of the National Archives, but it does not substitute for more detailed inding aids to the records themselves. Historians doing research at the National Archives should search the main Web site or contact the agency directly for more specific information. They should also check ProQuest's *National Inventory of Documentary Sources in the United States* [see 911] for more detailed descriptions of finding aids, or see if any are available electronically through the National Archives and Records Administration Web site.

839. *A Guide to Research Collections of Former Members of the United States House of Representatives, 1789–1987.* Bicentennial ed. Prepared under the direction of the Office for the Bicentennial of the United States House of Representatives, Raymond W. Smock, historian and director, Cynthia Pease Miller, editor in chief. Washington, DC: United States House of Representatives, 1988. 504pp. House Document no. 100–171.

840. Congressional Collections at Archival Institutions. http://www.archives.gov/records_of_congress/repository_collections This guide, a product of the staff of the Office for the Bicentennial of the House of Representatives, contains information on research collections containing historical material on 3,300 former members of the House of Representatives located in 592 archives throughout the United States. The House members covered include all former representatives and territorial delegates from all 50 states through December 31, 1987. Based on a survey conducted by the Office for the Bicentennial, the work is arranged alphabetically by representative. Each entry gives the name of the individual, their birth and death dates, abbreviation for state or territory they represented, and an alphabetical listing of repositories that hold historical material on their career. Information on individual collections includes such things as dates of the collection, size of the collection, and a brief description of the type of material available. If the former members' papers are part of a larger collection, that is noted. After the main part of the volume covering research collections, there is information on members whose papers location is unknown, a listing of repositories by state, a listing of current documentary editing projects related to the history of the federal government, a listing of the dates of each congressional session, and a copy of the survey reporting form. This *Guide*, along with the *Guide to Research Collections of Former United States Senators, 1789–1995* [see 841], provides researchers with ready access to the amount and locations of historical material on former members of Congress at archives all over the United States. A part of the National Archives and Records Administration Web site, Congressional Collections at Archival Repositories, supplements this printed guide by giving researchers the opportunity to search online for archival material relating to former members of the House of Representatives. Arranged alphabetically by member of Congress and by

archival institution, this site links directly to archival Web sites throughout the United States containing specific collections of documents related to these individuals.

841. *Guide to Research Collections of Former United States Senators, 1789–1995.* Compiled by Karen Dawley Paul. Prepared under the direction of Kelly D. Johnston, secretary of the Senate. Washington, DC: U.S. Government Printing Office, 1995. 743pp. Senate Document no. 103-35.

842. Congressional Collections at Archival Institutions. http://www.archives.gov/records_of_congress/repository_collections This guide, which revises and updates an earlier 1983 edition, is a companion to *A Guide to Research Collections of Former Members of the United States House of Representatives, 1789–1987* [see 840]. It is put together by the U.S. Senate Historical Office and provides access to research materials of 1,658 former Senate members in 594 archives throughout the United States, including personal papers, staff papers, correspondence with key individuals and organizations, and oral history interview transcripts. The main part of the work is arranged alphabetically by name, with each entry giving the name and location of the archive where the papers and other material are to be found, as well as a brief description of the scope of the collection. Several appendixes list state and party abbreviations; senators for whom no collections have been located; senators by birth and death dates, party affiliation, dates of service, service as governor, and service in the U.S. House of Representatives; a listing of archives by state and in alphabetical order; a list of documentary editing proj-

ects; and a copy of the survey form. A part of the National Archives and Records Administration Web site, Congressional Collections at Archival Repositories, supplements the printed guide by giving researchers the opportunity to search for archival material relating to former members of the U.S. Senate. Arranged alphabetically by member of Congress and by archival institution, this site links directly to archival Web sites throughout the United States containing specific collections of documents related to these individuals.

843. *Guide to the Records of the United States House of Representatives at the National Archives, 1789–1989.* Bicentennial ed. By National Archives and Records Administration. Washington, DC: United States House of Representatives, 1989. 466pp. Index. House Document no. 100-245.

844. *Guide to the Records of the United States Senate at the National Archives, 1789–1989.* Bicentennial ed. By National Archives and Records Administration. Washington, DC: United States Senate, 1989. 356pp. Index. U.S. Senate Bicentennial Publication no. 7; Senate Document no. 100-42. http://www.archives.gov/records_of_congress/about_the_roc/finding_aids_to_legislative_records.html
Both of these guides, originally compiled by the staff of the National Archives and Records Administration (NARA), were published to commemorate the bicentennial of the Congress. They are searchable electronically through the NARA Web site, providing detailed descriptions of nearly 46,000 cubic feet of House and Senate records located in the National Archives.

Each guide follows a similar arrangement; after a brief introductory chapter on researching the records of Congress, the bulk of each volume is arranged alphabetically, with chapters on individual committees. Within each chapter, there is information on the history and jurisdiction of the committee and detailed descriptions of the types of records produced. Following these chapters, there are additional chapters on other records and recent records of both branches. There are a number of useful appendixes at the end of each volume, such as listings of Congressional leaders, select bibliography, glossary of legislative and archival terms, session dates, National Archives finding aids, and microfilm publications of Congressional records. Both volumes are indexed. Each of the volumes is also searchable through the NARA Web site, as well as the *Guide to the Records of the Joint Committees of Congress, 1789–1989*, and some resource guides to recent Congressional committee records. Having all these finding aids searchable online makes it very easy for congressional researchers to locate and learn detailed information about Senate and House records stored in the National Archives.

845. *Members of Congress: A Checklist of Their Papers in the Manuscript Division, Library of Congress*. Compiled by John J. McDonough, with the assistance of Marilyn K. Parr. Washington, DC: Library of Congress, 1980. 217pp. ISBN 0-8444-0272-9.

Although dated for material published in the past 20 years, this checklist still provides information on locating the papers of members of Congress from 1774 to 1979 (First Continental Congress to the end of the 95th Congress) that are located in the Manuscript Division of the Library of Congress. The volume lists material on the papers of 894 senators, members of the House of Representatives, and delegates to the Continental Congress. Based on the members listed in the *Biographical Directory of the American Congress, 1774–1971* (Washington, DC: U.S. Government Printing Office, 1971) and other biographical sources, the work is arranged alphabetically by name. Each entry lists the member, dates of their service in Congress, state they represented, type of material and number of items in the collection, and *National Union Catalog of Manuscript Collections* number, if they are listed in that source. There are two appendixes listing members by state and Congress. Although selective, this volume does provide researchers with a convenient source of information about congressional research collections located in the Manuscript Division of the Library of Congress. The guide definitely needs to be supplemented by searching the main Library of Congress Web site, the NARA Web site, and the World Wide Web in general for other archival collections of papers and correspondence of former members of Congress.

846. *National Security Archive*. http://www.gwu.edu/~nsarchiv

This Web site provides access to searching the holdings of the National Security Archive, a nongovernmental, nonprofit institution located at George Washington University in Washington, DC. The holdings of this archive include over 100,000 records, totaling more than 2 million pages of material from declassified documents, focusing primarily on U.S. government policy decisions from 1945 to the present.

National Security Archive was founded in 1985 and is considered by many to be the most successful user of the Freedom of Information Act. The archive's publications include 20 microfiche collections, largely focusing on American foreign policy in Europe, Latin America, Asia, and the Middle East. Fifteen of these collections are available full text on the World Wide Web as part of an institutional subscription to the Digital National Security Archive, produced by ProQuest Information and Learning (Chadwyck-Healey). Nearly 40,000 declassified documents are available and searchable through this resource. The National Security Archive has also published more than 20 books written by members of their staff. Making this collection searchable and digitally available in university and research libraries has opened up direct access to thousands of documents for many researchers working on the history of U.S. foreign policy since 1945.

847. *National Union Catalog of Manuscript Collections.* Washington, DC: Library of Congress, 1959–1961–1993. http://www. loc.gov/coll/nucmc/nucmc.html
Although superseded by databases such Archives USA, the *National Union Catalog of Manuscript Collections* (*NUCMC*), is still a major source for locating manuscript collections in the United States. It began as a print catalog with 29 volumes covering from 1959–1993. The print volumes contain descriptions from 72,300 collections in 1,406 repositories. Since 1986 *NUCMC* records are searchable online in the Research Libraries Group (RLG) database and some can be searched in the OCLC database. They are also searchable online through the *NUCMC* Library of Congress

Web site and are searchable from 1959 to the present through ProQuest's Archives USA database, which includes NUCMC records for over 90,000 collections. Chadwyck-Healey has also published an *Index to Personal Names in the National Union Catalog of Manuscript Collections, 1959–1984* (2 vols., 1988) and an *Index to Subject and Corporate Names in the National Union Catalog of Manuscript Collections, 1959–1984* (3 vols., 1994). Basically, NUCMC's thousands of records are searchable electronically from 1959 to the present through Archives USA and from 1959 to 1984 through Chadwyck-Healey's print indexes and the individual print volumes. However, databases such as Archives USA and OCLC's World-Cat include more material than NUCMC and are a better starting point for the researcher trying to locate collections of archival material in the United States.

848. *Presidential Libraries.* http://www. archives.gov/presidential_libraries/index. html
This site, which is part of the main National Archives and Records Administration site, provides easy access to information about and links to the holdings of libraries that are part of the Presidential Library System. The 10 Presidential Libraries include those of Herbert Hoover, Franklin D. Roosevelt, Harry S. Truman, Dwight D. Eisenhower, John F. Kennedy, Lyndon B. Johnson, Gerald R. Ford, Jimmy Carter, Ronald Reagan, and George Bush. Also part of the Presidential Library System are the Richard Nixon Presidential Materials Staff and the William J. Clinton Presidential Materials Project. The site has information about the history of the Presidential Library System, library and museum hours, access to

records, and information about researching presidential materials. There are direct Web links to each presidential library and links to online finding aids for each library. Researchers looking for material on recent presidents from Hoover to Clinton should start with this site. They should then contact the appropriate presidential library if they need more detailed information.

849. *Presidents' Papers Index Series.*
Washington, DC: Manuscript Division, Library of Congress, 1960–1976.
This series of indexes is worth mentioning because it provides access to the microfilm editions of 23 presidential collections located in the Manuscript Division of the Library of Congress. The presidents included in this series are: Washington, Jefferson, Madison, Monroe, Jackson, Van Buren, William Henry Harrison, Tyler, Polk, Taylor, Pierce, Lincoln, Andrew Johnson, Grant, Garfield, Arthur, Cleveland, Benjamin Harrison, McKinley, Theodore Roosevelt, Taft, Wilson, and Coolidge. There is an individual computer-generated index to the papers of each of these presidents, arranged by correspondent and date. One drawback of using these indexes is that they do not provide access by subject. However, they do provide access to a wealth of primary documents for researchers in the history of these presidents and their presidencies. These indexes can be supplemented by the *Public Papers of the Presidents of the United States* series (Washington, DC: Federal Register Division, National Archives and Records Service, General Services Administration, 1930–1932/1933, 1945–), which index and include many of the papers of recent presidents from Hoover to Clinton, and the direct links through the

NARA Web site to the individual Presidential Library Web sites for each of these presidents [see 848]. The Library of Congress, through its American Memory Project, has begun digitizing some of the 23 presidential collections, beginning with those of Abraham Lincoln. This project, which will continue for years, will eventually digitize other major presidential collections such as those of George Washington and Thomas Jefferson.

850. *State Archives and Historical Societies.*
http://www.ohiohistory.org/ links/arch_hs.html
This site, regularly maintained by the Ohio Historical Society, provides direct Web access to state archives, which house the records of state government, and state historical societies, which house manuscript material and rare documents, of almost all of the states. The directory is an easy way for researchers to connect to each state's major historical repositories and then search or browse many of their collections.

851. *U.S. National Archives and Records Administration.* http://www.archives.gov
This is the main government site to federal records preserved by the National Archives and Records Administration (NARA), which include huge collections of documents and historical information. NARA has developed a strategic plan that provides for online access describing all of its archival holdings by 2007, and it is well on its way to meeting that goal. The Web site provides a number of direct links to material in NARA's nationwide research collections. A key starting point is the Archival Research Catalog, or ARC, which is an online catalog to the agency's holdings in

Washington, DC, regional archives, and Presidential Libraries. It currently covers about 20 percent of NARA holdings, including nearly 300,000 textual items and 124,000 digital images. Material can be searched by key word, organization, person, topic, digitized image, and location. There is also a link at the NARA Web site to the Access to Archival Data, or AAD, system, which allows searching of some of the agency's holdings of electronic records. The AAD system provides access to almost 50 million electronic records from more than 20 federal agencies on a variety of topics. Besides the ARC and AAD systems, there are many other links to finding aids for locating agency records. Among these are the online version of the Guide to Federal Records in the National Archives of the United States [see 838], the Records of Congress [see 843, 844], which links to holdings of individual Congressmen at archival institutions throughout the country, and the Presidential Libraries [see 848], which links to the individual Presidential Library Web sites containing detailed holdings information on the records of presidents from Herbert Hoover to Bill Clinton. The main NARA site provides one-stop access to a wealth of federal records and, with its links to a number of search systems and sites, is an excellent starting point for researchers seeking information on the holdings of the National Archives and Records Administration. Not all of the agency's records are online but more are appearing every day. The researcher may still need to use other print sources and contact the agency directly for further information, but this electronic site is a wonderful tool for initially locating material.

Canada

852. *Canadian Archival Information Network.* http://www.cain-rcia.ca
Begun in October 2001, through the efforts of the Canadian Council on Archives, the National Archives of Canada, and the Department of Canadian Heritage, the Canadian Archival Information Network (CAIN) is the closest thing to a search engine for locating material in the holdings of many Canadian archives. It provides detailed capabilities for searching descriptions of more than 30,000 archival records in over 800 archives in every Canadian province and territory. There are basic and advanced search screens, with the advanced search allowing Boolean searching by key word, provenance, administrative history/biographical sketch note, scope and content note, physical extent note, repository key word, CAIN number, and by territory or province. CAIN also has links to national and provincial archival networks and to virtual exhibits at the national and provincial level. It is an excellent site for researchers to initially search descriptions of Canadian archival collections and then use this information to contact a particular archive directly.

853. *Canadian Archival Resources on the Internet.* Created and maintained by Cheryl Avery, University of Saskatchewan Archives, and Steve Billinton, Archives of Ontario. http://www.usask.ca/archives/menu.html
This is the most comprehensive list of links to the home pages and resources of Canadian archives on the World Wide Web and is much more current than any printed guide. Links in this directory are mainly to archive

sites, but some museums and special collections departments are included. This site is updated periodically and the researcher can search for archival resources alphabetically, by type of archive (provincial, university, municipal, religious, medical, and other), and by region (western, central, eastern, and national). There is also a separate resource section with links to sites focusing on archival education, association sites, listservs, multisite databases, genealogical sites, miscellaneous sites, a listing of new links, a place to customize your search, and a link to CAIN (Canadian Archival Information Network). The Canadian Council of Archives is currently working on constructing a national Web database which will provide links to over 800 archives throughout Canada.

854. *National Archives of Canada.* http://www.archives.ca/08/08_e.html
The National Archives of Canada has developed an excellent Web site that allows for a significant amount of research online. Visitors to the site can find digitized collections arranged by theme, time period, and media type. Themes include First Peoples, New France, Newcomers, Women, War, Politics and Government, and Arts and Culture. Time period material is arranged by The Early Years, 1565–1760, From Conquest to Confederation, 1760–1867, The First Century of Confederation, 1867–1967, and Into the Second Century. Media type searches include Documentary Art, Audio-Visual, Manuscript and Private Collections, Postal Archives, Maps, Photography, and Government Records. There is also a separate genealogy page with links to family history material, and the researcher can use ArchiviaNet, the National Archives online search

engine. ArchiviaNet allows the researcher access to a wide variety of archival holdings through the options of searching a number of finding aids by theme and by type of document. The National Archives of Canada Web site is easy to navigate, colorful, and well-designed overall. While it does not provide total access to all the National Archives holdings, it is a good starting point for searching the collections of the major Canadian archival repository.

Latin America

855. *Archivo General de la Nacion Republic Argentina.* http://www.archivo.gov.ar/mc_general.htm

856. *Arquivo Nacional.* http://www.arquivonacional.gov.br

857. *Archivo General de la Nation-Mexico.* http://www.agn.gob.mx
These three sites are the national archival sites for Argentina, Brazil, and Mexico. For the researcher they contain a great deal of material about these collections, but the Argentina and Mexico national archives sites are only available in Spanish and the Brazil National Archives link is only available in Portuguese.

858. *The Nettie Lee Benson Latin American Collection, University of Texas, Austin Texas.* http://www.lib.utexas.edu/benson/index.html
There are a number of major collections of primary documents on Latin America in the United States. One of the most significant is the Nettie Lee Benson Collection at the University of Texas. Named after its for-

mer director, the collection has an extensive number of documents on Mexico, Central America, the Caribbean, South America, and areas of the United States that were part of the Spanish empire and Mexico. The collection contains over 2 million pages of manuscripts on Latin and Spanish America and over 800,000 books, periodicals, and pamphlets. Researchers accessing the Benson Collection Web site can search collection descriptions, connect to online exhibits, find out information about visiting hours, and access information about the use of materials in the collection. There is a listing with links to archival collections processed by the Benson archive. Besides links to Latin American collections in the United States through Archives USA, the Library of Congress, and a comprehensive Web search, there are also a number of printed guides to these materials. Greenwood published a series of guides in the early to mid-1990s providing detailed information on particular areas of research interest. These include Louis A. Perez, *A Guide to Cuban Collections in the United States* (Greenwood, 1991); Thomas M. Leonard, *A Guide to Central American Collections in the United States* (Greenwood, 1994); and Thomas Whigham, *A Guide to Collections on Paraguay in the United States* (Greenwood, 1995). Although these guides may need to be checked for the currency of their information, they provide a useful listing of Latin American collections in the United States on a state-by-state basis.

859. *Repositories of Primary Sources: Latin America and the Caribbean.* http://www.uidaho.edu/special-collections/MEXICO.html
Part of the Repositories of Primary Sources

main site, this directory is the most comprehensive guide to Web links listed alphabetically by country to archives in Latin America. Also useful are two other sites, the Latin American Network Information Center (LANIC) site at the University of Texas, http://lanic.utexas.edu/la/region/library, which has a section on Libraries and Archives in Latin America, and H-Net's Latin American Archives site, http://www2.h-net.msu.edu/~latam/archives. Both of these sites list library and archive home pages alphabetically by country. The LANIC site lists mainly libraries, while the H-Net site lists only archival sites. Both the Repositories of Primary Sources and the Latin America Network Information Center sites are updated regularly and link directly to the archive sites. The H-Net Latin American Archives site does not link directly to the archives but instead contains brief information about holdings, photocopying facilities, transportation, and nearby restaurants. However, the researcher should be aware that some of this information is not current and may no longer be accurate.

Europe

860. *EAN: European Archival Network.* http://www.european-archival.net
EAN, which is operated by the Swiss Federal Archives, is the key site for searching all the major European archives. It is searchable by key word, alphabetically, and geographically by clicking on countries on a map. A second important Web site is Gabriel: Gateway to Europe's National Libraries, http://portico.bl.uk/gabriel/index.html, which provides links to 35 European national library sites.

Great Britain

861. *Archives Hub.* http://www.
archiveshub.ac.uk
The Archives Hub, operated by the University of Manchester, serves as a gateway site to descriptions and finding aids for archival collections available at over 60 universities and colleges in the United Kingdom. It is a project run by a steering committee made up of representatives of the Public Record Office, the Historical Manuscripts Commission, and other archive networks. The Hub includes descriptions of individual collections, family collections, and organizational collections, dating back to the medieval period. Researchers can browse by subject, place, and personal or corporate names. There is also an advanced search capability, which allows combining of search terms and limiting by date and repository. The descriptions of the collections are detailed and there are links to directory information in ARCHON, the archival directory of the Historical Manuscripts Commission, and other related collections. The researcher can do a more complex search or just browse the finding aids of a particular repository. Archives Hub is one of a series of projects that are part of the United Kingdom's National Archives Network and a good place to start for locating collections on British history.

862. *British Archives: A Guide to Archive Resources in the United Kingdom.* **3rd ed. By Janet Foster and Julia Sheppard. London: Macmillan; New York: Stockton, 1995. 627pp. Index. ISBN 0-333-532-554.**
Although it is no longer current and its information is accessible through a number of Web sites, this work remains the standard printed guide to information about locating British archival materials. In its third edition containing more than 1100 entries, the *Guide* is arranged alphabetically by town; entries include name and address of the archive, telephone number, fax number, where to send inquiries, open hours, and a brief description of their major collections, finding aids, and publications. There is a good name and subject index, as well as an alphabetical list of repositories, a list arranged by county, and a list of key addresses and publications. This guide has been largely superseded by Web sites such as the Archives Hub and the Access to Archives part of the Public Records Office Site, which also allow much more flexibility in searching for records on a particular topic. In addition, ProQuest's *National Inventory of Documentary Sources in the United Kingdom and Ireland* [see 911], produced by Chadwyck-Healey, reprints many of the finding aids available at these local archives.

863. *The British Library Manuscripts Catalogue.* http://molcat.bl.uk
The British Library has one of the leading historical manuscript collections in the world, and this searchable online manuscripts catalog is available through its main Web site. This online catalog attempts to provide a single access point for searching catalogs of the Department of Manuscripts accessions from 1753 to the present. Researchers can search the index by name, language, state, and date, as well as find index records for a specific manuscript. In addition, they can search the descriptions or find a specific manuscript by number. While more and more material is searchable online, not all of the library's total holdings are searchable electronically. A significant

number of catalogs are still not searchable through the World Wide Web. A brief print guide, Margaret Nickson, *The British Library: Guide to the Catalogues and Indexes of the Department of Manuscripts* (London: British Library, 1998), provides the most complete list of these finding aids. The Manuscripts Catalogue online Web site also lists those catalogs available online and those still only available in print form. Researchers should contact the British Library Department of Manuscripts for information about catalogs still not searchable online.

864. *The National Archives.* http://www. nationalarchives.gov.uk

In April 2003, there was a major change involving the reorganization of British archives at the national level when the two key agencies in charge of access to archival records, the Public Records Office and the Historical Manuscripts Commission, were combined into one larger agency called the National Archives. This has created an archival collection that is one of the largest in the world and contains records dating from the Domesday Book in the 11th century to recent government papers. Currently the main National Archives page links to the Web sites of the Public Records Office and the Historical Manuscripts Commission, but over the next year the services of these agencies will merge into a single national organization. Since each of these agencies plays a major role in Great Britain's archival network, each will be discussed in this chapter under the next two entries.

865. *The National Archives: Historical Manuscripts Commission.* http://www. hmc.gov.uk

The Historical Manuscripts Commission, which has merged with the Public Records Office, serves as the central advisory organization on archives and manuscripts relating to British history. A difference between the Historical Manuscripts Commission and the Public Records Office is that it is not an archival repository. It does not hold any manuscripts or historical records, but it does maintain the National Register of Archives (NRA), a key place for locating manuscripts dealing with British history, and ARCHON, a key directory and portal for information about archives holding collections of British historical documents and archival research projects. The National Register of Archives provides indexing access to 43,000 unpublished lists and catalogs of repositories both in Great Britain and in other countries. These can be searched by corporate name, personal name, family name, and place-name. The material contained in the NRA lists and catalogs includes the dates of the collection and a very brief description of the main groups of records. ARCHON, the other key part of the Historical Manuscripts Commission site, is mainly a gateway to directory information about archives in Great Britain and in other countries and archival resources and projects. It is divided into two parts, the ARCHON Directory and the ARCHON Portal. The ARCHON Directory can be searched by ARCHON reference number, repository, town, and county, as well as part of the United Kingdom, such as Scotland or Wales. There is also an alphabetical list of professional organizations. The entries for the archive contain the name, address, phone number, fax number, e-mail address, days and hours it is open, and Web address, if it has one.

It also has links to entries for this repository in the National Register of Archives. The National Register of Archives likewise has links to the ARCHON Directory. Another part of ARCHON is the ARCHON Portal, which links to information about archival resources, projects, and initiatives. It is searchable by title, key word, and region. The entries themselves provide contact information, a brief description, and a Web link to that site. Using both the National Register of Archives and ARCHON through the Historical Manuscripts Commission site opens up a wide range of information for the British history researcher just by searching through their home or office computer.

866. *The National Archives: Public Record Office.* http://www.pro.gov.uk

The Public Record Office, which has been combined with the Historical Manuscripts Commission, is the organization that maintains British state and central court records from the 11th century to the present. Its online Web site is easy to navigate and provides searchable access to a wide variety of public records, including births, deaths, marriages, census records, wills, parish registers, migration, military records, and adoptions. Included in the Public Record Office database are the records of the Public Record Office of Northern Ireland, General Register Office of England and Wales, General Register Office for Scotland, National Archives of Scotland, National Library of Wales, and the British Library Oriental and India Office Collections. Material at the Public Record Office is searchable through PROCAT, its online catalog, which provides access to holdings from over 9 million files, arranged by department that created the file. Another

key search engine available through the Public Record Office site is Access to Archives (A2A). A2A allows the researcher to search catalogs from English archives separate from the Public Record Office. Regularly updated, this database includes more than 4.3 million cataloging records from over 300 record offices. It is searchable by key word, location, and region, and you can limit your search by date, leading the researcher to the location of specific records. There is also a Web link to the archive that has the records. Also searchable through the Public Record Office site are catalogs of tax records, hospital records, and electronic data sets. Researchers can also access records that have been digitized and are available online. The Public Record Office site contains a wealth of information for the researcher in British history. It should be supplemented by another non-governmental Web site, English Record Offices and Archives on the Web, http://www.oz.net/~markhow/englishros.htm.

This site, arranged alphabetically by county, provides direct links to those British records offices that have a Web page. It does not search the records of a site but only provides links to that repository. The main British Library Web site also has a number of links to other parts of its collections.

France

867. *Archives Nationales de France.* http://www.archivesnationales.culture.gouv.fr

The best guides to French archival resources are available online through two main sites, the French National Archives site and the French National Library site. The Archives Nationales de France was established during the time of the French

Revolution, and it continues to preserve the key documents of the history of France. It is comprised of five centers: the Historical Centre Historique of National Archives, which contains documents published before 1958 and the archives of the Heads of State; the Centre for Contemporary Archives, which mainly includes documents published after 1958; the Centre for Archives of Overseas Territories, which contains documents on former French possessions overseas; the Centre for Archives of the Workplace, which has material on companies, unions, associations, and architects; and the National Centre for Microfilms, which has original microforms of documents preserved in other national or territorial centers. There are links to each of the five centers from the main Archives Nationales Web site and the main site also contains contact information and general information concerning rules of usage and operation. The initial screens for the main site are in French and English but the rest of the searchable material on the five centers is in French.

868. *Bibliothèque Nationale de France.* http://www.bnf.fr

The second major site for locating French archival resources is the French National Library, or Bibliothèque Nationale de France, site. Rich in importance to the country, the history of the collections of the Bibliothèque Nationale dates back to the 15th century. These vast resources are mainly divided between two main libraries, the Richelieu Library, which houses 225,000 volumes of manuscripts, and the François Mitterrand/Tolbiac Library, which houses huge collections of printed, microform, and digitized materials. The Bibliothèque Nationale has an extensive digitization program underway and has roughly 100,000 digitized images available at its Web site. These are drawn from collections outside the library and from its own collections. This digital library, known as Gallica 2000, covers documents from the Middle Ages to the early 20th century. Both the library manuscript collections and digitized documents can be searched online. The introductory information about the history of the Bibliothèque Nationale and its collections is available in English but the online search tools are only in French. There are also links to virtual exhibitions from the library's collection.

869. *Les Centres de Ressources Documentaires.* http://mistral.culture.fr/culture/sedocum/ceresdoc.htm

This site, maintained by the French Ministry of Culture, provides the most complete and current access to the holdings of a large number of French archives. Arranged by broad subject areas, such as Archaeology, History of Art, and Museums, there are links to individual repositories. The information available includes address, hours of operation, major holdings, and history of the library. One drawback for the beginning researcher is the site is only in French.

Germany

870. *Archives in Germany: An Introductory Guide to Institutions and Sources.* Edited by Frank Schumacher, with the assistance of Annette M. Marciel. Hypertext version by Raimund Lammersdorf. Reference Guides of the German Historical Institute, no. 13. Washington, DC: German Historical Institute, 2001. 178pp. http://www.ghi-dc.org/guide13/#anchor_1

This introductory guide, published by the German Historical Institute, is the most current print source for information about archives in Germany. The work is divided into seven parts by type of archive: State Archives, Church Archives, Business and Economic Archives, Parliamentary, Party, and Association Archives, Media Archives, University Archives, and Other Archives. Within each of these seven categories, information on 162 archives is listed by city. This information includes name of the archive, address, phone number, fax number, e-mail address, and Web address, if one is available. Also included are its hours, the name of a contact person, a broad description of its holdings, and information about finding aids. There is a Web version of this guide, and it links to the individual archival Web site if the repository has one. Schumacher's work is a good introduction to the holdings of a number of German archives, but there is more detailed and current information on the Internet through the University of Marburg site, Deutsche Archive im Internet [see 872].

871. *Bundesarchiv Online.* http://www. bundesarchiv.de
This is the main National Archives of Germany Web site, with links to its wide range of holdings. The Bundesarchiv collects papers of individuals, political parties, and associations of national importance. Its focus is on the modern history of Germany with documents on different periods, including the Deutscher Bund (1815–1866), the Reich (1867/71–1945), the Zones of Occupation (1945–1949), the German Democratic Republic (1949–1990), and the Federal Republic of Germany since 1949. At this site researchers can

search indexes and descriptions of its major holdings and a list of its publications. This is the principal German national archival site but, after the initial introductory page, which has an English translation, its material is completely in German.

872. *Deutsche Archive im Internet.* University of Marburg, Germany. http://www. uni-marburg.de/archivschule/fv61.html
This site, which is part of a larger directory of archives site at the University of Marburg, is the most comprehensive guide to the holdings of German archives. Updated regularly, the site is divided into categories of archives, including national archives, local archives, church archives, literature archives, business archives, parliament archives and archives of political parties and federations, university archives, and archives of other institutions. Within each of these categories, the archives are arranged alphabetically by location and there are direct links to the archives Web site, which often has detailed information about its holdings. This site is a good place to start for researchers in German history seeking particular collections in their subject areas. The researcher will have to know German to navigate through this site because there is no English-language version. The site is entirely in German.

The Vatican

873. *Vatican Archives: An Inventory and Guide to Historical Documents of the Holy See.* New York: Oxford University Press, 1998. 588pp. ISBN 0-19-509552-9.
This work, prepared by historians and archivists who were part of the Vatican

Archives Project at the University of Michigan, is by far the most detailed guide to the records of the Vatican. It has much more detailed information than the Vatican Web site. The guide provides an overview of Vatican documents dating from the ninth century and is organized into seven sections: College of Cardinals, Papal Court, Roman Curia (Congregations, Offices, and Tribunals), Apostolic Nunciatures and Delegations, Papal States, Permanent Commissions, and Miscellaneous Official Materials and Separate Collections. It begins with an introduction focusing on a brief history of the Archivo Segreto Vaticano, or Vatican Secret Archives. The main body of the work covers the seven sections, with the entries divided into two parts: agency histories and series descriptions. Each entry includes the name of the series, dates, amount of material in the collection, organization, scope, references to guides and finding aids, and location of the physical records. Three appendixes include material on Vatican City and Palatine Offices and Administration, the Original Armaria of the Archivo Segreto Vaticano, and an Inventory of Numbered Indici in the Archivo Segreto Vaticano Index Room. There is a detailed bibliography and the work is indexed by agency, series title, and chronologically. This work is an excellent guide to the wealth of historical documents in the Vatican Archives.

Eastern Europe

874. *National Archives of Hungary.* http://www.natarch.hu/mol_e.htm

875. *State Archives of Poland.* http://www.archiwa.gov.pl

The National Archives of Hungary Web site and the State Archives of Poland Web site are two key locations linking to information on archives in Eastern Europe. The National Archives of Hungary traces its beginnings back to the Middle Ages. Located in Budapest, the National Archives of Hungary contains 68,000 linear meters of material. Among its holdings are the Archives of the Hungarian Chancellery (1414–1848), Archives of the Transylvanian Chancellery (1686–1848), and the Archives of the Age of Absolutism (1848–1867), plus many other collections of records. Individual databases allow searching of the archives inventory, parish records, and medieval documents. There are also links to other Hungarian archives. Researchers can navigate the site in Hungarian, German, or English.

The State Archives of Poland site offers a great deal of information about the structure of Poland's numerous archives and how they can be accessed. Poland's State Archives is a collective body of three archives, all located in Warsaw. The Central Archive of Historical Records preserves government documents produced prior to 1918; the Archive of New Records preserves records of national importance produced after 1918; and the Archive of Audiovisual Records preserves photographic and film materials from the early 20th century to the present. There are links to other Polish archives, and the main pages of the site are in English as well as Polish. However, the material beyond the main pages is only in Polish.

The best way to find additional major archive sites for the rest of the countries in Eastern Europe, such as those of the Czech Republic and Slovakia, is to go to one of the main archival directory sites—Repositories of Primary Sources and the

UNESCO Archives Portal—for links to the key archives in those countries.

Russia and the Countries of the Former Soviet Union

876. *ArcheoBiblioBase: Archives in Russia.* http://www.iisg.nl/~abb/#search
This Web site provides the most detailed information and English-language searching capability for material in the archives of the Russian Federation. The material is drawn from a larger ArcheoBiblioBase information system, which is located in Moscow under the direction of Patricia Kennedy Grimsted working with the Federal Archival Service of Russia (Rosarkhiv). Grimsted is a well-known authority on Russian archives and the archives of the countries of the former Soviet Union. The Archives in Russia site is divided into four parts: the fourteen federal archives administered by the Rosarkhiv, the archives of the major federal agencies that retain their own records, the local state archives in Moscow and St. Petersburg, and regional archives of the Russian Federation. Within each of these sections there is information about individual archives, including contact information, such as address, phone and fax numbers, e-mail, hours, and Web site address; previous names; brief history; access for research; descriptions of holdings; and a listing of recent guides and finding aids. All this material is searchable, and the amount of material on each archive will vary. This site contains the most current information on archives of the Russian Federation. Its coverage is more current than that found in the two-volume work, *Archives of Russia: A Directory and Bibliographic Guide to Hold-ings in Moscow and St. Petersburg*, edited by Patricia Kennedy Grimsted (Armonk, NY: M. E. Sharpe, 2000). Grimsted's directory contains more detailed descriptions of these archives than those found at the Web site. A more comprehensive Web site for archives in the Russian Federation is being developed at http://www.rusarchives.ru, but it is entirely in Russian.

Researchers seeking archival information located in any of the countries that were part of the former Soviet Union should search for archival sites in those countries, such as the National Archives of Estonia, http://www.ra.ee, and the State Archives of Latvia, http://www.archiv.org.lv. Links to the archives of those countries that were once part of the Soviet Union can also be found by searching any of the general sites, such as Repositories of Primary Sources and the UNESCO Archives Portal.

Africa

877. *Africa Research Central: A Clearinghouse of African Primary Sources.* http://www.africa-research.org
This is the best and most up-to-date site for locating African primary source collections. Put together by Susan Tschabrun and Kathryn Green, both African historians, the site broadly interprets African primary sources to include records, manuscripts, personal papers, photographs, film, and artifacts. The main part of the site is the Repositories section, in which the researcher can search for material on nearly 500 African archives, museums, and libraries. Repositories can be searched by type of institution, country, and type of primary sources, such as business records or manuscripts, as well as by an

alphabetical list arranged by country. Material included for each institution varies, but the entries contain contact information, access information, information on holdings, and Web address, if available. On many of the smaller archives the material is very brief and incomplete. In addition to information on African archives, Africa Research Central contains links by country to repositories with strong African collections in Europe and North America. There are also links to guides to African studies resources, other sources of repository information, associations and organizations, and preservation and conservation information. The site is a good starting point for researchers seeking primary source material on African history. Other meta sites, such as Repositories of Primary Sources and the UNESCO Archives Portal, have sections with links to archival Web sites in individual African countries.

878. *International Directory of African Studies Research/Repertoire International des Etudes Africaines.* 3rd ed. Edited by International African Institute. Compiled by Philip Baker. London: Hans Zell, 1994. ISBN 1-873836-36-8.
This work is an expansion and updating of the second edition, published in 1987, and it includes more than 1,800 entries with information on academic institutions, research centers, and public and governmental agencies that carry out African studies research. Covering countries all over the world, the entries are arranged alphabetically by country and, within the country, by name of the organization. Information for each entry includes address, telephone number, fax number, e-mail address, year the organization was founded, head of the organization, other staff engaged in African studies, principal areas of current African research, courses offered, degrees awarded, number of students taking courses in African studies, sources of funding, library holdings, publications, affiliations/exchange programs, and other additional information. Five different indexes make it easier for the researcher to get at certain kinds of information. They include a thematic index arranged by geographic area and subject, an index of international organizations, an index of ethnonyms and language names, an index of serial publications, and an index of personnel. The currency of the directory's entries needs to be checked through searching the World Wide Web and other sources, and there are certainly a number of Web sites with more current information on these organizations' resources. However, this is still the best printed guide to worldwide research in African studies, and it remains important to researchers working in that area. For material on Africa in the 20th century the researcher should also check Chris Cook, *The Making of Modern Africa: A Guide to Archives* (New York: Facts on File, 1995).

Asia and Australia

879. *Chinese Archives: An Introductory Guide.* By Ye Wa and Joseph W. Esherick. China Research Monograph, no. 45. Berkeley, CA: Institute of East Asian Studies, University of California, Berkeley, 1996. 355pp. ISBN 1-55729-047-4.

880. *Chinese Archives.* http://orpheus.ucsd.edu/chinesehistory/chinese_archives
Chinese Archives is the most recent printed

guide to archives in the People's Republic of China. Containing material on 597 archives, the work is arranged by type of archive. After a detailed introduction and sections on Chinese national archives and specialized national archives, the rest of the guide is devoted to coverage of provincial, municipal, and local archives. Drawing on local gazetteers, the data included for each archive includes the date it was established and brief information about its history, the size of its collection, and specific information on its contents. At the end of the work there is a section on archives in Taiwan, a list of sources used, and a glossary. This introductory guide is being updated by a Chinese Archives Web site at the University of California, San Diego. It lists additional archives not found in the printed guide and is arranged by region. The Web site is still under construction and currently covers archives by province through Jiangxi Province. The Web site is also useful for linking to those Chinese provincial archives that have a location on the World Wide Web. Researchers should also search the Web and check the larger electronic archival directories for additional links to Chinese archives. The Web is always the best source for the most current information.

881. *Directory of Archives in Australia.* http://www.archivists.org.au/directory/asa_dir.htm

882. *Register of Australian Archives and Manuscripts.* http://www.nla.gov.au/raam The two best places for current information on Australian archives are on the World Wide Web. Produced by the Australian Society of Archivists, the Directory of Archives in Australia began as a project to

create a Web directory from the original print directory, published in 1992. As of November 2002, the Web directory included over 500 entries. There is an alphabetical list with links to those archives with locations on the Web. The directory can be searched by subject, or the researcher can browse alphabetically or geographically by state. Each entry includes contact information such as address, telephone number, fax number, e-mail address, and URL address for the Web site. There is also information about hours, access, major holdings, and when the entry was last updated. The most recent updates to the site were in November 2002.

While the Directory of Archives in Australia provides brief factual information on a particular site, the Register of Australian Archives and Manuscripts (RAAM) is an actual guide to material in collections of personal papers and nongovernmental organization records located in Australian libraries and archives. Produced and maintained by the National Library of Australia, this Web guide is an updating of a printed guide published by the National Library of Australia from 1965 to 1995. Using the RAAM, researchers can do an online search of over 37,000 records. They can search by name, occupation, or other indexing terms, as well as browse by name of the repository or by state or territory. A more advanced search capability allows for Boolean searching. Information contained in the register comes from published and unpublished catalogs, lists of accessions, and other sources. Entries contain detailed descriptions of the collections, including the size and type of records, and link to the archives' listing in the Directory of Archives in Australia. These two Web sites are a good starting point for researchers seeking to locate material on Australian history.

883. *National Archives of Japan.* http://www.archives.go.jp/index_e.html
The National Archives of Japan was established in 1971 for the purpose of acquiring and preserving important documents from various government ministries, as well as making these documents available to researchers. Its Web site, which is available both in English and in Japanese, contains a detailed description of the archives, its organization and facilities, and information about its key holdings. There is also a guide for researchers and a list of the archives of Japanese prefectures and certain Japanese cities.

Researchers looking for material on other Asian countries need only to locate the Web site for that country's archives, such as the National Archives of India, www.nationalarchives.nic.in, the National Archives of Malaysia, www.arkib.gov.my/bi, and the National Archives of Singapore, http:www.nhb.gov.sg/NAS/nas.shtml. They can also use a search engine like Google to locate the Web sites or find them in one of the larger directory sites for locating archives around the world, such as Repositories of Primary Sources.

SPECIAL COLLECTIONS AND SUBJECT ARCHIVES

There are a large number of special collections departments and subject archives in the United States and worldwide. This section is meant to show the variety of material available at these sites that is searchable through the World Wide Web and not be a comprehensive guide to these locations. Many of these sites have digitized collections and additional finding aids that are available for researchers at their Web site.

884. *CESSDA: Council of European Social Science Data Archives.* http://www.nsd.uib.no/cessda/index.html
This Web site, maintained by the Council of European Social Science Data Archives, provides links to a wide variety of digital social science data in both Europe, North America, and other countries all over the world. It provides links to over 20 European country data archive sites, 14 United States and Canada sites, and five other country sites. Sites include the United Kingdom Data Archive, the Banque de Donnees Socio-Politique in France, and the Inter-University Consortium for Political and Social Research in the United States. Researchers can click on the individual site or search 10 of the sites at one time through CESSDA's Integrated Data Catalog, which allows for more advanced searching. This site serves as a central site providing access to country sites with a wealth of raw social science data in electronic form.

885. *Directory of Corporate Archives in the United States and Canada.* Society of American Archivists, Business Archives Section. Edited and maintained by Gregory S. Hunter. http://www.hunterinformation.com/corporat.htm
This print directory, in its fifth edition, is available on the Web through the auspices of the Society of American Archivists. Maintained since 1999 by Dr. Gregory S. Hunter, the site provides access to descriptions of the historical records of companies, both

those that maintain their own records and those that contract this out to other firms. The directory also provides access to information on the historical records of professional associations, such as the American Medical Association. It is arranged alphabetically by the name of the company or association. There are indexes by name of archivist and by state. Entries contain contact information, information on the type of business, access information, and brief information on the size of the holdings and a description of those records. The directory is a useful starting point for those researchers seeking material in business archives.

886. *Ex Libris Special Collections Directory.* http://www.colby.edu/~zechandl/index. htm
This Web site, maintained by Ex Libris, a worldwide company leader in library automation and linking software with such products as MetaLib and SFX, is designed to provide a single world-wide directory to special collections departments that have digitized some of their content and made it available on the Internet. The material includes manuscripts, art images, and electronic texts. Special collections are arranged by broad subject areas such as history, religion, geography, political science, music, art/architecture, and literature. Within these broad subject areas, there are links to digitized documents available on the Web. The history material is further divided geographically by material from Europe and the Americas, as well as documents on the history of the book and the history of science. There are also separate links to electronic texts and online catalogs. The Ex Libris site makes it easy for the researcher to navigate a wide variety of special collection

documents that have been digitized and made available on the World Wide Web. It is a very comprehensive site for locating digital material in all areas of the humanities.

887. *A Geographic Guide to Uncovering Women's History in Archival Collections.* http://www.lib.utsa.edu/Archives/ WomenGender/links.html
This Web guide, produced by the Archives for Research on Women and Gender Project at the University of Texas at San Antonio Libraries, is the most comprehensive place to start for links to women's history resources in the United States, with some links to repositories outside this country. The main part of the site is a geographical listing of sites with primary source material on women's history, arranged alphabetically. Within each state, there is an alphabetical listing of archives, special collections, and libraries, with short descriptions of their women's history holdings. Each entry has a hypertext link to that site's home page for easy access to further descriptive material. This site is an excellent starting point for researchers in U.S. women's history because it links to a number of collections in a single location.

888. *Subject Collections: A Guide to Special Book Collections and Subject Emphases as Reported by University, College, Public, and Special Libraries and Museums in the United States and Canada.* 7th ed., rev. and enl. **Compiled by Lee Ash and William G. Miller. New Providence, NJ: R. R. Bowker, 1993. 2 vols. ISBN 0-8352-3141-0.** Although much of its usefulness has been superseded by searching on the Internet, Ash and Miller's work still remains the standard printed guide to special book collec-

tions material in the United States and Canada. The seventh edition of this massive work contains 65,818 entries from collections held in 5,882 institutions. There are over 13,000 new entries since the previous edition of the guide, published in 1985. Based on questionnaires sent to libraries, the volumes are arranged alphabetically by subject, with the subject headings being adapted from the most recent Library of Congress Subject Headings. Within the subject headings entries are arranged by state, with information about the institution holding the collection and a description of the number and type of materials included; some of the descriptions are quite lengthy. This work, because of its detailed subject indexing, remains a good source for special collections information found in libraries in the United States and Canada. However, with the material in the volumes more than 10 years old, the researcher needs to supplement this with searching the Internet for more recent special collections material on their topic. The institutions and departments listed in Subject Collections will have their own Web sites, often with a number of finding aids available for searching electronically through individual collections. This has made it much easier for the researcher; the printed subject guides cannot provide the depth or currency of the Web guides or department Web sites.

DIGITAL SITES

With the emergence of the Internet, many sites provide access to extensive collections of digitized documents. The following sites represent a sampling of the best available

and give an idea of the wide variety of primary source material located on the World Wide Web.

889. *American Memory: Historical Collections for the National Digital Library.* **http:// memory.loc.gov/ammem/amhome.html** The Library of Congress American Memory site has one of the largest collections of digitized material on the history and culture of the United States. It provides access to more than 7 million digital items drawn from more than 100 collections in the Library of Congress. Drawing on the superb Library of Congress collections of historical photographs, maps, correspondence, sound recordings, and motion pictures, the American Memory digitizes material ranging from baseball cards to sheet music to books and pamphlets on women's suffrage. The collection is easily searchable through the American Memory site by broad topics such as Agriculture, History, and Recreation and Sport, or you can search by individual collection, format, or search the entire list of collections. American Memory is updated regularly and more collections are constantly being added.

890. *The Avalon Project at Yale Law School: Documents in Law, History, and Diplomacy.* **http://www.yale.edu/lawweb/avalon/ avalon.htm** The Avalon Project at Yale provides access to the full text of a large collection of digitized documents in the areas of Law, History, Economics, Politics, Diplomacy, and Government covering the pre–18th century, 18th century, 19th century, 20th century, and 21st century. Documents in the collections range from "Acilian Law on the Right to Recovery of Property Officially

Extorted," 122 BC, to the "September 11, 2001: Attack on America—A Collection of Documents." The emphasis of the collection is on American documents but there is also European and other world coverage. Avalon can be searched in its entirety, by period, title of the document, subject, and major collection. There is a bibliography of sources listed at the end. The Avalon Project brings together an extensive collection of primary documents, mainly from the 17th century to the present.

891. *Berkeley Digital Library SunSITE.* http://sunsite.berkeley.edu

This site, maintained by the University of California, Berkeley, contains an extensive amount of digital collection material as well as providing information for starting digital library projects. There are two key parts of the Web site, the Catalogs and Indexes part, which can be searched for locating historical documents, and the Collections part, which leads to the texts of primary source documents. Primary source collections included are the Tebtunis Papyri Collection, the Digital Scriptorium, which includes medieval and early Renaissance manuscripts, and the Jack London Collection on American literature. Researchers can search the entire site or go directly to a specific part of the collection. The Berkeley Digital Library SunSITE contains a wide variety of digitized text and image material on California, United States, ancient, and world history.

892. *EuroDocs: Primary Historical Documents from Western Europe.* http://library.byu. edu/~rdh/eurodocs

Maintained by Richard Hacken, European studies bibliographer at Brigham Young University, EuroDocs brings together an extensive collection of primary Western European historical documents, which have been transcribed, reproduced in facsimile, or translated. There is no search engine for the entire site, but it is arranged alphabetically by country from Andorra to Vatican City. Within each country section the primary source documents are arranged by historical period. There are also sections on medieval and Renaissance Europe and Europe as a supranational region. A nice feature of the site is that many of the documents are translated into English from the original language. One of the best sites for locating an extensive array of primary Western European documents, EuroDocs is a good place to start for searching for key primary sources on European history.

893. *Making of America.* http://moa.umdl. umich.edu

The Making of America site, maintained by the University of Michigan, is a digital library of primary source book and journal material focusing on the United States between 1850 and 1877. Initially begun as a joint effort of the University of Michigan and Cornell University in 1995, the site contains the full text of 8,500 books and 50,000 journal articles produced during the 19th century. It is particularly strong for providing a social history of the United States during the pre- and post–Civil War period. Researchers can search the entire books and journal articles databases individually and focus their search to full text, title, and subject. They can also alphabetically browse both the book and journal article databases for material.

894. *National Archives and Records Administration Online Exhibit Hall.* http://www.archives.gov/exhibit_hall/index.html Part of the main National Archives and Records Administration (NARA) Web site, the Online Exhibit Hall links to a large number of exhibits on American History, drawing upon documents from the huge collections in the National Archives. There is an American Originals section highlighting key documents in American History such as the Emancipation Proclamation and the Louisiana Purchase Treaty of 1803.

Other exhibits focus on a century of American photographs, World War II posters, the 1970 meeting between President Richard Nixon and Elvis Presley, and American women. The site has information about new and traveling exhibits and direct links to all the material in these collections. Online Exhibit Hall also links to other parts of the NARA Web site and the researcher can quickly locate additional material by searching the entire site for additional digital documents.

14

MICROFORMS AND SELECTED MICROFORM COLLECTIONS

In recent years there has been a tremendous increase in the amount of material available for historical research in microform, including both microfilm and microfiche. The availability and accessibility of these sources and the ease with which they can be identified has been enhanced by the emergence of the Internet and the World Wide Web. Another rapidly emerging trend is the development of imaging technology leading to the digitization of large microform collections, making these materials much more accessible for researchers. This chapter is an attempt to make historians, graduate students, and undergraduate students in history aware of the potential use of some of these sources. There are three main purposes of this chapter: (1) to familiarize the reader with the main guides to microforms, (2) to list and describe the major history microform publishers and some of their key publications, and (3) to describe a selection of the major history research collections available in microform and digitally on the World Wide Web, noting their usefulness for historians.

GUIDES TO MICROFORMS

895. *Bibliographic Guide to Microform Publications, 1986–1993.* Farmington Hills, MI: G. K. Hall/Gale Group, 1987–1994. Annual.

This annual guide, which began publication in 1987 and ceased publication with the 1993 edition, contains information on all the microform materials cataloged during the past year by the New York Public Library and the Library of Congress. The microforms covered in the *Bibliographic Guide* include both original microform publications—materials filmed for archival or preservation purposes—and commercially available microforms purchased or received by these libraries. Material covered includes U.S. and foreign books and nonserial publications, government publications, pamphlets, and ephemeral material. In terms of the records included from the New York Public Library, the *Guide* also contains information on dissertations, technical reports, and manuscript collections.

The *Guide* is arranged by author, title, and subject in a single alphabetical sequence. Entries include information such as the bibliographic entry, number of reels, format, content statement, call number, and subject headings. This annual publication superseded the *National Register of Microform Masters*, which was discontinued in 1983; it contains information on an extensive number of specialized microform publications available for historical research in these two libraries. For more recent microform material, check OCLC WorldCat.

896. *The British Library Microform Research Collections.* London: British Library. http://www.bl.uk/services/document/microrescoll/mrcframe.html
This site provides online Web access to a list of the major microform research collections held by the British Library. Information on 219 collections is accessible alphabetically, with each entry containing a description of the material in the collection. The entries give a brief description of the collection, including the size of the collection in terms of reels of microfilm or sheets of microfiche. This list serves as a starting point for researchers looking for microform research collections available at the British Library. They can then search for more detailed guides to individual collections.

897. *Canadian Newspapers on Microfilm Held by the National Library of Canada.* Ottawa, Canada: National Library of Canada. http://www.nlc-bnc.ca/8/18/index-e.html
This list, which is updated online, is the most current and extensive list of Canadian newspapers, containing over 2,300 titles, including ethnic, native, and student newspapers. The list is organized by province/territory and then alphabetically by city. In each individual entry the newspaper is listed by the masthead title, with extensive see and see also references to variations in title and to changes in place of publication. Each entry lists the name of the paper, whether it is on film or fiche, and the dates of the National Library of Canada's holdings. This is by far the best historical list for the names of Canadian newspapers.

898. *Chinese Materials on Microfilm Available from the Library of Congress.* By James Chu-yul Soong. Bibliographical Series, no. 11. Washington, DC: Center for Chinese Research Materials, Association of Research Libraries, 1971. 82pp.
Although lacking current items, this volume attempts to provide a single listing of Chinese books and serials on microfilm located in the Library of Congress. The guide is divided into two parts: (1) survey and (2) checklists. Part 1, Survey, is divided into broad chapters by type of publication, for example, monographs, newspapers, periodicals, and translations. Each chapter in this part briefly describes the Library's holdings. In part 2, Checklists, individual items are listed alphabetically by type of publication, such as monographs, newspapers, etc. Individual entries in each chapter are arranged by title and include information on the number of reels and size of the collection. The first part of this work contains a good overview of Chinese material held at the Library of Congress. Soong's work is dated; its coverage needs to be updated using OCLC WorldCat and the Library of Congress, *A Guide to the Microforms Collections in the Humanities and Social Sciences Division: Guide to Microforms in Print. Author, Title.* Munich: K. G. Saur, 1978–.

ISBN 0-88736-364-4. ISSN 0164–0747. Annual.

899. *Guide to Microforms in Print: Subject.* Munich: K. G. Saur, 1978–. ISBN 0-88736-363-6. ISSN 0163-8386. Annual.

This annual four-volume work, while perhaps more useful as a library acquisitions source, provides a great deal of information to researchers about historical materials available in microform. The present series of volumes replaced three separate earlier publications: *Guide to Microforms in Print* (1961–1977), *Subject Guide to Microforms in Print* (1962/63–1977), and *International Microforms in Print* (1974–1975). There is an annual supplement updating the main volumes.

This *Guide* is international in its coverage of microform titles, including books, journals, newspapers, government publications, archival material, and collections. The *Author-Title* volumes are arranged in a straight alphabetical listing, with both interfiled in one sequence; the *Subject* volumes are arranged by broad Dewey Decimal Classification subject headings, for example, Philosophy or Law. Entries are arranged alphabetically within these headings. Information given in each entry includes author or editor, title, place of publication, date of publication, collation information, type of microform code, ISBN, extra distributor or copublisher, further title information, publisher code, and subject class. There is an index of persons at the end of the second subject volume, as well as a survey of Dewey classes and of subjects. The *Guide* is useful to historians for seeing whether a particular work or collection is available in microform. However, the subject index is very general, and researchers may first have to find the broader heading and then look alphabetically under their subject.

900. *Guide to Russian Reprints and Microforms.* New York: Pilvax, 1973. 364pp.

The objective of this work is to provide a complete listing, as of July 1, 1973, of available Cyrillic Russian reprints and microforms. This includes items available from both foreign and U.S. publishers such as books, pamphlets, serials, and newspapers, but it does not include manuscripts. The main part of the *Guide* is basically an alphabetical author list, with the entries containing bibliographic information such as author, title, edition, and original place of publication. Following the bibliographic information, there is material on the source of the reprint or microform, type of reproduction used, publisher's serial or identification letter and number, and price. The second part of the volume is a title list, which refers back to an entry number in the main part. Although broader in its coverage than just microforms, this guide includes information on over 8,000 items, and provides a good starting place for Slavic researchers trying to locate the availability of microform material in their research areas. For more recent material researchers need to check the World Wide Web and OCLC WorldCat.

901. *A Guide to the Microform Collections in the Humanities and Social Sciences Division.* Washington, DC: Humanities and Social Sciences Division, Library of Congress. http://lcweb.loc.gov/rr/microform/guide This Web-based edition updates a series of earlier printed guides, the most recent of which came out in 1996, adding a number of collections received from that time to the present as well as several previously undiscovered collections. The guide provides an introduction to the holdings of the Microform Reading Room at the Library of Congress, which includes over 7 million pieces. It is updated regularly online as new collections become available. The entries are arranged alphabetically by collection title, with cross references to personal and corporate names. Each annotated entry briefly describes the size and content of the collection and lists a guide, if there is one. There is an alphabetical index to the entries by format (books, pamphlets, etc.) and subject. This ongoing guide serves as a starting point for researchers looking at the microform holdings of the world's greatest research library, the Library of Congress.

902. *An Index to Microform Collections.* Edited by Ann Niles. Meckler Publishing Series in Library Micrographics Management. Westport, CT: Meckler, 1984, 1988. Vol. 1, 891pp. Vol. 2, 1,002pp. ISBN 0-930466-75-6 (vol. 1); 0-88736-061-0 (vol. 2).

This two-volume work serves as an index to a total of 70 microform research collections containing over 20,000 items. The items indexed in the first volume were taken from the second edition of Dodson's *Microform Research Collections*, while those in the second volume were selected individually. A major criteria for inclusion was that the collections included were those causing the most problems for users, especially collections containing a large number of individual monographs and not having an adequate guide already available. The collections indexed are wide-ranging and include material in history, literature, architecture, and religion. Each of the two vol-

umes is divided into three parts: (1) an alphabetical list of each of the titles covered, along with a detailed contents list of the monographs in each collection, (2) an author index, and (3) a title index. Most information found in these volumes is taken from the catalogs of micropublishers. This work, although selective and no longer current, does provide detailed indexing for a wide range of microform research collections. It needs to be updated with more recent sources such as OCLC WorldCat and Internet searches of publisher Web sites.

903. *Microform Research Collections: A Guide.* 2nd ed. Edited by Suzanne Cates Dodson. Meckler Publishing Series in Library Micrographics Management, no. 9. Westport, CT: Meckler, 1984. ISBN 0-930466-66-7.

This is the definitive single-volume guide to large microform research collections, covering almost 400 items. Dodson has nearly doubled the number of entries contained in her first edition, *Microform Research Collections: A Guide* (Westport, CT: Microform Review, 1978). The guide is obviously selective, but it provides the researcher with detailed information about a wide variety of major collections. Entries are arranged alphabetically and contain title, publisher, format, price, location of reviews (if available), arrangement and bibliographical control, listing of bibliographies, indexes, etc., and scope and content. A detailed index provides access by subject, title, author, editor, and compiler. Researchers need a new edition of this work to include the many recent collections now available in microform. Detailed reviews of these recent collections can be found in *Microform Review* and its successor, *Microform and Imaging Review*. More information on new collections can also be found through OCLC WorldCat.

904. *Microfilm Resources for Research: A Comprehensive Catalog.* Washington, DC: National Archives and Records Administration, 2000. 109pp. ISBN 1-880875-22-5.
The National Archives is the major repository of America's historical records, and a large number of those records are available on microfilm. This catalog serves as the most recent guide to these microfilm and microfiche publications. Covering more than 2,000 microform publications available from the National Archives, the guide is organized first by numbered record groups, which group records by agency. These are followed by donated materials and miscellaneous items. Within these broad categories the information is arranged by record group and lists a microfilm publication number as well as the number of rolls. At the end there is a general index, an alphabetical list of record groups, a numerical list of record groups, and a numerical list of microfilm publication numbers. For historians interested in more specialized areas of research, the National Archives has published other microfilm catalogs, including ones on American Indians, black studies, immigrant and passenger arrivals, military service records, and the population censuses. These sources may be accessed through the National Archives Web site at www.nara.gov.

905. *Microform and Imaging Review* (formerly *Microform Review*). Munich: K. G. Saur, 1972–. Quarterly.

This is the outstanding journal covering microforms and, for the historian, it is particularly helpful for its definitive reviews of research collections available in microform. Its coverage and title have been expanded to include articles on digital imaging. Published quarterly since 1972, the early issues of *Microform and Imaging Review* (then called *Microform Review*) contained a number of detailed reviews of collections available in microformat as well as reviews of books concerned with microforms. The reviews, written by both teaching faculty and librarians, were lengthy; some covered several pages. They critically analyzed the collection being reviewed, provided background, evaluated the microform format of the collection, and listed any finding aids available. More recently, there are two to three articles, plus a review item. The focus of the publication is much more on digital imaging and projects using that technology.

There are two cumulative listings of reviews published in *Microform and Imaging Review—Cumulative Microform Reviews, 1972–1976* (Westport, CT: Microform Review, 1978) and *Cumulative Microform Reviews, 1977–1984* (Westport, CT: Meckler, 1985). These volumes make researchers' task a great deal easier by arranging the reviews done from 1972 to 1984 into broad subject categories such as black studies, government documents, and U.S. cultural and historical materials. *Microform and Imaging Review* is the best current source for reviews of new microform and digital imaging collections.

906. *Newspapers in Microform: United States, 1948–1983.* 2 vols. *Newspapers in Microform: Foreign Countries, 1948–1983.* 1 vol. Compiled and edited by the Catalog

Management and Publication Division, Library of Congress. Washington, DC: Library of Congress, 1984.

This three-volume cumulation lists in separate volumes U.S. holdings of American newspapers and world holdings of foreign newspapers that are on microform through the end of 1983. These volumes replace earlier cumulative volumes for the United States and foreign countries, as well as additional annual supplementary volumes. The U.S. volumes are arranged by state, then city, and alphabetically by the title of the newspaper; the foreign countries volume is arranged by country, then city, and alphabetically by title. Within each volume the entries give information such as the date of publication, frequency, libraries that hold microform copies, and the dates of their holdings. Information is also given about the type of microform copy available, and there is a title index at the end of each set of volumes.

For researchers working today there is no recent printed source that duplicates *Newspapers in Microform,* but they can do much of the same work online. They can locate libraries that have a particular newspaper through OCLC WorldCat and then search the library's online catalog to see what holdings they have. Since 1984 University Microfilms International, the world's largest producer of newspapers on microfilm, has published, either separately or together with *Serials in Microform*, its own version of *Newspapers in Microform*. This version is basically a UMI newspaper catalog and does not include any library holdings. The most current information about UMI's more than 7,000 newspapers is available online at http://www.umi.com.

MICROFORM PUBLISHERS

907. Gale Group
27500 Drake Road
Farmington Hills, MI 48331

A newcomer to microform publishing, Gale has been a leading publisher of reference materials and creator of full-text magazine and newspaper databases. Gale Group companies include such leading microform publishers as G. K. Hall, Primary Source Microfilms, and Munich-based K. G. Saur. It currently maintains over 300 microfilm and microfiche sets pertinent for history. It is strong for U.S. and U.K. history and politics—particularly social and administrative history. Among its list of holdings are the *British Culture Series I and II* covering the 18th and 19th centuries (recently acquired by Primary Source Microfilm from Readex). Gale's list of holdings may be accessed by subject or publication type at www.galegroup.com.

908. LexisNexis Academic and Library Solutions
4520 East-West Highway
Bethesda, MD 20814

With its acquisition of Congressional Information Service (CIS), LexisNexis Academic and Library Solutions has become the leading micropublisher of U.S. government documents, including federal, state, national, and international publications. In addition, through the merger with University Publications of America (UPA) it has gained strong collections in 20th-century U.S. and British history. CIS has had strong indexing of government documents, such as the *Serial Set Index,* and extensive collections of U.S. legislative publications on microfiche such as *U.S. Congressional Committee Hearings, 1833–1969, U.S. Serial Set, 789–1969,* and *U.S. Congressional Journals, 1789–1978.* CIS also publishes a number of executive branch publications including *Presidential Executive Orders and Proclamations, 1789–1983,* the *Federal Register,* and *Code of Federal Regulations* on microfiche. For international coverage, CIS publishes the *International Statistics Library* on microfiche, including the statistical sources indexed in *Index to International Statistics.* It also publishes a large set of individual statistical publications. CIS has expanded its World Wide Web service with the development of LexisNexis Congressional, which provides access to the *CIS Index* and hypertext links to the full text of related congressional documents.

Also now part of LexisNexis Academic and Library solutions, UPA brings a strong emphasis on American history microform collections and 20th-century American history materials. Its research collections include collections on politics (John F. Kennedy Oral History Collection), radicalism (Department of Justice Investigative Files on the Industrial Workers of the World), women's studies (Papers of Eleanor Roosevelt), and presidential documents (Minutes and Documents of the Cabinet Meetings of President Lyndon Johnson). UPA also publishes a number of international collections including U.S. State Department and U.S. military intelligence collections on other countries. Although UPA remains weak in pre-20th century materials and British, Canadian, and Russian primary source materials, it has strengthened its pre-20th-century U.S. history sources with sets such as the Bexar

Archives, 1717–1836, Colonial Archives during the Spanish Period, and Jesuit Relations and Allied Documents, 1610–1791. To access lists of both CIS and UPA research collections, visit the LexisNexis Academic and Library Solutions Web site at www. lexisnexis.com/academic.

909. Newsbank
Corporate Headquarters
5020 Tamiami Trail North, Suite 110
Naples, FL 34103

910. Readex Office
397 Main St.
P.O. Box 219
Chester, VT 05143

Newsbank merged with Readex in 2000, thus taking over one of the oldest microform publishers in the United States. Readex published two major document collections originally on microprint (now on microfiche): *United States Government Depository and Non-Depository Publications* and *United Nations Documents and Publications,* which includes the Official Records of the United Nations since 1946. Readex also published research collections in American and British history, including *Early American Imprints,* which reprints the texts of all the titles in Charles Evans, *American Bibliography, 1639–1800,* and is also available in digital form, and Ralph Shaw and Richard Shoemaker, *American Bibliography: A Preliminary Checklist for 1801–1819,* as well as *Early American Newspapers,* which includes the full run of many 18th-century newspapers. Readex also has collections covering British history. The list of Newsbank/Readex microform holdings may be accessed at www.readex.com.

911. ProQuest
300 North Zeeb Road
P.O. Box 1346
Ann Arbor, MI 48106
ProQuest, formerly known as Bell & Howell/University Microfilms International, is the oldest of the major history microform publishers, beginning micropublishing in 1938. It absorbed UMI in 1985 and Chadwyck-Healey in 1999, making it one of the largest private publishers of microform materials in the world. ProQuest's collections on Great Britain and the United States are among its strongest. Many of the Chadwyck-Healey and UMI materials are available on microfilm or microfiche, including *National Inventory of Documentary Sources in the United States* (Chadwyck-Healey), *American History and Culture* (Chadwyck-Healey), *Dissertation Abstracts* (UMI), *American Periodicals Series* (UMI), and *Early English Books Series* (UMI). ProQuest is becoming very active in making some of these collections available on the World Wide Web in digital form. These include the American Periodical Series Online, Digital Sanborn Maps, 1867–1970, and the Early English Book Online. The full list of ProQuest products is available at http://www.umi.com/proquest.

912. Scholarly Resources, Inc.
104 Greenhill Avenue
Wilmington, DE 19805
Founded in 1971, Scholarly Resources is a major microform publisher whose area of emphasis is in the humanities and social sciences. They have strong microform collections in American history, British studies, Asian studies, black studies, and military history. The American history collections include the Papers of Andrew Jackson,

1770–1845, a number of Civil War–era newspapers, early American newspapers, and the New American state papers. For 20th-century American historians, publications include the recent FBI files on Malcolm X, Nelson Rockefeller, and the Bureau of Social Hygiene Project and Research Files, 1913–1940. In addition, Scholarly Resources is a distributor for all National Archives microform publications, including U.S. census material on microform. The company also publishes British historical documents, for example, the *British Foreign Office Correspondence* concerning Japan, Russia, and the United States. It also has major collections in diplomatic history, specifically Latin America, including the U.S. Department of State Decimal Files for Latin America, which contain 20th-century U.S. diplomatic correspondence with individual Latin American countries. Listings of Scholarly Resources microform holdings may be accessed online at www.scholarly.com.

MAJOR HISTORICAL MICROFORM COLLECTIONS

913. *American Culture Series, 1493–1875*. Ann Arbor, MI: ProQuest. 669 reels of microfilm.
This interdisciplinary series is a massive collection on microfilm of early American books and pamphlets from 1493 to 1875. Covering 5,850 titles, the collection is divided into two parts—ACSI, which covers from 1493 to 1806, and the much larger ACSII, which covers 1806 to 1875. The titles included in this series were selected from David R. Weimer, *Bibliography of Amer-*

ican Culture (Ann Arbor, MI: University Microfilms, 1957) and cover many different subject areas, including history, literature and languages, science, economics, philosophy, politics and law, military and naval history and science, art and architecture, anthropology and sociology, education, journalism, and music. History is the largest part of the collection, with over 1,500 titles, and the selection includes primary material on colonization, exploration, frontier life, the American Revolution, and the Civil War. There is an excellent finding aid to the collection, *American Culture Series, 1493–1875: A Cumulative Guide to the Microfilm Collection American Culture Series I–II*, edited by Ophelia Y. Lo (Ann Arbor, MI: University Microfilms International, 1979). The guide provides author, title, subject, and reel number access to this collection. For the historian and specialist in American studies, this collection provides access to a wide range of primary source materials.

914. *American Periodicals Series, 1741–1900.* **Ann Arbor, MI: ProQuest. 2,770 reels of microfilm. Also available electronically through ProQuest.**
This series provides access to the complete text of more than 1,100 American periodicals published from 1741 to 1900. The series is divided into three parts: Series I, which is the smallest of the three, running from 1741 to 1800; Series II, covering from 1800 to 1850; and Series III, which includes material from 1850 to 1900. Covering from the very beginning of American journalism, this collection includes Benjamin Franklin's *General Magazine*, Thomas Paine's *Pennsylvania Magazine*, William Lloyd Garrison's *Liberator*, as well as standard publications such as the *North American Review* and

Godey's Lady's Book. Many of the magazines contained in this collection are indexed in *Poole's Index to Nineteenth Century Literature* and the *Nineteenth Century Readers' Guide to Periodical Literature, 1890–1899.* There is also a separate guide to the collection, *American Periodicals, 1741–1900: An Index to the Microfilm Collections* (Ann Arbor, MI: University Microfilms, 1979), which provides title, subject, editor, and reel number access to the material in this series. This collection has a wealth of information for historians of the colonial, revolutionary, Civil War, and Reconstruction periods in American history. The collection is also searchable online and available full text through ProQuest's Digital Vault Initiative, which makes 7 million pages of material available to researchers.

915. *Columbia University Oral History Microfiche Collection.* **Westport, CT: Meckler, 1973–.**
The Columbia University Oral History Collection, begun by Allan Nevins, is the largest ongoing oral history archive, containing interviews with major figures in 20th-century American history. A number of memoirs from this collection are now available on microfiche from Meckler Publishing. This is an ongoing project and currently six parts of the collection are available, a total of 1,149 individual memoirs, including memoirs from 20th-century leaders in areas such as politics, media, science, economics, business, journalism, and the arts. There are printed guides available for the first five parts, but the most recent general guide is Elizabeth B. Mason and Louis M. Starr, *The Oral History Collection of Columbia University* (New York: Oral History Research Office, 1979), which

provides name and subject access to the collection. This has been supplemented by a brief publication, *Columbia University Oral History Microfiche Collection: A Cumulative Index to Memoirs in Parts I-V* (Westport, CT: Meckler, 1985), which is strictly an alphabetical listing of names and locations. The Columbia collection is a must for social, economic, and political researchers in 20th-century America.

916. *Documents on Contemporary China, 1949–1975.* White Plains, NY: Kraus International. 525 microfiche.

This specialized research collection on modern China was originally published by Johnson Associates in 1977, in cooperation with the Social Science Center of the Columbia University Libraries. The collection is divided into five parts: (1) Cultural Revolution: Red Guard translations, (2) enactments of party and government, (3) research and analysis reports, (4) bibliography/research and leadership information, and (5) provincial/municipal data. There is also a two-volume index to the five parts, which includes a bibliography of the items available on microfiche and detailed subject indexes to the documents. This set includes translations of primary documents and reports, as well as secondary studies on China. It is an excellent source for researchers interested in China during the Communist period, including the period of the Cultural Revolution, and an example of the more specialized materials currently available on microfiche.

917. *Early American Imprints, 1639–1800.* New Canaan, CT: Readex/Newsbank, 1981–1982. 26,057 microfiche.

918. *Early American Imprints, 1801–1819.* 2nd series. Chester, VT: Readex/Newsbank. 60,508 microfiche.

Charles Evans, *American Bibliography* (Chicago: Charles Evans, 1903–1934), is regarded as the major compilation of early American books, pamphlets, and periodicals. This collection, published by Readex, contains the complete text of all the works listed in Evans, 39,162 titles, plus an additional 10,035 titles discovered since the publication of Evans's work. There is also a second series of microfiche, based on the work of Ralph Robert Shaw and Richard H. Shoemaker, *American Bibliography; A Preliminary Checklist for 1801–1819* (New York: Scarecrow, 1953–1963), which chronologically continues Evans's work through 1819. The company originally issued the first version of *Early American Imprints* on microcard during the 1950s and then in the early 1980s began making it available on microfiche. Historians of early American history are fortunate to have access to this wealth of primary documentation, as well as excellent indexes to these collections. The two-volume work by Clifford K. Shipton and James E. Mooney, *National Index of American Imprints Through 1800: The Short-Title Evans* (Worcester, MA: American Antiquarian Society/Barre Publishers, 1969), corrected errors in Evans, added other titles, and serves as an index to the first Readex series. The multivolume work by Shaw and Shoemaker aids researchers working through the second series. Readex has started making available an Evans Digital Edition, which began in July 2002. When completed, the Evans Digital Edition will include the full text of more than 36,000 works and over 2.4 million images.

919. *Early American Newspapers.* **Chester, VT: Readex/Newsbank, 1962–.**

In 1962 Readex Microprint Corporation began publishing on microprint (6x9-inch opaque cards) the more than 2,000 U.S. newspapers published prior to 1821, including all titles listed in Brigham's *History and Bibliography of American Newspapers* [see 331]. The project was completed in the late 1970s, and the collection became widely available in U.S. research libraries. In 1979 Readex decided to make the collection available on 35 mm reel microfilm, an ongoing project. More than 700 titles have been filmed and researchers can access lists by state and more detailed descriptions of specific newspapers at Readex's main Web site, www.readex.com. This is the most valuable historical collection available of early American newspapers. Other American newspaper collections on microfilm include *Civil War Newspapers*, *Newspapers from the Depression Years, 1929–1938*, and *South Carolina Newspapers, 1732–1782*, all produced by UMI/ProQuest.

920. *Early English Books I, 1475–1640.*

921. *Early English Books II, 1641–1700.*

922. *Early English Books Tract Supplement.* **Ann Arbor, MI: ProQuest.**

These collections, based on A. W. Pollard and G. R. Redgrave, *Short-Title Catalogue of Books Printed in England, Scotland, and Ireland, Wales, and of English Books Printed in Other Countries, 1475–1640* (London: Bibliographical Society, 1976–1986) and Donald G. Wing, *A Short-Title Catalogue of Books Printed in England, Scotland, Ireland, Wales, and British America, and of English Books Printed in Other Countries, 1641–1700* (New York: Index Committee of the Modern Language Association of America, 1972–1988), attempt to reprint the complete text of every English book published in Great Britain or British North America from the invention of printing to 1700. The first collection is complete and includes almost all the 26,500 titles listed in Pollard and Redgrave. The second collection is ongoing and includes over 64,000 titles. The *Tract Supplement* provides access to small items, such as broadsides and pamphlets, that were often collected into scrapbooks or tract volumes. These tract volumes, primarily from the British Library, allow users to see the material in the same order as they would when leafing through the original volumes. The material in this supplement corresponds to the dates of parts 1–2. These collections provide an unparalleled primary source collection for researchers in subject areas such as English literature, British and American history, philosophy, linguistics, and fine arts. There are reel guides and a cross-index listing entry numbers from Pollard, Redgrave, and Wing. This vast collection is also available online through ProQuest's Digital Vault Initiative. Known as *Early English Books Online* (EEBO), this collection is accessible to researchers electronically through libraries paying for the access.

923. *Early English Newspapers.* **Farmington Hills, MI: Gale Group.**

This is also an ongoing project to film a large collection of 17th- and 18th-century British newspapers and make them available to researchers in one location. It was begun by Research Publications and is being continued by Gale through its Primary Source

Microfilm imprint. The newspapers in this collection are drawn from two large archival collections at the British Museum and the Bodleian Library at Oxford. Although the collection mainly covers the 17th and 18th centuries, recently titles printed in London and its suburbs through 1900 have been added. The collection includes newspapers such as the *Gentleman's Magazine* and the *Gazetteer* and *New Daily Advertiser*. There is a brief guide to the collection, *Early English Newspapers: A Bibliography and Guide to the Microfilm Collection*, compiled by Susan M. Cox and Janice L. Budeit (Woodbridge, CT: Research Publications, 1983). However, this work is arranged alphabetically by title and does not provide any kind of subject access. It does give information about publication dates, title changes, and reel locations. This collection brings together a wide range of primary source material for historians interested in cultural, political, and social currents during the Stuart, Hanoverian, and, to a lesser extent, Victorian eras in England. The complete collection will total over 6,000 reels of microfilm. Another related, more specialized British newspaper collection is *Eighteenth Century English Provincial Newspapers*, available through Thomson/Gale's Primary Source Microfilm.

924. *The Eighteenth Century*. **Farmington Hills, MI: Gale Group, 1983–.**
The *Eighteenth Century* is an ongoing microfilm project based on the *Eighteenth Century Short Title Catalogue (ESTC)*, a machine-readable database of works printed in any language in Great Britain or its territories, or in English anywhere in the world, between 1701 and 1800. Like *Early English*

Newspapers (see above), it was begun by Research Publications and is being continued by Gale through its Primary Source Microfilms imprint. Ultimately the *ESTC* will contain 500,000 items and 200,000 will be available in this collection, making it one of the largest microfilm projects ever. The collection has been organized into eight broad subject areas—religion and philosophy; history and geography; social sciences; law; literature and language; fine arts; science, technology, and medicine; and general reference and miscellaneous. It includes a wide variety of materials such as books, broadsides, tract books, and sermons by individuals such as David Hume, Edmund Burke, and Thomas Paine. Eventually containing over 12,000 reels of microfilm, this collection is accessible through temporary unit listings, arranged by main entry. There are also separate volumes, *The Eighteenth Century: Guide to the Microfilm Collection* (Woodbridge, CT: Research Publications, 1984–), which supersede the unit listings and provide better access by main entry, title, and broad subject area. In 2003 Gale started producing the Eighteenth Century Collections Online, which will eventually digitize this entire collection, totaling over 33 million pages. This collection is indispensable for historians of the Enlightenment and 18th-century England.

925. *Latin American and Caribbean Official Statistical Serials, 1821–1982*. **Ann Arbor, MI: Chadwyck-Healey/ProQuest.**
This collection, which contains over 4,000 microfiche, represents an attempt by Chadwyck-Healey, now part of ProQuest, to publish historically the statistical volumes issued by the governments of the Latin American and Caribbean countries from

the earliest efforts to the early 1980s. To accomplish this, Chadwyck-Healey reproduced statistical volumes from the holdings of libraries in Great Britain and the United States. The aim of the collection is a good one, but the title is a bit misleading, in that most of the material covers the 20th century, with much less country coverage available for the 19th. Also, the coverage for each county varies, depending on when statistical compendia first began appearing on a regular basis. Despite these problems, this set does open up a great deal of historical statistical material on Latin America and the Caribbean. Chadwyck-Healey has also published several other large statistical sets for other areas of the world, including *African Official Statistical Serials, 1867–1982* and *European Official Statistical Serials, 1841–1984*.

926. *National Inventory of Documentary Sources in the United Kingdom and Ireland.* Ann Arbor, MI: Chadwyck-Healey/ ProQuest.

With the publication of this microfiche set and its American equivalent, the *National Inventory of Documentary Sources in the United States*, Chadwyck-Healey (since 1999 a subsidiary of ProQuest) has performed a real service for historians. It has published many of the local finding aids, previously only available at the repositories themselves, for locating in detail what material is available in individual collections at particular locations. In publishing the *National Inventory* Chadwyck-Healey is publishing these inventories or finding aids for national and county record offices; national, university, and public libraries; and private, special, and other repositories in Great Britain and Ireland. This is a long-term project that is

being produced on microfiche at the rate of 3,000 fiche per year and includes more than 14,000 unpublished finding aids. The microfiche is published in units, with a new cumulative index for each unit. Each cumulative index contains a list of finding aids and a name and subject index. This collection is quite expensive, but it will eventually provide researchers with access to the finding aids of many of the archives and libraries throughout the United Kingdom. Guides to archives on the World Wide Web have made some of these finding aids available, but this collection is still useful for researchers. They will not have to make unnecessary trips or spend months trying to find out whether a particular collection would be appropriate for their research.

927. *National Inventory of Documentary Sources in the United States.* Ann Arbor, MI: Chadwyck-Healey/ProQuest. Pt. 1, *Federal Records* (2,054 microfiche); Pt. 2, *Manuscript Division, Library of Congress* (924 microfiche); and Pt. 3, *State Archives, State Libraries, State Historical Societies, Academic Libraries, and Other Repositories* (ongoing).

This microfiche collection does the same thing for American History as the *National Inventory of Documentary Sources in the United Kingdom and Ireland* does for those countries. It provides access to many of the finding aids—registers, calendars, inventories, guides, etc.—to archival repositories in the United States. The *National Inventory* is divided into three parts: (1) federal records, which includes records in the National Archives, Smithsonian Institution Archives, and the Hoover, Roosevelt, Truman, Eisenhower, Kennedy, Johnson, and Ford presidential libraries; (2) Manuscript Division, Library of Congress, and (3) state archives, state libraries, state historical societies, academic libraries, and other repositories. Each of the first two parts is complete and has a printed index; the third part is ongoing at the rate of 10 units a year, which are accompanied by a cumulative index on microfiche and on CD-ROM. This is a wonderful tool for historians seeking to find out whether a particular collection meets their research interests, but it is important to keep in mind that the inventory is dependent on all the libraries involved cooperating with the project and making all of their finding lists available for filming. This is also an expensive project, which may dissuade some libraries from acquiring it. Guides to archives on the World Wide Web have made some of these finding aids available, but the *National Inventory* has certainly made it more convenient for historians to learn more about a collection, without having to travel to or contact that archive.

928. *Pre–1900 Canadiana*. Ottawa: Canadian Institute for Historical Microreproductions.

This microfiche project claims to be the "most comprehensive collection of Canadian research materials in existence," with 57,850 monographs and pamphlets printed prior to 1900. The collection covers a wide range of subject areas, including history, geography, native American studies, sociology, psychology, anthropology, economics, religion, philosophy, law, political science, education, and science. Title lists are available for the collection as a whole as well as each unit, and libraries can purchase individual segments of the collection, such as history and geography. The records in the collection are also accessible through

OCLC WorldCat, which greatly improves access to these records for the individual researcher. This collection provides access to an enormous amount of pre-1900 Canadian primary source material in a single location, making things much easier for the researcher in Canadian history.

929. *Russian History and Culture*. Ann Arbor, MI: ProQuest, 1978–.

With this still ongoing collection, University Microfilms International, as part of ProQuest, is providing researchers in Slavic studies and Russian history, politics, literature, and culture with access to the Slavic collection of the Helsinki University Library, recognized as the best Slavic collection outside Russia for the period 1820–1917. The goal is ultimately to make available 5,000 scarce titles from the Helsinki collection. These titles are being selected by the staff of the Slavic and East European Department of the University of Illinois Library, with a goal of not duplicating Russian material already in American and Canadian libraries. The collection includes books in eight main subject areas—politics and government, industry and trade, military history, literature, biography, education, state and law, and social questions. There is an author, subject, and title index to that part of the collection thus far published. This is a valuable collection of diverse sources for researchers in 19th and early 20th-century Russian history.

930. *U. S. Congressional Committee Hearings on Microfiche, 1833–1969*. Bethesda, MD: Congressional Information Service.

Congressional Information Service (CIS) (now an imprint of LexisNexis Academic

Library Solutions) is the major indexer and micropublisher of U.S. government documents. One of its major document collections is the *U.S. Congressional Committee Hearings on Microfiche*. This massive collection, which covers 1833 to 1969 (23rd–91st Congress), when the more recent CIS collection began, contains more than 40,000 titles on over 84,000 microfiche. The collection contains a full-text copy of virtually all U.S. House and Senate hearings published during this period. It is divided into four groups of hearings, depending on when different collections of hearings were located and reproduced on microfiche: Group 1—hearings contained in the U.S. Senate Library's bound collection of hearings, 1869–1934, and the Senate Library's bound *U.S. Serial Set* collection, 1833–1934; Group 2—hearings not contained in the U.S. Senate Library, 1839–1934, found in the Library of Congress and other locations; Group 3—hearings contained in the U.S. Senate Library bound collection, 1935–1969; and Group 4—hearings not contained in the three previous groups identified by CIS researchers examining other major collections and sources. More recently CIS has published a second set of committee hearings, the *CIS Unpublished Congressional Committee Hearings, 1823–1980*. Both of these hearings are indexed electronically through *Congressional Indexes, 1789–1969* on LexisNexis Congressional and also through CIS print hearings indexes.

INDEX